MODERN
FISHING LURE
COLLECTIBLES

VOLUME 2
IDENTIFICATION & VALUE GUIDE
Russell E. Lewis

COLLECTOR BOOKS
A Division of Schroeder Publishing Co., Inc.

Cover design by Beth Summers
Book design by Karen Smith

Photography by Russell E. Lewis

COLLECTOR BOOKS
P.O. Box 3009
Paducah, Kentucky 42002-3009
www.collectorbooks.com

Copyright © 2003 Russell E. Lewis

The current values in this book should be used only as a guide. They are not
intended to set prices, which vary from one section of the country to another. Auction prices as well as dealer prices vary greatly and are affected by condition as well as
demand. Neither the author nor the publisher assumes responsibility for any losses
that might be incurred as a result of consulting this guide.

Searching For A Publisher?

We are always looking for people knowledgeable within their fields. If you feel
that there is a real need for a book on your collectible subject and have a large com-
prehensive collection, contact Collector Books.

Contents

◆ Dedication

Dedicated to my loving wife, Wendy, the best design any Weber ever produced. With parents having the last names of Weber (see Volume 1, Chapter 8 for a complete history of this company) and Richardson (a famous Chicago rod maker), she must have been destined to end up with a "lure nut." For the past year she has tolerated more than one can imagine with lures, rods, reels, decoys, magazines, and catalogs constantly filling up her home and my time. Without her and her constant patience, this work truly would not have been possible. It is with joy and love that I dedicate both Volumes 1 and 2 to her.

I also am thankful that my two sons, Justin and Rob, have been able to share in some memories of fishing on Clear Lake by experiencing the same clean spring fed waters and learning the importance of casting a lure while being tutored by a patient hand. Regardless of fish caught or not, this is an experience that can never be replaced by any amount of classic lures, and my books are thus also dedicated to my two sons for helping me create memories of a lifetime.

Clockwise from top: Author and son Rob with friend West Docker on Michigan's Upper Peninsula; author's Canadian excursion; Wisconsin farm visit with sons Rob and Justin; dog-tired constant companion Art.

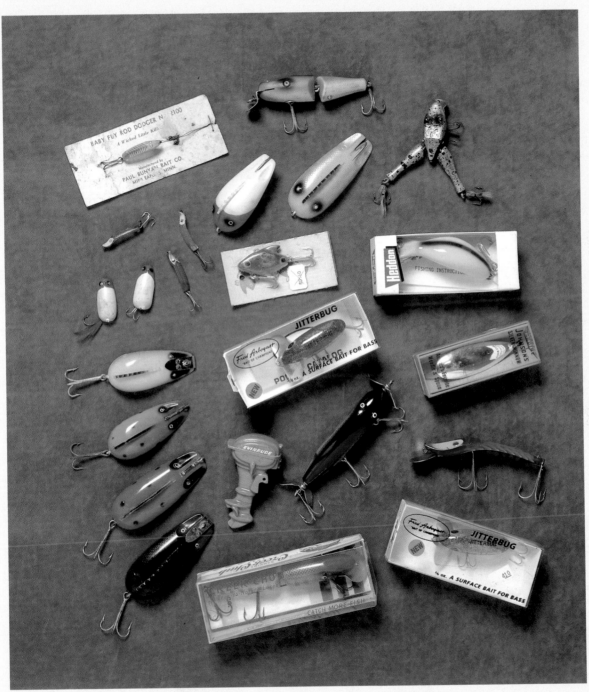

A variety of collectibles, starting with the Creek Chub Bait Company Fireplug Jointed Pikie on top to left; Paul Bunyan on card; eleven Paul Bunyans; bottom has a Creek Chub box and catalog with a Paw Paw Pikie in it; two of the better colored more recent Jitterbugs; Paul Bunyan Transparent Dodger; Johnson's Silver Minnow; Paw Paw Injured Minnow; a Heddon Magnum Tadpolly in box; a little Sonic copy on card; (maybe Atlantic lures); and a nice Evinrude Motors pin given to sales people upon entering the convention. The top right lure is a small Paw Paw Wotta-Frog. Many of the above items were featured in Volume 1.

◆ Acknowledgments

First, my editor, Lisa Stroup, who had the foresight to contact me after nearly a year and say, "What about that book you wanted to do?" Without her gentle reminder, it may have stayed on the back burner forever.

Second, all the friends that have sold and traded with me for years and some that are new friends that have really helped me find some of those unusual plastics and newer items in this book.

Special thanks goes to the following:

West Decker for being the best picker, lure trader, pike trolling expert, and friend that one could ever have in this crazy business of old lures. If he had let me have that old Heddon Bat Wing decoy in the box that day, we may never have gotten to know each other so well!

Capt. John Kolbeck for trading with me, selling to me, buying from me, beating me to all the good lures at shows while "I watch his stuff," and in general for keeping this business interesting. He is also a great fishing guide and works hard to find good stuff that is still out there!

Tony Zazweta for finding me tons of plastics the last year and a half and supplying me with some great lures shown in this book for the first time. A friend developed through the Internet and to whom I'm still waiting to say "Hi" in person.

Mike Anderson for letting me be second to look at and buy from his recent find of a complete collection of fishing items, some of which found there way into this book.

Charles "Bud" Hartman for selling me his accumulation of fishing lures kept for the past 50+ years as a representative in the fishing tackle trades. With his collection came many of the baits shown in this book.

Bob Slade for showing me that a lure book with some history in it is more fun to read than just a picture book and for selling me his photo equipment used for some of the photos for this book.

Stewart Phillips for becoming a friend when needed and for sharing some good lures with me, a few of them now in print.

Ken Syrjala for finding some great Heddon plastics and others that have rounded out both my collection and the book project.

Larry Menard for loaning me the "left-over" lures from his hardware store to photograph for the book.

Terry Wong and John Muma for shipping their books to me when needed and showing me two fine examples to follow.

John Shoffner and Art Kimball for always answering any of my questions and providing inspiration through their own efforts.

Sherman Dewey and Walter Welch for taking time to talk to me about fish carving and decoy use.

My wonderful neighbors in Watton, Covington, and L'Anse, Michigan for sharing with me a few nice items, some wonderful trout streams, and the peace needed to write a book such as this.

My clients in the law practice that allowed me the time off needed to meet the deadlines in writing this book.

My great customers on eBay for trusting my judgment and my descriptions for the past few years and for helping me reach that magic 1000+ mark for feedback.

All the honest sellers on eBay and at shows that have shared some good lures with me.

Roxanne Coleman of Shakespeare for finally giving in to my requests and loaning me a unique resource only available from Shakespeare and allowing me to reprint materials needed for this book.

Remer Hutchinson, the last president of Weber Tackle Company, for selling me the remaining Weber inventory and archival materials of Weber and Frost that have been such a great help in writing this book.

Phil Jensen of Luhr Jensen & Sons, for being so helpful in general, giving me specific answers to some of my questions on things that happened in the 1980s and 1990s, allowing me to use printed materials of the company, and for being willing to work with me in the future on more research and books. But most of all, just for being able to find someone else equally interested in the history of modern fishing collectibles.

The friends that have been there for me over the years, Rich Allington, Gerd Dallmann, Jim Godek, Steve Keerl, Dan Perrin, Charlie Schmidt, and Leon Stout.

Most of all, to my sons, Justin and Rob, for sharing some time with me on Clear Lake and helping me learn what is truly important in life.

I have been "collecting" fishing lures since 1950, the summer of my third year here on planet Earth. My neighbor living on a glacial pothole bass lake connected to our lake via a shallow channel (both of which were private at the time) gave me three Creek Chub Plunkers, two in regular size and one baby Plunker. A few years thereafter, once I was able to cast, I fished with the baby, and still do, and put the other two in my tackle box to admire over the years. Nick, my neighbor, was a rather wealthy man with an extensive selection of fishing lures, and I would spend hours going through his various lures and rods and reels in amazement, even in my youth. Of course, I was also fortunate to have grown up in a time period when companies would send you a catalog for 25¢ or free (and no, I was not smart enough to keep them all). I would spend hours admiring the newest Heddon items, or staring at an Ambassadeur 5000 and wondering how I could afford one at age seven. Oh, to go back in time for a visit to the local tackle shop in 1955. How many of us say that with some regularity!

Ultimately in 1995, my wife Wendy and I opened a business called Heritage Tackle 'n Tiques, which placed on display hundreds of lures, rods, and reels in our collection. One of the first events that I recall is learning about the National Fishing Lure Collector's Club (NFLCC) only after opening the store. We had no idea that there was an organization dedicated to what we simply thought was an interesting piece of our cultural heritage that we wanted to share with others. Again, knowledge is power in the collecting business, and much was soon learned from fellow collectors and dealers.

Heritage Tackle 'n Tiques is now a virtual company, http://www.wwbait.net only doing business on line and at shows. However, our goal is the same, to share with others the joy and pleasure found only in fishing collectibles. I spent the first 15 years of my academic career as a field archaeologist and now bring to lure collecting the same dedication of learning as much as possible about the material cultural items we simply call "fishing lure collectibles." I have written this second book on modern fishing collectibles using my own experience for the past seven years selling thousands of fishing collectibles at shows, on eBay, out of our store, and out of antique booths in antique malls. It is hoped that others will benefit from my experience and that this book will add important information about a growing aspect of our hobby: "the modern era." It is not hard to figure out why more collectors are now starting to concentrate on the modern items: the pricing of vintage items is driving them to another part of the hobby. However, pricing of some modern items is also shocking, such as the recent sale of a new-in-the-box '70s Crazy Crawler for $1,650.00 on eBay[1]. I have also met many collectors that relate to the modern items the same as the older collectors related to the vintage items, items that bring back childhood memories. What I recall as a fishing lure from 1952 is quite different than what my neighbor Nick would have recalled from 1932! Finally, some collectors of vintage lures are switching to plastic lures because of the horror of having a very rare wooden bait deteriorate in front of their eyes due to paint flaking or instability of a related nature. This very fact was brought to my attention four years ago at a show in Ann Arbor where an older gentleman was selling all of his "vintage" lures and beginning a collection of Heddon plastics because of the recent loss of some fine lures due to paint deterioration. Granted, this does not happen to many early lures, but one could see the discouragement if a $350.00 lure fell apart as one admired it!

But, for whatever the reason, "modern" fishing lure collectibles have come of age. I recall the first show I did in 1995 where most of the folks were laughing at my "Heddon Plastics" tackle box and the fact that I was offering "choice out" for $10.00. Many scoffed at my "high" prices and said, "who cares about this modern junk?" Well, I sure wished I had some of the tough color River Runts and Sonics that I have sold over the years; on the other hand, that little tackle box of "Heddon Plastics" paid my way to each and every show that I attended and always resulted in a positive cash flow for me. The point is simple: what appeared at the edge of the hobby seven years ago has now become central to the hobby.[2] Without an interest in "modern" items, most of the new members would not have anything to collect, and frankly would be priced out of a most fascinating hobby. Hopefully, this book will help those individuals wanting to know more about these interesting collectibles.

The cover of Volume 1 illustrates many of the beautiful items described in Volumes 1 and 2 of the author's series on modern fishing collectibles.

This book begins coverage of fishing lure collectibles with the year 1940. This is the second book on the market that concentrates on the more recent items of collector interest, those items that I refer to as "modern" as opposed to "vintage." In my opinion, many modern lures are also "classic," and this term should be reserved for lures of distinction regardless of their precise age. Thus, those of us interested in what I have referred to as the more "modern" items will now have a benchmark reference that earlier books tended to cover only at a minimum, or in many instances, not at all. This is the second volume in a series of works on modern fishing collectibles with a third volume upcoming.

The date 1940 is historically relevant to begin a treatise on "modern" fishing lure collectibles because it is a time period that saw the beginning of the end for the so-called "vintage" wooden lures and the introduction of many new materials and manufacturing techniques. Some of these changes were brought upon lure companies by the outside forces of WWII, and some of the changes were born of opportunities afforded by inventions in the making of modern plastics. Another important change was the introduction of spinning technology with its related reels, lines, and new lighter lure weights. The result of all of these historical forces working together was the birth of many new lure manufacturing companies, some of which were long lived and some of which contributed to the body of lures and fishing memorabilia for only a short time.

There are many excellent references for lure collecting on the market; however, I know there is a need for detailed references, for items of this so-called "modern" age. Volume 1 covered important changes in the big companies, and Volume 2 introduces the readers to some of the lesser known companies, presented alphabetically, and provides a history of the changes that ultimately led to the closing or selling off of most major companies by 1988. As a lover of all fishing items, old and new, classic or clever, it is my hope to leave the reader with a solid foundation of knowledge on which the collector of modern fishing items can forge ahead with the power that only information provides.

It is difficult to give values for any particular item with precision due to the constant flux in the market for collectible fishing items. The suggested values in this book are based upon actual observations of items sold by us and others selling on eBay during 1998 – 2001, sales of items at shows specializing in fishing collectibles (both NFLCC-sanctioned and general shows), sales by private treaty, and discussions with other specialists in the field. However, the data given is just that, data based upon past performance. It cannot guarantee that future prices will continue to rise or that values will hold. It also cannot guarantee that future prices will remain anywhere near as low on some items. If I had a crystal ball, I would have bought every Punkinseed and Crazy Crawler in sight the past 10 years. I tried but ran out of money!

As a general rule, I think it is a fair statement to assume that most lures of any collectible interest will bring a minimum of $20.00 new-in-the-box by the time this book is published or within a year or two thereafter. This is based upon the general principle that a lure is usually worth double its value new-in-the box, and most lures are worth at least $10.00 now. Collectible lures are a lot like land, they are only available in a limited supply, and this is the driving force on price. The catch is determining which lures are collectible. Some new Pradco lures are already commanding high prices while others are only worth the face value for fishing purposes. For a lure to become collectible, it normally had to be produced in a limited supply for a limited time period and have some collector interest either due to its design or the company that produced it. Thus, one does not usually recognize a collectible item until some time has passed. As a general rule, I would not speculate on collectibility by hoarding large numbers of newer items in the hopes that they will go up in value.

Condition is also of utmost importance in any field of collectibles, and fishing items are no exception. Although dents caused by the teeth of a Northern Pike lend credibility to one's fishing stories, the same dents do not add value to the lure! Collectors love "minty" items. The NFLCC has a grading system used to grade old lures and also one to grade reels. This system is fine but in many ways does not apply to many of the plastic items that make up a vast portion of modern fishing collectibles. I would suggest the following categories:

1. New in the sealed box or on the sealed card, i.e., never opened.
2. New in the box with any original paper inserts.
3. New in the box.
4. Excellent in the box, i.e., no nicks, scars, abrasions, cracks, rust, etc.
5. Used in the box, i.e., some sign of wear or use but box still present.
6. Excellent without box, same as #4 without the box present.
7. Used without box, same as #5 without the box present.
8. Example bait only, poor condition but bait complete.
9. Parts bait or reel or rod only.

I have purposely avoided the word "mint," as it is so hard to define unless something is actually new and undamaged in the original packaging. Many sellers of lures have claimed on eBay that "this bait looks like it never saw the water," yet how can they know when it is out of its box! Many better quality plastics could be fished with for years without showing any signs of use if properly stored and cleaned after use, something many cautious individuals do. I was recently at a public auction sale where the auctioneer thought everything was "new" because it was so clean, but in reality the owner simply cleaned every item after use and reinserted it into its original packaging for storage. I knew because the owner was a friend of mine.

Yes, I could break the above 9-point scale into more refinements with mint, excellent, very good, good, fair, and poor. One can also grade the condition of both the packaging and the contents. But, I believe that a simple scaling of items as to new, excellent or used is more appropriate when dealing with items of more recent vintage, especially plastic items. I believe the key to these newer items is the presence or absence of packaging as well as the condition of the lure, rod or reel. In the final analysis, each individual collector will judge the item on its own merits, and each seller will use their own language when "hawking" their items on eBay or at a show. But, if one keeps in mind the rules about boxes and paperwork being present, this will assist in making a more well thought out purchase.

Finally, it is important to keep in mind that fishing collectibles are "luxury items" and as such the values will go up and down with the stock market and the available discretionary income of the public. This was obvious in the late 1990s and the early years of this century! A strong market and abundant discretionary income drove prices to unheard of levels for the rare and semi-rare items. In the months during which I wrote this volume (February through July of 2001), the market was weak, and prices for lures were not as strong. Good items maintained their values, but we are not seeing the strong prices for fairly common items seen a year ago. Our market for lures has been weaker since 9/11/01 but is slowly making a recovery along with the stock market. Only time will tell how America fully responds to the devastation brought to our wonderful country, but I am certain there will always be a strong interest in our cultural heritage related to fishing.

Hopefully, one is not collecting solely for the potential monetary gain of amassing a large collection but for the satisfaction of owning a piece of our cultural heritage and "little pieces of art." One has to keep in mind both the intrinsic and extrinsic value of one's collection. Another problem with fishing collectibles is that one cannot always "buy low" as it is absolutely true in this hobby that one must seize the day and buy items when available since they often are not available at a later date. So, buy wisely when possible, and keep some general rules in mind for your own goals. However, do not always expect to make money on lure sales and be aware that the market will continue to fluctuate in the future just as it has in the past. But, with good judgment being used, your collection should continue to grow in value over the years.

From top: Fin-Dingos, Bug-N-Bass, Doll Top Secrets, Eddie Pope on a card, Paul Bunyans, and a Depth-O-Plug in a box. Some of these items are featured in both Volumes 1 and 2.

One of the most puzzling areas for any collector new to the field of fishing collectibles is how to reliably date an item. Many of the reference works cited later in this book detail how to date very early items but do not assist the collector with post-1940 items to any great extent. Hopefully, the following discussion will assist collectors of modern items.

1. Catalogs and magazines are invaluable aides to dating items. However, the catalogs themselves are too expensive for the average collector to acquire just for dating purposes. Such purchases would soon require more invested in Heddon catalogs, for example, than in the Heddon River Runts in one's collection to determine some simple facts. Magazines, on the other hand, are very affordable and can assist one in determining the first year of production of an item, short-run lure identifications, and trends in lure manufacturing. I have identified many lures only by scanning through old fishing magazines and seeing the "only" advertisement ever run by a small company. It is common to still find magazines from the 1950s for only a few dollars each in mint condition (although as I am writing this book I am being outbid more and more on eBay as the prices are going up at this time for these items). See also Benchmarks on page 14.

2. Club literature of the NFLCC is another wonderful source of data. One can now purchase on CD-ROMs (the biggest drawback is that they are only reproduced in black and white) the entire lure history that the club had in print prior to 2001. This includes dozens of catalogs, brochures, patents, letters, and other documents to assist the collector. In addition, old issues of the *NFLCC Gazette* (the newsletter) and of the NFLCC magazine can assist one in identifying "unknown" lures. Again, there has been a bias in the club toward only early items, but more and more interest is being shown in some of the plastics and other "modern" items even within the club itself (again, witness the more recent issues of the publications).

3. Packaging is a big clue in dating if you are lucky enough to find a lure in its box or on its card. The first thing to look at is the address to determine if a zip code is present. Zippy[3] introduced the zip code for the U.S. Postal Service in 1963, and the zip code started appearing immediately on some packaging. However, the lack of a zip code may also simply mean that the company used up "in stock" packaging first or simply failed to comply with new postal regulations. The lack of a zip code is not a guarantee that an item is pre-1963, but it is one possible indicator. Also, I have noted that many companies used the zip code on a coupon or mailing label but not on the front of a package or catalog for the first few years of the 1960s. So, again, beware,

lack of zip code was often only a sign of a company being slow to react to new postal regulations and/or the layout department not being real creative and using old copy for catalogs and advertisements. My archival material of Weber Tackle Co. shows many examples of the secondary use of the same layout in following years. Also, the last four Heddon catalogs produced prior to the sale to Ebsco, Inc./Pradco are very, very similar.

4. What is in an eye? Well, for Heddon plastics, it is the easiest way to identify certain cut-off years for lures, in some cases. Some examples are reviewed in the Heddon chapter which should help the collector know an early Heddon plastic from a more recent Heddon or Pradco plastic, just by looking into the eyes of the lure! This was not true for all companies; however, many companies also had other changes that date a lure similar to eyes, such as variations in hook hardware, line ties, paint schemes, packaging, and so on as detailed below. Some of these details are very minute, and it takes time and experience in examining items to notice them all. I am still finding tiny differences that become clues to dating on many of the lures in my own collection.

5. Hook hardware is another major obvious item on a lure that can often assist one in dating it. Again, Heddon had significant changes documented elsewhere that help identify a range of years for any given item. Some other companies also had changes in hardware, for instance a Ropher Fin-Dingo may have rivets, flat blade screws, or Phillips screws, and one never finds the first option on a South Bend Fin-Dingo. Also, the early Doll Top Secrets had a very small hook hanger that was enlarged only when Heddon started painting Dolls and inserting its hook hangers.

6. There are other nuances that one can find in small detail changes to help date lures but always begin with the eyes and the hardware. Maybe the name was placed on the lure in a different fashion, such as on a Fin-Dingo. When Ropher made them, there was no name on some of them, and some had the name along with the model on the right side above the fin. South Bend placed the name across the back, as they did on most of their lures. When Luhr Jensen took over South Bend, they added the words "Original" to the classic South Bend lures. Numerous examples abound in other companies.

7. Package colors and materials also evolved and are an obvious indication of approximate time of manufacture. The two-piece cardboard box did not live too long into the 1950s for most companies. I have detailed one example with Heddon packaging in Volume 1, Chapter 1. However, in general, one finds smaller companies going to a solid two-piece plastic rectangular box without hinges for typical bass baits of 2 to 4 inches long by the mid-1950s. Examples include those shown for Hellbenders and others. Lures were also packaged in hinged one-piece plastic boxes for the smaller lures. Both cardboard and cellophane were used as seen on Doll Top Secrets and many Heddon lures. Eventually, lures were sold in bubble packs with little resemblance to the earlier beautiful packaging for lures. Regardless of the style or material, a package can usually be dated to a range of years at the very least. For example, the Millsite chapter in Volume 1 shows some very small differences that detail some year changes in the lettering on its box ends.

8. Lure colors are also an important indication of the time of production. Of course, this is somewhat a circular argument as only the catalogs or a lure insert will assist you with specifics; however, there are some general signs that help. Gantron fire lacquers were introduced as early as 1950 on some fly rod poppers, including Weber, and had a short run of popularity on lures at the same time, running out of general interest by the mid '50s. Thus, some of the fireplugs of CCBC bring such high dollars today. The one exception here would be the many orange plugs that signify the boom in Coho salmon fishing in the Great Lakes during the early '60s. Look for some of these in Bass-Orenos and others. Obvious color relationships also include red/white/blue combinations that one finds at the end of World War II and especially during the U.S. Bicentennial. Then, of course, we have a peanut-shaped lure to commemorate our peanut-farming president, Jimmy Carter. As a general rule, some of the more advanced color schemes of the late 1970s simply could not be done earlier without the computer graphics to support the concepts. Complexity of paint schemes usually is related to a more recent lure. But, again this is not written in stone.

9. Quality of manufacture is something that is hard to explain in a book but is easily recognized when examining an item. After looking at thousands of lures, one can usually date a plastic lure by the type of method used to make it, the feel of the plastic, the presence or absence of "white scum residue" on the lure, hook attachment, survival condition of the gloss, hardness of the plastic, etc. As a general rule, the higher the quality, the more recent the lure. But, of course, this does not always hold true, one example being the poor quality paint, eye placement, and loose cup hardware found on the 1987 reintroduction of Pikies and other wooden lures by Creek Chub/Dura Pak.

10. The most important way to date an item is to handle as many items that you already know the dates on and can learn to compare by examination of similarities and differences. This is one of the main advantages to the lure shows. You are able to walk around, pick up lures, ask questions, make comparisons, learn, and not spend a cent. I know I have spent many days as an instructor, talking as I have set up my sales table, and have enjoyed the opportunity to teach others what I have learned. Most people that do the shows also enjoy helping one learn about the lures they have for sale, so go, ask, learn, and maybe even buy an item or two! I no longer go to shows in anticipation of selling as I believe the Internet is a far superior tool. However, I still enjoy seeing thousands of lures, decoys, creels, rods, and reels in one spot, and shows are a great social activity, too.

11. Company names and packaging. This is an area that is key to look for when identifying modern items, such as some of the examples shown below (see also patents & trademarks, etc).

Heddon. By 1940 the earlier names of Dowagiac, James Heddon, James Heddon and Sons had become James Heddon's Sons, Dowagiac, Mich. By 1951 it was the same name but "Mich." becomes "Michigan," and the back of the catalog says "James Heddon's Sons of Dowagiac, Michigan." The trademark is "Heddon" set inside the offset rectangle. By 1962 there is still the same trademark with "of Dowagiac, Michigan" added along with Subsidiary, Daisy Manufacturing Company. By 1965 the company is referred to as Daisy-Heddon. In 1967, the name is James Heddon's Sons, Dowagiac, Michigan, Division of Daisy Manufacturing Company. In 1968, it evolves into Daisy/Heddon, Division of Victor Comptometer Corporation after another change of ownership. In 1970 the catalog advertises blister pack presentation for lures for the first time. The blister pack is again advertised in 1971. In 1972 the trademark is changed to Heddon with a registered mark going up at an angle on a solid triangle. The year 1975 sees the addition of the service mark of "The Great American Tackle Company." In 1977, it becomes James Heddon's Sons, Division of Victor Comptometer Corp., Dowagiac, Michigan 49047. This same year sees Heddon spelled out in green and black diamonds and the introduction of the green and black logo on rods, reels, and lure boxes. The 1978 catalog had Heddon spelled out in diamonds on the cover. There is a short-lived use of the green diamond boxes with Kidde on the boxes and also brief runs of the green diamond boxes that say simply "James Heddon's Sons" on only one side of the box. James Heddon's Sons was used early by Ebsco, and the first Heddon lures after the 1983 purchase by Ebsco did not have Pradco on the packages but only had Ebsco, Inc. and a trademark of 1984, with the packages being a light green or a light beige. As a matter of fact, beware as some of the early Pradco packages are really Ebsco, Inc. 1984 packages with only a little sticker added to the top backside of the package, adding the word "Pradco" and covering the original Ebsco, Inc. found on the package back top. I say beware for the simple reason that many of the early Ebsco, Inc. lures with Pradco "over-marked" lure packages actually contained old stock Heddon items that the company received from Heddon when they purchased it. I confirmed this when speaking to the president of Pradco in 1999, and he informed me that "we would simply find a container of older (Heddon) items and put it (the lure) in our packaging," responding to my asking why I was finding Heddon items from the early 1970s in some of the Ebsco, Inc. packages. The mark has varied since 1984 with the famous offset Heddon in a rectangle reappearing at times. This should give the reader an idea of the subtle nuances available in Heddon packaging. More details are given in the Heddon chapter in Volume 1.

Creek Chub Bait Company always used the same name; however, they had the subsidiaries of Allcock, Laight & Westwood in Canada and Sure Strike in the USA. One can date more recent wooden Creek Chub lures and plastics by looking at the place of manufacture on the box, with the Sioux City, Iowa, address being used after the company left Indiana in 1978 when CCBC was purchased by Lazy Ike. There were also slight box design changes for some of the plastic lures, and the script on the boxes became similar to the one used on the Sioux City boxes prior to the company's leaving Indiana. Lazy Ike and CCBC were eventually sold to Dura Pak while still in Sioux City and then purchased by Pradco in 1991 with the trade names of Creek Chub and Lazy Ike still being used by Pradco. The last few years of Creek Chub history, the company moved as fast as one of its Pikies on a 5-to-1 bait-casting reel!

South Bend became Gladding-South Bend by 1964. During that era one usually finds lures with the words "Original" added to the name on the back of the lure, and the trademark was "modernized" to a capital SB with a little dot in the upper part of the B. A review of the 1969 Parker Distributing catalog shows South Bend rods and reels available in a wide variety, all under the name Gladding-South Bend. Eventually, the rights to make the lures were acquired by the Glen L. Evans Company of Idaho, and in turn, the rights to make and sell the Oreno line of lures were purchased by Luhr Jensen & Sons, Inc. of Hood River, Oregon, in 1982, and they are still being made by a subsidiary of Luhr Jensen, Classic Woods, at this time. The words "Original" no longer appear on the back of the lure. South Bend

Sporting Goods Inc., with a current address of 1910 Techny Rd., Northbrook, Illinois 60065 and a former address of 1950 Stanley Street, Northbrook, IL 60062 as given in 1992, in the Chicago area, lives on as a major distributor of fishing items, primarily rods, reels, and terminal tackle.

Pflueger became part of Shakespeare in 1966; however, it was operated as a separate company with its own trade names used until at least the 1970s. The 1966 Pflueger catalog Number 102 shows the complete line of rods and reels and a decent assortment of fishing lures. It also has a mini-catalog inserted in the middle showing 16 pages of terminal tackle, taking Pflueger back to its roots as a hook company. Its boxes changed in modern times from the classic "canoe box" to a stylized and modernized Pflueger being spelled out in blue on either a white background with a large "P" in Pflueger or the same design on a paper label on the end of a neat gold box with a repeating fish design on the box. Also, slide-top plastic boxes were used by Pflueger with the early ones being the green versions as shown in the Pflueger chapter and later ones being the stylized P on white with a slide top.

Shakespeare took over both Paw Paw and Pflueger in the 1960s and was a subsidiary of Anthony Industries by 1992 with an address of 3801 Westmore Drive, Columbia, South Carolina 20223. The company is still headquartered in South Carolina and markets rods, reels, and terminal tackle only. As Luckey points out in his book, at one time Creek Chub purchased Shakespeare in the 1950s (the period during which the mice of both companies were co-mingled) only to see Shakespeare survive and Creek Chub be consumed in consolidations by Lazy Ike, Dura Pak, and most recently, Pradco. Only Shakespeare lives on today as an independent fishing tackle company with its beginnings in 1897. Even though it is part of a bigger corporation, Shakespeare is now headquartered in one of the original Shakespeare operations, dating back to at least 1951, according to facts found in the 1951 Shakespeare catalog. The Kalamazoo works are gone, but the company still has ties to its past in a more direct way than any of the remaining "big five" companies.

Many of the smaller lure companies were first consolidated with one of the big five, such as Paw Paw being purchased by Shakespeare, prior to having their names disappear from history forever. Regretably, most of the consolidating companies, such as Shakespeare, Pradco, and South Bend[4], kept no records of these events other than accounting ones that, in most cases, no longer exist. Thus, our knowledge has to be based upon the same type of reconstruction history one finds being done by an industrial archaeologist! There are many gaps to fill, and I shall do my best to continue to fill them in future editions with the assistance and contributions of my readers. So, please contact me if you have additional information for the history of any of the companies, or corrections to my work.

12. Benchmarks. What I refer to as benchmarks include literature or advertising introducing a lure or item as "new." Be aware that some companies used the designation "new" for more than one year to sell their products; a review of the Heddon catalogs from 1970 – 1984 demonstrates this over and over again. These can be catalogs, magazine advertisements, company brochures, lure box inserts, separate wholesaler fliers or advertisements, or company histories. Once a direction for the collection has been decided, the wisest investment the new collector can make is the purchase of the company catalog for the particular year of the beginning of the collection, if available. Then, attempt to follow the changes in following years through catalogs and advertising in trade magazines and popular literature. For instance, if you collect only South Bend Fin-Dingos, you need not go any earlier than 1952 for your catalogs. Then, you can trace Model 1965 until it disappears from production. Research and collecting must both have a beginning, and once you have this foundation, the rest of your collection is built on the strength of the knowledge of your product. Of course, we often, as collectors, only do the research once we accidentally discover some irresistible lure or rod or reel that must become ours!

13. Oral history. As a former working anthropologist and folklorist, I long ago learned the importance of paying attention to oral history and seeking out "informants" when attempting to learn the history of an area or subject. This is no different in lure and fishing collectible history. Phil Jensen, current owner and son of the founder of Luhr Jensen, is a prime example. Here is a man who has literally lived through all of the major changes in modern fishing lure manufacturing, and we are fortunate in the fact that he is also interested in lure history and collecting. It is most important to the future of fishing collectibles that we document all we can about the history of items by seeking out individuals with knowledge and writing down what they have to say while the information is still available. I have learned much of my information through discussions with lure makers, decoy carvers, jobbers, and retailers in the trade, and I can only hope that others are also documenting all they can while it is fresh in the minds of those involved.

14. Patents, trademarks, trade names, and copyrights. One final way to date an item is to complete a patent search for the item on the U.S. Patent and Trademark Office website found at http://www.uspto.gov by entering the appropriate data. The site is quite easy to use and will result in finding great details on an individual piece. Sometimes the only information about a lure or an item we have is the patent number, printed on it, and this will help in a complete history of the item by entering the number in the search process. There are limitations on certain searches unless you know the patent number, and keep in mind that the patent year only indicates when the item was actually granted a patent. Sometimes this is years after an item was "used in commerce." It is also possible to conduct trademark, trade name, and copyright searches for items; however, this is a bit more complicated than entering the patent number. Trademark and trade name searches are conducted through the U.S. Patent and Trademark Office, and copyright searches would be completed through the Library of Congress, the organization in charge of protecting copyrighted material in the United States. You can go from the http://www.uspto.gov site to the copyright site, or the address for copyrights is http://lcweb.loc.gov/copyright/ which tells one how to go about searches. Also, keep in mind that if you are printing items for publication, some of the materials on the U.S. government sites are protected by copyright, and you will need permission to reprint certain items for publication.

The author is always willing to appraise collections of fishing items, buy collections large or small, and sell collections for others. Also he has a variety of modern fishing lure collectibles by direct sale and on eBay. He may be reached in any of the following ways and will respond to all legitimate inquiries.

Mail: Dr. Russell E. Lewis
      Bishop Hall 515
      1349 Cramer Circle
      Big Rapids, MI 49307

E-mail: findingo@netonecom.net or lewisr@ferris.edu

Website: www.wwbait.net

Phone: (231) 591-3581

The link found on the eBay website may be used to e-mail the author via his eBay user id: findingo.

What I have referred to as the modern era begins with the year 1940, a foundation upon which we can build our understanding of lure and fishing collectible history in the United States. Most of the vintage lures and collectibles up to now have been from the period prior to World War II according to most collecting literature. Only a few of us have been actively seeking the newer items the past five or 10 years. This has helped me amass a large number of items at rather reasonable prices, but I have been frustrated by the lack of reliable information on modern items. Even Luckey's 5th Edition which has an expanded section on "plastics" still fails to solve many mysteries and does not really go into depth as to the historical processes involved in changing lures from vintage classic wood to modern neo-classic plastic. Please do not misunderstand, I think Luckey's book is one of the best, and I could not live without it for its wonderful treatment of many companies. I am simply stating that collectors needed books to fill in some gaps, and I am hoping this is one of those books.

If it were not for the fact that it is necessary to give some background on what had led to the changes in vintage lures, I would begin my treatise with December 7, 1941. Yes, Pearl Harbor! This is, of course, the triggering event for the entry of the United States into World War II. We were in a war build-up period prior to that time with more and more of our lure companies also doing defense production; however, the act of declaring war had not happened until after the bombing of Pearl Harbor. This really hit home for me when I was reviewing a 1942 fishing magazine for this book, and most of the lure company advertisements made some reference to the bombing of Pearl Harbor and/or the war effort itself. Creek Chub Bait Company even came out with a new lure with the SOS symbol for victory as a response to the war. This late date in 1941 would also be accurate for a beginning as most catalogs for 1942 had already come off the press, and the 1942 catalogs were the last ones produced by most major companies until either 1946, or in many cases, 1947.

So, our era begins in 1940 but develops slowly until 1947 for reasons beyond the control of tackle companies and the fishing public. The only exception to this statement is that one of the first major advertisements for spinning reels and lures that I have found appeared in the same 1942 fishing magazine mentioned above and returning service personnel started bringing home spinning equipment from 1942 until after the end of the war in 1945.[5] So, the stage was set for major changes to come in the tackle industry with the introduction of a new type of fish-

ing and a post-war economic boom that would last at least until the late 1960s.

Another thing happened that is directly related to modern fishing collectibles in 1946 and 1947, the birth of an entire generation of potential collectors known as "baby boomers." I am a baby boomer of 1947 and know that my interests in "classic tackle" relate more to the Ambassadeur 5000s and early Heddon plastics than to Heddon 150s that I had only seen hanging on the neighbor's garage wall pegboard. Not that I would not love to have those old 150s, but I feel more nostalgia for a Heddon Meadow Mouse, Creek Chub Spinning Plunker, and Shakespeare Wonderod than for the earlier items. It is with this in mind that I have written these books.

The next historical period that would later have an impact on lure collecting would be the recessive economic conditions of the 1970s and early 1980s, starting with the oil embargo of 1973. This saw the consolidation and closing of many companies in the tackle industry due to a number of factors. Important factors included the fierce competition created by Japanese imports, and imports from Taiwan and Hong Kong, the general economic downturn associated with the first "energy crisis" of 1973, and the high cost of money during the inflationary period of 1978 to 1983. When floor plans on inventory were costing a company up to the usurious limits of interest, it is not difficult to see how it was impossible for them to survive. That is why in reviewing the Weber archives, one finds an appraisal in 1984 looking at other uses for the physical plant of the company and discussions of the need to downsize all inventory. That is also why Heddon discontinued dozens of lures in 1982. Companies could no longer afford to produce and finance large inventories in the hopes of selling them within a year or two. Turnover had to be instant to avoid paying "floor plan interest" on goods being held for sale.

Another factor was yet another change in fishing technology. Injection molding of plastics had become very advanced by the early 1970s, and a company no longer needed to be large to be cost effective in producing lures for a specialty market. Also, BassPro Shops saw their beginning in 1970 as a specialty store dealing in items for tournament fishing. Many fishing enthusiasts and tournament fishing contestants (for tournament fishing was now becoming big business) were "hooked" on the new technique of using rubber worms, jigs, jig and pig techniques, and the not so new but now widespread use of scented baits. So, while the classic companies were producing thousands of plastic and wooden lures to stock the shelves of the bait stores, the public was turning to those companies producing any form of "new and improved" rubber worm or scented bait! As with spinning in the 1950s, this new interest in rubber worms added one more wound to a dying industry. Of course, now we may have come full circle with the revitalization of "crank baits" that started to be in vogue in tournament circles in the 1990s, and our future collectors of our "post-modern era" will have numerous choices of short-lived runs of bass and walleye baits from which to choose for their collection of "vintage" lures.

Finally, one other historical event that has changed lure collecting is the high prices that became common in the late 1990s and early 2000s for vintage lures. As more and more entered this wonderful hobby of lure collecting and the stock market continued to make many collectors "rich on paper," NFLCC members and non-members alike started paying hundreds of dollars for certain vintage items. This drove more and more of us to plastics and newer wooden lures to keep us busy collecting. As I write this paragraph, May of 2002, the stock market is still not doing so well, and prices are a little soft. Yet, the days of picking up a classic Heddon 150 in excellent shape for a few dollars are gone forever, and the interest in "modern era fishing collectibles" is here to stay.

So, for now I shall define the modern era as 1940 through 1988. The reasons for the initial date are well defined in history. The reason for the concluding date is the closure of most vintage tackle companies by then, with Weber closing officially in 1988, the last to go, having produced its final catalog in 1985. Heddon became property of Pradco in late 1983. Creek Chub Bait Company had joined forces with Lazy Ike and others under the Dura Pak label by then. Shakespeare (having purchased both Pflueger and Paw Paw), Luhr Jensen and South Bend are still in business. Shakespeare now exclusively sells rods and reels, and South Bend imports most of its goods for retail. Luhr Jensen remains solid on its own foundation, and it has in turn purchased many former companies and added their products to its line. Throughout the book I shall refer to some post-1988 developments and events; however, this treatise shall officially end at 1988.

One final note, this book is not meant to be exhaustive but rather exemplary and illustrative by nature. I now know how Capt. Luckey must have felt after completing his first edition of his classic text on fishing collectibles: "the feeling that one simply cannot cover it all in enough detail." To cover just one company in detail is difficult enough, to attempt to give a good cross-section of modern lures and fishing collectibles becomes mind boggling at times. Regardless of what I put in the book, others will criticize my work due to the omissions and the lack of completeness. So, with this said, I know there will be future volumes in which additions, corrections, and even deletions may occur. But, I, and the collecting world, had to begin somewhere, and this is it. I welcome all correspondence to make future works better and hope that given my editorial and publishing limitations on the number of pages and photographs that you will forgive me if your favorite fishing lure, rod, reel, or accessory was omitted from these two volumes. I simply hope that you find these two volumes useful texts as foundation builders in the exciting area of modern fishing lure collectibles. Enjoy!

The author is always willing to appraise collections of fishing items, buy collections large or small, and sell collections for others. Also he has a variety of modern fishing lure collectibles by direct sale and on eBay. He may be reached in any of the following ways and will respond to all legitimate inquiries.

Mail: Dr. Russell E. Lewis
Bishop Hall 515
1349 Cramer Circle
Big Rapids, MI 49307

E-mail: findingo@netonecom.net or lewisr@ferris.edu

Website: www.wwbait.net

Phone: (231) 591-3581

The link found on the eBay website may be used to e-mail the author via his eBay user id: findingo.

Volume 1 covered 14 major companies and this volume takes on a new task. This is the most fun of all, attempting to cover the rest[6] of the companies and their contributions to modern fishing lure collectibles. This chapter has examples of baits new in the boxes that are identified for the first time in print and many examples that are detailed better than ever before. Part of my own collection is the foundation for this chapter, and I have included detailed photos of all lures identified. Some of the most valuable of all plastic and modern wooden baits are found in this

miscellaneous category and were manufactured by a small company in either small production runs or for a short time period. This section is organized on an A-Z basis with the name of the lure and a cross-section table to the manufacturer when known.

A-Lures to Zimmy Lures are detailed with photos. I have included text in this section with enough detail to assist the collector; however, each entry could be expanded upon as more details are known. I have included data related to company location(s) and time of production when known.

A-Lure

A-LURE, Inc., P.O. Box 2385, Portland, Oregon or 118 N.E. 24th Ave., Portland 12, Oregon. Both addresses appeared on the same advertisement and both are pre-zip code. It appears this was a single lure company, making and selling a lure known as the Keel-Fish "The Revolutionary All-Purpose Fishing Lure." This is a lure that looks nearly identical in body and eye design to the odd goggle-eyed lure known as the "Lucky Lady," pages 90 – 92. Both are West Coast lures, one California and the other Oregon. The quality of the Keel-Fish is excellent, some of the best I have seen in a plastic lure. This lure was promoted as an all-purpose lure and came with three sizes of hooks in a single hinged plastic box with one lure. The fisherman could change the hook size depending on the fish being targeted. The paint on the lures is beautiful with excellent scale patterns. "Made in 12 Basic Tested Colors" says the brochure included with each lure (printed on the same type of paper as the early Eddie Pope brochures): 101 Fluorescent Red; 102 Fluorescent Red, Black Spots; 103 Gold; 104 Silver; 105 Green Frog; 106 Orange, Black & Red Spots; 107 Yellow, Red Spots; 108 White, Red Spots; 109 Pearly, Pink Striped; 110 Perch Scale; 111 Gold Scale; 112 Silver Scale. The lure cost $1.25 new and should fetch at least $15.00 – 20.00 new in box today. These are some of the nicest small company lures out there. Each box was marked with the color number on top and had a black heavy paper liner separating the lure and the brochure. This really added to the color visibility when marketing the lure in the bait shops. The black paper also served as a hook protector, and the lure was shipped with its hook and the two spares tucked nicely under this paper to protect the lure. Hopefully, one of my readers will write and tell me there was a complete line of these lures and others by this company, but for now we have only this one set of lures to go by.

Shown is Keel-Fish with brochure and all three hooks removed from its box and one in the original box on black background. $15.00 – 20.00 each.

Abbey and Imbrie
(A & I)

This brand was around for a long time prior to the Modern Era, and actually the lures were normally, if not always, produced by someone else. Some of the vertical stripe patterns typical of this company were later typical of the Horrocks-Ibbotson 1950s wooden lures. Shown is a nice Nature Lure, Rubber Cricket No. 01, new on card, and a very high quality jointed wooden runt type bait new from its box. This second bait has cup hardware similar to a South Bend, a Shur-Strike type diving lip, and tack eyes. It is so well made that I first thought it was plastic and had to take out the front cup to be certain it was wooden. This is a typical scale pattern for Horrocks-Ibbotson, and Abbey & Imbrie used it previously. It was found new in a two-piece cardboard box with no markings, and a woodgrain pattern in gray tones. The lure is 3½" long.

Cricket No. 012. $10.00.

Likely an H-I Jointed Go-Getter, surface/washer tail and cup belly hardware. $25.00 – 35.00.

Abu Aktiebolag

Located in Svangsta, Sweden, the makers of the famous Ambassadeur and Cardinal reels also made some early spinning lures in the 1950s and some plastic lures of note. The 1973 catalog illustrated two pages of plastic lures, some of which show up fairly often in trading. One of higher interest is the Hi-Lo series of lures that have an adjustable diving lip, thus the name. These lures were made under contract for Abu by Heddon and have Heddon colors, for the most part. The lures vary in length from a short 2½" river runt type to a 6" vamp type lure. These are marked on the belly as Abu Hi-Lo and the type of lure. New-in-the-box lures run about the same as the Heddon River Runt, $15.00+ depending on color and size.

The 1973 catalog also lists a Rapala/Rebel copy known as the Killer. Cello and Cello Dip appear to be lures like Burke's soft lures detailed below and maybe were even made by Burke for Abu. The Kynoch is a J-Plug type lure for Salmon. Finally, new in 1973 was the Snoky, a fish-shaped plastic lure in diving and floating models.

The Snoky is an interesting looking plastic bait, especially the floater, and will likely go up in value over the years. Altogether, the 1973 catalog listed a total of 79 size and color combinations for its lures. Again, a fairly large number for a collector to find them all! Other items of interest would be the Optic Flies, some of the metal baits not often found, and the early Old Pal/Abu tackle boxes. Add to this a complete collection of Ambassadeur and Cardinal reels and one has quite a collecting goal from a single company.

Hi-Lo Lure Box. $5.00 – 10.00.

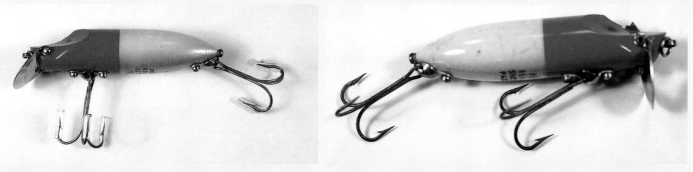

Two different Hi-Lo lures in same color. 3¼" long, surface hardware, painted eyes, second one is from box shown, note how lip moves. These two are common. $15.00+ depending on color/size. Add $5.00 – 10.00 boxed.

HI-LO

HI-LO is a "MUST" Lure for Pike and Salmon
The deadliest wobbler, taker of many thousands of double figure Pike and Salmon. Adjustable lip clicks into 6 different positions to fish Hi-Lo at any depth or across the top as a "popper". Floating versions allow the lure to be drifted into just the right position before retrieve sends it searching at the depth you have set. Luminous colour (LYS) is best for really deep fishing.

Unless otherwise stated available in colours: BGL, BO, D, LYS, M, RH, T, XRY.
³/₇ oz. 2¹/₂" Sinking. In all colours. **Price 72p**
⁵/₈ oz. 3¹/₄ Sinking. In all colours. **Price 80p**
³/₄ oz. 3¹/₂" Jointed. Slow-sink. In all colours except LYS. Also in L = Brown/Green/Yellow and XRS = Silver/Black Ribbing. **Price 95p**
1 oz. 4¹/₂" Floating. All colours except LYS. **95p**
1 oz. 4¹/₂" Sinking. In colour LYS only. **Price 95p**
1¹/₂ oz. 6" Floating. BGL, BO, LYS, M. **Price £1.55**

KILLER

A MUST for big Lake Trout, good for Bass, Salmon and Pike too! A sinking lure that can be fished at any desired depth. Last year two of the best fish reported — a 17 lbs. Brown Trout and a 32 lbs. Salmon, taken on "Killer" in Scotland. The ABU "Killer" has many imitators for none have such a superb long lasting or glistening finish, none seem quite so effective in fish getting as the ABU original.
¹/₈ oz. 2³/₄" G & S only. **Price 75p**
³/₈ oz. 3¹/₂" G, S, BGL. **Price 85p**
¹/₂ oz. 4¹/₂" G, S, BGL. **Price 95p**
³/₄ oz. 5¹/₂" G, S, BGL. **Price 99p**

Tight Lines 73 catalog, page 96.

CELLO & CELLO DIP.
Lures fish love to chew and can't spit out! Cello has taken specimen after specimen, Pike, Salmon, Trout, including a monster Pike of 35 lb. 5 oz. When a fish takes Cello it takes a body as soft as the real thing, so flexible that the fish finds it difficult to eject until it's too late and the hooks are home. Cellular cavities allow the lure to float no matter how badly punished. Available in 2 models. Cello Dip has a special lip for deeper swimming. Colours, D, S, RH, BGL.

Cello	¹/₂ oz./2¹/₂"	Price 85p
Cello Dip	⁵/₈ oz./3¹/₂"	Price 99p

KYNOCH.
The MUST-Lure for Salmon — good for Pike and Lake Trout too! Specially designed for trolling and harling from a boat, but can be cast and fished equally well from the bank. Countless thousands of really heavy Salmon are taken on Kynoch every year. Concave face gives an irresistible shimmy and darting action. Special hook shackle allows the body to move up the line leaving the hook only in the fish's mouth. Available in colours: BGL, T, BO, LYS, G, WP also. RH = Red head, White Body and K = Coppertone. ³/₇ oz./4" Floating.
Price 75p

New! SNOKY.
Here is a wonderful new wobbler that on extensive trials has measured up to ABU standards in fish getting ability. Killer and Hi-Lo had better look to their laurels now that Snoky is on the scene! This great new lure has a superb reflective glitter-scale finish and is destined to become a great favourite with Pike, Salmon, and Bass. Available in two versions in colours S, K, BGL.
Sinking: ³/₈ oz. 85p. ¹/₂ oz. 95p. 1 oz. £1.05.
Floating (with lip): ³/₁₆ oz. 85p. ³/₈ oz. 95p.

Colour Guide: *There are 79 size/colour combinations of the ABU lures illustrated. The full range of colours is shown, with the exception of XRS. Please refer to descriptions for size/colour availability.*

Tight Lines 73 catalog, page 97. Trade value $5.00 – 15.00.

Early Abu boxes for its spinner baits and a bait in the box; the one shown is Model 129, ³/₇ oz., the other two are shown in Chapter 3. $10.00+ boxed, $3.00 – 5.00 loose.

A-C Shiners

Made by A. C. S. Industries, 5747 Jenkins Rd., Okeana, Ohio 45053. These nicely made, colorful wooden lures, new-in-the-box have sold for $10.00 – 15.00 each on eBay. With a plastic top cardboard box, Model 256 DR (deep running) is 2⅛" long and has the more rounded head, simple screw hardware, painted eyes, and marked on bottom with name and model number. The dive lip is held in place by two flat blade screws. The Model 250 looks like a Rapala and is made of balsa, with staple-type hook hangers forced into the wood, also clearly marked.

Two new-in-the-box A-C Shiners. $8.00 – 15.00 each.

Accetta

Tony Accetta, 853 East 144th St., Cleveland, Ohio. This company is now one of the many owned by Luhr Jensen and Sons, Inc. Shown is an early Weed-Dodger, new in its two-piece cardboard box, with an insert touting that only five baits are needed in Tony's tackle box! To no one's surprise, one is the Weed-Dodger by Accetta. The other four are the River Devil, in my opinion one of the nicest looking Al Foss type lures ever made; the Spin Dodger; the "Pet" Spoon; and, the "new" Jigolet. The Jigolet was a popper bait made of Tenite with the addition of the "Hula Skirt" by Arbogast. Accetta licensed the rights to use the skirt on this bait and a new version of the Weed-Dodger with a Hula Skirt instead of a feather. The Jigolet lists no colors, and I have only seen red/white ones. Tony Accetta made his fame first as the U.S. Professional Bait and Fly Casting Champion. This made his lures very marketable, much in the same way as Pradco today is using professional contest fisherman to market its lures. Accetta went on to make a number of unique lures, and there is growing collector interest for his items. However, inasmuch as many of the lures are metal, they do not have the value of some others. One interesting note is that Accetta made and marketed the Weber Champ starting in about 1987, and this may have been an infringement according to letters in the Weber's archival material. However, it does not appear Weber pursued this as it was ready to close its doors. But Accetta may have also had a license to produce the lure for which I did not find the evidence in the files.[7] Values for early lures in two-piece cardboard boxes should be $15.00 to $20.00, maybe even a little more for the River Devil and a perfect Jigolet. The spoons are common and not worth as much.

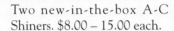

Just Five Favorite Baits
THAT'S MY TACKLE BOX!
Says **TONY ACCETTA**

U. S. PROFESSIONAL BAIT and FLY CASTING CHAMPION

They give the Advantages of 1001 Baits
Here is one of them

WEED-DODGER
PAT. NO. 2,145,283

An older Accetta box for a Weed-Dodger. $20.00+ in box.

A nice looking Tony Accetta Bug-Spoon, $10.00+, and a common Hobo, $5.00.

Allcock Laight & Westwood Company (A L & W)

206 Parkhurst Blvd, Leaside, Toronto, Ontario was the address given in the 1955 catalog. Allcock Laight & Westwood was the licensing agent for Creek Chub Lures in Canada, and it manufactured and distributed both its own line of baits and Creek Chub baits. The first year they packaged the famous Creek Chub Pikies (see page 2 of their 1955 catalog) and other baits in a one-piece hinged plastic box with the name AL&W on the upper left hand side was 1955. The box would also have the catalog model number and lure name on the top in gold letters. Shown is a "Popeye"-Wabbler, Model No. 928, 2¾" long, in gold with a ruby eye. This AL&W bait was invented in 1935 according to the catalog, and the lure is described on page 32 of the 1955 catalog. It was available in two sizes, 4" and 2¾" as shown in Silver, Gold, and Copper colors. Some of the AL&W Creek Chub baits are worth even more than the ones from their parent companies,

well over $100.00 each for some examples. The Popeye would bring about $25.00 new in its box. This metal bait has more value than most because of the manufacturing company's association with Creek Chub.

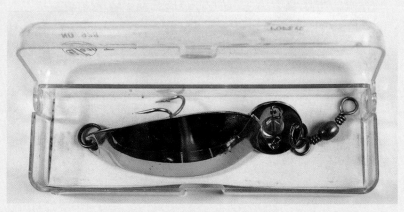

Popeye lure in box. $25.00.

Atlantic Lures

Providence, Rhode Island. Atlantic made many "copycat lures" of the major companies, including the Jitterbug and Hula Popper, River Runt, Bayou Boogie, Rapala/Rebel Minnow, and even Flatfish copies known as Flatheads. Some of these lures are shown below. The Flatheads shown are all new in the tube and have a sales price of $1.20; the model number is 804 on both the orange with black spotted ones and the red/white one. These lures were not marked; however, many Atlantic Lures are marked. These are likely pre-1963, pre-zip address on the cards. The value on most of the Atlantic Lures is not very high and would average about $5.00, unless new in package, then they should bring at least $10.00 each. A nice side collection would be adding Atlantic Lures to your main collection if you favor the look-alikes. Again, an interesting question that remains unanswered is whether or not these were true knock-offs or if they were being produced under a licensing/royalty agreement with the owners of the trademarks/patents. Only future research will answer some of these questions.[8] Part of an Atlantic catalog from 1966 follows on pages 24 – 30.

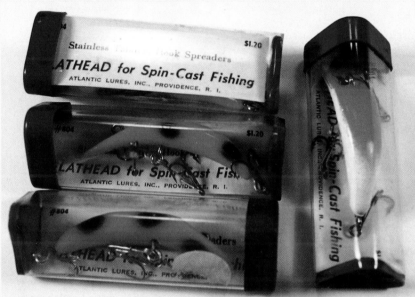

Flatheads in tubes, lure is 2¼" long, front gang hardware, rear treble hook. There is a half-moon indentation at the screw line tie. $8.00 each.

Atlantic Lures' versions of Hellbenders, the frog is a ½ oz. Plunger-Pup, clearly marked on lip. Tail spinner and lip also have lighthouse trademark, belly hooks are inset into molded body, and eyes are slightly raised. The attractive black shore/scale pattern is a ⅝ oz. Plunger-Pup made the same way and also clearly marked. $6.00 – 9.00.

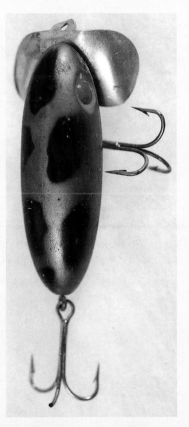

Jitterbug-type Atlantic lure, the Frantic Antic, 2⁹⁄₁₆", surface belly hardware, simple screw tail hardware, carved eyes, lip marked with company and lure name. $10.00 – 12.00.

"BARON"

DEEP-RUNNING
PROPERLY-BALANCED
FAST-DIVING

Made of tough tenite, perfectly balanced to float and swim with the proper wiggle and counter balanced with the correct weight and shaped scoop. This is an ideal Lure for spinning, casting and trolling. Comes with a pre-set snap-bar to which the line is attached. The final action may be "Field Adjusted" by bending the snap-bar to the left or the right until the desired retrieve is found.

COLORS: USE SAME CHART AS PLUNGER-PUP BELOW.

ONE EACH ON A PEG-BOARD BUBBLE CARD

#845	BARON ¼ OUNCE SPINNING	$1.15 list
#847	BARON ⅜ OUNCE CASTING	1.15 list

"PLUNGER-PUP"

BULLET CASTS
CONTROLLED DEPTH
AMAZINGLY EFFECTIVE

USED EFFECTIVELY AND WITH PROVEN RESULTS ON BASS, PICKERAL, MUSKIE, PIKE, BLUES AND OTHER GAME-FISH. COLORS FOR DAY AND NIGHT FISHING

A size for spinning, spin-casting and casting, decorated in time-tested and proven colors, and assembled with the finest hardware available. The "Plunger Pup" will cast with great ease, sinks to the desired depth quickly and will stay there with a steady retrieve. Will swim over objects where other Lures would snag and hang-up.

★ STOCK COLORS BY THE DOZEN OF A COLOR		
RW	RED HEAD, WHITE BODY	★
FR	FROG, WHITE BELLY	★
BK	BLACK WIDOW	★
CW	COACHDOG-BLACK WHITE	★
WR	WHITE, BLACK RIBS	★
YR	YELLOW, BLACK RIBS	★

(ALSO: MINIMUM 10 DOZEN OF A COLOR AND SIZE)

SP—SILVER PERCH	YW—YELLOW w/BLACK WAVE
BR—BLACK w/WHITE RIB	RF—RIB BED FLUORESCENT
WW—WHITE w/BLACK WAVE	PM—PURPLE MINNOW
WD—WHITE w/BLACK DOT	YD—YELLOW w/BLACK DOT

ONE EACH ON A PEG-BOARD DISPLAY CARD

#870	PLUNGER-PUP ¼ OUNCE	$1.15 list
#871	PLUNGER-PUP ½ OUNCE	1.15 list
#872	PLUNGER-PUP ⅝ OUNCE	1.15 list

Atlantic Lures 1966 catalog, page 3.

"BASS'R-PLUG"

This bass plug needs no description other than the picture. Has been used for over 50 years. It floats at rest, swims just under the surface, and pops loudly.

Colors: Red-White
          Spotted Orange
          White-Belly Frog
          Yellow Perch

ONE EACH
ON A PEG-BOARD
BUBBLE CARD

#890	BASS'R-PLUG	3/8 ounce	$1.10 list

"GAYLORD"

For Spinning and Spin-Casting

EACH ON A
PEG-BOARD
BUBBLE CARD

THE BASS-BUSTING "FISH-CALLER" PLUG

Colors: Silver Blue   Silver-Shad
        Red-White   Frog

A terrific surface lure, the "Gaylord" is an exceptionally effective bass and game-fish bait. It can be popped, trolled or jumped with little effort. The churning props attract fish for great distance

#881	GAYLORD	3/8 ounce	$1.10 list

"POP-TAIL"

EACH ON A
PEG-BOARD
BUBBLE CARD

The Fishermen's BASS friend

A popping Bass-plug with stainless hook spreaders and a "TEASE-TAIL" attracter. At rest, this lure will float with hooks down and in ready position. You can fish it by slowly reeling in, popping, and moving rod tip.

Colors: RED-WHITE MULLET, BLACK ADDIS
COUNTRY FROG, YELLOW PERCH

#865	POP-TAIL	¼ Ounce	$1.10 list

"LAZY-SUSAN"

Jointed-Action

SENSATIONAL UNDERWATER SWIMMER

A fantastic lure that swims just under the surface. This "Lazy-Susan Jointed Plug" will give off fish-calling sounds during retrieve that attracts the game-fish to it. The motion of this lure in action makes them hit hard. Available in a wide range of colors for every weather conditions, it has a place in every tackle box.

Colors: RED-WHITE   WHITE BELLY FROG
        BLACK MULLET   BLUE MULLET
        YELLOW PERCH ORANGE SPOTTED

#835	LAZY-SUSAN	3/8 ounce	$1.10 list
#836	LAZY-SUSAN	5/8 ounce	1.10 list

EACH ON A
PEG-BOARD
BUBBLE CARD

Atlantic Lures 1966 catalog, page 4.

"FLATHEAD"

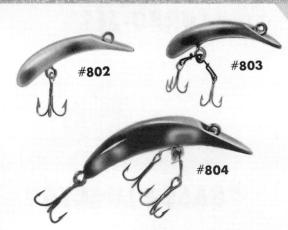

TANDEM SPREADER OF STAINLESS STEEL NEEDLE SHARP HOOKS

For the past several years, the Flathead Plug has been taking it's place among the top ten lures in the country.

"MILLIONS and MILLIONS HAVE BEEN SOLD"

RW	RED WHITE	OR	ORANGE-BLACK
P	YELLOW PERCH	BK	BLACK DRAGON
FR	FROG	GL	RED FIRE-GLO

ONE EACH ON A PEG-BOARD BUBBLE CARD

#802 FLATHEAD "ULTRA-LITE"	$ .85	list
#803 FLATHEAD LIGHTWEIGHT	1.00	list
#804 FLATHEAD SPINNING	1.10	list
#805 FLATHEAD SPIN-4 HOOKS	1.20	list
#806 FLATHEAD SPIN-CASTING	1.10	list
#807 FLATHEAD CAST-4 HOOKS	1.20	list

"SOUNDER"

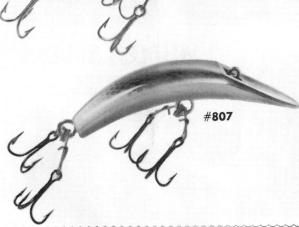

EACH ON A PEG-BOARD BUBBLE CARD

"The Plug That Sounds Off!"

Bullet casts and fast sinking to desired depth. Properly weighted and balanced. Has a fish-calling rattle. Swims on a even keel with vibrating action.

Colors: WHITE BELLY FROG — BLACK-YELLOW ARROW
RED-WHITE   YELLOW-BLACK ARROW

#819 SOUNDER 3/32 ounce ULTRA-LITE	$1.00	list
#820 SOUNDER 1/4 ounce SPINNING	1.00	list
#825 SOUNDER 3/8 ounce CASTING	1.00	list

Atlantic Lures 1966 catalog, page 5.

26

"TURBO-JET"

SOLID BRASS SHALLOW SWIMMER

Will cast with no wind resistance, swims with a side wiggle to tease and attract. Stays just under the surface. Polished to a high lustre and assembled with stainless spreaders and needle point hooks for quick set.

ONE EACH ON A PEG-BOARD BUBBLE CARD

#901	TURBO-JET GOLD or NICKLE PLATE	$1.10 list
#904	TURBO-JET CRYSTAL PEARL	1.10 list

"BASS-PLUGGER"

WITH GOLD-PLATED HOOKS

A favorite on all game streams and ponds for years, this plug is nationally advertised and accepted. It floats with hooks at the ready. Belly hooks are gold plated and all hardware used is the strongest made.

Colors: RED WHITE, YELLOW PERCH, FROG DESIGN

EACH ON A PEG-BOARD BUBBLE CARD

#841	BASS PLUGGER, Feather Tail Hook	$1.00 list
#843	BASS PLUGGER, 2 Gold Plated Hooks	.85 list

WEEDLESS SPOONS 4 SIZES

MASTER BOX OF 6 SPOONS, EACH IN INDIVIDUAL ORANGE BOX

SPARKLING CRYSTAL PEARL

A "Critic's-Choice" PRODUCT
WEEDLESS SPOON

INDIVIDUAL RACK CARDS

AMERICAN MADE

ORANGE and BLACK BOX WITH SLEEVE

Change for the better

VALUE PACKED — LOW RETAIL LIST

The weedless "Silvertone" spoons made by Atlantic are forged brass, needle sharp and non-tarnishing. The guard will always retain it's tension. The lures are not to be confused with copies of light-guage metal and tarnishing finishes. Insist on brand name. Look for the Atlantic Name.

GOLD or SILVERTONE PLATED				SPARKLING CRYSTAL			
#W1B	1 3/4"	$1.10	DOZEN BOXED OR CARDED	#W1BSP	1 3/4"	$1.35	DOZEN BOXED OR CARDED
#W2B	2 1/8"	1.10		#W2BSP	2 1/8"	1.35	
#W3B	2 3/8"	1.10		#W3BSP	2 3/8"	1.35	
#W4B	2 7/8"	1.10		#W4BSP	2 7/8"	1.35	

Atlantic Lures 1966 catalog, page 6.

"FLASHTAIL"

A "DEEP-RUNNER" WITH CONTROLLED ACTION

TEASING "FIRE GLO" TAIL

A jointed swimmer of non-breakable tenite with proven colors. Non-tarnishing hardware with needle point hooks. This is a fisherman's game-fish Lure.

Colors: Yellow with Black Arrow   Red-White
Black with Yellow Arrow   Golden Perch   Frog Design

#830	FLASHTAIL	3/8 ounce	$1.15 list

EACH ON A PEG-BOARD BUBBLE CARD

NEW! "CRYSTAL PEARL"

"SPOONLURE"

Designed to bounce off the bottom during retrieve — the Spoonlure will tease and attract. Finished in Colors for day or night fishing, in all bodies of water.

Finishes: 24K Gold Plate, Bright Nickle, Black Crystal Pearl

#902	1/4 ounce	PLATED FINISH	$1.00 list
#903	1/4 ounce	CRYSTAL PEARL	1.25 list
#908	3/16 ounce	PLATED FINISH	1.00 list
#909	3/16 ounce	CRYSTAL PEARL	1.25 list

EACH ON A BUBBLE CARD PEG-BOARD

"SWAMP-FOX"

ONE OF ATLANTIC'S "PERFECT-DOZEN" LURES

"Swamp-Fox" enters the water quietly and trolls beautifully. A real teaser for any fish that feeds on minnows. Bass, pike, muskies and all game fish find it a treat!

Colors: Red-White   Yellow Perch
Black Minnow   White-Belly Frog

#885	SWAMP-FOX	1/2 ounce	$1.10 list

EACH ON A PEG-BOARD BUBBLE CARD

"PARADISE POPPER"

with FLEXIBLE "TEASE-TAIL"

A beautiful floating popper type plug with hooks set at the ready. The colors are vivid and expertly applied. It has a belly hanger to insure no hook locking. By far, the "BASS-POP" type of popper is used by more fishermen than any other.

Colors: Swamp Frog   Yellow Perch
Black Widow   Red and White

(Fluorescent Red also, minimum — 6 Dozen)

#809	PARADISE POPPER	5/64 ounce	$1.00 list
#810	PARADISE POPPER	1/4 ounce	1.10 list
#815	PARADISE POPPER	3/8 ounce	1.10 list

EACH ON A PEG-BOARD BUBBLE CARD

Atlantic Lures 1966 catalog, page 7.

"FRANTIC-ANTIC"

Made of Tenite Plastic and assembled with the finest hardware and treble hooks made. This Popper lure has been completely field tested for casting ease and retrieving action under actual fishing conditions. "FRANTIC-ANTIC" is a fish producing lure from the very first cast.

Colors: Red-White
Yellow Perch
Black Dragon
Spotted Orange
White Belly Frog

Colors Assorted to Dozen

ONE EACH ON A
PEG-BOARD BUBBLE CARD

#859	ULTRA-LITE	1/16 OUNCE	$1.00
#860	FRANTIC-ANTIC	1/4 OUNCE	1.10
#861	FRANTIC-ANTIC	3/8 OUNCE	1.10

"SWANEE"

Designed for Shallow and Underwater fishing. Made of tough tenite, properly weighted and balanced for bullet casts and good retrieve.

1. "Swanee" will cast with bullet-like accuracy
2. "Swanee" is guaranteed not to wist your line
3. "Swanee" takes bass under all fishing conditions

Colors: FROG, BLACK, YELLOW COACH DOG, WHITE COACH DOG
EACH ON A PEG-BOARD BUBBLE CARD, 12 ASSORTED

#855	SWANEE	3/16 ounce	$ 1.00 list
#856	SWANEE	1/4 ounce	1.00 list
#857	SWANEE	3/8 ounce	1.10 list

"FINGER-FISH"

A SWIMMING DEVIL

The floating "Finger-Fish' swims with a swaying motion during retrieve. The prop starts spinning immediately. This slender lure is a "Game-Fish" killer, being deadly to bass and pike. Colors available give the fisherman a wide choice for any kind of weather or place. Spreader hooks are on a stainless spreader and the tail skirt responds to the slightest water current.

Colors: Yellow Perch   Red Mullet
Frog   Black Dust

| #866 | FINGER-FISH | 1/4 ounce | $1.00 list |
| #867 | FINGER-FISH | 3/8 ounce | 1.15 list |

EACH ON A
PEG-BOARD
BUBBLE CARD

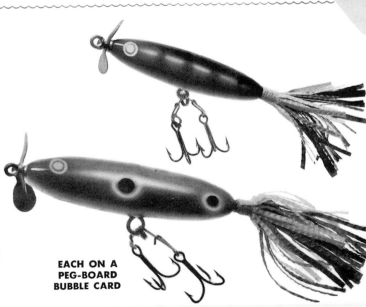

Atlantic Lures 1966 catalog, page 8.

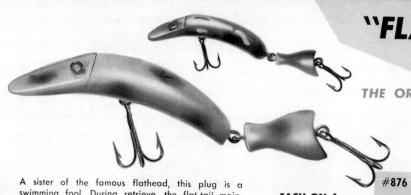

"FLAT-TAIL"

THE ORIGINAL SWIMMER-KILLER

Colors:
Yellow Perch   Red White
Country Frog   Orange Dotted

A sister of the famous flathead, this plug is a swimming fool. During retrieve, the flat-tail maintains it's depth, yet will have a wildly wobbling and erratic action. Game fish hit hard because the lure resembles a live swimming minnow.

EACH ON A PEG-BOARD BUBBLE CARD

#876	FLY FLAT-TAIL	$1.00 list
#877	SPIN FLAT-TAIL	1.10 list
#878	CAST FLAT-TAIL	1.10 list

"MAGIC MINNOW"

100% "BRASS" BODY

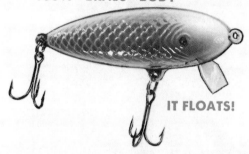

IT FLOATS!

Made of brass and thermo sealed with enough buoyancy so that the "MAGIC - MINNOW" floats with hooks down. During the retrieve, it will swim medium shallow. It swims in a natural life-like manner. This plug has no equal.

ONE EACH ON A PEG-BOARD BUBBLE CARD

Colors: 24K Gold Plate   Bright Silvertone   Black Dust

#900	MAGIC MINNOW	¼ OZ.	$1.25 list

NEW! "FLY-WEIGHT" PLUGS

#802   #803

ACTUAL SIZE

Baby Sounder

Carefully scaled from the larger spinning sizes, the fly-weight plugs are as active and action-packed as the fisherman could desire. Use them with a light spinning outfit or with your favorite fly rod. Each has been designed to do a special job.

Colors: Red White, Baby Frog, Black Jet. Orange with Black Spots, Yellow Perch,

#802	FLATHEAD	FLY WEIGHT	$ .85 list
#803	FLATHEAD	FLY WEIGHT	1.00 list
#809	PARADISE POPPER	5/64 oz.	1.00 list
#819	BABY SOUNDER	3/32 oz.	1.00 list
#859	FRANTIC ANTIC	1/16 oz.	1.00 list

INDIVIDUAL BUBBLE CARD

Frantic Antic

The only Set of it's Kind in America

$3.98 list

PROFESSIONAL "ULTRA-LITE" PLUG KIT

Bass, Trout, and all Game Fish.

#8999 "U-L PLUG KIT"

Bagley's Lures

Jim Bagley Bait Co., Inc., P.O. Box 110, Winter Haven, Fla. 33880. This company was sold to Bill Stuart lures in about 1990 and then recently sold to Ric Willie who calls the company Bagley International. The original Bagley lures were made of "Tru-Life" balsa, and some have become quite popular with collectors, bringing up to $40.00 on eBay for new-on-the-card square lip versions. Some of the Small Fry look like real fish, and this series is also now commanding a decent price and will likely garner lots of collector interest in the future. Look especially for the Baby Small Fry, tiny balsa replicas of the Small Fry. The interest in Bagley's Lures is a clear indication that fishing items need not be ancient to be collectible. The nice thing about these lures is that they came in many colors, sizes, and models, giving the collector a range of items to locate. They are also recent enough to be found in perfect condition and new in the package. See also page 117.

A nice patch, $10.00, and a little rainbow-colored Bagley, $10.00 – 15.00.

New-on-the-cards Bagley Lures, including a Chatter Shad 3" Black on Chartreuse, CS3 09; a 2¼" Mama Cat; an older Divin' B, 2¼" long, DB2-GOS, from when it was still called Jim Bagley Bait Co. Shad and Mama Cat are trading for $12.00 – 30.00 new on cards. The older Divin' B, $20.00 – 40.00.

New-on-the-cards, including another earlier one, a sink-n-swim Kill'R "B" II in SDKB2-6C4, 2¼" long sinker; a Slo-dancer #4, 3½" long Flatfish type bait in frog with orange belly, Model SD4-6E, also from Jim Bagley Bait Co.; a Kill'r B1, 2" on another early card; another earlier one, a Divin' B, Model DB1-6G4, a 2" balsa bait. Some, but not all, Bagley Lures are marked Bagley's on the clear diving lip, as on the little B1 shown here. $15.00 – 40.00 with values highest for earlier models.

Barracuda Brand Lures
(Florida Fishing Tackle Manufacturing Company, Inc.)

St. Petersburg, Florida, U.S.A. This company made a wide array of lures, and one could build a major collection around the company. This company is now owned by Luhr Jensen. I have shown some of the lures new in boxes, and some used in boxes. As shown, even a Barracuda Reflecto Spoon new in the cardboard box makes a nice display piece. Values for these lures vary from a low of $10.00 to $50.00 for some of the items new in boxes. The toughest piece to find is the salesman's tie clasp, a rare piece.

Typical Barracuda colors. This wooden surface bait is very collectible and worth $40.00+.

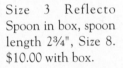

Size 3 Reflecto Spoon in box, spoon length 2¾", Size 8. $10.00 with box.

Older example of Barracuda lure, 3¾" long, recessed cup belly hardware, washer/screw tail hardware, painted eyes, two belly weights, Barracuda in small red letters on belly. $20.00 – 30.00.

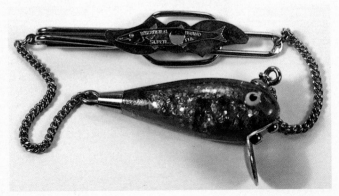

Rare Barracuda salesman's tie clasp. The lure is a 1¹³⁄₁₆" Spark A Midget without hooks marked Barracuda Brand, St. Pete, Fla. $100.00+.

Bass Bird Lure Company

P.O. Box 3397, Bloomington, Illinois 61701. This Bass Bird shown new in its little package with a patent number of 4,232,469 was invented by Howard P. Shiverdecker of Bloomfield, Illinois; he applied for the patent on April 2, 1979 which was granted on November 11, 1980. This little plastic Red Wing Blackbird, also in black, yellow and brown, and red and white (shown on cover), is one of the neatest of the fairly recent entries into the plastic lure cadre. The little plastic bird is only 2¼" long, has a rubber skirt, and one large treble for bass. These already command a premium at shows and should continue to increase in value. One new in package is shown and two close-ups of lure. These were available as "new" in the 1979 BassPro catalog shown in three colors; a year later only the Red Wing Blackbird was shown, and within a few years the Bass Bird had disappeared from the catalog altogether.

Side view of Bass Bird.

Bass Bird, new in bag. $50.00+ in bag.

Top view of Bass Bird. Note wings are poorly attached and often come unglued as can be seen on the top wing (left) in photo, but they readily re-attach. $35.00+ loose.

Bear Creek Tackle

Kaleva, Michigan. This company produced a rather popular bait called the Sucker Bait and also was a major producer of ice fishing decoys, early in wood, later in plastic. The brand name is still in use today, however the company has since moved and the fish decoys are not as collectible as the early plastic ones. The earliest plastic ones were actually a hard rubber-type material, and one can easily identify the difference between the early plastic versions and the recent lightweight plastics. The first ones were solid and now are hollow with drain holes in top and bottom of fish. The large one shown below is 9¾", and the smaller ones are 6" long.

Three red and white Bear Creek plastic decoys, see Chapter 5 for more details and photos on the decoys. $50.00+ for early models; $15.00 – 30.00 for later ones.

Beno Baits

Shown is an example of a Beno with four segments. These are now manufactured by Luhr-Jensen & Sons, Inc. of Hood River, Oregon. They came in a variety of jointed versions and a number of colors. They are worth between $8.00 – 12.00 each at this time, more if packaged. This one has inverted belly and screw tail hardware. The eyes are molded with a slight raise in the pupil and an indentation at the gill mark behind the eyes.

Beno bait, 4⅞" long.
$8.00 – 12.00.

Blakemore Lure Company, Inc.

P.O. Box 505, Branson, Missouri, 65616. We know this company was in business in the 1970s from a 1972-73 catalog. One collectible lure they produced is called the Blakemore Crab, and a few are showing up in old tackle boxes, but the exact years of production are not yet known.

The box back, a new crab in the box. Paid $30.00, summer 2001, private treaty sale.

Loose Orange Blakemore Crab, 3⅝" long, tip to tip, including diving lip. $25.00+.

35

Bleeder Baits

The wooden versions of this company are fairly well known and very collectible. However, it appears they made a plastic version as well for distribution by Lucky Strike lures in Canada (see page 93). This has a similar "bleeder" compartment to their wooden lures and is the same color as the Cardinal Translucent bait of Millsite, shown in Volume 1. This is the only example I have ever owned.

Bleeder-type plastic lure, 3" long, protruding pupils from a concave eye socket, Lucky Strike in trademark horseshoe on diving lip, bleeder compartment identical to Bleeder Baits. Scarce, $50.00+.

The Bomber Bait Company

Texas, now owned by Pradco. (My thanks go to John Kolbeck, capt.john to the virtual world, for contributing this coverage of Bomber Baits. I recommend visiting his website for more details.) The Bomber Bait Co. was started in Texas during WWII. Shortages of just about everything forced the founders, Ike Walker and C. S. Turbeville to improvise. Using telephones poles for wood, shoe eyelets for cups, staples and Copenhagen lids for line ties, and Coleman stove tops for diving plates, they kept turning out this hot new lure. These early "handmade" Bombers are highly sought by collectors. The line tie easily identifies them. The painted eyes on these early versions are normally yellow and crudely rendered. When priming these baits, the makers just dipped them and hung them to dry. This causes a "paint-circle" to form on the nose. This very fragile thin nose is easily broken off. Very few examples exist with full nose paint, so they command a premium.

A translucent plastic Bomber in plastic slide-top box. $10.00 depending on colors, see text.

In 1949, Bomber Bait Co. wanted to jump on the bandwagon of manufacturers producing plastic lures. After all, this was a much cheaper way to make lures, and the lures held up better. Unfortunately for Bomber, their first attempt was a near disaster. Their new plastic lure, or "49er" as collectors like to call them, didn't work very well. Fishermen quit buying them, and the company found itself in trouble. A switch back to wood found favor with anglers, and Bomber was off and running again. They expanded the Bomber line from three sizes (400s, 500s, and 600s) to include two new smaller sizes (200s and 300s). Bomber expanded their line of lures to include the famous Water Dog (1500, 1600, and 1700 series). Other less well known wood lures that Bomber made include the Knothead (1200 & 1300 series), Stick and Spinstick (7200, 7300, and 7400 series), Bomberette (700 and 800 series), Midget Bomberette (2700s), Jerk (4300, 4400, and 4500 series) and the Top Bomber (4000 and 6000 series). They also made numerous metal lures.

From time to time Bomber would produce special order lures. The most famous of these is the Looboyle Special. It is similar to a regular Bomber in shape (a little thinner and longer) but has the eyes painted on the front and has a small floppy blade on the rear. There are many examples of special-order paint jobs found on regular Bombers and over 100 different colors on Bomber lures. The majority of the colors were listed in Bomber catalogs at one time. Jerks were made for use in salt water and offer the wildest color assortment.

There were many types of boxes used over the years. The oldest are yellow 2PCCB with the picture of a no-eye Bomber on top. One rare variety of the yellow boxes says "Bomber Manufacturing Co." These are very hard to locate.

In 1972, Bomber quit making wood lures and switched to plastic. These new plastic models worked better than the 49ers but were soon discontinued in favor of the current Model A. While the Model A is a proven fish catcher, many anglers still like the old wood models better. There is a strong after-market for wood "beaters" by fishermen.

Bomber prices have increased dramatically in recent years. Nobody seemed to want these well-made wood lures a few years ago. Now it is not unusual to see rare ones fetch over $300. Common types in rare colors will also bring hefty sums. Prices for common color wood Bombers are still affordable. They usually sell for $20 – 25 new in plastic-top sleeve boxes. In older orange 2PCCB boxes expect to pay an extra $10. When the correct vintage lure is new in a yellow box, expect to pay about three times as much. Waterdogs trade in the same price range. Sticks and Spinsticks are only a little higher in price. Jerks and Midget Bomberettes are harder to find and usually sell for about twice what comparable Bombers would fetch. Top Bombers are much harder to find and usually start at $50 new in the box. 700 and 800 Bomberettes are nearly impossible to find new in the box so expect to pay at least $100. Most costly are the Knotheads. Even nice used ones go for at least $100 with new in box bring $300 or more. Plastic 49ers sell lots better now than they did in 1949, expect to pay $75 or more if new in box.

Like any brand of lure, certain colors are very rare on some Bombers. While common on the Jerk, a catalog color like #30 (bee) would be extremely rare on a regular Bomber. With the thousands of possible combinations, it is not practical to try to list all the rare colors. To learn more or just to view examples of Bomber colors, boxes, and styles check out the website devoted to Bombers: http://www.bomberbaits.com.

Close-ups of a small (actual measurement is 2³⁄₁₆" long) red/gray scale wooden Bomber. Note the screw holding in the diving lip, a sign of a wooden Bomber bait on either a Bomber or Water Dog. $25.00 – 35.00 new in box.

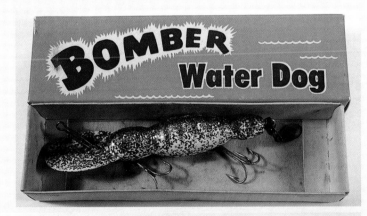

Two wooden Water Dogs in two box types. The top photo is the Model 1615 Christmas Tree pattern. The bottom photo is a wooden white coach dog, Model 1655. Christmas Tree sold for $35.00 in 2001 on eBay. Coach dog, $20.00 – 25.00.

The Bomber Baits Pinfish new in its box. $15.00 – 25.00.

Speed Shad in the same pattern as Pinfish in Yellow. $10.00 – 15.00 loose.

Boone Baits

The neat wooden lure shown here is a Boone Bird bass bait. I am not sure of year, but BassPro Shops were offering similar ones in more "modern" colors in the early 1990s. The red and white might be a little earlier model. This is a very unusual bait, and I have only found the one so far, but if available from BassPro, there should be lots of them out there. No trade data is known.

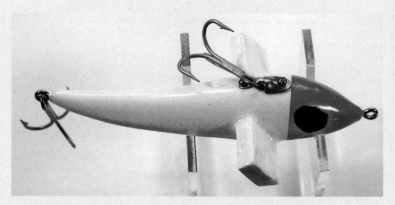

Boone Bird Bait, 4¼" long, simple screw tail and surface belly hardware, marked on back, painted eyes. No trade data.

Brooks Baits Brand

By R-Jay Industries, Inc., Box 107, Cuyahoga Falls, O., also simply Cuyahoga Falls, Oh., pre-zip code boxes. The boxes shown are not new-in-the-box baits but are shown as examples. The No. 7 bait is the Frog patterned Al Foss type bait in a Pat. Pending box and is the correct lure for that box. The Brooks Reefer has a jointed tail and is yellow with black and red spots, 4" long with belly surface and tail screw hardware, no model number on box. I included it to show the type of white "plastic scum" that is formed on some early plastic lures from the 1960s.

Being stored in a damp environment likely causes this, and I have seen it the most often on lures made by Brooks, Cisco, and Creek Chub. The good news is that it cleans off with plain water and a little elbow grease. The lures as shown would only be worth $5.00 to $10.00 each due to poor condition of the boxes, although the Patent Pending box could bring a little more. I have also shown two additional Brooks Reefers, one with a little rubber plug that can be removed to add weight or a split shot for rattling. The lures are approximately 4" long.

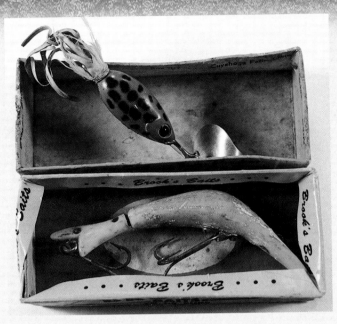

Brooks Baits in boxes. $10.00 – 15.00.

Brooks Reefers, common examples of the many lures produced by this company. $8.00 – 12.00 loose and in excellent condition.

Bumble Bug

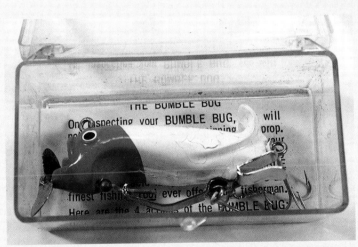

A Bumble Bug new in hinged plastic box. $35.00 – 50.00.

Gowen Mfg. Co., Gowen, Michigan. This lure was developed in a little town just east of where I grew up in Michigan, near Lincoln Lake and a chain of great fishing lakes. It was a surface bait that had an unusual propeller device to make a commotion. This lure is from the 1950s and came in a variety of colors: Frog, Gold, Silver, Black, Red/White (shown), and Black/White. It is 2⅞" long and the eyes protrude as part of the mold. It is uncommon and usually trades for $35.00+. It was packaged in a one-piece hinged plastic box with a paper insert that also served as an "Emergency Order Blank" if the tackle shop was unable to supply the needs fast enough. I have a number found in storage, and it is clear that the plating on the metal parts was not very well done and easily corrodes in damp storage, especially the propeller. Yet, ones stored properly in dry conditions remain perfect.

Burke Lures

Box 72, Traverse City, Michigan 49684; by 1984 the address becomes 19609 S. Airport Road, same city and zip. This company manufactured numerous fly rod and ultra light rubber baits and bugs. Being a Michigan native, I have used these for years with success on panfish, trout, and largemouth bass. These are of some collector interest if found on the cards.

Beginning in 1968 Burke also marketed a unique type of fishing plug called the "Flex-Plug" and did a pretty nice job of copying some Heddon and Creek Chub type baits in flexible rubber. They also added some really unique looking baits of their own design. Luckey's 5th Edition refers to a flyer about the Flex Plugs that he believed was prior to 1965; however, I could not docu-

A pair of Burke Ants new on the card, Model T-114, address on card is Dept. OL, P.O. Box 72, Traverse City, MI 49685. $5.00 – 10.00 for pre-1984 cards.

Front of Bassassin packaging, note the pre-1984 address on the card.

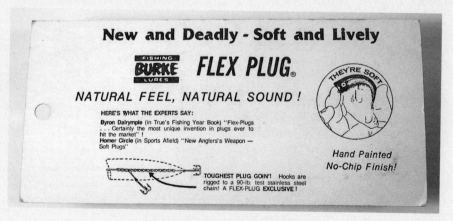

Back of Bassassin packaging.

display pack of six, or six to a "Peg Pac" for peg board displays. They could be all the same color or assorted colors in the six-packs. If copying is the ultimate compliment, Burke complimented Jitterbugs, Lucky 13s, Plunkers, and Zaras very well. The Big Dig is also not too unlike a Bomber, especially in design function. In 1984 Burke added Weedless Top Water Plugs by adding Bing type weedless rigs to three of its lures, the Pop Top, the Bassassin and the Top Dog. These were available in 16 color patterns. The early 1980s also saw the addition of "lifelike colors" much like those available through Heddon on its Sonics and some other baits. The Leopard Frog is really quite sharp and realistic, especially in the Bassassin (the Jitterbug copy).

The Flex Plugs included Model #2014 Pop Top in 3¼"-⅜ oz. W/2 #4 Trebles; Model #2017 Bassassin in 2¾"-⅜ oz. W/2 #6 Trebles; Model # 2010 Bandit in 2¾"-⅜ oz. W2 #4 trebles; Model # 2021 Hunchback in 3¾"-½ oz. W/1 # 1/0 treble; Model #2015 Big-Dig in 4½"-½ oz. W/2 #4 trebles; Model 2016 Little Dig in 3"-⅓ oz. W/1 #6 treble; Model 2018 Top Dog ½ oz.; and others as shown. Weedless versions of the models simply added W to the model number.

Colors included perch, red head, frog, midnite black, shad, and skeleton (shore minnow). New lifelike colors added Natural Perch, Natural Shad, Leopard Frog, chartreuse, hot green, pearl pink, pearl/green spots, yellow/green spots, and pearl green. Not all lures were available in all colors. The eel was available in a gray color as shown, the first jointed Flex Plug called the La-Z-Liz, 6¼" long, ¾ oz. #2/0 double hook on front section and #1/0 double hook on rear section. The little Model #2020 called the Soft Touch was a 1½" long-⁶⁄₁₆ oz. #6 Treble lure in a foam body that looked like the old Paw Paw Trout Eat Us. I have found this in fluorescent orange in addition to the hot green.

Also shown is the cover of a 1987 Burke catalog received with this collection of Flex-Plugs and some other Burke items of inter-

ment this. I was lucky enough to buy from a fishing tackle dealer's representative, Bud Hartman, all of the lures he had saved from the time period of 1951 to 1996 and in his displays was a fairly complete set of Burke Flex-Plugs, only some of which are shown here. These lures came individually boxed, in a dealer

Four examples of Bassassin. This is the Jitterbug type lure by Burke. $12.00 – 20.00.

Three examples of Top Dog. $15.00+.

est. One future collectible will likely be the "Frogbait" shown on page 17 of the Burke Lures catalog (page 47). Doug Hannon and his "wildlife artist wife, Lynn," developed this, and is part of what Burke called the Hannon Field Guide System of lures. The frogs were initially available in six very realistic patterns as shown in the photo on page 47, a Green Leopard Frog, a Brown Leopard Frog, a Bull Frog, a Spring Peeper Frog, a Pine Barrens Frog, and a Northern Pickerel Frog. It was only recently that I found my first one of these in a tackle box and wondered what it was. Another interesting item from the 1987 catalog is the Skitterfish, also a Hannon Field Guide System lure. These were available in a number of fish scale patterns and should garner some interest in the future.

I would look for the small Burke items new on the card. Values range from $5.00 to maybe $25.00 for some of the Flex-Plugs boxed or mint.

Burke La-Z-Liz, $25.00+.

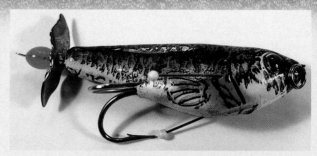

Burke Shadoo, $12.00+.

Zara type, $25.00+.

Burke Muddler, $6.00+.

Burke Big Digs, $12.00 – 20.00 each.

Unusual Sonic type, $12.00 – 20.00.

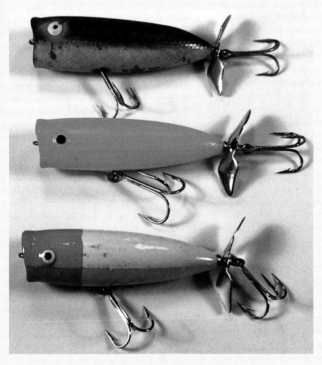

Pop Tops, $12.00 – 20.00.

Weedless Pop Tops, $12.00 – 20.00.

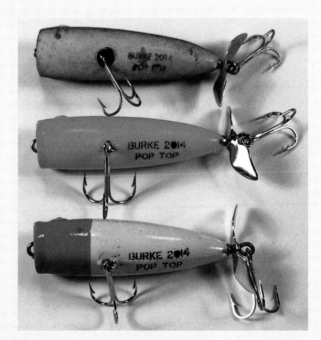

Bottom view of Pop Tops on left.

A Burke Pulsar made along the same principles as a Heddon Sonar, even to the three different line ties. It is 2⁹⁄₁₆" long and the line tie and hook hanger are one piece of metal with the lure molded around it. $12.00 – 20.00.

Flex Plugs *Natural feel...natural sound...natural action!*

Sound like food on the water – feel like food on the strike

You have more time to set the hook with Flex Plugs because fish hang on for critical extra seconds. They bend during the fight too, so fish can't throw them easily. Tough

90-pound-test stainless steel chain runs through the flexible lure. No screws to

loosen. Permanent lifelike paint job can't chip, crack or peel. Punctures seal over. Closed cell foam bodies have thousands of tiny air cells so lure never gets water logged like plastic or wood.

Shadoo!

Tail prop, top water Flex Plug. Whenever gamefish are bustin' crippled minnows or schooling shad, Shadoo! shines. Twitch it slowly, or rip it across the surface. It's hard to find a way to fish it wrong!
#2003 – 2½" long – ⅓ oz. – #6 belly hook, #8 tail hook with prop $4.95

Pop Top

Top-water classic. Pop Top hits with a soft plop, then should be worked back in a series of jerks. The dished-in face scoops water, forms a bubble and goes "bloop!" When retrieved in short spurts Pop Top bobs and bloops in a lunker-getting dance big fish can't resist!
#2014 – 3¼" – ⅜ oz. – #4 treble hooks $4.95

Bassassin

It Walks! It Talks! It Wiggles across the water like it wants to be eaten. This soft sensation is bound to be the last meal for a lot of lunkers. Work it top water with very small, short jerks and it "Spits" back at you. On a steady retrieve it waddles back and "Talks" to the fish with a "Plip-Plip-Plip" sound that says chowtime!
#2017 – 2½" long – ⅜ oz. – #4 treble hooks $4.95

Top Dog

Top water action puts you in the driver's seat. Top Dog can be twitched (and it will "walk the dog"), skittered (looks like a terrorized food fish) or just bobbed up and down like a dying minnow. Designed to take Salt or Fresh Water fish.
#2018 – 4¼" long – ⅝ oz. – #4 treble hooks $4.95

La-Z-Liz

First jointed Flex Plug! The lazy, free swimming action turns on fish feeding re-action. Designed for Big Bass, Muskies, Pike, Stripers. LA-Z-LIZ is a must for trophy fishermen. You can even reverse the extra strong double hooks and it's snag-free!
#2023 – 6¼" long – ¾ oz. – #2/0 front double hooks, #1/0 rear double hooks $5.75

COVER: Doug Hannon "The Bass Professor" has teamed up with Burke Lures to produce the "Hannon System" series of products that promises better and bigger bass fishing!

Burke Lures 1987

Flex Plugs *Catch more fish...naturally!*

Crankstar

No rattle, clatter, buzz or bang, Crankstar relies on its soft, natural "silent sound" – low frequency vibrations that duplicate a frantic swimming minnow. Perfectly balanced, it throws like a streamlined crowbar and you can't crank it back fast enough. But most of the time, you won't get it back until you land a Bass.
#2022 – 2¾" long – ½ oz. – #4 belly hook, #6 tail hook $4.95

Big Dig

Floats at rest, "digs" for the bottom when retrieved or trolled. The soft body actually flexes from side to side, giving a true "feeding minnow" appearance. Practically snagless, it flips over most obstructions. Salmon and Striper trolling champ!
#2015 – 4½" long – ½ oz. – #4 treble hooks $4.95

Little Dig

Spin-size version of Big Dig. Great for light tackle enthusiasts. Does everything its big brother does...and in spades! When the fish are looking for an appetizer instead of a full meal, Little Dig is the answer! A proven Salmon killer, too!
#2016 – 3" long – ⅓ oz. – #6 treble hook $4.75

Hunchbak

New star of the salmon trolling troops. Flex plug soft construction has a natural sound and feel, plus an erratic, darting, fish exciting action. Because Hunchbak feels like food, fish hang on and try to "kill" the plug. That extra time means more hooked fish, especially on downrigger strikes.
#2021 – 3¾" long – ½ oz. – #1/10 extra strong treble hook $5.95

Soft Touch

Drift fishing or trolling, Soft Touch has a deadly wobbling action, and the exclusive flex-plug foam body offers natural sound and feel. This combination sets Soft Touch a step above standard hard bodied lures: you have more time to set the hook because the body feels like food.
#2020 – 1½" long – ⁶⁄₁₆ oz. – #6 extra strong treble hook $2.25

Flex Plugs Color Chart

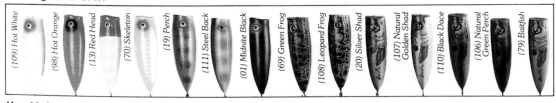

(109) Hot White   (98) Hot Orange   (13) Red Head   (70) Skeleton   (19) Perch   (111) Steel Back   (01) Midnite Black   (69) Green Frog   (108) Leopard Frog   (20) Silver Shad   (107) Natural Golden Shad   (110) Black Dace   (106) Natural Green Perch   (79) Baitfish

Hunchbak and Soft Touch Color Chart

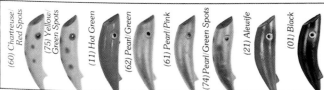

(60) Chartreuse/ Red Spots   (75) Yellow/ Green Spots   (11) Hot Green   (62) Pearl/ Green   (61) Pearl/ Pink   (74) Pearl/ Green Spots   (21) Alewife   (01) Black

Burke Lures 1987

Burke 1987 catalog, page 3.

Weed Beaters *First truly weedless surface plugs!*

Weed beaters solve an old top water problem. Because you can fish where fish *live* – not just the edges of cover.

Imagine throwing a surface plug into brush covered water and chugging it back over branches, logs and limbs and lily pads! You can do it – with a Weed Beater! Extra strong double hooks and unique ball-head wire guards (patent pending) are the keys to this new concept in surface fishing.

So the time-proven action of top water plugs can finally be used in the heaviest cover. It's "cardiac casting" time when you fish places that were impossible to fish before – places where the fish may have never *seen* a plug before!

Pop Top

The time-tested chugging action of the original Pop Top can now be fished where the fish live! Cast it back in the brush and chug it back over logs and around branches – places you could never reach before! You'll hang fish that never saw a plug before!
#2014-W – 3¼" long – ⅜ oz. – #5/0 XX strong double hooks $4.95
#2004-W – 2½" long – ¼ oz. – #2 hooks $4.75

Bassassin

Some folks called the first Bassassin their "Holy Plug" 'cause it walked across the water so well! The new model is sort of a miracle too! Fish it any place you find water …'way back in the pads where big fish wait for that frog to jump off the bank. It's a "twitch bait" and a popper too. Don't just crank it back – tease that lunker into his last lunch!
#2017-W – 4" long – ⅜ oz. – #5/0 XX strong double hooks $4.95
#2007-W – 2½" long – ¼ oz. – #1 hooks $4.75

Top Dog

"Walkin'-the-dog" with the old Top Dog was fish gettin' fun. Now you work it where the fish are 95% of the time – in heavy cover. Timber, bushes, brush, pads, grass weeds, reeds, snags or stick-ups are no problem anymore. Just twitch this "Weedless Wonder" through any kind of cover and get the landing net ready!
#2018-W – 4⅜" long – ½ oz. – #5/0 XX strong double hooks $4.95
#2008-W – 3⅝" long – ⅝ oz. – #3 hooks $4.75

Shadoo!

The weed beater version of our shad-shape bait opens up all kinds of new top water territory. Chunk it in the weeds, pads, grass or stumps – back where big fish live most of the time. The plump shape and prop-tail sputter combine to give fish in heavy cover a case of the hungries!
#2003-W – 2½" long – ⅓ oz. – #2 double hooks, prop tail $4.95

WEED BEATER COLORS: See chart on page 3 for Weed Beater colors. Note, however, that Weed Beaters are not available in the Special Hunchbak and Soft Touch colors shown.

Burke Lures 1987

Burke 1987 catalog, page 4.

The Hannon Field Guide System

Frogbait *A natural selection for big bass!*

NEW

FROGBAIT

DOUG HANNON REPORTS ON FROGBAIT DEVELOPMENT:

"Thousands of hours of observation and study showed that frogs are one of the most favored items in the bass diet. Since a bass learns that a certain forage food is safe to eat by general cues (size, profile, outline, color, etc.) it was necessary to incorporate – even exaggerate – the things about a frog that say "food" to a big bass. Large protuding eyes, powerful rear legs and a ridged back seemed to be the main cues.

"After several prototypes proved we were close to a good design, my wife, Lynn, applied her talents as a wildlife artist/sculptress and carved a beautifully detailed master model. The engineers at Burke then reproduced the master perfectly in their production molds.

"Even our early prototypes caught some great fish, but when the "Lynn-bodied" frog was tested it exceeded our expectations, taking big bass with regularity.

"Frogbait is the latest in the Hannon Field Guide System of lures. I hope you find it as effective as we have!"

#2025 – 4" – 3/8 oz. – #4/0 XX strong double hooks $3.95
COLORS: Shown below.

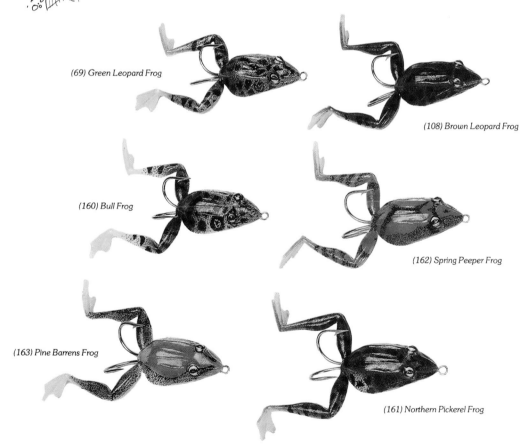

(69) Green Leopard Frog

(108) Brown Leopard Frog

(160) Bull Frog

(162) Spring Peeper Frog

(163) Pine Barrens Frog

(161) Northern Pickerel Frog

Burke Lures 1987

Burke 1987 catalog, page 17.

Muddlers *"Lifelike!" They cast and troll better than the real thing!*

Stone Cat

#905 – 2" long – ¹⁄₁₆ oz. – #4 double hook Baby stone cat or river cat. Colorado spinner on wire shaft. Red and gold beads. $2.15
COLORS: (22) Silver, (46) Mud Brown, (49) Red Dace, (50) Moss Green.

Willow Cat

#903 – 3" long – ¼ oz. – #1 double hook Willow catfish or muddler. Colorado spinner on wire shaft. Red and fold beads. $2.25
COLORS: (22) Silver, (33) Gold, (46) Mud Brown, (49) Red Dace, (50) Moss Green, (51) Blue Cat.

Ripple Cat

#904 – 4" long – ½ oz. –#2/0 double hook Medium catfish. Silver ripple spinner on wire shaft. Red and gold beads. $2.50
COLORS: Same as #903 Willow cat.

Livin' Minnows

Our lifelike minnows have been popular for over 30 years. The old harness rig caught it's share of fish, but nothing like the new jig-minnow series has been doing lately. The "Livin' Minnow" combines the incredible lifelike detail of the original with special body-balanced jigs. The result is a natural, fish catching system that's hard to beat. Try these "super-naturals" and see!

Small Livin' Minnow

#901 – 2" – ¹⁄₁₆ oz. – #8 hook, small minnow $1.25
COLORS: Shown in chart below.

Medium Livin' Minnow

#902 – 2⅝" – ⅛ oz. – #6 hook, medium minnow $1.50
COLORS: Shown in chart below.

Large Livin' Minnow

#900 – 4" – ¼ oz. – #4 hook, large minnow $1.75
COLORS: Shown in chart below.

Livin' Minnow Color Chart

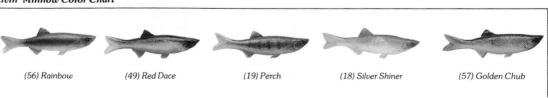

(56) Rainbow   *(49) Red Dace*   *(19) Perch*   *(18) Silver Shiner*   *(57) Golden Chub*

Burke Lures 1987

Burke 1987 catalog, page 18.

C.C. Roberts Bait Company

Mosinee, Wisconsin; later address was J. J. Rheinschmidt, Prop., 1201 W. Main Street, Mosinee, Wisconsin. Both Mud Puppies shown are from this later era. John Kolbeck has written an excellent article on this company, found in the *NFLCC Gazette*, December, 1997, Vol. 22, No. 74, pages 20-21, and readers are referred to it for details. However, this company made a wide array of interesting baits for the collector, and some are shown below. In addition, most people do not realize the company, specifically Roberts and Rheinschmidt themselves, also made for family and friends some very beautiful and rare duck and goose decoys (fewer than 100 total). I was fortunate enough to buy and trade for 17 of them, Canada Geese, Canvasbacks, Redheads, and a couple of Mallards. I have shown some of them to alert collectors to the types of auxiliary items to be on the lookout for when collecting lures.

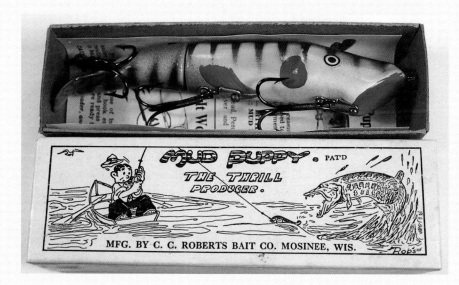

"Cartoon Box" with new-in-box Perch pattern Mud Puppy, river version, Model 0102-L.M.P.-R.M. $40.00+.

Comparison of a River version Perch with a Lake version Natural, Model 0100-L.M.P., Mud Puppies. These are actually "Little Mud Puppies" at 5½", 1¼ oz., and the Mud Puppies were 7" at 2 oz. The River version has permanent hooks; the Lake version had a hook that allowed the Muskie to throw the bait itself, and the hook harness would then come free of the lure and stay with the fish. This prevented hooked fish, in theory anyway, from escaping. Once the fish was landed, the fisherman would find the lure, reassemble, and be back in business. $40.00+ each new in boxes.

A rare find, three decoys made by Roberts and his partner Rheinschmidt. Very rare tin goose and a nice pair of Canvasbacks. I also have some Magnum Canvasbacks carved for Lake Michigan shooting that are as large as the goose shown. Values on these would be negotiable.

A close-up of one of 12 Canada Geese made of metal (the body and the legs) with a wooden head and neck and glass eyes. This is number 7 of 12, one of only two still known to exist. The other goose sold for over $500.00, and I have been offered more for this one. Assigning a value to such a rare piece is tough, but it should trade for $750.00 – 1,500.00 at least.

Cats Paw Lures

Wilson W. Hargrett, 2623 Grand River Ave., Detroit, Mich. Although this lure has been shown in other books, I had to include such a great item to find, and it was patented in May of 1940, the beginning of our modern era. Shown below with hooks in "striking position" and closed, this was another great attempt to make a bass plug weedless to get into those lily pads.

Cats Paw Lure, painted eyes, diving lip is marked with U.S. Pat. 2200670, no other markings. Uncommon lure, $30.00+, depending on condition.

Clark

Makers of the famous Water Scout lure which is covered in detail in other volumes. However, many collectors are unaware of the recent evolution of the Water Scout, so a brief entry is made here. These were beautiful wooden lures made in the 1940s and 1950s, packaged in a two-piece cardboard box. Bill Dance marketed the lures again under the Strike King label in the 1970s and 1980s and then the rights were sold to Cordell, and the lures were marketed again under that label in a version not nearly as attractive as the first wooden Water Scouts, but they are still collectible. Thanks to my wife, Wendy, for use of a small part of her Water Scout collection.

From top left: Original Clark Water Scout new in two-piece cardboard box (these trade for good money, $100.00 plus), Perch, Model 322, carved eye; below it is a Bill Dance Strike King version, also in wood, Model 245-2, gray scale with skirt, carved eye; the last entry into the Water Scout business is Cotton Cordell, shown in a plastic box glued onto a pegboard card, plastic, Model 6538, molded plastic eyes and diving lip with skirt. The Strike King versions averaged $25.00 – 40.00 on eBay in May of 2001. Cordell models. $15.00+ (see next page).

Cordell Tackle Company

P.O. Box 2020, Hot Springs, Ark. 71901, now owned by Pradco (see page 113). Early Cordell items are gaining collector interest. Shown are three new from their hinged plastic box examples of the smaller Spot lures, a close-up of the lure in its box, and an example of the fine Big-O lure. Early Big-Os new in the box are gaining interest now, and one can put together a great color collection of these. There were numerous Big-O copies, and they would also make a nice collection. Also, remember that they picked up the rights to Pflueger's Gay Blade and produced it in at least eight catalog colors. They also owned the rights to the Doll Fly, formerly a Thompson bait. Finally, their Crazy Shad, shown on page 262, Volume 1, has some collector demand. I would value the lures shown at $10.00 – 15.00 each; Model 2011 with the papers in box, $20.00+.

Series 2000 Spot lures, ⅓ oz., 2½" long, raised letters naming company on left side and Spot on right side. $20.00.

Big O #4634, orange belly in box. $12.00+.

Series 2000 Spot lures, ⅓ oz., 2½" long, raised letters naming company on left side and Spot on right side. $15.00 – 20.00 each new in boxes, $5.00 each loose.

Crème Lure Company

P.O. Box 87, Tyler, Texas 75710. This lure company was founded in 1949 by Nick Crème. He is famous for being the originator of the plastic worm. A 1986 catalog only shows plastic worm type baits, however, earlier the company produced some standard baits as well. Shown are two of the nicest Jitterbug type lures made by this company, the diving lip says Crème's, Akron, O and Tyler, Texas, much like Arbogast markings. The shorter lure is a 2¼" Du-Dad with indented eye sockets, protruding eyes, hula skirt tail, marked on back, and spoon type lip. The longer lure is a 3" Mad-Dad with inverted bell/screw belly hanger, one spinner on tail, wobble spoon lip, flattened out bottom, and carved eyes. The Mad-Dad has both spoon lip and back markings. Both lures are in Perch color.

Top, Crème Mad-Dad, and bottom, Crème Du-Dad, $15.00 – 20.00 each.

Demon Lure Company

1510 S. Olive St., San Antonio, Texas, made one of the most collectible of all plastic lures, the Sail Shark. This little lure is developing collector interest due to its cute little size, ease of display, multiple colors and sizes, and the fact that it was available in a variety of packaging from three different lure companies, including Creek Chub Bait Company when owned by Dura Pak. A number of lures are shown in packages, dealer cartons, and loose in this section and in the sections on Creek Chub in Volume 1 and Kautzky (Lazy Ike) pages 79 – 83. Of course, most of these have to be found in the box or package to be certain of the lure's heritage. Although it appears that early Sail Sharks were marked on the belly when sold by Demon, some of the early Demons said Demon's Sail Shark, and some

said Sail Shark. Also, some of the very early ones had color markings such as PEP 35 standing for Pink Eye Pearl or BF 65 standing for Bar Fish/Grey Body. Later, Lazy Ike went to only a letter code on some. Also, eye placement varied on Demon versions but was usually at the front of the lure on Lazy Ike versions. Future editions will be able to add more information on eye variations, hook variations, and markings. Bringing only a couple of dollars in the late 1990s, this lure is now selling loose for at least $10.00 and in the box for at least $15.00 – $20.00 depending on age, manufacturer, color, and so on. Dealer packs will go up in value just as those with Heddon Sonics have over the last couple of years. Lastly, a small ultra-light or "fly rod"[9] version would command more money.

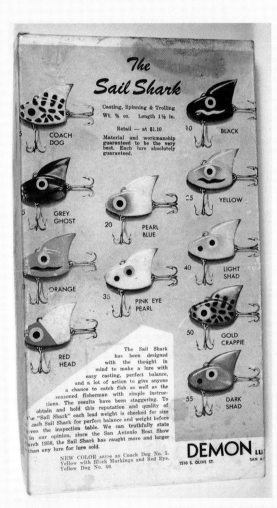

Rare dealer carton, loaned by John Kolbeck. $100.00+.

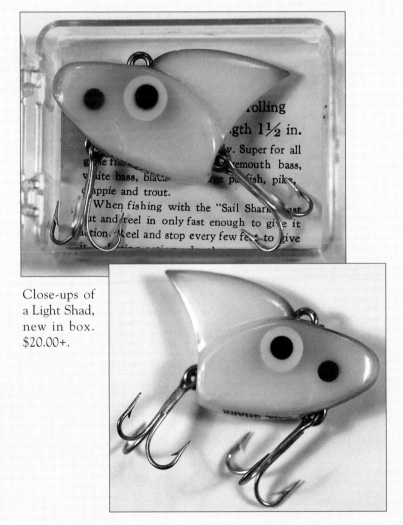

Close-ups of a Light Shad, new in box. $20.00+.

Three more original Demon colors. $15.00 – 20.00 loose.

A variety of Sail Sharks, tough jointed and ultra light, likely are Lazy Ike versions. Jointed one is 2¼" long, Model 100 ultra light is just over 1". The 200s are 1½". Note that the paint on the weights can come loose as on Heddon Sonics. $15.00 – 30.00 for ultra light and jointed versions.

Introductory box for Lazy Ike with an original Demon pattern. The one shown is a 200 series Coach Dog number 205, ⅜ oz. Shark Ike. It is on a pre-zip code card with the address of Fort Dodge 22, Iowa, making it from the early 1960s. The nicest thing about this particular lure from a collector's view is that not only is it mint in the box, it is in the "Introductory Box!" These lures are rather hot as a collectible, and this introductory box could bring a premium of up to $40.00. I paid about half that amount on eBay in late 2000, but the seller did not indicate anything about the importance of the box or it would have gone up in price.

Diamond Jim

Manufactured by Fastex, Des Plaines, Illinois, pre-zip box. These are some great spinning lures from our modern era and should really gain in collector interest due to uniqueness of design and colors. I have shown two new-in-the-box spinning lures, an unmarked jointed lure that appears to have been made by the same company, and a floating bass plug with similar eyes. I paid $15.00 each for the two in the box four years ago. Loose, they should bring that much now.

Two new-in-the-box Diamond Jim lures. Model DS-5 is called a Gold Scale Minnow, the red/white is Model DS-1. These jointed lures are 3⅛" long and have L&S type diving plate and hardware. The paper insert indicated nine colors, all in ¼ oz. spinning lure size. Also, the paper insert had Fishin' Tips authored by famed Joe Bates, Jr. Suggested retail was $1.35. $20.00 – 30.00 each boxed.

A 3⅞" jointed hard plastic lure with diamond eyes, fin-shaped tail, and a little concave mouth molded into lure. This has the heart-shaped diving lip held on by two flat blade screws, and the hook hangers are both screw type inserted through a protective inverted cup to protect the lure. A most attractive plastic lure that is very well made. No trade data.

A floating bass lure with diamond eyes, 3¾", Pflueger scramble type paint, diamond protrusion around diamond eyes, simple screw belly hardware, and unmarked propellers. $15.00 – 20.00.

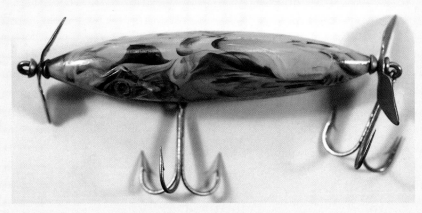

Dickson

This is a company name without an address, actually a Japanese import claiming lures are made of "Belco Balsawood." An early copy of a Rebel Minnow or Rapala type, this is a box for Model No 613-G but it looks like an S for silver. The lure shown is actually a plastic Rebel copy and not a balsa Rapala copy. A nice addition to a Rebel/Rapala type collection. New price was 59¢.

Dickson 4½" lure and box. Sold on eBay in early 2002 for $12.00.

Doctor Spoon

Brainerd Bait Co., St. Paul, Minn., pre-zip box. Though an obvious metal, I have placed some metal baits in this chapter as well. This is a common spoon in many sizes and varieties, but look for examples new in the box. Value is about double face value to $10.00.

Doctor Spoon new in box, Model No. 175, Thin Doctor Chrome, 3¾" long, cardboard box with plastic top. Sold on eBay in early 2002 for $15.00.

Dura-Pak Corporation

Dept. FS, Box 3410, Sioux City, Iowa 51102 was once the owner of Creek Chub (see Volume 1) and Lazy Ike (see discussion under Demon for the Sail Ike). They also jobbed lures that were copies of famous lures through the brand name "Golden Eagle." I assume that these were produced with licensing agreements and know it dates to as early as 1973. Lures made included a "Hilo Popper" (Hula Popper), "Wiggle Bug" (Jitterbug), "Tadpole" (Tadpolly), "Jointed Flasher Minnow" (L&S Miracle Minnow), "Lazy Min" (Lazy Ike), "Rocket Lure" (Bomber), "Spot Minnow" (Cordell Spot), "Tenite Minnow" (Rebel Minnow), and more. Some of the lures collectors heretofore assumed

were Herter's are likely Golden Eagle copycat lures. I do not know if they were made in the U.S.A. or Japan at this time. They also marketed a number of flies and fly rod baits under the same name, including the Golden Eagle Beetle Bug that is an exact copy of a Weber and Luhr All fly rod beetle. Weber appears to have been making flies for Dura-Pak from the looks of it. However, this shows the danger of attempting to identify some lures common to many makers such as the cute little beetles without a card or packaging. Some of those mint fly rod beetles that collectors paid dearly for may be from a 1973 Dura-Pak carton!

Eddie Pope and Company

Altadena, Calif., was later purchased by Luhr Jensen & Sons, Inc., Hood River, Oregon 97031. This company made the excellent plastic bait called the Hot-Shot shortly after World War II and first marketed it in a two-piece hard plastic box with a pink colored catalog insert. It then placed the lure on a cardboard backing with the graphics of a man catching a fish in blue color with red letters outlined in white and shrink-wrapped it all for a peg-board type display at the tackle shop. One of these little packages sold in April 2001 on eBay for $16.00; new it would have been about 95¢. The blue packaging dates from the 1960s. Luhr Jensen took over and also used a peg-board type package but with its own graphics. There are also packages that say "now made by" after Luhr Jensen bought the rights to the lure.

The ones in two-piece plastic boxes are worth at least $20.00 each, and the little shrink-wrap packs from the 1960s are worth nearly as much. The newer Luhr Jensen models would be worth less than $10.00 at this time, except maybe the introductory Luhr Jensen packaging worth a few dollars more. Another lure with some collector interest is the Eddie Pope Fishback as shown below and in Chapter 8.

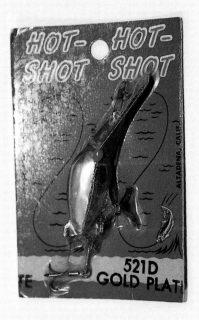

New on the card 521 D Gold Plate model. $16.00+.

New in the box 3¼" Orange with papers, first box, Model M102. $20.00+ in new condition as shown.

Three older fly rod models, two 2⅛" M5 Models and M3. $4.00 – 6.00 each loose.

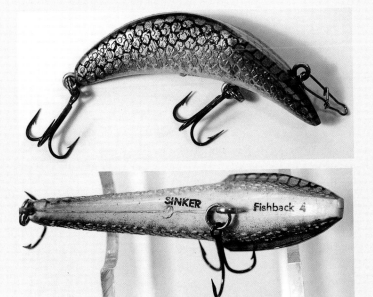

Fishback Model 4 Sinker in Purple Scale, 2½" long as measured on the curve. $8.00 – 12.00 loose.

Electro Lure

Chicago, Illinois. According to Luckey's 5th Edition, this lure dates from 1946 and 1947. The model shown is from 1947 since it has the little round knob on the back, and the earliest model did not. This is a rare modern lure and would command $50.00 or better, $100.00 or better in the box. According to the company, this version only produced light underwater when in motion. I would imagine the color was limited to the famous red and white as the illumination was the special feature, not the color of the lure. The lure is 3½" long counting the propeller. Hook hardware is a washer screw in belly, and a screw through the propeller on tail. Eyes protrude from the lure, and the lure disassembles with a flat blade screw on its back. Lure is clearly marked on the lip "Electro" above line tie and "Lure" below the protruding plastic line tie.

 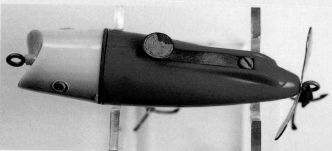

Left, side view of Electro Lure; right, top view showing 1947 knob. $50.00+.

Glen L. Evans, Inc.

Caldwell, Idaho, now owned by Luhr-Jensen & Sons, Inc., Hood River, Oregon. Evans made a wide array of fishing items and lures for a number of years, including many fly fishing items. It is thought that many of Evans' items were tied by Weber, and it may be that Evans made the Weber Dive-n-Wobl bass baits for them. Evans was purchased first by Gladding and at that time Evans became associated with the Oreno line of lures of South Bend. When Luhr-Jensen received Evans, they also received the Oreno line of lures. In Chapter 8 is shown a bass spinner new on an Evans card and at right are a couple of nice fly rod items. Hopefully, in the future I will be able to really detail this company's history with the cooperation of Phil Jensen of Luhr-Jensen and the use of his company archives.

 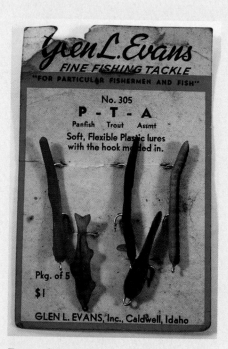

No. 465 "Top-Walker" cork popper w/rubber legs on card. $20.00+.

Evans lifelike fly rod lures on card, Model 305. $10.00 due to poor condition of card; $20.00+ if clean.

Fin-Wing

Grand Rapids, Michigan. This beautiful wooden bait from the 1950s is similar to a CCBC Injured Minnow. They have glass eyes, quality cup hardware, and front and rear propellers. They came in at least two sizes with hook variations. They trade for a minimum of $50.00 each loose, more with the box.

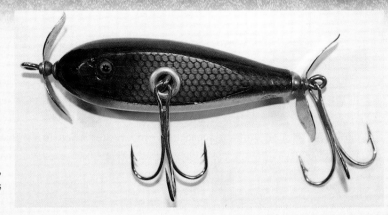

A 3" Fin-Wing from Grand Rapids, Michigan, round decal type, marking on bottom of tail says Fin-Wing, Grand Rapids, Michigan. $50.00+.

Fincheroo

Distributed by Robfin Tackle of Arizona, made by Katchmore of Wisconsin, see Ubangi Lure on page 137. This is a unique plastic lure, and it is marked on the back. It is 3⅜" long, has surface side hardware, one protruding eye, and tail spinner with inverted barrel hardware. No trade data is known, but it should bring $20.00 – 25.00+ due to unique design and short production run. The hole was to grasp the fish without a gaff. This lure dates from the early 1970s.

 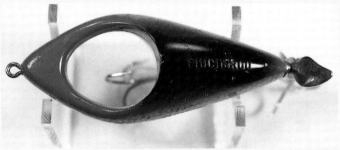

Fincheroo. $20.00+.

Flathead Lures

No manufacturing data known. These are five of the coolest plastic lures I have ever seen, and I know nothing about them. I found them in a tackle box that had made its way from the Midwest to Sun City, Arizona, and back again when I bought it. The box was made up mainly of Bombers, Jitterbugs, a South Bend Tease-Oreno, a Miracle Minnow, Heddon Sonics, a Cordell Big O, a Doll Top Secret, metal baits, and these Flathead lures (most baits were from the late 1960s, early 1970s). Atlantic Lures made a Flathead as shown on page 23, a copy of the Helin Flatfish. There was an Atlantic Lures Jitterbug copy in the box, but I do not think they made these unless they had changed the lure and not the name, something companies have indeed done through history. At any rate, any help with these is welcome; it is unusual to find so many of one type in one box, so the owner must have liked them! The colors are bright and all have a "shore minnow" design on them. The lure is two-piece plastic with the head being one mold and the body another. The line tie and both hook hangers are simple screw eyes. The face has a "smiley face," and the tail has two dots and the name Flathead with little radiant marks coming off it. Whoever designed these must have been a very creative artist, and maybe they even worked. I know I am not going to try one until I find a double!

Five Flathead Lures, 2¹³⁄₁₆" long, painted eyes. No trade data, scarce.

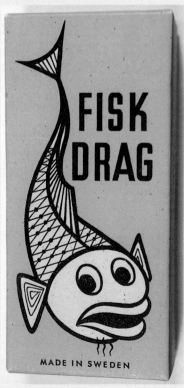

New-in-box Fisk Drag. No trade data.

Ford Lundquist

A unique spoon made in Sweden is shown because of its box and plastic tail. Called the F. L. Draget on the spoon and box end and the Fisk Drag on the box top, this nice brass spoon with fish scales on tail and a plastic fin is well-built and attractive. It is shaped much like the modern Little Cleo but not as wide. The box is a two-piece cardboard box with great graphics. How this ended up in the Great Lakes is a mystery, but it makes a unique addition to any collection. No trade data is available.

Al Foss

See the section on Tru-Temper, page 133.

Garcia Corporation

329 Alfred Ave., Teaneck, N. J. The Garcia Corporation imported fishing lures in addition to high quality reels. The most commonly found models are the Eelet shown below and a little Plucky type bait called the Lippy Lure. The Eelet says "Depose France" on the diving lip and is about 3⅞" long. Its hooks and line tie are molded into the lure. Of the Lippy lures shown, the smaller one is a Model 7280, ¼ oz., 3⅛" long including diving lip, the larger one is 4³⁄₁₆" long, both imported from France and likely made by the same company that originated these spinning baits in the 1940s or early 1950s. Both of the Lippy Lures have France in small block print on the left rear of the belly ridge. The smaller one has the letter B on the same ridge in the left front and the larger one the number 3 in the same place. These lures were coming into America through importation by Airex as well. These lures are trading for $5.00 – 12.00 each without packaging.

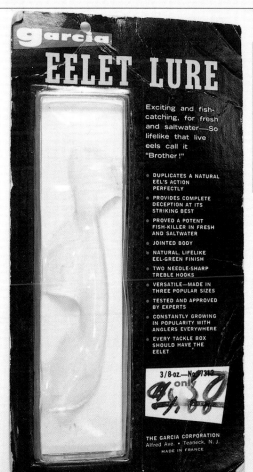

Eelet package and lure. $15.00 – 20.00 in package.

Two Lippy Lures. $5.00 – 12.00 loose.

Unknown Lippy/Plucky type spinning lure, this clear red diving lip, weight on bottom, 2¾" lure is not marked. Quality is excellent. $10.00 – 12.00.

Lippy Lure on blister pack, ¼ oz. size, No. 7280. $15.00 – 20.00.

Gee Wiz Bait Company

Richland Center, Wisconsin. This company's products actually are borderline for our modern era, but they were still made in the early 1940s and are neat lures to add to your collection. The Gee Wiz Frog was one of the many frog moving leg type lures to be invented, based on the same principles of the Rhodes Frog. The photo shows a nice two-piece cardboard box and a clean example of the bait. I paid $100.00 for this piece in June of 2001 by private sale.

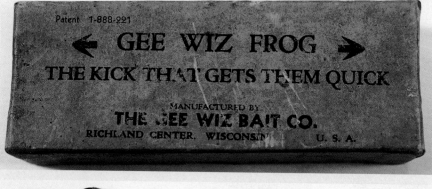

Gee Wiz Frog, 4½" long, and box. Also available in red and white. $100.00.

Go-Get-tum

G&G Industries. These diminutive baits actually could go in the fly rod section, but they seem like "classic" plastic lures and I included them here. These were made in Michigan but the exact date is not known. Note the ingenious clip hardware used. Face of lure is stamped Go Get-tum Pat. App'ld For. Protruding eyes, white with black eyeballs, 1" long, single treble.

Go-Get-tums.
$10.00 – 20.00 each.

Top and bottom view of Bippie, 2" long, eyes protrude. No trade data.

Gudebrod Bros. Silk

12 So. 12th Street, Philadelphia, Pennsylvania. These makers of famed fishing lines also made some plastic lures of interest. I had not seen the Bippie before 2001, an odd "chunk" type bait with the name printed on the bottom. Most Gudebrod lures can be recognized by the oversize eyes they used, as seen on the other examples. It may be possible that L & S, or Miracle Minnow, made lures for the company. No trade data exists, but I would rate them as a little above common, and they should bring $8.00 – 15.00 each, depending on type, color, and condition.

Blue and yellow Viper with CCBC-shaped diving lip, marked Gudebrod and Viper on lip. Simple screw hardware, large raised eyes, 2¹³⁄₁₆" long. $8.00 – 15.00.

63

Small gray shiner minnow, Gudebrod printed within a fish on diving lip, simple screw hardware, 1¹¹⁄₁₆" long, raised eyes. $8.00 – 15.00.

A 2⅞" long top water dual propeller bait in red/white. Each of the propellers is marked M inside a fish. Gudebrod type eyes and hook hardware, although the rear has an inverted bell also to allow the propeller to work. This could be a Miracle Minnow instead, but it has the same type of foil scale inserts as the Gudebrod lures. $8.00 – 12.00.

A Gudebrod plunker type, Trouble Maker stamped on lure bottom, Model 1400, color 42, ½ oz., 2½" long. $8.00 – 15.00.

Butch Harris

No manufacturing data. The Fas-Bak lure shown here is one of a number of outstanding colors on a body shape similar to a Heddon Hedd-Hunter. The lures are all clearly marked on the back as shown. The ones I have sold have ranged from $12.00 – 15.00.

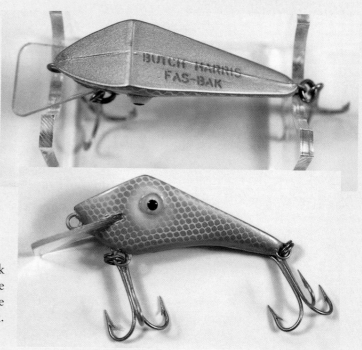

Butch Harris Fas-Bak lure, 2¼" long, staple hardware molded into the casting, marked on back. $12.00 – 15.00.

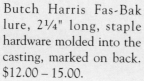

Harrison Industries, Inc.

250 Passaic Street, Newark, N. J. This company made the very collectible Bill Plummer Bass Frogs. These frogs come in a variety of sizes, and the older ones have more of a "raised" forehead. I sold a new-on-card with pocket catalog one for over $100.00 on eBay in 2000. Shown here are a new-on-card Skitter Frog version and a Bass Frog off the card. One thing to be aware of is that BassPro Shops offered these through their catalog outlet recently, and those would not be of much collector value. However, BassPro included some very unusual color patterns that could go up in value in years to come. I have only had one Skitter Frog in the last seven years. The company also made a collectible spinning reel, the Harrison's #100 Auto-Max, designed for 2 to 8 lb. test line.

Skitter Frog on card, Model #SK-F, ⅜ oz., 1½" long, 3/0 Nickel Hook and 1¾" Bass Frog. $125.00+ for carded lure; $20.00+ for frog alone.

Hawk Lures

See Bayou Boogie in Chapter 12 of Volume 1. At left is a Hawk lure, a neat little plastic lure with raised eyes, that came in numerous colors. The interest in these has really risen the past four years, and a color collection of them is attractive. They currently trade for $8.00 – 12.00 each.

Hawk lure in orange w/black spots. $8.00 – 12.00.

Helin Tackle Company

Detroit 7, Michigan. Similar to the Dardevle and the Jitterbug, one or a number of Flatfish are usually found in every tackle box since the early 1940s. This lure was developed in the largemouth bass waters of southern Michigan at the beginning of our modern era. I have a prototype in orange given to a fishing guide to try out (the gentleman mentioned in Volume 1). It looks about like the production models. One thing originally unique to this lure was the "gang" type of hook hardware. This really hooks fish, but it also tangles some on casts and in the tackle box. For that reason, I think more of these are found still in their boxes which keeps the hooks from tangling in storage. It would be quite a task to collect the hundreds of color, size, hook pattern, box pattern, etc. of Flatfish. There is little serious collector interest at this time due to the availability of the lures. The company lives on today, being recently purchased by Worden. There is some interest in the wooden Flatfish, as they were produced in both wood and Tenite, and some of the early and introductory boxes. Also, the pre-zip code boxes are more valuable than the recent ones. Shown are a variety of boxes; some are tough to find, such as the green and black one. The green/black box has a new U20, SAS;

the box is cardboard with plastic slide top and it dates from 1950. The mailing address in 1950 was 6342 Pulford Ave, Detroit 7, Michigan. The insert claims that 6,000,000 were sold by the end of 1949! Most Flatfish sell for $4.00 – 8.00 new in the box if they are post-zip code; double that for pre-zip code in the box; wooden ones sell for a little more. Wooden Musky size Flatfish sell for $15.00 – 20.00 each in good shape.

A more collectible version is the Swimmerspoon, some of which are shown. This was advertised to combine the qualities of a spoon with a lure and reap the benefits of the marriage. This lure is worth about double what a Flatfish of the same vintage would bring.

The most collectible of all Helin baits is the Fish Cake, a great surface bait in different sizes and a variety of colors. It also had gang hardware and the size number was printed on the back. These sell for $20.00 – 40.00, a little more boxed. They had a shorter history than the other lures and also have a little more style.

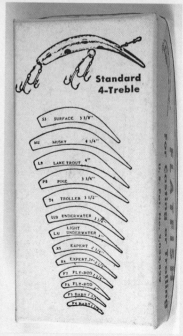

A variety of Flatfish boxes and a Model F5 FR (frog) Flatfish new (hook removed for shipping by Helin). I have a gross of these with no hooks; hooks were included to be added after shipping depending on size wanted, but I do not think this was a common practice. Sold in a pre-zip cardboard box with plastic top. See text for values; most are valued at only $4.00 – 8.00 boxed.

Introductory box for the Swimmerspoon, one new in same box, Model SP 175 SS, 1¾" long and two more. The larger one is 2¼" long, Model 225. $18.00 – 25.00 boxed.

Yellow Fish Cake, Model #9, 2¼", same as at right. $25.00 – 40.00.

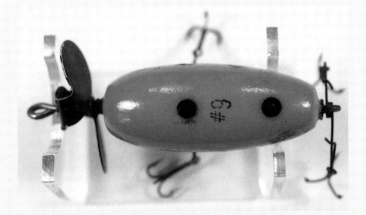

Orange Fish Cake Model #9, 2¼", typical Helin gang hooks with simple screw hardware, front propeller. $25.00 – 40.00.

Herring Magic

Model No. 3. This is a Pacific Northwest company that makes this minnow holder for trolling. The bait is not special, but the graphics on the box are nice. The bright aluminum on the box caused photo reflections, but the box is quite stunning. The box back says it is right for a number 3. I sold two of these on eBay in early 2000 for $15.00 – 20.00 each.

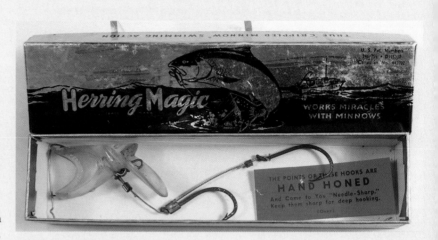

Herring Magic in box. $15.00 – 20.00.

Herter's

This famous Minnesota hunting and fishing supply house has sold some wonderful lures through the years, mostly copies of major lures. However, Herter's put its own brand of color on some great lures, such as Sonic types, River Runt types, etc. In the year 2000, I sold a complete Herter's-made River Runt type lure collection, and the lures averaged over $18.00 each. Many of the Herter's lures are marked Japan on the lip in very small print, so look for this. Also, Herter's catalogs are readily available, and one from the 1960s or 1970s gives nice color charts to study. Herter's also made a Finnish Minnow similar to the Rapala, and I think the box shown is theirs, but I am not sure of that. They made a Rapala type with fins as shown and a plain Rapala type as well. The unusual thing is to find them boxed or bagged, as the two shown. The Tiny Tad copies are really nicely done and came in a little plastic box as shown (one per box). The nice thing about Herter's is that there is a double market to sell items as many collectors collect the brand name, hunting, fishing, camping, etc., while others are only interested in the lures. But, as with Airex/Lionel, this interest increases the demand and the prices a little bit. Of the following, only the Tad copies would have much interest, maybe $8.00 – 12.00 each. The minnows are just too common but are always worth at least $5.00 for catching walleye. The bagged one is worth $10.00.

Herter's version of a Rapala Minnow, although I am not certain this is by Herters. $5.00.

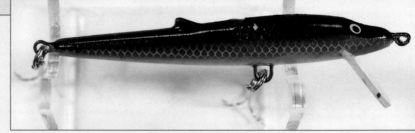

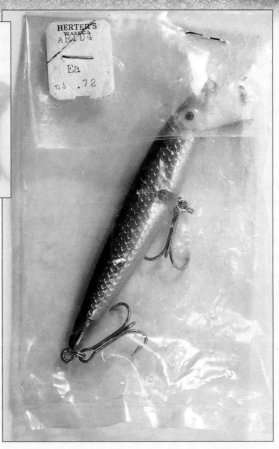

Definitely Herter's, one still in the bag. The raised fin version is 3½" long, and the one in the bag is 3¼" long. $5.00 – 10.00.

Two Tiny Tad copies, note the nice eyes, likely from the 1950s or 1960s, found in a marked one-piece hinged plastic box. The lures are 1⅞" long, Model No. 6501. $8.00 each, $12.00 in box.

Highland Group, Inc.

Crankbait Products Division, 5 Mill Street, Sheffield, Penna. 17. This nice looking early crankbait is marked on the lip only with Crankbait Corp., called the Hi-Catch, and came in a bubble pack with the name in block letters. The packaging was copyrighted in 1981, and the gentleman who had a new one told me that he remembered buying it in 1981 – 82, one of the last lures he purchased. The few others of these I have seen were never in their packages. They were designed after a fingerling fish, and the realism is outstanding. I recently discovered this bait became the rare 1980s Heddon Preyfish which trade for $75.00 new in a box. Given the relationship, the Hi-Catch should bring $25.00+ loose.

Hi-Catch Crankbait, 3" long, hook hangers molded into lure, protruding plastic eyes are part of mold. $25.00+ loose.

Hildebrandt

John J. Hildebrandt Corp., Logansport, Indiana 46947, makes primarily flies and spinners; however, this company has been around since 1899, making it one of the oldest continuous bait companies in America. Most lures are of little value off the cards; however, shown is a box of spinners new on cards. An item such as this would normally bring up to $8.00 per card based upon sales the last two years, and the dealer dozen in the box should bring over $30.00 easily. But, of course, it depends on how many are on the market at any one time. I have sold some individual items for nearly $20.00 and then can hardly get that much for a dealer dozen at other times. The most important thing to remember is that items such as this cannot be soiled *at all* or the value is greatly reduced. Also, if the card is moist or musty, it is nearly worthless. Items must be crisp, clean, and dirt-free to command the prices mentioned. Early Hildebrandt items on cards or in boxes would be the most desirable due to identification ease and the ability to assign a date to the rather common items. One modern item is also shown on page 71, the Jigolo Lure. This rather attractive deep running vibrating lure with a tail spinner was available in three sizes and six finishes. A nice little addition to sonic type lures. The Jigolo Lure would likely only bring $6.00 – 9.00 each at this time.

Hildebrandt lures new on cards in dealer box, size 3½" double spinner blades on 4⅛" shaft marked with company name and size of blades. $8.00+ each card.

Hildebrandt's # SKITTER - SPOON
For Bass

A PROVEN BASS BAIT FOR THE REAL FISHERMAN

No. 2 SKG

This is the bass spoon the fishermen want. Designed so that it can be reeled in on top of the lily pads and weed, it is also effective underwater. Use with a pork rind or plastic worm or lizard.

Made of solid brass, plated all over and weighted in the rear. Extra sharp bass hook. 5/0 hook size.

No. 1 SKS

SKITTER-SPOON		
1/4 oz.		3/8 oz.
No. 2 SKS	Silver	No. 1 SKS
No. 2 SKG	22-K Gold	No. 1 SKG
No. 2 SSS	State Color	No. 1 SSS
No. 2 SKB	Black	No. 1 SKB

No. 2 SSS (Skirted)

PLEASE STATE COLOR

Gold and Nickel Models, $1.65 ea.
SSS Models, $1.95 ea.
PACKED: Individually carded, one dozen baits per box. Blister pak.

SEE COLOR CHART ON BACK PAGE

Hildebrandt's ## Jigolo Lure

No. J-2 $1.25 ea.
1/2 oz. No. 6 hook.

(Actual Size)

No. J-3 - $1.25 ea.
5/8 oz. - #6 hook

No. J-1 $1.25 ea.
1/4 oz. No. 8 hook.

IDEAL FOR WHITE BASS, BLACK BASS, TROUT, AND PANFISH

The JIGOLO is a deep runner with a vibrating action and lots of flash. The curved angle blade spins at the slightest motion and makes the whole bait vibrate. Fish hit the sharp treble hook before they know it. This bait takes the work out of fishing. Solid construction in lead and stainless steel.

COLOR CHART FOR JIGOLO LURES	PLEASE STATE FINISH	Nickel Gold Spotted	Shad Flash (White) Perch Flash (Yellow) Tiger Stripe

Nickel   Shad Flash   Perch Flash

Spotted   Tiger Stripe   Gold

Hildebrandt catalog, page 8.

Hildreth Brand

Mike Hildreth, West New York, Gunnison, Colorado. The Wonder Bug by Hildreth is a handmade wooden plug with deer hair wings introduced in 1963. The maker claims to have discovered, patented, and manufactured this lure based upon a bug found on a fishing trip to Mexico 36 years earlier, in 1927. This is a unique lure hand made from wood and hand painted. The lure has two simple screw eye hook hangers and the same screw eye for a line tie. It is about 2½" long, exclusive of metal lip. It came presented in a hinged plastic box with an insert showing the lure being attacked by bass and explaining the story of the lure. These lures trade for $50.00 or more.

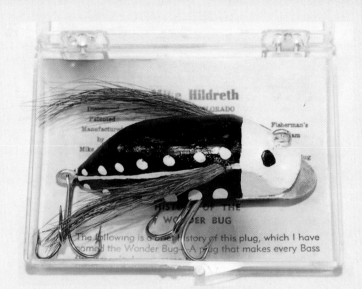

New-in-box Wonder Bug. $50.00+.

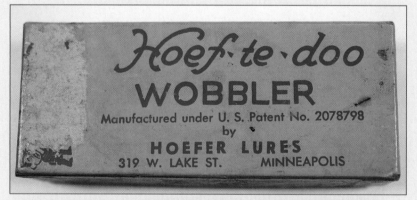

Hoefer Lures

319 W. Lake St., Minneapolis, Minn. Shown is a Hoef-te-doo Wobbler, U.S. Patent No. 2078798. This nice spoon bait came in a two-piece cardboard box with great graphics in red on a yellow background. The lure cost $1.50 new. The spoon itself is marked on the top Hoef-te-doo. It was available with three different colored streamers attached, red head, black head, and blue head. All I know about the company is that they made flies mainly for Crappies, Bass, Pike, Bream, and Sunfish. One interesting note is that the spoon bait came with a polishing cloth included in the box (as shown)! The lure shown is the Blue Head, and there is a little blue dot next to the price on the box as a color code.

Hoef-te-doo box and lure, uncommon in two-piece box. $20.00+ with box.

Hofschneider Corporation

848 Jay Street, Rochester 11, New York, pre-zip code box. This old New York state spoon maker has a long history, and its spoons are very common. However, a new in the box example like the one shown makes them interesting. You can see the original price on this was scratched out and the item was on sale years ago! This is likely from the 1950s in this package. A colorful addition to a modern lure collection which should be available for $8.00 – 20.00.

Red Eye new in 1950s box, lure is 2¼" long, Model No. 2P-C. $8.00 – 20.00.

Hornet Lure Company

El Dorado, Arkansas, nice pre-zip two-piece cardboard box with an attractive plastic lure. I paid $50.00 for this in May 2001. Note this is a Patent Pending box, so there may be variations of it.

Hornet Lure new in Box, 2" long, screw hardware mounted into a slightly protruding convex circular mold on belly and at tail, hand soldered hooks, no marks on diving lip, and flat painted eyes with no eye balls. The box is all yellow, the white is from water damage. $50.00+.

Horrocks-Ibbotson Company (H-I)

Utica, New York. See the Abbey and Imbrie listing also on page 18. I am uncertain of the relationship between these two companies, but many of the lure lines and color patterns of the early A & I lures become common again in the H-I offerings of the 1950s. This was a complete tackle company offering a full line of items. An entire book could be written on the variations of this one company, but I cannot do it much justice in this short entry. Just be aware that H-I items often look like early A & I items and that they marketed a complete line of wooden baits in 1958, including Tango types, fly rod baits that look like Trout-Orenos, Plunker types, and more. Many of the baits were named after "Old HI" an advertising creation, or were called HICO. I am planning a major chapter on this firm for Volume 3.

Hubbards Lures

4 Main Street, Brooklyn, Indiana. This nice lure found new in the hinged plastic top box has become somewhat collectible. The Sparkle Tail was a ½ oz. Floating lure that dove deep with a fast retrieve. It has an inserted barrel type cup hardware to keep the hook away from the plastic finish and an extended line tie. It was recommended to use a leader with a snap or a snap swivel for tying lure to line. The Sparkle Tail came in a variety of colors, and the values will vary as to the color, but the lure would start at $15.00 or so new in the box. The color shown is 66F.

Sparkle Tail in box, jointed lure, 3" long. $15.00 – 20.00 boxed.

Hump Lure Company, Inc.

Box 1013, El Campo, Texas, pre-zip code, one-piece hinged plastic box with paper insert. There slogan was "Don't Get Bumps — Get Fish With Humps," and they produced a lure similar to the Bingo lure. Shown is the Mighty Midget new in the box, 2" long with a #6 treble in front and a #8 in rear, surface hardware, large teddy bear style eye. The paper insert reads "Hump Mighty Midget with the magic eye." Hopefully we can unwind the Bingo/Hump mystery in Volume 3. These are attractive little lures in a variety of colors and are already getting collector attention. They do attract the dreaded "plastic scum" that needs cleaning. A similar Texas lure is called the Bingo Lure, and they are hard to differentiate since they both have the trademark big eye. However, Bingos also came in larger sizes, and I am not sure about the Humps. One series of Bingos on eBay in March of 2001 averaged nearly $22.00 per lure, and up to $38.00 for some of the translucent colors. Humps should have the same or higher value.

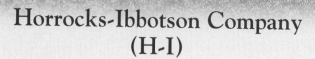

Hump lure new from box. $22.00+ loose; $30.00+ boxed.

Paul Huppertz

Dupont, PA 18641, maker of the Hoopy Lures. This may be more recent than 1988, I am not certain, but it was packaged in a stapled plastic bag with the card insert shown. It is a very large, 6¾" wooden Musky bait, raised teddy bear glass eyes, simple screw hardware, and unmarked diving lip. I thought it was nicely made and painted.

Hoopy Jointed Musky Bait. Sold for $18.00 on eBay early 2002.

Jamison Tackle Corporation

3654 Montrose, Chicago 18, Ill., the address on a pre-zip code card new in box with a Shannon Twin-Spin. Formerly known as the W. J. Jamison Co., 5559 W. North Avenue, Chicago 39, Illinois. Twin Spins were made over a long period of time, and you will find them in a two-piece cardboard box, a cardboard box with a plastic top, and, a shallow cardboard box with a plastic top with the lure mounted to a cardboard with all the data printed on it. The top lure on page 76 is a Model 1011, Black Head, White Feathers, new on card in mint box. Value for this is $15.00 to $20.00. Twin Spins are very common; new in box is not common. Jamison made a number of collectible lures over the decades and has one great contribution to the modern era, the Jamison Wig-L-Twin, a unique looking plastic bait with twin spinner blades. This has been selling for $20.00 to $35.00 if in excellent shape since the late 1990s. New in the box it should be worth $50.00. Shown on page 77 is a great brochure showing 11 colors available for the Wig-L-Twin that is likely the introductory advertisement, given the description of the lure. It was stated that the lure was individually boxed in a ⅝ oz. weight with two No. 2 trebles and two No. 2 spoons. It was also stated, "This indestructible plastic lure, moulded of Tenite, has full length action." I have never seen a Wig-L-Twin deteriorating like the early Heddons. The Wig-L-Twin was introduced in 1939, according to Streater, so one would expect some poor plastics to show up yet. See Streater on page 220 for illustrations of some more collectible Jamison lures. The 2" Beetle Plop looks like a Millsite Floating Beetle. The Shannon Torpedo was new in 1941 and looks like a cross between a Wig-L-Twin and a Heddon River Runt. And finally one I have not seen yet is a Shannon Wig-L-Tail that according to the reprinted advertisement in Streater's book: "Swims like a living fish-flexible rubber tail-14 colors-2 spinners-No. 2000 made of Tenite Plastic." According to the color selection, Wig-L-Twins should have been available in the same 14 colors, one would assume. Jamison also marketed Tenite River Runt type lures claiming its No. 1500 was the most popular bait in all America. Again, according to Streater, either Jamison had a marketing agreement or a licensing agreement with Dillon-Beck Mfg. Co. of New Jersey for many of the above lures.

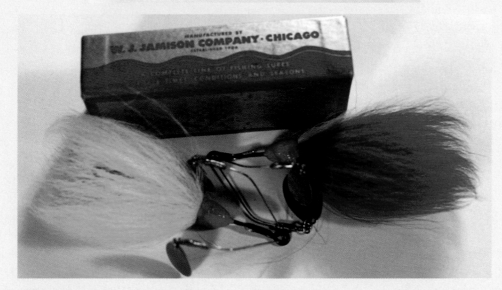

Twin-Spin and box examples. $15.00 – 20.00 for new-in-box versions. $5.00 – 10.00 loose.

THE W. J. JAMISON CO.
5559 W. NORTH AVENUE
Chicago 39, Illinois

SHANNON WIG-L-TWIN

FOR YOU . . . another Shannon prize-winning fish-getter! This indestructible plastic lure, moulded of Tenite, has alluring full length action. Shannon Spinners in the streamlined lifelike fins make the lure a living thing from head to tail. Can be fished at any desired depth. Sinks slowly if allowed to rest; if retrieved immediately lure travels 12 to 14 inches below the surface, an ideal fishing depth. May be cast or trolled with equal success. Use it for bass, walleye and northern pike, pickerel and muskies.

MOULDED OF TENITE

Non-chip finish. No. 2 Hollow Point treble hooks. No. 2 spoons. Popular ⅝ oz. weight.
INDIVIDUALLY BOXED, $1.35
PATENTED

Let's Go Fishing

All Shannon Lures made in U.S.A. under J. P. and J. M. SHANNON Patents – Prices quoted include Federal Excise Tax.

Full Length Action – Catches Short Strikes

W.J. Jamison Company catalog, back cover. These are very collectible lures. $20.00 – 35.00 loose.

77

J.C. Higgins Brand

Like Meadow Brook Lures, another Sears Roebuck & Co. brand name for fishing tackle. This was available in the classic blue and white packaging that Sears used on its Higgins brand items for hunting and fishing. Shown is a new in the box Shur Strike type small pikie in wood with screw eye hardware, a Shur Strike or Isle Royal type diving lip, and simple yellow spots outlined in black shading for eyes. Again, exact maker is never certain as more than one company provided lures for Sears. Value on the one shown is around $30.00 new in box. A nice collection of J. C. Higgins items could include a tackle box, rod, reel, line dressing, snelled hooks, lures, and more. Again, I would only recommend new in the box or marked items. Higgins lures were often marked on the bottom but as the new one shown demonstrates, not always.

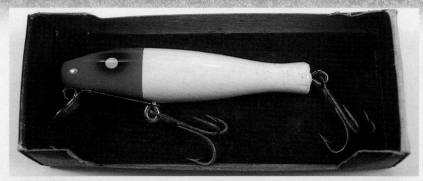

J.C. Higgins Pikie, new in the box, Model 14 RH, 3½" long. $30.00+.

Johnson's Silver Minnow

The address in 1977 was Louis Johnson Company, P.O. Box 21, Amsterdam, MO 64723. Pre-zip address of Louis Johnson Co. was Highland Park, Ill. This was a very successful and thus common lure, shown in one of the box types. These came in two-piece cardboard boxes for quite a while into the 1950s. Again, the only interest in these lures is in the variations in lure and box types and finding the introductory models. A common one such as this is of little value, maybe $6.00 – 9.00 in the box. But, my 1977 catalog shows over 95 variations in the Silver Minnow, Sprite, and other spoon offerings from this company. Quite a little collection in itself.

Johnson Silver Minnow in plastic top cardboard box, Highland Park, Ill. address, Model No. 1310, 2¾". Weber also made these for Johnson at some point in the 1970s or 1980s as I have about 40 of them from the Weber archival purchase molded, but they did not yet have the scurs removed and polished. $6.00 – 9.00.

Bob Josefiak Lures

Kaleva, Michigan. A nicely made lure of a diving wobbler type, 2⅜", washer/screw hardware, and painted eyes. His paint jobs are excellent. His lures should trade for $15.00 – 25.00, but little data is known.

Josefiak lure.
$15.00 – 25.00

Kautzky Lazy Ike Company

Fort Dodge, Iowa, later the Lazy Ike Corporation, Fort Dodge, Iowa. This company made the largest competitor of the Helin Flatfish, and few tackle boxes are found from the 1950s, 1960s or 1970s without a "Lazy Ike" or two. There are numerous variations and scads of colors. Shown is a Lazy Ike 2, Model KL2 in Fluorescent Red, 2⁹⁄₁₆" long counting its reinforced diving lip. It is new in the box with a new pocket catalog showing the whole line of lures. Mint in the box with catalog, it should bring $8.00 to $16.00. The problem is that they sold so well, and there are many out there. However, again, there are not too many new in the box so look for those.

Also shown is something a little different: a school of Shark Ikes! Again, thanks to John Kolbeck for the loan of his dealer carton of Sail Sharks on page 53 and his Shark Ike dealer dozen on page 83. The Sail Shark was first made and distributed by the Demon Lure Company of San Antonio, Texas under the name "Sail Shark" with great success. Then, Lazy Ike acquired the patents, trademarks, and original molds of the company, took over production, and changed the name to Shark Ike. See also the Demon Lure Company for photos of a few of these little gems out of their boxes and a Demon Lure Company box. See Creek Chub Bait Company in Volume 1 for the last version of these to be distributed by Creek Chub/Dura Pak. The trade value of these is $10.00 – 15.00 loose, more if boxed or on the card.

An older Lazy Ike two-piece cardboard box ($8.00), two common Lazy Ikes ($4.00 – 6.00), and the Fluorescent Red KL2 lure ($8.00 – 16.00), new in the box described above.

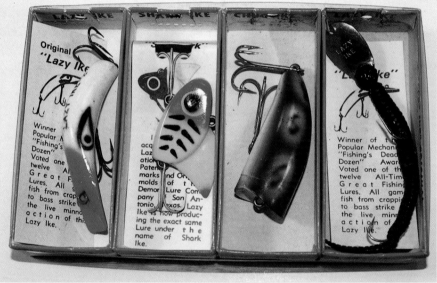

A little more valuable Lazy Ike item, a "Bass Kit" with a Lazy Ike plastic worm, a Series 200 Shark Ike, a Chug Ike, and a Lazy Ike-2. $40.00 – 60.00.

A more uncommon plastic Lazy Ike lure, the Skitter Ike, protruding eyes, simple screw hardware, 3" long, and marked on bottom. $8.00 – 12.00.

A collectible Natural Ike, these were a short run for the company and made in many sizes and natural fish finishes. I have been selling these for $14.00 – 22.00 each new in the box. Early in 2001 I sold a collection of 22 of them for $14.00 each, and one usually gets more when just selling one or two lures at a time. This one is a Model NIM 25 MA (Medium Diver) new in slide-top plastic cardboard blue box that was standard for the Natural Ikes. See the 1980 BassPro Shops Catalog for a complete color display of these colorful lures.

An ultra light Shark Ike, Model 140, new in the box. $25.00 – 35.00 due to size and box.

A more common 200 Shad new on a Lazy Ike card, $25.00 – 35.00 due to early card.

Lazy Ike dealer display carton for Model 200s with three shown, it had four of the six in it. Model 200 BF, Barfish, I paid $100.00 in May of 2001 by private sale.

Another shot of the Introductory Box for a Model 205 white coach dog. $25.00 – 35.00.

A Model 200 GG new on newer Lazy Ike card, $20.00 – 30.00.

A selection of Sharks on display, mostly Model 200s. $10.00 – 15.00, more depending on size/color.

A selection of Sharks on display, mostly Model 200s. $10.00 – 20.00 loose.

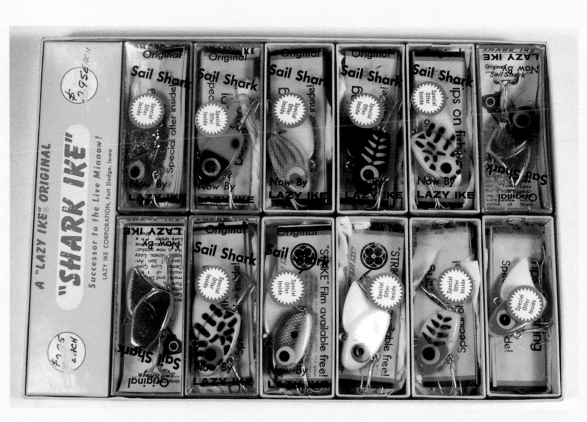

A rare find indeed, a dealer's dozen of Shark Ikes as nice as can be. Note the lure in top right corner is actually an earlier version in the introductory packaging, as is the one in the bottom left corner. There may be a significance in the color of the paper insert in the two introductory boxes, but at this time I am not certain of its meaning. Rare piece, no trade value.

Kush Spoons

This Michigan lure maker produced a most distinctive spoon with the waving center ridge that has some collector interest now. Shown is a plastic top box from the 1950s with a yellow/silver spoon, and three loose versions are also shown. As with some other collectible lures, there is also a demand for these for fishing as they are very successful and well constructed. The boxed one is Model B & Y, Pat. No. D 158873 (design patent), ¾ oz., 3⁵⁄₁₆" long. The spoons are marked Kush Spoon on the lure bottom, stamped into the raised wave pattern. Also shown is another ¾ oz. in a nice pink/white pattern and two fly rod sizes, 1¼" long. The small ones are not marked.

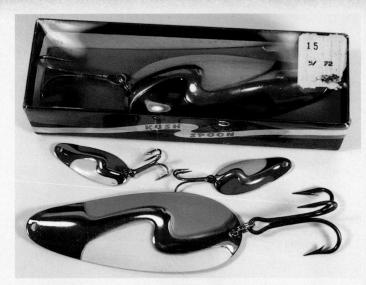

Kush Spoons. Boxed, $20.00+; others, $8.00 – 15.00.

Two-piece plastic box.

L & S

Addresses vary from Illinois to Florida, makers of the famous Mirrolures. This company is well documented in other references and mentioned here to introduce the reader to the company's interesting top water plunker type bait. I do not know the exact production details on these lures but find them attractive and an interesting addition to a collection of Mirrolures. Mirrolures themselves are becoming somewhat in demand due to color collectors and of course for fishing. This is a very successful lure and still in demand. It is difficult to tell the older from the newer versions without packaging, so beware if you are interested only in the very first models. But, for color collecting, this company offers many possibilities. I have sold many Mirrolures on eBay from 1999 – 2001 for up to $15.00 each for the larger, more difficult to find models. Also, the fly rod sizes are fairly hard to find compared to the spinning and casting sizes. See Miracle Lures on page 104 also.

Two of the jointed minnows. $8.00 – 15.00.

A small collection of the Plunker types, the jointed ones (left bottom and center tray) are Models 12M19, about 2⅞" long. The small ones without skirts are Models 12M23, 2" long. The skirted small ones are Models 1621, 2" long. All have surface hardware, screw tail hardware, and are marked L&S and USA on bottom. A bottom marking would be as an example: L&S 12M19 USA. This would be a jointed skirted model. $8.00 – 20.00.

Homer LeBlanc

Traverse City, Michigan. The Swim Whiz is a common modern lure used for Great Lakes trolling, but this small one shown is more unusual in terms of size. These baits are now being sold with a Rockford, Michigan address on the card. The original Swim Whiz baits have some collector interest but beware of recent copies. The small one shown was in the plastics collection I purchased, and I have not seen another one since; no trade data is available.

A 4" casting Swim Whiz, raised plastic eyes, Perch, and hook hangers molded into body and attached with swivels. No trade data but this size is uncommon.

Les Davis Fishing Tackle Company

1565 Center Street, Tacoma, Washington 98409, trademark of a fish with Les Davis with a Registered trademark symbol as the dot for the i in Davis. The company dates from 1926 from typical one-person invention beginnings at home, according to the history of the company given by Luhr Jensen & Sons, although the trademark says "since 1934." It was sold off to Luhr Jensen & Sons in 1983. Les Davis made a variety of terminal tackle items and some lures. Sometimes the tackle is not as important to a collector as the graphics, as shown on the Herring Aid shown here. This is a simple live bait holder that holds the bait while trolling. The graphics are wonderful and make the piece worth keeping for display. The Herring Aid was formerly known as the Strip Rig. Also shown are two Herring Dodgers new in packages, the old Herring Dodger should bring over $20.00 as it still has the older name of Davis Fishing Tackle Co. and is in a paper package. The trade name is still Les Davis at the top of the package and on the Dodger itself. The newer one should fetch about $8.00 to $10.00 tops. The Original Canadian Wonder Trolling Spoon Model #5, 3⅜" long new on the card is worth $5.00 to $10.00 new on card, but of very little value off the card. As with any company that has consolidated with another, the pre-1983 items will continue to rise in value but beware if buying items off the card, as they could be new. Check the Luhr Jensen website at www.luhrjensen.com for an excellent history and a complete product line still being produced at www.luhrjensen.com/products.HTM.

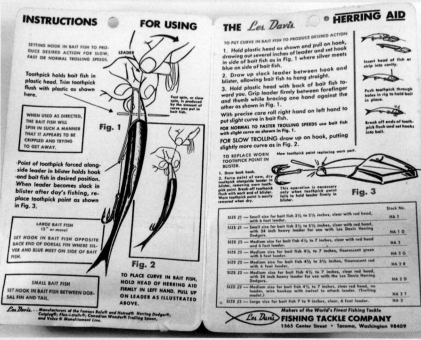

Front and back of Les Davis Herring Aid. $20.00.

Paper Herring Dodger, $15.00 – 20.00. Carded Herring Dodger, $8.00 – 10.00. Canadian Wonder on card, $5.00 – 10.00.

Lou J. Eppinger

1757 Puritan Ave., Detroit 3, Michigan. More recently, Eppinger Mfg. Co., 6340 Schaefer Highway, Dearborn, Michigan 48126. Manufacturer of Osprey and Dardevle Products. This Detroit company was the most successful marketer of spoons in the world. One cannot find a tackle box without a Dardevle or Dardevle copies in it, at least if pike are in the local waters. One day my son Justin, 12 at the time, started casting a Dardevle spoon while his younger brother, 8-year-old Rob, and I were catching crappies to beat the band. I asked him what he was doing, and he said he was going to catch a big pike. Well, about 40 minutes later, undaunted by not getting one sooner, he hooked up with what was one great fight and eventually landed a 39" Northern pike on his trusty Dardevle spoon. To this day, I

think Rob was more excited to watch the action than Justin was to catch it as he knew all along he was "going to catch a big pike." This story, or one like it, has been told by thousands of anglers the world over using this lure. The problem is that metal baits in general have not caught the enthusiasm of the collector, let alone spoons. So, we resort to spoons new in the box, especially the older two-piece cardboard boxes, and then it gets interesting.

But, Eppinger made other interesting items, including a rare baitcasting reel. The company also made a small Trout-Eat-Us type bait they either copied from or purchased from Moonlight/Paw Paw. Their metal Osprey lure to which one could attach other baits was also interesting. They also made some terminal tackle. Values would be from a low of

87

$5.00 for the newer items to up to $30.00 for some of the older Dardevle or Osprey boxes. An early 1970s catalog I have shows 39 color variations available from what was at one time a list of 65 colors.

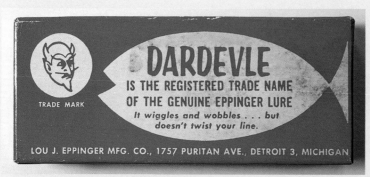

Color No. 30, Rainbow Dardevle and pre-zip box. $15.00 for pair.

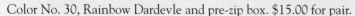

Fred Long Baits

Morton, Illinois. Long made bass and musky baits of wood with wonderful color schemes from the mid-1950s until he passed away in the late 1990s. His baits are little known nationally but have an excellent regional reputation for fish catching, and the collectors are getting interested in them too. Each bait is one of a kind as they were hand painted and assembled by Long and his girlfriend. Most are signed somewhere on the lure, but not all models are signed, also many are dated. Long copied many successful lures and also made his own unique models. I could show you over 50 varieties, but we do not have the space for them all now. Shown are three examples to give you an example of his work, two are signed, the one with a feather paint pattern is not.

Examples of Fred Long Bass Baits. The little fat one is unusual in design. These trade for $15.00 – 35.00.

Another view of the Fred Long Bass Baits.

Live-Lure

Made by Rice Engineering, 912 Stephenson Bldg., Detroit, Mich., pre-zip. This minnow tube type bait is shown in its box and with the color insert as an example of one of the many live minnow type baits made to fool fish and/or the fishing public. These show up often here in Michigan but still command about $30.00 each if new in the box; this one cost $15.00 at a flea market in 1996. As a comparison, I have also shown another plastic minnow tube type lure.

Live-Lure Bait, 4" long, line tie and hook hangers are one wire running through the lure. $30.00.

Comparison of another plastic minnow tube, 4⅜" long, three breathing holes on head, two on tail, brass piece on rear hook hanger and line tie that moves to open the tube. Paid $25.00 in an antique shop in 1999.

L.B. Charley Lucy

Little Rock, Arkansas. This 1940s plastic lure is unique. Called the Fancy-Dancer with the box top showing a picture of the lure as a dance girl strutting her stuff! The label says: "Action! Action! Action!" and is a great example of lure companies playing on sex to sell a lure. The lure had a hollow shaft through the center with the line tie secured to the rear hook hanger's last screw. The hook hangers were surface type similar to a Pflueger. The lure is 3¼" long at the bottom and 2½" long at top with a slanted front accordingly. Its eyes are molded like the carved eyes of later South Bend lures. This is my only example, and I would have to guess it is fairly rare. Value is likely upwards of $40.00 new in the box. One with an insert would be nice for more historical data.

Fancy-Dancer in two-piece box. $40.00+.

Lucky Lady Tackle

130 N. Ave. 50, Los Angeles 42, later became Lucky Lady Fishing Tackle Co. at same address, and then it moved to P.O. 4398, Pasadena City, Calif. This company made only the Lucky Lady fishing lure, marketed as the lure with the "Inner Glow" and a neat little plastic tackle box, to the best of my knowledge. The lure was a goggle-eyed, banana-shaped lure with a vertical tail, large protruding eyes, a little ventral and dorsal fin, and two hooks. As the chart says, it came in a few colors and sizes and was first packaged in a nice yellow cardboard box with a very high quality plastic top; then packaged in a little shrink wrap plastic with a sliding cardboard back; then packaged in simple plastic wrap stapled together with the lure placed over a catalog which shaped the package. It also came in the little shrink wrap packages stapled 12 to a display card, two are shown. These lures have been selling for $25.00 or better on eBay, new in the package. I understand that they are exceptional salmon and walleye lures and that drives up the demand somewhat.

The sizes are ¹⁄₁₀ oz., 1¾ inches; ⅛ oz., 2⅜ inches; ⅕ oz., 2⅝ inches; ¼ oz., 3⅛ inches; and, ⅝ oz., 3⅝ inches. This is the length of the lure itself, not including any protruding hook hanger. The hook hangers are a simple screw-in variety, and some lures came with a swivel clip on the hook tie, others did not. Also, at least on the larger lures, the front hook was sometimes mounted on a split ring and then attached to the screw hook hanger.

Catalog colors from the first catalog included Goldfish; Frog; Black Flash; Silver Flash; Red and White; Red and Yellow; Perch; and Cherry Fluorescent. I have examples of later colors that include Silver with Red Dots, color code SR; Salmon Egg Fluorescent; and Orange with Black Dots. The Salmon Egg Fluorescent came in at least two versions, one with yellow eyes and gold foil and one without the yellow eyes and silver foil. Most of the ones I have seen are in the Fluorescent color. I have seen only one Frog. I should think the rarest item is the little plastic tackle box shown in the catalog. What a neat item it is, the advertisement shows the back of the tackle box has a checkerboard and states that "if you don't catch fish you can play checkers." What a neat concept — Isaac Walton would be proud!

Display board with a dozen Lucky Lady Lures. $250.00+.

Close-up of the largest size Lucky Lady. $25.00+ in package.

Another display board of a dozen Lucky Lady Lures. $250.00+.

Oldest to newest packaging for Lucky Lady Lures. Boxed items, $35.00+; others, $18.00 – 25.00.

Lucky Strike

A Canadian lure company still in production. Address on this box is Lucky Strike Bait Works, Peterboro, Canada. This company made many baits similar to both Heddons and Creek Chubs. This Pi-Kee Minnow found in a two-piece cardboard box would date from the 1940s or early 1950s. Note the larger than CCBC cup hardware. This is Model 832, brass tack and washer eyes, cup hardware, 4½" long, and diving lip marked Lucky Strike in horseshoe symbol, the company's trademark. Also, see the entry earlier under Bleeder Baits (page 36) for an unusual plastic version of a Bleeder runt type lure.

Lucky Strike Pi-Kee in two-piece box. $50.00+ boxed.

Lur-All Tackle and Manufacturing Company

Berkley, Michigan. This nice Lur-All Beetle Bug Bait is new in the box with insert. This is the predecessor to the Millsite Beetle (see Volume 1). This is a tough box to find and nice to have the insert and bait unused. This was purchased privately in 2001 for $75.00.

Lur-All Beetle Bug in two-piece box, Model No. 164, yellow body with red/black trim. 1" body; propeller is marked with lure name and manufacturer. $75.00.

Lutito Lure and Novelty Company

Denver, Colorado, maker of the Kitchen Sink lure. This is one example where the packaging is as interesting as, or more so, than the lure. The lure is a novelty lure, looks like a two-section kitchen sink, to try when all else fails. I have two of these lures, both on different cards. Shown here are both colorful packages, great for framing. I have seen these trade for over $75.00 new on cards.

Kitchen Sink graphics. $75.00+ with lure.

Smaller version of similar lure made by San Michell's Novelties & Lures, PO Box 95242, Atlanta, Georgia 30347, 2" long version. $75.00+.

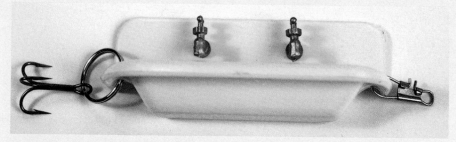

Contents to package, above left, Kitchen Sink lure, 3" long. $35.00+ loose, $75.00+ with card.

94

Mac's Squid Salmon Plug

Floyd Tucker Co., Gig Harbor, Washington, pre-zip address. This simple white plastic salmon plug is presented in a crisp two-piece white cardboard box with red and blue lettering. The one shown is a #15 Point Special and had a suggested retail price of $2.25. The literature says it is the proven, old reliable bait that "fools fish, not fisherman." Sorry to say, the Payless store put the price tag of $1.79 right over the head of the Salmon taking the plug on the box top! I sold one on eBay recently for around $20.00 used in the box. This crisp box and new plug should bring $30.00 or more.

Mac's Squid Plug, 4" #15 Point Special, in two-piece box. Hardware is a ball-bearing swivel held onto the body by a Phillips screw. The line tie has a ring that was mounted prior to affixing the screw onto the body. $30.00+ new in box.

Makinen Tackle Company

Kaleva, Mich. Just as the Finns of Finland have added much to fishing history with the Rapala and other baits, the Finns of America, mainly residing in Michigan, have contributed much to fishing history. One of the famous names is Makinen (pronounced Mack eh nun) Tackle Co. This company was an early user of plastic in its production of lures, and some lures were available in both plastic and wooden varieties. It was from the same town as the famous Bear Creek Company, maker of lures and fish decoys. From an insert included with a Muskie-sized Holi Comet lure, we learn that, in speaking of the Holi Comet, "This faster tail action is the result of the ingenuity of a Finn, who is an old-time fisherman. By inserting a 17/64-inch opening at the head, water is forced through this opening when reeling the Lure, thus giving the fast action in the tail."

This company's collectible lures include the Holi Comet available in two sizes, The Merry-Widow, The Makilure, The Wonder Lure, and The Waddle Bug. These are all shown in the 1947 catalog available on the NFLCC CD ROMs. Any of these lures are worth $20.00 by themselves, double that in the two-piece cardboard box. The Waddle Bug is the hardest to find. Shown is a Tenite Muskie size Holi Comet in an early white box and a Makilure in Tenite in Model 10E in the more common green and white box. According to the 1947 catalog, Bill Makinen had been carving lures of wood for years, and in 1946 the hobby became a business. The catalog also points out that in 1947 virtually all of the lures will be made of Tenite. In addition to the green and white box appearing in the 1947 catalog is the phrase "Stream Tested Baits." One could conclude that most wooden Makinen lures are older than Tenite ones and that boxes in just white without "Stream Tested Baits" are older than the green and white ones. However, the catalog does say that "most" new lures will be made of Tenite, leaving open the door for yet some wooden baits after 1947.

Wonderlure, 2½" long, Makinen marked on flat metal diving plate on bottom of lure, Tenite, Wonderlure marked in silver letters on left side of mouth. $30.00+ if in crisp condition.

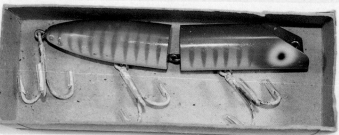

Muskie Holi Comet in the box. $75.00 due to early box, papers, and lure size.

Newer two-piece box with a Model M 10 E Makilure in Tenite, screw/washer hardware, shiner scale with spots, hand soldered hooks, extended line tie, and 3" long counting tail cap. $40.00+.

A wooden Merry-Widow, 3¾" long, no eyes, screw and raised washer hardware, back stencil says Merry-Widow in gold letters. $8.00 – 20.00.

The Waddle Bug

THE WADDLE BUG—the aristocrat of all surface baits, used for casting or trolling. Gives best results when reeled in at a medium speed.

It's a surface Waddler; it really stirs the ire of the big ones, and its unique waddle and colors make it a great Bass and Pike killer.

It's the Waddle and splatter that stirs 'em up. Try this Lure the early part of the season and prove it to yourself. For best results, use snap-on swivel. Do not use a long, heavy wire leader.

The Wonder Lure

THE LURE with THREE outstanding action features combined into ONE lure,—the Lip for diving, the Spinners that flash, and Tandem Treble Hooks for action and shimmy.

Can be used for casting and trolling. For proper action retrieve slowly.

Try this WONDER LURE that has eye appeal and action.

MAKINEN LURES and BAITS

Manufactured by

MAKINEN TACKLE CO.
KALEVA, MICHIGAN

The Merry Widow

THE MERRY WIDOW LURE, with its wobble and shimmy action at tail, travels at a very narrow area when reeled in at an average speed. This particular lure attracts the bass and pike and travels at approximately 6 to 10 inches under the surface.

For deeper depths lead sinkers are required and that is up to the judgment of each individual fisherman as to how great a depth he wishes to reach, by attaching lead sinkers about 18 inches ahead of his lure.

There are times when fish migrate to deeper depths, depending on the weather and water temperatures, and a little skill by the average fisherman is all that is required to regulate his lure.

There is one caution to heed when reeling the Lure in, not to retrieve it too fast as this will cause imperfect action.

The Holi Comet

THE HOLI COMET LURE is similar to our Merry Widow lure but has a faster tail action and travels approximately within a ¾ to 1¼ inch width area.

This faster tail action is the result of the ingenuity of a Finn, who is an old time fisherman. By inserting a 17|64-inch opening at the head, water is forced through this opening when reeling the Lure, thus giving the fast action in the tail.

The weather and water temperatures vary at different times and fish are known to migrate deeper. The depth you want the Lure to travel can be regulated by fastening sinkers ahead of the Lure.

Perfect performance is secured by proper reeling. Avoid retrieving the Lure too fast.

The Makilure

THE MAKILURE in M type is the Lure with the zig-zag action caused by a hollow hole at the head of the Lure. The resistance of the water at this insert gives the Lure this zig-zag action and causes it to travel at a deeper depth. The depth the Lure will travel is governed by the speed of the retrieve.

Front and back of Muskie Lure insert.

Mann's Bait Company

P.O. Box 604, Eufaula, Alabama 36027 in 1986. A more modern addition, but some of the early baits are getting collectible. Shown is an early slide-top box, the Big-O like Mann's Loudmouth new on the card, and a new without box Mann's Rattlin Finn Minnow, a most stunning underwater sonic type bait with rattles; this bait is 3⅜" long with screw hardware. Some of the baits in the 1986 catalog I would watch for include the hard plastic Hardworms, the baby bass copy in plastic, the Leroy Brown lure in green and in silver, the Zara shaped with a fin, Mann-Dancer, and the Shad-Mann fish finish crank baits. I sold some Hardworms for $15.00 each back in 1996; no other trade data is available.

Examples of Mann's Baits. $12.00+ boxed; $8.00+ on cards.

Marathon Tackle

Rte. 2, Mosinee, Wisc. 54455, "Quality Since 1925." Marathon made a wide variety of terminal tackle, some metal baits, and a complete line of flies. When one finds a spoon with the two little trailing spinner tails, it is often a Marathon. Marathon also provided terminal tackle, clips, and some other items to other manufacturers, including Weber Tackle Company.

Shown is also a Marathon catalog that must date from the late 1920s according to the cover photo and the dress of the fisherman inside the covers. Sorry to say, it is undated. However, it gives us a good idea of a wide selection of fly and deer hair baits available that were likely tied by the same women working at different times for Weber Lifelike Fly Fishing Co. and Frost Flies. Wausau, Wisconsin, is just north of Stevens Point, and though ladies would not likely have been commuting, I am sure there was some interchange between these companies in terms of personnel. Items the collector will most definitely find include the unique scale patterned Fishtail Casting Spoon with a distinctive painted eye, made of brass and enameled to look like a pike-minnow, according to page 2 of the catalog. Another nice item is the Jack's Bass-Houn, a fly rod bait similar to those

Marathon Fishtail Casting Spoon

NEW thrills await the fishermen who use these spoons. More strikes and more fish is the verdict of both professional guides and experienced fishermen, who have unqualifiedly pronounced the Fishtail Casting Spoon one of the best and most successful casting rod lures ever designed. The spoon is made from heavy gauge brass with the concave side heavily nickeled and highly buffed to a mirror-like finish; and the convex side is enameled in five colors that blend into a beautiful, natural 'pike-minnow' appearance. The extra sharp hooks are dressed with genuine northern bucktail hair, giving Fishtail Spoons a lifelike action that is entirely missing in other spoons. Made in three popular sizes and six hair color patterns, each in an individual box. Blade sizes: small (2 3/16 in.), medium (2⅞ in.), large (3⅝ in.).

Hair Color	Catalog Number			Hair Color	Catalog Number		
	Small	Medium	Large		Small	Medium	Large
White	71	81	91	Natural	74	84	94
Yellow	72	82	92	Red	75	85	95
Gray	73	83	93	Black	76	86	96

List Price: Small, ea. 55¢, doz.,$6.60; medium, ea. 65¢, doz., $7.80; large, ea. 75¢, doz. $9.00.

Fishtail Casting Spoon Display

HERE is a colorful, attractive, sales producing display unit which, experience has proved, makes fast and profitable sales of Fishtail Casting Spoons for every fishing tackle dealer who has one or more in stock.

One dozen Fishtail Casting Spoons of a size are assorted two of each hair color in an attention arresting, transparent top box.

Assortment No. 70, one doz. small Fishtail Spoons, list price $6.60
Assortment No. 80, one doz. medium Fishtail Spoons, list price $7.80
Assortment No. 90, one doz. large Fishtail Spoons, list price $9.00

FISH WITH FLIES -- More Fun -- More Fish

Jack's Bass-Houn
Series 100
The Deadliest Fly Ever Made -- Successful Beyond Belief

JACK'S BASS-HOUN
Series 100
A Hound for Bass

THIS is the fly that fishermen rave about because it will actually take bass when other lures have failed. It is the one fly that will take bass in July and August. Made entirely of bucktail, and its floating qualities leave nothing to be desired. The durability of the Bass-Houn is surprising, over two hundred bass having been brought to net with one fly. Bass-Houns are tied only by experts of many years experience as it is our aim in making them to produce only the highest quality and most successful bass fly that money can buy. It is not necessary to be expert at fly casting to take bass with this fly. Simply cast to likely bass water and let the fly lie still. If a bass sees it,—Wham! a fight is on. Complete instructions furnished with each Bass-Houn. If these instructions are followed, successful results will follow.

Jack's Bass-Houns are dressed on size No. 1 extra sharp, Model Perfect hooks. Made in twelve color patterns listed below, of which Nos. 110, 112 and 114 are the most popular. Any fisherman who likes to catch large or small mouth bass will be a booster for these flies after the first trial. Jack's Bass-Houns are imitated but never equalled. Insist on the genuine.

No.	Wing	Body	Tail
110	Gray	Black	White
111	Tan	Black	White
112	White	Black	White
113	White-Red	Green	Red
114	Sand	Sand	Black
115	White-Black	Bee	Red
116	White	Red	White
117	Yellow	Black	Yellow
118	White	White	White
119	Yellow	Yellow	Yellow
120	Black	Black	Black
121	Gray	Yellow	Red

Packed one in a box, twelve boxes in a carton.

List Price each_____75¢   Dozen_____$9.00

MARATHON FLIES -- Tested on the Stream

Marathon catalog, pages 2 and 3. Showing two collectible Marathon items. $5.00 – 10.00.

by South Bend and Creek Chub. This is a winged, torpedo-shaped bass bait with a long tail that was available in a dozen colors. It was also available in a cork body. One of nicest of the Marathon baits is the Hair Frog, followed by the Marathon Mouse. The Frog was rather triangular-shaped and came in many colors, and the mouse was available in three sizes and made of quality deer hair with a wool tail. I believe the ears are leather, some may also be made of wool. The Marathon Mouse has a higher back than the Weber mouse, and the frogs cannot be confused due to shape either. Another bait encountered here in the Midwest is the Musky Houn. This bait had a football-shaped head in the first few years, and that is the one col-

lectible, as it was made well into the recent years. Any flies in packages would also be of interest. Musky Houns are often found in the box which greatly increases value. Likely the most collectible of all Marathon baits would be the Musky Munk, a wooden plug with deer hair trim. The earliest of these had glass eyes and would bring $50.00 or more in decent shape. Any of the previous baits described would be worth $10.00 to $30.00, early Musky Houns in perfect shape in the box should command over $50.00, glass eyed Musky Munk in a box even more. Unique packages, dealers dozens, etc. of the flies would also bring a premium. They were out of business by 1992, maybe a little before. See the chapter on Fly Rod Baits for fly examples.

Common Marathon spinners, $3.00 – 5.00.

6   MARATHON BAIT CO., Wausau, Wisconsin

Introducing to Fly Fishermen and Bait Casters Everywhere -- A New, True-to-Life Frog

THE MARATHON HAIR FROG

Made Entirely of Deer Hair

A FROG is a delicacy to every game fish -- In any waters it is a sure lure! Irresistable to bass, pike, pickerel, muskellunge and other game fish and when other baits fail, the experienced fisherman starts searching along the edge of the water for frogs. He knows how the big fellows go for 'em.

There have been a score or more artificial frogs on the market. Some of wood, others of metal, rubber or whatnot. The Marathon Frog is made of genuine deer hair, giving it appearance, action -- everything but the croak! No wonder fishermen have taken to it -- no wonder it gets the fish!

The Marathon Hair Frog is the product of the most highly skilled deer hair workers in America whose knowledge is taxed to the limit in making this frog. An examination of the Marathon Hair Frog will reveal the expert workmanship in its production. Beware of imitations!

Use the Marathon Hair Frog with fly rod and leader as a floating lure or with weighted spinner for casting and trolling.

	Hook Size	Pattern			
No. 901	1	Spotted Green Back, White Belly	Each 90¢	”	$10.80
No. 911	1	Black Back, White Belly	” 90¢	”	10.80
No. 921	1	Black Back, Yellow Belly	” 90¢	”	10.80
No. 931	1	Spotted Green Back, Yellow Belly	” 90¢	”	10.80
No. 904	4	Spotted Green Back, White Belly	” 80¢	”	9.60
No. 914	4	Black Back, White Belly	” 80¢	”	9.60
No. 924	4	Black Back, Yellow Belly	” 80¢	”	9.60
No. 934	4	Spotted Green Back, Yellow Belly	” 80¢	”	9.60
No. 936	6	Spotted Green Back, Yellow Belly	” 70¢	”	8.40
No. 938	8	Spotted Green Back, Yellow Belly	” 70¢	”	8.40
No. 560w	Weighted Spinner only, for Size 1 Frog		” 20¢	”	2.40
No. 570w	Weighted Spinner only, for Size 4 Frog		” 20¢	”	2.40

Packed one in a box—Twelve boxes in a carton

MARATHON HAIR FROG *with Weighted Spinner for Casting or Trolling*

AMERICAN FLIES -- *for American Waters*

MARATHON BAIT CO., Wausau, Wisconsin   7

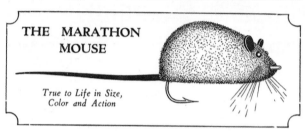

THE MARATHON MOUSE

True to Life in Size, Color and Action

A Floating Lure for All Game Fish

Unlucky is the field mouse that finds himself in water inhabited by fish. Once he is spotted by Mr. Fish, he is doomed for he is a great delicacy to the finny tribe. Many imitation mice have been made but the Marathon Mouse is the nearest thing to a real mouse ever introduced. This mouse casts nicely, floats like a cork and will not flop on its back when it hits the water. Made to stand up under severe abuse. It is dressed by a special process that packs and ties hair so that it will not mat when wet. Only especially selected deer hair is used. Tails are hand made of pure wool and will not dry out hard, or deteriorate with age. Packed one or six on a card -- one card in a box.

No. 308—Size 8	Trout	Natural	Each	55¢	Doz. $	6.60
No. 304—Size 4	Bass	Natural	”	70¢	”	8.40
No. 301—Size 1/0	Bass	Natural	”	85¢	”	10.20

Marathon Fly Rod Minnow
Series 20

The Marathon Fly Rod Minnow is the only feather minnow with a lifelike action joint in its make-up. The head construction being on a separate

Series 20

MARATHON FLY ROD MINNOW

shank from that of the hook, gives this minnow the life and action to get more strikes. The Marathon Fly Rod Minnow will take bass and other game fish either with or without a spinner. Supplied in size No. 1. Patterns: (No. 21) white, (No. 22) Yellow, (No. 23) Black and White. Packed 1 on a card, 12 cards in a box, assorted or all of one pattern. **Each 50¢; Doz. $6.00**

FISH WITH FLIES -- *More Fun -- More Fish*

Marathon catalog, pages 2 and 3. Clean examples of the mouse or frog will bring $10.00+.

Martin Fish Lure Company

Seattle, Washington. Shown is an injured minnow type bait in cup hardware and glass eyes. Also shown is a two-piece cardboard box from the 1940s or early 1950s. Martin made a wide range of quality lures, and interest is growing nationally in this company. The company has been actively collected for some time on the West Coast, and these lures should command even more interest in the future. The wooden Injured Minnow is 3⅝" long, marked Martin on the bottom in red letters, has cup hardware, teddy bear glass eyes, and unmarked propellers.

Martin Fish Lure Co. examples. Lure, $30.00+; two-piece box, $5.00 – 20.00.

Maxwell Manufacturing Company

Vancouver, Washington, no zip code or street address. A partially full display card of neat Grizzly Red Feathered Treble Hooks in size 3/0, three missing. This is a colorful card and although these hooks themselves have little value, the card of hooks with the colorful graphics should be valued at $10.00 to $15.00 in new condition such as the one shown.

Grizzly also made a number of spinner baits, including one called the Half Nelson Synchronized Spinners. These are fairly recent, likely the 1970s and 1980s, and the value would be $5.00 or less. However, I love the name "Half Nelson," having lettered in wrestling in high school!

Grizzly hook display. Sold for $22.00 on eBay, 2001.

Meadow Brook

Sold only by Sears, Roebuck and Co. (see also J. C. Higgins, page 78). These lures were available throughout the 1940s, 1950s, and 1960s and came presented in a two-piece cardboard box and cardboard box with plastic sleeves. Shown is a new-in-the-box example of a small Surf-Oreno type lure with painted cup hardware and tack eyes and only a front spinner blade. This lure was made either by South Bend in their Best-O-Luck series or by Paw Paw. It is hard to say since Paw Paw also made some of the South Bend lures and/or painted them. As Surf-Orenos are very collectible, this lure would likely bring $50.00+ on the open market.

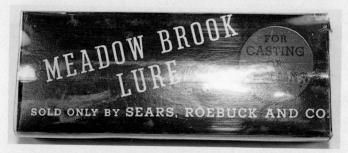 

Meadow Brook Surf-Oreno in box and box, Model No. 33-173 M, 2¾" lure, painted cup hardware, single unmarked front propeller, tack eyes. $50.00 or more new in its box.

Mepps Brand

Mepps is famous for its squirrel hair treble hooked spinner baits and is not too collectible due to production numbers and the fact that most are still in production. I have shown a Mepps Killer Kit, the Mepps Trouter, still in its shrink-wrapped shipping package, likely from 1980. I know that I purchased these types of kits in the late 1960s without the shrink wrap, stock number K1D. The fishing value alone of this with six mint Mepps spinners should be $20.00. Also, this is the only company that you can barter with for lures; send them a certain number of squirrel tails (the numbers have varied over the years), and you will receive in lures return. This bartering angle alone is worth mentioning! I wonder how many IRS audits have turned up a non-reported squirrel tail for Mepps spinner barter? Reminds me of an old "Tammy" movie, the name of which I have forgotten!

Mepps Trouter Kit. $20.00.

Mermaid Baits

Shown below is one of many Mermaid type bass size baits available to modern lure collectors. Mermaid also made spoons, bobbers, and fly rod baits. The second photo shows a comparison of two spoons and a small fly rod lure. See also Chapter 2 for another fly rod size. The bass size trade for $20.00 – 30.00 normally, bobbers about the same, fly rod sizes will trade for up to $100.00 without packaging.

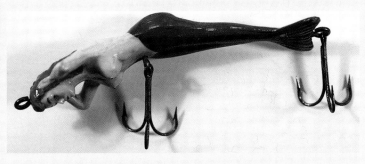

Example of Mermaid Bass Bait, 4" long, red hair, brown eyes and eyebrows, red lips and nipples. $20.00 – 30.00.

Two Mermaid spoons. Bronze one is 1⁷⁄₁₆" long and has front and rear views cast into spoon; the silver is 2¹³⁄₁₆" long and also has front and rear views as an insert into the spoon. Also a fly rod Mermaid, 1⁹⁄₁₆" long, blonde hair, orange tail, blue eyes, red lips and nipples, and black eyebrows. Spoons are scarce, $50.00+, and the fly rod sizes run $75.00 – 100.00.

Millie Mouse

Dunstable, Mass. Shown are two really nice wooden mouse lures with bead eyes, leather tails, and leather ears. Screw-type hangers and hooks are gold colored. These came in a two-piece plastic box typical of the mid-1950s, but I have no manufacturing data for the lures. These trade for $80.00 – 100.00 each on eBay.

Large Millie Mouse lure, just under 2" long. $80.00 – 100.00.

Small Millie Mouse lure, just under 1½" long. $80.00 – 100.00.

Miracle Lure, Inc.

Miracle Lure, Inc., East Bay Drive, Largo, Florida. Shown is a box back and insert for a unique plastic lure with metal diving planes similar to a Heddon 1600. The lure came in three sizes, Big Mo, Middle Mo, and Little Mo. These baits are gaining in collector interest and should trade for $15.00 – 20.00 each, more boxed.

COLOR NO.	BACK	BELLY	FLASH	HEAD
1	Clear	Clear	Silver	Clear
2	Green	Yellow	Gold	✿Std
3	Black	Black	Silver	Black
4	Black	Yellow	Gold	✿Std
5	Clear	Clear	Gold	Clear
6	Red	Yellow	Gold	✿Std
7	White	White	Silver	Red
8	Black & Green	Yellow & Cream	Silver	✿Std
9	Black & Brown	Yellow & Cream	Silver	✿Std

✿Standard Head—Yellow, Black Eye Shadow & Red Chin

CODE NUMBERS

First Letter of Code Indicates Size of Plug,
B—Big Mo   M—Middle Mo   L—Little Mo

Second Letter of Code Indicates Depth
S—Surface Runner   D—Deep Runner

Third Letter of Code Indicates Color No.
Example: LS—4   Little Mo—Surface Runner Color No. 4

WEIGHTS

LITTLE MO	MIDDLE MO	BIG MO
S—1/3 oz.	S— 3/4 oz.	S—1-3/4 oz.
D—1/2 oz.	D—1-1/3 oz.	D—3 oz.

Naturalure Bait Company

104 E. Colorado St., Pasadena 1, Calif. This company should not be confused with the Actual Lure Co. of New York. The Naturalure baits were made of a plastic material and had unusual fins and tails that actually became pliable in water and "waved" like the real thing. These lures are fairly often found but not usually in the box.

Shown is a new-in-the-box Strikee Minnow, a ⅝ oz., 3⅞" long (3" body without tail) deep running jointed minnow with a lifelike tail and fins. The one shown is model SM 85 Green Perch, but the box is for an SM 82 Black and Silver Scale. The box is marked with the lure company, address, and trade name LifeLikeLure. The lures were available in five sizes and a variety of colors, the Strikee Minnow, the Strikee Floater, the Tropical Floater, the huge (7") King Strikee; and, the diminutive (1½") Lucky Strikee. These lures usually bring less than $10.00 loose but should bring over $20.00 boxed. Here in the Midwest I have had about 20 of these lures the past seven years, so they do show up either in transplanted tackle boxes or folks were sending away for them back in the 1950s and 1960s. The fins were always shrunk up on them, and this should not detract from their value, since this was part of the design, for the fins to become pliable when wet.

Strikee Minnow in Box.

Neon Mickey

Similar in design to a Mercury Minnow, a salmon type plug with a liquid insert to make it wiggle and shine, the Neon Mickey "lights as it swims," says the box advertising. Shown are some examples of both boxes and lures. The lures shown are 3¹³⁄₁₆" long, have simple screw hardware, concave eye socket, and protruding eyes. Should trade for $20.00+ and double with the box.

Examples of Neon Mickey lures and boxes. $40.00 each with box, $20.00 each loose.

Nielsen Bass Appeal

No manufacturing data, but shown is a photo of two identical lures, top and bottom. This appealing jointed bass bait likely dates from the 1950s – 1960s. It has a plate joint and screw hardware. No trade data is known but likely a $15.00 – 20.00 lure.

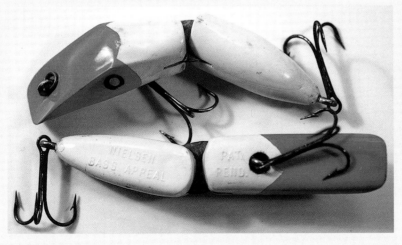

Lure is 4" long, painted eyes, simple screw hardware inserted into round opening on belly, split ring on line tie, name clearly stamped into the belly of the lure. No trade data.

Nils Master Warrior

No manufacturing data other than being Finland made in the 1970s. Imported by Nils Master, 275 57th Avenue, New York, N.Y. Shown are three photos of this nice balsa bait with a plastic diving lip, marked on the belly "Tank Tested." It is 3" long, and the blue one is Model 201, white one is Model 204. Both lures have simple screw hardware. No trade data is known, but nicely made lures available in a variety of colors should bring $15.00 – 20.00 each.

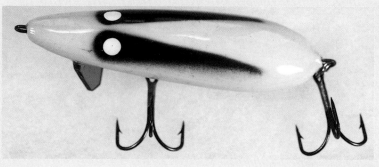

Nils Master Warriors. $15.00+.

Norman Manufacturing Company, Inc.

P.O. Box 580, Greenwood, Ark. 72936, previously Norman Mfg., P.O. Box H, Greenwood, Ark. Again, many of these baits are more recent than 1988, but shown are three box types and one of the company's Deep Big N lures in a green pattern, similar to a Big O. Watch for these new in the box as the potential seems to be there for some interest in this early crank bait company.

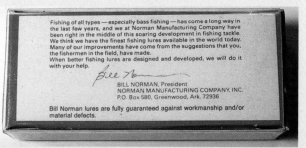

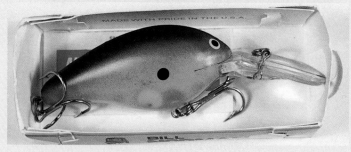

Examples of Norman box types & a Big N. No trade data, but should start at $8.00+.

Normark

1710 East 78th Street, Minneapolis, MN 55423, 1976 address. Sellers of the famed Rapala Minnows, see Rapala, page 118. This company also recently acquired Storm Lures, also detailed later.

OK-doke

The box insert shows the lure design; this lure, a competitor of the Lazy Ike design, was made in plastic only and came in a cardboard plastic top box shown here.

OK-doke box and insert. $20.00+ with lure.

Old McDonald Lif-Lik Lures

P.O. Box 70, Lees Summit, Missouri. These colorful lures with a clever company name trade for $20.00 – 30.00 for the Sonic type bait shown. They used the attractive red and yellow box for even the spoons and spinners. I found a number of these recently in a closed tackle store, and they must date from the 1960s given the advance design of the plastics and the inserts. There is no zip code on the box. Shown are two unique designs in Sonic type baits, both new from the box.

Lif-Lik Sonic type lures, 2¹⁄₁₆" long, and boxes that say Merry Minnow on both ends. These traded for $20.00 – 30.00 in 1999. In 2002 a spoon in a box sold for $16.00 on eBay.

Orchard Industries

Detroit 5, Mich. The manufacturers of the famous glass Action Rod (see Chapter 6) also made three very distinct and recognizable plastic casting lures. Shown top, right to left, are the Slippery Slim, a jointed 2½" lure, cup hardware, black/yellow; the Kick-N-Kackle, Model 202-YB, 2½" surface popper with surface side hardware and inverted bell tail hardware; and the Bottom Scratcher, Model 100-RW, 2½" diving wobbler with surface hardware. The Kick-N-Kackle is similar to a Bud Stewart offering, and sometimes collectors get them mixed up. These are classic plastic baits that epitomize our era of a plastic rod maker also marketing lures made of the same materials. These would easily trade for $40.00 – 50.00 in boxes with papers as shown.

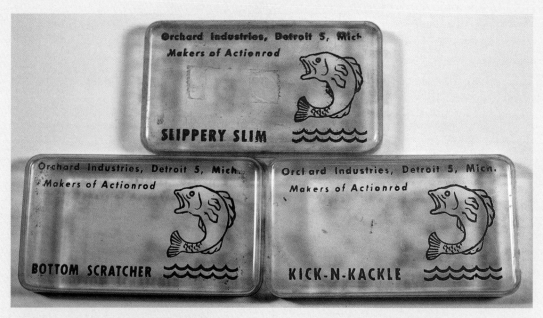

Box tops and lures of Orchard Industries. $50.00+ each in boxes as shown.

Ozark Woodchopper

This bait is now owned and being sold by Luhr-Jensen. This is one of the highest quality wooden baits made in fairly recent years, and the spinners and hardware are also very high quality. I have a large collection of these new in the boxes and have found they sell well, for up to $28.00 new in the box for some colors. The last one I sold on eBay was for fishing, and he paid $28.00 for it. Normally, they sell for around $15.00 new in the box. They also made a Zara type wooden lure for which I believe Charlie Campbell was involved in development and promotion. The lures are not marked, but the boxes are marked and easy to distinguish. The two lures shown in the first photo are the two sizes in casting plugs in the same blue scale pattern. Shown out of its box is a Rainbow pattern large Woodchopper in the second photo.

Ozark Woodchoppers new in boxes, large 3¼", ½ oz., and small 2¼", ⅜ oz. both in blue scale pattern. Painted eyes, simple screw belly hardware, heavy duty and high quality propellers. Boxes, $18.00+ each.

Rainbow colored ½ oz. size Woodchopper from box, boxes were not marked with color numbers, only the weight class. $12.00 – 18.00.

Fly rod size rubber P&K mouse, 1½" long, gold painted eyes. $30.00+.

P & K Incorporated (Pachner and Kohler)

Pachner and Kohler of Momence, Illinois. This smaller company made many collectible baits, including frogs, mice, and lures, in a two-piece red cardboard box with white lettering. They also had a line of fly rod baits called Hook-Loc Bugs, and one is shown new on the card. Most of the P & K baits can be found with regularity; however, new in the box is harder. The P & K Whirlaway is growing rapidly in popularity and has gone up in value the past five years, now about $15.00 or 20.00, even loose. The company's rubber baits need to be boxed to bring that much. The fly rod bait shown is the only one I have had and is likely worth double the other lures due to rarity.

Finally, the P & K Walkie Talkie Plunker type lure is increasing in demand with certain boxed ones bringing nearly $50.00, rare colors bringing the most. They are 2¹⁵⁄₁₆" long, have surface belly and screw/washer tail hardware. The eyes are depressions with raised pupils in a reverse tear dropshape, and the lure came with a wire line tie about 1¾" long. Also shown is one of the small Walkie Talkie Plunkers. I have no trade data for them, and I do not see them as often. The small Walkie Talkie is 1¾" long, and has surface belly and screw/washer tail hardware. It is marked on the belly as Walkie Talkie Junior and has raised molded eyes. As with its big brother, its tail fans out, making it easy to distinguish from most plunker types.

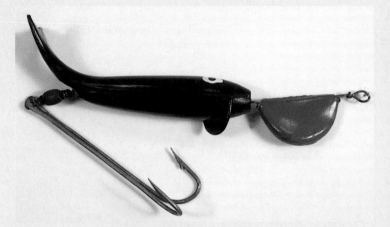

P&K Whirlaway, 2¾" long, painted eyes, 2" line tie wire is missing on this one. $15.00 – 20.00.

P&K Popper on card, catalog No. 3P, size #4. Rare find, $35.00+.

P&K Walkie Talkie, new from two-piece box, Cat. No. 43-P. $15.00 – 20.00 loose; $30.00+ boxed.

P&K Walkie Talkie Junior. More uncommon than larger size. $15.00 – 20.00 loose, $30.00 boxed.

Phillips Fly & Tackle Company

Alexandria, Penna. This company made very collectible flies, as shown in the next chapter, and many spinning baits worth finding. Luhr-Jensen acquired the rights to this company through its purchase of Glen L. Evans and is distributing some of the spinning lures. Shown is a new-in-the-box Series 300 Floating Crippled Killer, ¼ oz. Class, 2" long, Color and Model 305; a 2⅜" injured minnow type with a nice gold foil insert and painted yellow eyes, name unknown; and a Model 808, ¼ oz. Flash-O-Mino new in the box. Any of these should bring $15.00 – 20.00 each. Crippled Killers are the most common of the three.

Phillips Spinning lure examples. $15.00 – 25.00 boxed, $8.00 – 15.00 loose.

Poe's

This company likely started with lures being made by Milton Poe in the 1950s. Lures were made in Ceres, Turlock, and Roseville, California, in that order. Poes are a high quality, hand crafted variety of lures made from cedar with some marketed in a clever fish-shaped package. These are starting to be of interest to collectors, especially the Ceres lures in a cardboard box with a plastic overwrap. By 1992, according to the December issue of the Fishing Tackle Retailer guide, Zebco had acquired the fishing lure rights to Poe's. Yakima Bait Co. of Granger, Washington, now owns this lure. The Zebco ownership of Poe's was the beginning of "Made in Mexico" on the cards. I have shown some of the various models below. I sold some on eBay in late 2000 for about $12.00 each and traded some for some plastic lures new in boxes. The earlier ones should bring $20.00 new in the box. The fish-shaped boxes, pre-Zebco lures, will do little better than $12.00 for the near future.

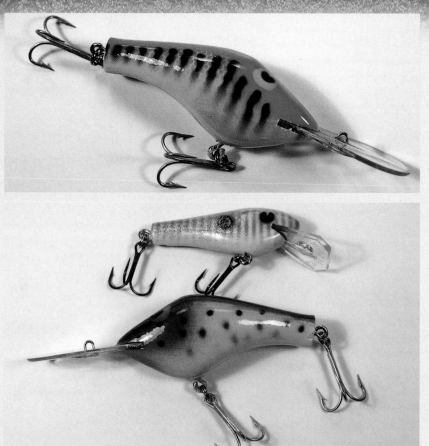

The two large lures are Ceres models, each 3³⁄₁₆" long. The Rainbow trout colored one has screw/washer belly hardware and simple screw tail hardware. The smaller one is a 2½", Model RC-1; the model number and Poe's are marked on the squared-off lip. I am not certain where it was made. It has simple screw hardware, both belly and tail, with hooks attached with split rings as on larger models. Any of these will trade for $8.00 – 15.00 loose, double that boxed.

Two of the fish-shaped packages from Turlock. $12.00 each.

Erv Pope Bait Company

929 Washington St., Wausau, Wisc. 54401. Although this is a post-zip code card, this one and more than 20 others were found in a closed bait shop in Wisconsin that had been closed in the late 1960s. The lures were not primed well, and the paint on new ones, as shown, is sometimes not real sharp and bright, note the tail area. Also, the little felt tails tear easily. But, with a name of Musky Lunch, everyone should own at least one of these. I sold about a dozen of them new on the cards for $12.00 – 24.00 depending on condition of the paint and the tail piece.

Musky Lunch new on card, lure body is 3¾" long, painted eyes, felt tail, diving lip, and double hook held on by flat blade screws, no markings on lure. $12.00 – 24.00 in 1999.

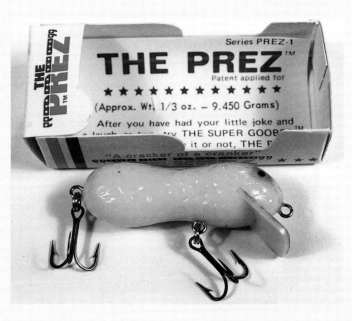

New from its box The Prez-1. $15.00 – 25.00 as shown.

Prez

The Prez, a ⅓ oz. Class spinning lure made of plastic, 2³⁄₁₆" long, is one of the interesting lures tied to a historical legacy. This lure commemorated the election of President Carter due to his peanut farming background and was also called the "Super Goober." These trade for $15.00 – 25.00 new in the box. Made by Cordell Tackle, Inc., PO Box 2020, Hot Springs, Arkansas 71901. (See page 52.)

Powerpak Lures, Inc.

Dallas, Texas. This is a great collectible, and it just barely beats the cutoff date of 1988 (1987) but I had to include it. The idea was invented by Frank G. Pearce of Garland, Texas, patent was granted June 23, 1987 and it had been filed on August 13, 1985. The invention was then assigned to Thornton-Denena Industries, also of Garland, Texas. By the way, this was all quickly researched in about two minutes on the patent site given under dating techniques earlier in the book. Rumor has it that these were distributed by driving around to tackle shops, wholesalers, etc., and a large chain never distributed the items. I do not know if this is true, but a tackle store owner told me that in about 1995 when I found the first ones in his "close-out" bin. I now buy all that I can find. This company made a number of different fish-shaped lures in modern chrome paints and a frog model, too. When you pulled the line tie, it activated a little spring-wound motor that made the tail wiggle, thus the patent. I have sold a few of these and see them trading for about $20.00 – 30.00 already new on the card. The copyright on the card is 1990.

One example of a Powerpak Minnow. $20.00 – 30.00 for minnows, more for frog models.

Psycho Lures

P.O. Box 53, Tarzana, Calif. Another card that is better than the lure it contained, however, the little Martini shaker is also cool. No trade data available, but most novelty lures trade for $10.00 or more, double with packaging. This should likely bring $50.00 with its card.

Martini Lure, 2¼" from tip of shaker to bottom of green bead.

Psycho Lures Martini Lure card. $50.00 for pair.

Pro-Line Plastics

P.O. Box 2641, Livonia, Michigan 48151, produced at least two lures, and the one shown is a "Pirate, Jr.". This is a neat little narrow-bodied lure made from plastic, likely during the mid-1960s. The Jr. is about 2⅝" long and has screw hardware, with the belly treble being inserted into an extension molded into the bait, two trebles and raised plastic eyes molded as part of the lure. Too late to add to this book, but I just received a larger version Pirate as well.

 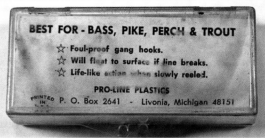

Pirate, Jr. new in the box and the box back, $15.00 – 20.00 in box.

Rabble Rouser Lures

By Doug Parker. With patents of 3,881,272 and 3,894,350, these lures are dated from January 28, 1974 and beyond, the date of the second patent application (granted July 15, 1975). The address at the time of filing the 1974 patent was Douglas W. Parker, 615 Rogers Avenue, Fort Smith, Ark. 72901. The next address given for the company is 500 South 7th Street, Fort Smith, Ark. 72901. The address on the blister pack shown is P.O. Box 644, New Philadelphia, Ohio 44663. According to the history on the blister pack, Douglas W. Parker carved the first Rabble Rouser Lure in 1951, now famous for the large "Bug-Eye" found on all Rabble Rouser lures. All of the lures had names protected by Registered Trademark and many by design or functional patents. The most collectible at this time are the Top-Water and Rowdy, Rouster, and Roo-Tur models. One great potential in this company is the fact that special order colors were accepted. Standard colors were the following: 1. Black-Silver; 2. Black-Gold; 7. Ivory; 8. Crawdad; 9 Chartreuse; 11. Sun Perch; 12. Pearl Shad; and 15. Fluorescent Red. I do not know what happened to the other numbers, but they were likely dropped from an earlier color list available. Some of the models are shown on the next two pages.

The values of course would vary on standard or special order color, age, and condition, but most in the box should start at $15.00 to $20.00, with hard colors to locate bringing a premium. The company also made a copy of a Hellbender lure called the Di-Dapper in three varieties: 3 hooks, 2 hooks and a tail spinner, and 3 hooks and a skirt. These might be a little more scarce as I have not seen many of them. Also, I am not sure of the Big-O types shown; they were found in Rabble Rouser boxes with unmarked lips and no other distinguishing features. Two are Bagley Big-O types in Rabble Rouser boxes, so the others may not be original either.

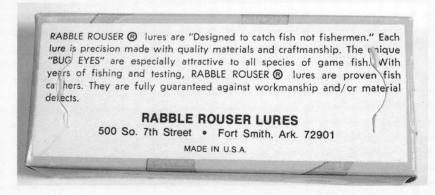

Typical box back from slide-top plastic boxes.

Upper lure is a new 2½" sonic type next to a smaller version. $8.00 – 15.00.

A ½ oz. Model RR Top-Water on the bottom, a medium diving Rowdy on top. $8.00 – 15.00.

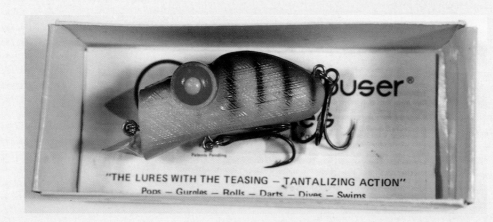

Rowdy in a box. $15.00 – 20.00 boxed.

Deep diving Rouster. $8.00 – 15.00.

Rainbow Trout Big-O type, not sure of maker. Maybe Bagley provided lures for sale to factory distributors and they ended up in these odd boxes. $12.00 – 20.00.

Rainbow Trout next to a Bagley Silver Shiner Big-O type. Found new in Rabble Rouser boxes. $12.00 – 20.00.

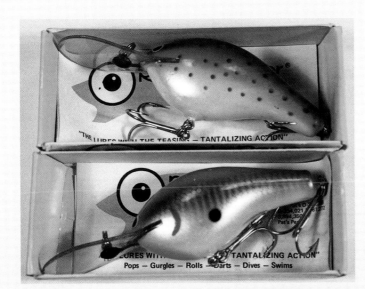

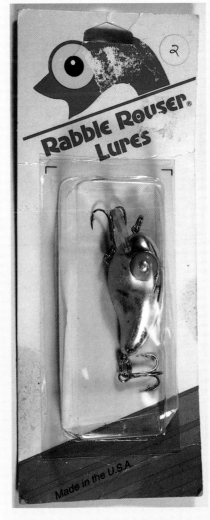

Rainbow Trout and Orange scale Bagley Big-O types (see page 31). Found new in Rabble Rouser boxes. $12.00 – 20.00.

A small lure on newer blister pack. $8.00 – 12.00.

Rapala Lures

Now marketed by Normark Lures. This classic balsa Finnish-made minnow is not real collectible due to the millions sold and available. Some things to look for include finding the earliest boxes written in both Finnish and English; I sold one of these for $12.00 on eBay. Also, some of the earliest types have different diving lips. The box shown is one of the earlier ones with hard plastic cover, late 1960s or early 1970s, but not the earliest. Without any doubt, this is one fish-catching lure. One of my sons cast out a 7" jointed Rapala in blue mullet only to find about a 10" Rainbow hit it instead of the expected Northern Pike. When a lure is this successful, do not expect it to be of any great value unless you find something unique or keep only new in the package with papers items.

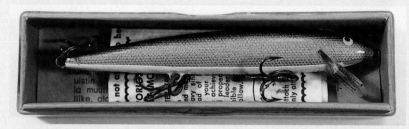

Rapala Minnow new in older box with papers, 4⅝", Model 11G, floating. See Chapter 8 for two more new-in-box models. $8.00 – 12.00.

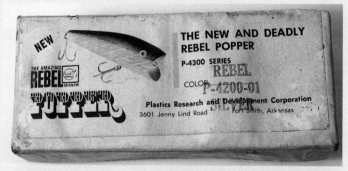

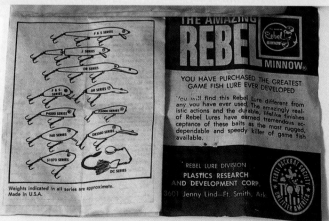

Plastics Research box and insert. $20.00+ for box, $30.00+ with lure and papers.

Rebel Brand (Pradco)

Plastics Research and Development Corporation, 3601 Jenny Lind Road, Fort Smith, Arkansas, pre-zip box. This is the very successful modern lure company known as Pradco. Rebel had a famous minnow that competed head-to-head with the Rapala Minnow, only made of plastic; see the Dickson lure for a copy of one. I was recently surprised to see fairly current Rebel Toppers, a surface plunker type bait shown on the box, bring $15.00 each on eBay. But, as the photos show, Rebel made many varieties of lures in many colors which is the key to collectors finding an interest in a company. The older Plastics Research box shown in the first two photos is worth at least $20.00 as they are not found often. Shown next is a typical Rebel plastic slide-top box. These are followed by a Joe Camel new on its card, these trade well at $12.00 – 20.00 with regularity if new on the card. Actually, I have sold loose ones for upwards of $15.00 on eBay. This is followed by the small Rebel plastic frog and a colorful Rebel crankbait example, the Rattlin' Firetail. The Rattlin' Firetail comes from my 1970s plastics collection, as have many of the earlier baits. The body is 3½" long, and the lip is marked Rebel Floater Made in U.S.A. The body cavity has four b.b. shot for rattle noise. Pradco now owns many of the companies featured in my two volumes and clearly has made its mark on fishing lures.

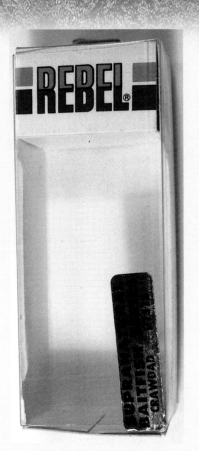

Typical slide box from the 1970s.
$5.00 – 10.00.

Joe Camel, new on card.
$15.00 – 20.00.

Rebel frog. $5.00 – 8.00.

Rattlin' Firetail Floater. $8.00 – 12.00 due to early model and unique color.

Red and Green Tackle Company

6030 Helen Avenue, Detroit 11, Michigan, pre-zip address, cardboard box with plastic slide top, address only appears on the paper insert. Shown is a new-in-the-box Bass King lure, a bait-casting size deep diving lure. I have three colors of these lures.

The one shown is a black lure with green frog spots, screw hardware, and painted eyes. These date from the 1950s and would trade for $20.00 – 30.00 in the box as shown. Do you think the Red Green Show got its name here?

Bass King new in the box with paper insert, black with frog spots, white raised eyes, deep diving lip, screw/washer hardware, 2¾ long. Retail price of $1.19. $20.00 – 30.00 boxed.

Bass King box side.

Republic Tackle Company

Republic, Wash. I have a collection of new on the dealer display card lures called the Demon. The pre-zip code card and graphics make it clear that it is an early 1950s lure and display. I have five of the cards which are not identical, some have many more of one particular color. The lures are a simple spinner with a bead at the end of the shaft and one treble hook with an injection-molded plastic fish-shaped body held on by the front wire of the spinner blade being inserted through a single hole in the lower part of the fish head. The lures have painted eyes, and most do not have a pupil; eyes are black on the red/white and orange and brown on the frog and the black lures. So, this lure was easy to assemble and had a one-step molding process, indicative of many of the "ma and pa" garage operations that started up right after World War II. No trade data exists, but the little lures should be worth at least $8.00 each, and the dozen new on a display card should fetch better than $100.00. I have also shown one metal bait that also came from the Washington area that may pre-date the plastic Demon. It is constructed in the same fashion and may have been made by the same company at an earlier date.

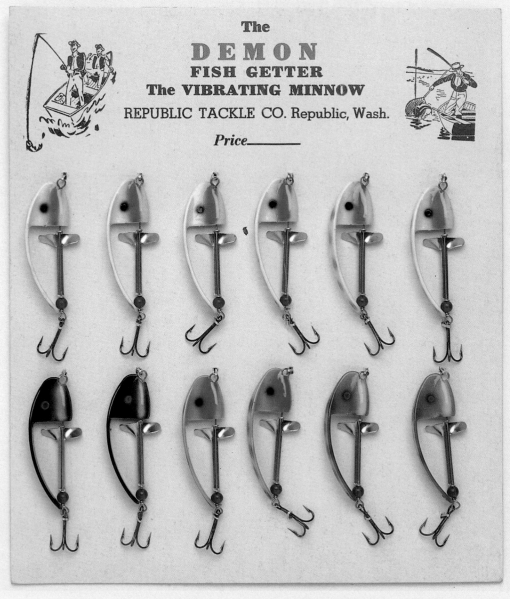

A display board of Demon Lures. I sold one on eBay in late 2001 for $90.00.

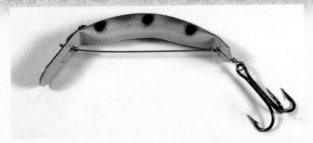

Metal Demon Type Lure, 2¾" long. $5.00 – 10.00.

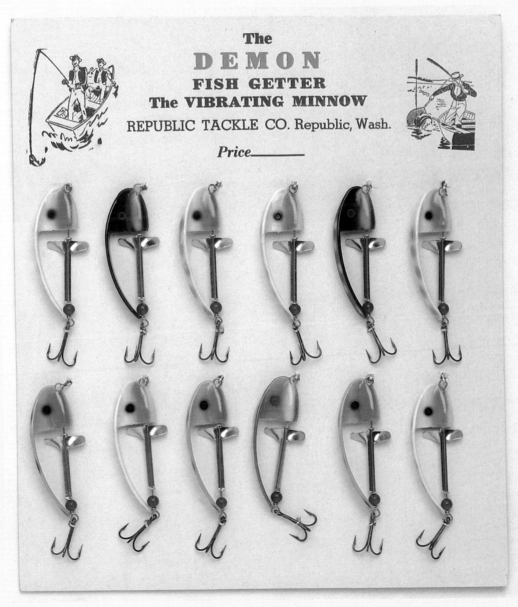

A second display board of Demon Lures. $75.00 – 100.00.

Rinehart Brand Manufacturing

By Fred Rinehart Tackle Co., Newark, Ohio, U.S.A. This company sold a very nice collectible lure called the Jinx made out of durable Tenite. The lure was in a number of sizes but all designed the same, a wobbler-type lure with an adjustable diving lip for shallow or deep diving. It came in many colors and sizes and had surface hardware and large protruding eyes molded into the body. Most of the lures are not marked, but they are distinctive and easy to recognize. The original box is likely the blue and white two-piece cardboard box shown, followed by a two-piece cardboard box in an

attractive green and yellow with an upward leaping bass grabbing onto a Jinx lure. The company, according to a box insert, also made a fly rod beetle — yet another company with a beetle offering. The harder to find models seem to be the muskie varieties. Also, the shore minnow colors do not appear as often as the perch and pike colors. Again, like most plastic lures, there was little interest in these lures two years ago, but one new in the box sold at the 2001 NFLCC show in Wausau, Wisconsin, for $30.00. I think they should be valued at $15.00 without a box and $30.00+ with a box.

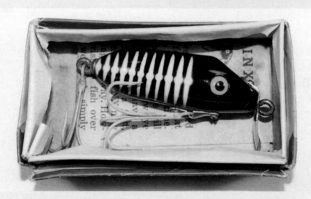

Newer, but still pre-zip, likely the 1950s, version of the Rinehart box, green and yellow, with a black with white rib shore pattern Jinx, Model 10M 475, made of Tenite, price of $1.09, raised molded eyes, opposite box end stamped WRB; and the lure's hook hardware. $30.00 in box minimum, $15.00 loose.

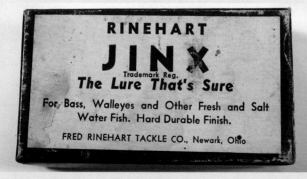

An older Jinx box in white and blue and its contents, a Luminous white with black ribs Jinx Lure, 2¼" long, rare color. This older box with a rare luminous color would bring over $50.00 in this condition.

A tough to find Musky size, 4¹³⁄₁₆" long, Jinx in a simple rainbow pattern, surface belly, screw/washer tail hardware, and raised molded eyes. I paid $40.00 for it in early 2001 in a private sale.

Rhys Davis Ltd.

2070 Lands End Rd., Sidney, B.C., Canada, V8L 3R9. This is a modern lure shown as another example of the same idea marketed by Les Davis, Herring Magic, and Luhr-Jensen. Even a set of all of these varieties makes an interesting and inexpensive display.

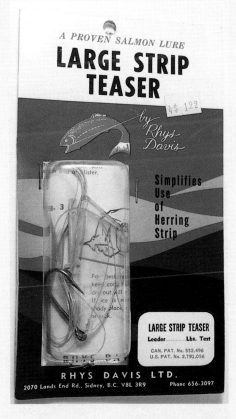

Large Strip Teaser.
$5.00 – 10.00.

Ropher

Los Angeles, California. See the detailed discussion under South Bend in Volume 1 for a full history of this company's famous bait, the Fin-Dingo! Fin-Dingos are shown on page 10 of this volume.

Russelure

Los Angeles, California. What kind of collector would I be if I did not like Russelures? These technically belong in the metals chapter but are shown here because of their general collector appeal. They came in at least three packages, a green and black one-piece cardboard box with a fold-out display cut-out; the common two-piece plastic box from the 1950s/1960s; and the plastic bag found in an old local hardware store. The one in the plastic bag is a 2½" model and had an address of P.O. Box 537, Chico, Calif. 95927. These trade for $10.00 – 25.00 depending on packaging, condition, and other variables. The real small fly rod sizes are more difficult to find than the spinning size. Also, some of the models had color jackets available, and the lures are more valuable with jackets but they were not available on all models.

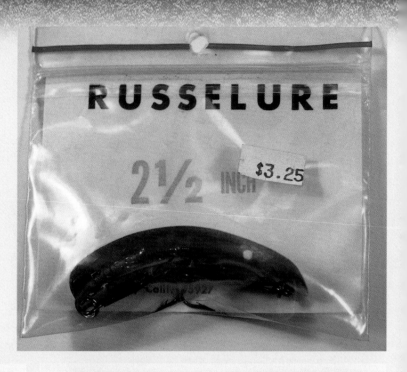

Examples of Russelures in packages. $8.00 – 15.00.

Top and side view of the oldest one-piece cardboard box. $25.00+.

St. Croix Tackle Company

Park Falls, Wisconsin. An uncommon plastic bait of the early 1960s (1961 – 1964 in the catalog) is the St. Croix Snipe. See a box example under Unner-Flash, page 137. The Snipe came in a 2" and a 2¾" size, and a number of examples are shown below. The bait is easily recognized as it is marked St. Croix on one side and Snipe on the other. Also, the rear double hook has the little flapper blade attached. They have simple screw hardware with the belly screw mounted in an indentation in the mold. The rear hook is a double and the belly hook is a treble, although some of the ones shown have one of the hooks cut off. The eyes are painted. Though a rather recent bait, it is also quite scarce and should trade for $20.00 – 30.00 loose and much more in the box new.

Examples of both sizes of the Snipe baits. $20.00 – 30.00 loose; $40.00 – 50.00 in box.

Safety-Lure

Glen Willow Lure Co. This is a unique lure that retracts its hooks so one can safely carry it in the pocket! Another neat gadget for us to collect years later. Recently purchased for this book for $75.00 privately.

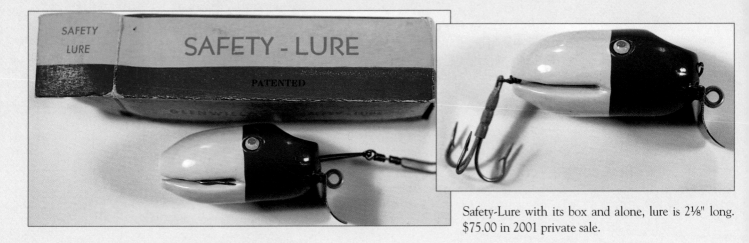

Safety-Lure with its box and alone, lure is 2⅛" long. $75.00 in 2001 private sale.

Salmon Lures

I have shown one nice rainbow salmon lure here to let you know that I have not forgotten the collectors of these nice plugs. Folks in the Pacific Northwest and the Great Lakes have been keeping some of these for years, but little has been written about their history, use, and the companies that made them. With the assistance of my friend Tony Zazweta in the Pacific Northwest and Phil Jensen, owner of Luhr-Jensen & Sons, I hope to put together another book dealing with salmon plugs or include them in a book on Luhr-Jensen & Sons.

Sample Salmon Lure, 4¾", rainbow, carved molded eyes, and hook hanger; line tie is one heavy-duty clip molded into the casting.

Seal Tackle Company

Union Lake, Mich. My only example is a flatfish-type lure found new in the box that is called "The Game Fish Lure," and the box claims a patent pending on the lure. The box is white with green trim and shows a wave pattern on the lure. The lure is similar to the Flipper Fish of Michigan Tackle. The lure is 2⅝" long and has two small trebles on hangers that look like cut-in-half Flatfish hangers mounted with one screw directly into the plastic. The eye of the line tie has a similar addition to it as the hook hangers. This lure is uncommon and would trade accordingly, especially in its box. I paid only $25.00 for this one in a deal when I bought a number of lures, but it is worth at least $10.00 more in its box.

Game Fish Lure on two-piece cardboard box. $35.00+ in box, scarce lure.

Shurebite Tackle Company

Bronson, Michigan. Shown is an early Shurebite Shedevil box from the 1940s, one of the more collectible Shurebite baits due to a wide variety of colors available. Also shown are two new from their boxes Shedevils; one is black and yellow, and the other is red and yellow. These would trade for over $30.00 new in the box.

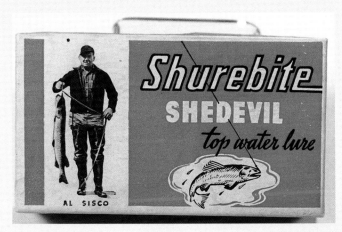

Shurebite box and two Shedevils. $30.00 – 40.00 boxed; $15.00 – 20.00 loose.

Smithwick Lures

A photo essay of Smithwick boxes and lures. I have not labeled these because they are all named on the lure and detailed in many reference works. But, there is growing interest in earlier Smithwick products, and this essay will help you identify the company's items. Lures in the two-piece cardboard box should start at $20.00, ones in slide-top boxes at $12.00. Loose lures will vary greatly but should be valued at $8.00+ depending on model.

Shreveport, Louisiana. This company is now owned by Pradco but was started as an independent company in 1947 by James Smithwick. Lures of interest include any of the early lures in boxes, such as the Devil's Horse or Carrot Top. Pradco is making many of the same lures, so beware if you are buying off eBay or at a show and the lure is not in original packaging. Most of these lures were made of wood, and the only major plastic products of the company were the Rattlin' Rogues and Water-Gaters, a sonic type lure. Smithwick Lures were featured in early BassPro catalogs and they are numerous. A color collection of Devil's Horse lures would surely be impressive. Most of the lures that follow came from the former collection of Bud Hartman and are believed to be original Smithwick examples. The Water-Gater shown is 3¼" long and has hook hangers molded into the lure.

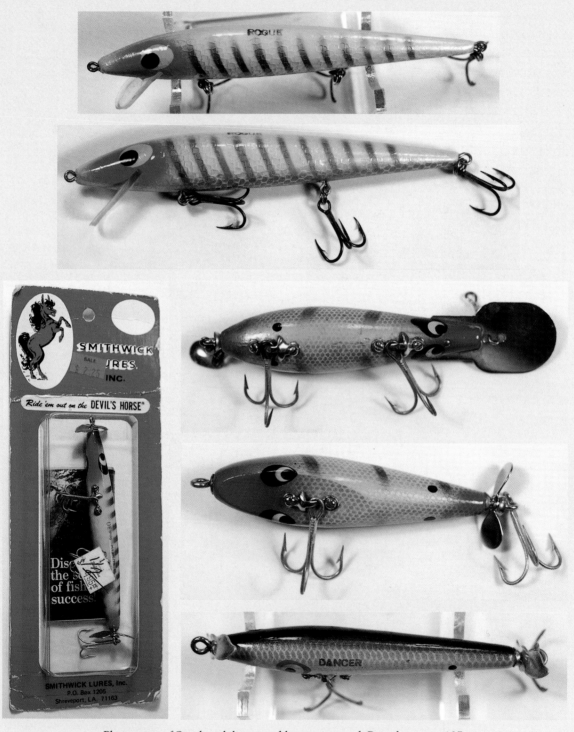

Photo essay of Smithwick boxes and lures continued. Priced on page 127.

More of the photo essay of Smithwick boxes and lures. Priced on page 127.

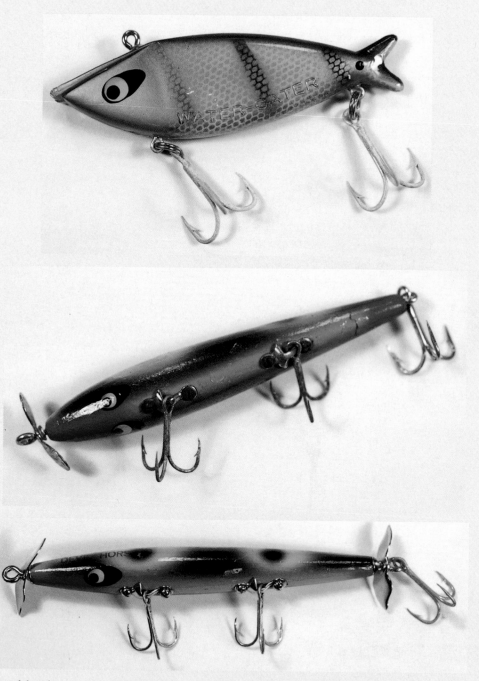

Conclusion of the photo essay of Smithwick boxes and lures. Priced on page 127. There is also a strong market for these lures for fishing, and many are still being made by Pradco so it is best to stay with packaged items.

Bud Stewart Tackle

There is a major work out on Bud Stewart[10], but I needed to show some examples of his work, one in plastic, a Minnie spinning size bait. The lure is about 2⅝" long, jointed, with a typical Bud Stewart tail addition. His lures are unmarked for the most part, so one needs to learn to recognize styles, hardware, and colors. Also, beware that some of his plastic lures are worth as much or more than the wooden ones, commanding over $100.00 each. This little plastic bait is worth at least $25.00. I have also shown two Pad Hoppers, circa 1960 valued at $100.00 – 250.00 each, made of wood with the typical Bud Stewart plastic weed guard over the hooks. Note how they are similar to the Orchard Industries Kick-N-Kackle. Stewart's painting and lure making creativity put his lures and his fish decoys in great demand, with some rare items bringing over $1,000.00 each. His lures are concentrated heavily in the eastern region of Michigan's lower peninsula, but he sold nationally through publications such as *Field and Stream* and *Outdoor Life*.

Painted eye Pad Hopper, side eyes painted, front eyes carved, 2" long, tail missing. $100.00 – 250.00.

Raised eye Pad Hopper in frog, 2" long but a little fatter than the one above with feelers added; left side of body has concave carving to produce an injured swim. $100.00 – 250.00.

Bud Stewart Minnie, 2⅝", sold new for $2.25. $25.00.

The recent (1982) but collectible Bug Plug, 3" counting diving lip.

Storm Lures

Storm Manufacturing Co., P.O. Box 265, Norman, Oklahoma 73070. This successful family lure company was sold in the late 1990s to Normark Corporation of Finland (makers of the famed Rapala Minnow), and some of the lures are still being marketed by Normark at this time. Although this is a more recent production than most lures in this book, I have shown one of the earlier Storm boxes for identification purposes. The box is cardboard with a plastic sleeve and a hang tab for pegs on one end. There is no indication of the lure model or color on the box (it is a Big Mac). One very collectible lure from this company is the Bug Plug from 1982, which came in a variety of colors and is most interesting in appearance. I would call this a "classic" plastic lure. Also shown are a box back, a Chug Bug, and a Thin Fin. Early Thin Fins in their boxes are gaining collector interest now also. Again with the company being owned by Normark, the early years will become more collectible. A 1981 Storm catalog in my collection lists 72 available color variations on the company's lures!

The Chug Bug was available in 15 colors in 1981. The company also made one of the best modern Pike baits I have ever used, the Hot 'N Tot. In 1981 it was available in nearly all color variations. With such color and lure variation, it is no wonder collectors are attracted to this modern company's products. Interest in Storm Lures is growing rapidly, and in May of 2002 early colors were in demand due to Normark's discontinuing many colors and models. Look for pre-Normark models in unusual colors.

A "likely" collectible, the Chug Bug, 3⁵⁄₁₆" long, concave eye sockets, protruding eyeballs, screw type hardware inserted into molding process with hooks held on by split rings, indented gill marks, Chug Bug on bottom of lure. $8.00 – 15.00.

A Big Mac and a box. $15.00 – 20.00.

A Thin Fin and its box back. $20.00+ new in early box.

132

Suick Lure Manufacturing

630 Industrial Park, Antigo, Wisconsin. A common musky bait from Wisconsin but seldom seen as a casting plug. This raised eye plastic casting bait has the number 3 stamped behind the rear hook on the bottom. It is 4½" long and uncommon.

Plastic Musky Thriller by Suick. $12.00 – 20.00.

The Actual Lure Company, Inc.

392 Fifth Avenue, New York 18, New York. I really do not understand why collectors have been avoiding these lures, but the value just is not there yet. I have sold some of these at shows for $20.00 new in tube, but they draw little interest on eBay right now. It seems these should actually command a small premium as they are "Real Bait-Sealed Tight" in a tube and have little value once used or ruined. Lures such as this were actually made on both coasts. The lures came as Wobblers formed with a curve for darting; Spinners with a spinner attached; and Side Fins which were actual shiners. I have shown two below.

Examples of Actual Baits. $12.00 – 20.00 new in tubes.

Tru-Temper Lures

An outgrowth of American Fork and Hoe Company, Tru-Temper Speed Shad and Crippled Shad and their Al Foss baits are all collectible, as are some of the rods and reels. According to one wholesale catalog, Tru-Temper Speed Shad was owned by Bomber Baits of Texas by 1973. Bomber is now owned by Pradco, along with the Speed Shad. In 1973, the American Wholesale Hardware Co. only lists Speed Shad as being available in the ⅓ oz. and ⅖ oz. sizes. Cost in 1973 wholesale was $2.25. The Shad baits were originally made in wood in 1941 but due to the war effort could not be produced, and all post-war Shads are of plastic. An excellent article in Vol. 10, No.2 of the *NFLCC Magazine* written by Dick Wilson & Jerry R. Martin titled "Al Foss Serve it with Pork" details all the Foss baits, many of which pre-date our era. As pointed out in that article, one interesting note is that Weber Tackle Co. produced the Shimmy Wiggler for a short time in the 1960s or 1970s, and it did not do very well (I received about 40 new in the box when I purchased the Weber inventory, see Volume 1). The jig 'n pig phase of rubber worm fishing was already starting to replace the interest in pork rind baits. As with most metal baits, there just is not the collector demand for them as for wooden and better plastic lures. The Speed Shad and Crippled Shad came in interesting colors and box presentations and should continue to increase in value. Shown are some common Al Foss baits and an example of a Speed Shad and a Side Shad. These are gaining in popularity, especially the early boxed versions. Trade value on the metal baits is low, as with most metal baits, but values for any of the following lures should be in the $10.00 – 30.00 range with the early models already bring over $30.00 new in the box.

A variety of collectible Foss baits. $10.00 – 30.00 each.

A Tru-Temper Speed Shad, 2⁵⁄₁₆" long, dented eyes, cup belly hardware, inverted barrel tail hardware, and no markings. $15.00 – 20.00 loose; $30.00 boxed.

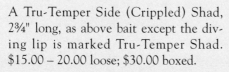

A Tru-Temper Side (Crippled) Shad, 2¾" long, as above bait except the diving lip is marked Tru-Temper Shad. $15.00 – 20.00 loose; $30.00 boxed.

Triple Action Lure

The Ogene Company, Abilene, Texas, pre-zip, sold for $1.10 new. This is a most interesting plastic bait with great advertising on the box. The advertising says it has "Three Distinct Actions Plus Action," sounds like the advertising man graduated from the Department of Redundancy Department. It appears the

uniqueness of the lure is its movable diving plane that would increase the wobble. At 2½" long with inverted bell tail hardware, surface belly hardware, painted black spots within an indentation on rear section, it is likely meant to appear as a crawfish to a fish.

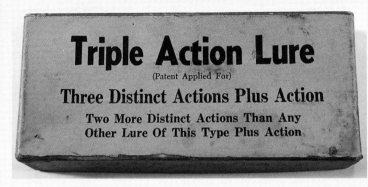

Triple Action two-piece box and lure. $100.00 by private sale, May 2001.

Troller Tackle Company

A division of Wise Products, Inc., 4225 N. W. St. Helens Rd., Portland 10, Oregon. This neat pre-zip code one-piece cardboard box and large rubber salmon plug are very colorful.

This was purchased with a number of other items but valued at $30.00+ at the time. The name of the lure is the Pirate, same name as a Pro-Line Plastics lure (see page 151). This is the Pat. Pend. Box and dates from the 1940s or 1950s. You can see in the second shot that the name and Patent Pending are stamped on the lure's fin. It is a large hard rubber plug with a more pliable tail and fin, one single hook, and glass or plastic eyes. Like many of the smaller companies, the box of this lure is as attractive as the lure itself.

Pirate box and lure. $30.00+.

Trout Louie

Made by Minser Tackle Company, Route 1, Box 621, Port Angeles, Washington (pre-zip). This little plastic trout bait, 1⅞" long, from the Pacific Northwest is a good example of small company offerings in the 1960s. The company also made the Lucky Louie Plugs, Minser Sinkers, and Minser Rod Holders. The Trout Louie came in six colors: White with Red Dots, Light Yellow, Light Orange, Pearl Pink, Blue Back, and Fluorescent Red. This lure had Patent No. 2236353 according to the paper insert, but Minser's patent for his Lucky Louie Salmon Plug was issued March 25, 1941. Another example of not believing everything one reads in catalogs or on advertising inserts. This should trade for at least $8.00 – 12.00 new in its little bag with papers.

Trout Louie and paper insert. $8.00 – 12.00 new with papers.

Turner Bros.

Wellington, Ohio. The pre-zip code box states "A Big Spoon for A Big Fish" with patents pending. It was No. 1 N and sold for $1.10 new, the front of the box was stamped with the price and F1551. The spoon is nearly 5" long with a giant treble attached by split ring and a barrel swivel on the line tie with a little propeller. One propeller is marked with name and address and the other lists three patents. This is indeed a "big spoon" and the only one I have ever seen. It likely sold well regionally for large fish such as muskie. However, out of the region it would be fairly uncommon. Value would depend on supply but I should think it is worth $20.00 – 30.00 in its box, $5.00 – $10.00 without a box.

Model F1551 Turner spoon in two-piece box. $20.00 – 30.00 boxed.

Ubangi Lure

This is a neat and fairly uncommon plastic bait first produced on the East Coast in Stamford, Connecticut by Forrest Allen, then Allen Tackle of Chicago, then the rights were acquired by Katchmore Bait Company of 700 3rd St., Palmyra, Wisconsin, according to the research completed by Bob Slade in his Wisconsin book. Slade also points out that Katchmore made the Fincheroo shown earlier for the Robfin Company of Arizona. Katchmore made a number of collectible plastic lures for themselves and for other companies, including the River Shiner and the jointed plastic Radtke Pikie made for Radtke Tackle Company, the bait that many think is a plastic Paw Paw Pike Caster. On its own merits, the Pikie is selling for at least $30.00 and is beautiful. The Ubangi is semi-rare, according to Bob Slade, I have only found two in my last seven years of seriously looking for plastics. As with many plastics, it is hard to determine the exact year and place of manufacture without packaging, but Katchmore ceased operations in 1975, so any Ubangi should pre-date that period.

Ubangi Lure, 2" long counting diving lip, concave eye socket, protruding eye ball, simple screw hardware, and plastic protrusion for simple screw line tie. $20.00 – 25.00.

Unner-Flash

Manufactured by O. M. Bait Co., Hazel Park, Mich. Pre-zip two-piece cardboard box is shown, along with a St. Croix Snipe box, for above and a lure that I believe belongs to the Unner-Flash box. The lure fits the general description, and one can see the inner foil to make it sparkle. A Lazy Ike-type shape with foil insert, simple screw hardware, double belly hook and rear treble, red gills, and raised molded fin, the lure is exactly 3" long. This lure and box are uncommon.

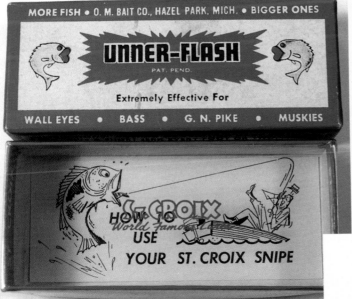

Unner-Flash box and lure. $30.00 pair.

Vivif

A classic French import during the spinning and spin-cast era of the 1950s and 1960s, this lure was copied by Weber (see Vol. 1, p. 216), as shown again, due to its success. This lure came in a variety of sizes and colors and is molded of a hard rubber material that remains quite pliable with age. As do a Fin-Dingo and Fifi, the Vivif also stands up for display purposes. These trade in the low end for $5.00 – 15.00 each, depending on color and size variables; they are common.

Vivif and a Fifi.
$5.00 – 15.00.

Voo Doo Lures

San Francisco, Calif. Not to be confused with the plastic worm maker Venom Manufacturing of Lithopolis, Ohio that discontinued making worms in about 1999. I only know of one Voo Doo lure, a jointed new-in-the-box example of a jointed Lazy-Ike type lure. The lure says Voo Doo on the left side and Pat Pend on the right side. No other company data has been researched.

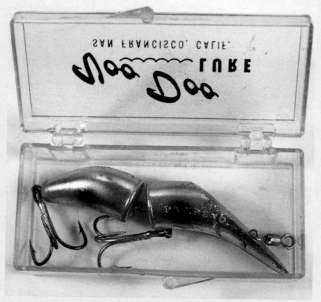

Voo Doo lure in box.
$12.00 – 20.00.

W. & J. Specialty Company

Detroit, Mich. This is an example of a great "local" knock-off bait. Detroit, Michigan is home to Eppinger Dardevle, the world's largest selling spoon bait. Well, another Detroit company decided to get in on the act and made a bait called the Haw King that looked a lot like a Dardevle to me! I have shown the two bait boxes together. This box does not have any address or zip code and is quite old, the side of the box says, "The W. & J. Made for Angler's Play" and the end is marked No. A-1, one standard spoon. It is 3⅝" long in a 4⅜" box. Original sales price on box back appears to be 25¢. I paid $25.00 for this by private sale. It should be worth that much or more in a two-piece cardboard box, and the bait is new, mint in box.

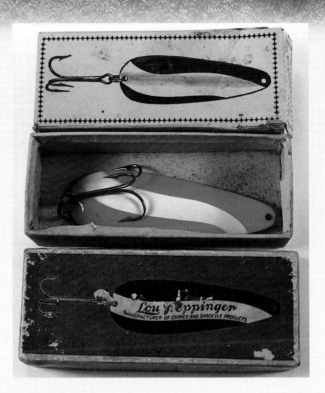

Haw King box, lure, and a Dardevle box. $25.00 each for these early boxes with lures.

Wallsten Tackle Company

Kenilworth, Ill., moved to Chicago in the early 1950s. Shown here is a dealer carton for a dozen Jointed Cisco Kid Pike Model 21 Lures, with one two-piece cardboard box containing one mint-in-box Orange – 7C version of the lure. I think this is the earliest Cisco Kid box and the only two-piece cardboard box for one I have seen. This lure was very successful, and the company produced many thousands of lures and was located in more than one location. The Cisco Toppers are gaining a lot of collector interest. Any of the boxed or packaged lures would be of most interest. The brand name on the early box showed it WT over a CO in a triangle. There is no zip on the box and the dress of the fisherman in the boat is late 1940s, early 1950s, and they are fishing (one is, the other is rowing11) with a baitcasting rod. The dealer carton shows the straight pikie type lure and the injured minnow type lure. The company made lures well into the 1960s and one can find complete listings in many jobber catalogs. One thing to note is that some of the Cisco lures are prone to "plastic scum" if left in damp areas, as shown on the one new in an older blister pack, but this cleans right off with a little work. More on this important company upcoming in my next volume because of growing collector interest.

Wallsten dealer carton, rare, even shopworn as shown. $100.00+.

One of the more collectible Ciscos, a Topper, 3⅞" long, surface belly hardware, screw tail hardware, painted eyes, and marked on back. $20.00+.

Wallsten dealer carton and new in mint box lure, Model 7C-Orange, 2½" long, surface belly simple screw tail hardware, and no name on diving lip. Dealer box is valued at $100.00+ and the perfect two-piece box and lure would bring $50.00+. Values on Cisco lures reached over $100.00 on eBay in 2002. Rarity and color are key elements.

1950s – 1960s Cisco Kid blister pack, front and back. This rare piece, $25.00+.

Wood's Manufacturing Co.

El Dorado, Arkansas. Makers of the famous Wood's Spot Tail and other minnow type baits. The 1947 catalog insert with the two-piece cardboard box describes only the Dipsy Doodle Series 500 available in 19 colors; the Deep-R-Doodle Series 800 also in 19 colors; and the Deep-R-Doodle 1000 Series in 19 colors. The Spot Tail Minnow is featured on the box cover but not the insert. The box shown is the Patent Applied For box. The Spot Tail Minnow is a plastic bait with excellent paint, a diving lip held on by two screws, cup hardware, and the trademark spot on the tail. The Wood's diving lips are easily spotted since they have a channel down the center unlike most others. The interest in Spot Tail minnows has gone up dramatically the last four years due to the wide array of colors, sizes, and models available. Other lures of interest from Wood's include Dipsy Doodles and Deep-R-Doodles, again available in many sizes and colors. The collectible baits by this company trade in the $15.00 – 30.00 range loose, more boxed.

Wood's Spot Tail early box, insert and 3" lure in a perch scale, cup hardware, inverted barrel rear hardware, painted yellow eye with large black pupils. $20.00 – 35.00 with box and catalog insert.

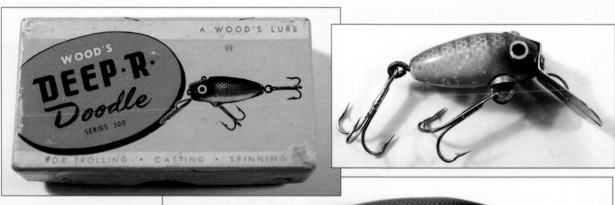

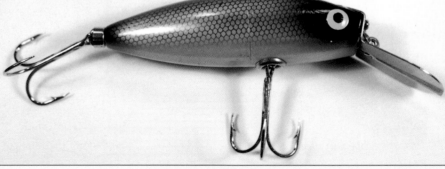

Wood's Deep-R-Doodle box, 1⅝" long (body only) Midget ½ oz. plastic version and ⅝ oz. plastic version Model 516, 3" long (body only). I recently paid $20.00 each for a dozen midgets in April 2002. Boxed models would bring at least $10.00 more.

Box types from the 1950s – 1960s, with the two-piece plastic box pre-dating the cardboard with plastic top box. $5.00 each.

Worden's Brand

Yakima Bait Co., Granger, Washington, both pre-zip code and zip code of 98932 shown. Worden's makes two of the best panfish and trout baits, and they have sold a bunch of them. I found an advertisement for the one now called Spin-N-Glo in a July 1937 issue of *Field and Stream* and it was a new offering then. The lure was also featured in the 1939 Gateway catalog. A recent visit to a tackle shop shows the Rooster Tail and Spin-N-Glo lures still on the pegs waiting to be sold new. However, I have heard of some folks trying to color collect the older Rooster Tails now. I do not have any trade data on them but would think that off their cards they would be worth only up to $3.00. However, new on the card the older ones should bring $8.00 to $10.00. The Rooster Tail came in a number of sizes and colors and indeed would be a fun, inexpensive beginning collection, maybe like the Heddon Sonics were six or seven years ago. The Rooster Tail shown is ⅛ oz. in pattern PBRT. It sold new at G.I. Joe's, Inc. for 59¢. The other bait shown is a Spin-N-Glo also known as a cork drift bobber with a treble hook, catalog number 112. I have fished with this lure for well over 40 years and know it is a killer on panfish and brook trout. Bluegills and punkinseeds cannot resist this lure in calm water in the evenings, especially when on their spawning beds. One does find a few in tackle boxes but not as many as Rooster Tails. I would guess this would be a good future collectible since the little wings on it make it something that can eventually damage. Not worth much off the card, but new on card older ones would have the same value as the Rooster Tail, $8.00 to $10.00.

Worden has also taken over a number of other companies, including Poe's Cedar lures and the famous line of Helin Tackle and its ever present Flatfish. This post-dates the coverage of this book but again alerts one to be cautious buying Flatfish out of a package as the lure could be very recent indeed. These would only have fishing value since they are too recent, but the first packages will likely increase in value over the years, and one may want to set aside an introductory blister pack for a Flatfish by Worden.

Rooster Tail and Spin-N-Glo on cards. Older ones on cards $8.00 – 10.00.

Worth Tackle

By the Worth Company, Stevens Point, Wisconsin. This is the final link in the trilogy of fly bait companies, Marathon, Weber, and Worth, that made the Stevens Point/Wausau, Wisconsin area the fly fishing capital of the world. Worth was an outgrowth of an Olsen Bait Company of Chippewa Falls, Wisconsin, buy-out, moving the company to Stevens Point, according to Bob Slade in his book on Wisconsin fishing tackle. The company's first address was 138 Clark Street, Stevens Point, Wisconsin, and then the company moved to 214 Sherman Ave., Whiting (a suburb of Stevens Point). The company then referred to itself as The Worth Company, Stevens Point, Wisconsin. The 1954 catalog I have verifies this name and address.

Worth's most collectible bait is without doubt the cute little Flutter Fin. In the early 1960s Worth purchased the rights to Nova Spinner Co. of Wild Rose, Wisconsin, and acquired the rights to this lure. The inventor Delbert Patterson originally produced this lure in a dozen or so wooden lures with glass eyes and then a wooden version without glass eyes. Once he sold the company to Worth, shortly after inventing the lure, Worth marketed it only in plastic in at least six different colors. I have not been able to find a Flutter Fin for less than $20.00 for some time.

The other items in the Worth Company's arsenal were mainly fly rod baits and metal lures. A review of the 1954 catalog shows many items similar to those made by Weber and even the tops of the display cards have a familiar look to them! Worth, Weber, and Frost all used little tubes to package some of the flies, and these are nice additions to a collection.

And yet another beetle comes to life! Lur All and Weber lead the way in beetle production, but Worth had a similar one that must have sold by the thousands. It came in a size 10 and a size 4-hook variety in a dozen assorted colors. In 1954 it was made of brass, and the catalog said it was the same high quality but a new lower price, also offering it packed three to a plastic box for the first time in addition to the standard card assortments.

Another item of some interest is the plug called Red-head made by Worth. This was a simple casting plug with one size 1/0 treble hook. 2½" long, ⅜ ounce. These were packed one to a "colorful individual box." This same bait came in a 1½" ⅒ ounce fly rod lure. One can tell it from the Trout-Oreno and H-I versions easily as the face is at a different angle. This had a size 6 double hook and came packed one on a two color card with six connected cards, or in a two dozen counter display box. Either of these cards would be a nice addition to a modern fishing lure collection. In 1954, the catalog listed as new Model 27 Worth Spinning Plug. This was old "red-head" again in spinning sizes ⅙ or ⅛ ounce in 1½" in length with a number 6 double hook. It was packed also the same way as its fly rod counterpart.

Common items one finds include most of the Worth metal baits, Worth June Bug Spinners, Worth Casting Spoon, and the Worth Water Demon spoon. Most of these are of little value unless new on card or on a display board. One also finds a little bait known as the Worth Fire Drifter fairly often, a floating drifting spinner bait from the Northwest that had the fire lacquers of the early 1950s. Again, it is of little value unless found on a card.

Worth also made some high quality hair poppers, a hair mouse, and hair frogs. The problem is figuring out a Worth mouse from a Weber mouse, as they are nearly identical. The frogs are quite different from Weber and Marathon and of a more square design. Also, the Worth hair popper was very different and unique with a bass bug body and a large disc type attachment before the tail. This produced the "popping" action of the fly rod bait. In addition to the hair lures, Worth made an extensive array of flies that were similar to those offered by Weber. As I said earlier, these lures were often tied by the same woman as piece work or work in both factories at different, or even the same, times. It is no wonder that Worth and Weber items appear similar.

Worth also made a complete line of terminal tackle. It did not sell any rods or reels in 1954. However, an examination of the 1954 catalog makes it clear that this traditional fly and terminal tackle company was also adding many items to its "spinning" line. By 1954 all of the American fishing tackle companies knew spin fishing was here to stay and responded with new products.

Flutter Fins. $30.00 plus, more boxed. $30.00+, more boxed.

WORTH While · FISHING TACKLE · "WORTH" Style

No. 109 Worth Water Beetle

Shaped like the underwater beetles which the various species of game fish are accustomed to feed on, this sensational new lure is outstanding for taking Trout, Panfish, Bass, and other game fish. Made from bright enamelled brass bodies decorated to resemble the live

**SAME
HIGH QUALITY
NEW
LOW PRICE**

NEW!

NO. 109AA

bugs that exist under water. Also used extensively for taking fish through the ice in winter fishing. HOOK: Finest quality plated Turned Down Eye. SIZES: 10 and 4. PACKING: One to an individual card, 12 cards connected, one or two dozen to a colorful counter display panel, one panel to a box. Patterns as described below.

12 COLOR COMBINATIONS AS FOLLOWS:

CODE	COLOR BODY	TAIL
BR	Black & Red	White
YR	Yellow & Red	Brown
RG	Red & Green	Gray
BY	Brown & Yellow	Brown
GS	Green Spotted	Gray
OS	Orange Spotted	Gray
WR	White & Red	Brown
YS	Yellow Spotted	Black
GY	Green & Yellow	Brown
OG	Orange & Green	Gray
GR	Gold & Red	Brown
BB	Black & Red	Black

NOTE: Illustrations are actual size of Water Beetle using No. 4 hook. Water Beetle using No. 10 hook is about one half size.

No. 109A ASSORTMENT
1 Doz. Size 10 (Retail 35c Each) **$4.00**
NO. 109BA ASSORTMENT
1 Doz. Size 4 (Retail 50c Each) **$6.00**
NO. 109A2 ASSORTMENT
2 Doz. Size 10 (Retail 35c Each) **$8.00**
NO. 109BA2 ASSORTMENT
2 Doz. Size 4 (Retail 50c Each) **$12.00**

WORTH
WATER BEETLE

NO. 109BA

**NEW -
FAST
SELLING
ASSORTMENTS!**

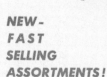

**SIZE 10
35c Each
3 For $1.00**

WORTH WATER BEETLE ASSORTMENTS

No. 109AA WATER BEETLE ASSORTMENT. A new popular assortment, containing three different patterns, size 10, beetles on a two color card in a re-usable clear plastic box. Six assortments on a three color counter display panel, one panel in a box.
PER ASSORTMENT (Retail **35c** Each) **$1.00**
PER PANEL (6 Assortments) **$6.00**
WEIGHT PACKED: 5 ozs.

No. 109BB WATER BEETLE ASSORTMENT. As above but size 4 hooks.
PER ASSORTMENT (Retail **50c** Each) **$1.50**
PER PANEL (6 Assortments) **$9.00**
WEIGHT PACKED: 8 ozs.

No. 109A6 WATER BEETLE ASSORTMENT. Contains half dozen of each twelve patterns, size 10 hook. Six dozen in all.
PER ASSORTMENT (Retail **35c** Each) **$24.00**
WEIGHT PACKED 8 ozs.

No. 109BA6 WATER BEETLE ASSORTMENT. Contains half dozen of each twelve patterns, size 4 hook. Six dozen in all.
PER ASSORTMENT (Retail **50c** Each) **$36.00**
WEIGHT PACKED 10 ozs.

Worth catalog, page 36.

WORTH While • FISHING TACKLE • "WORTH" Style

FLY ROD MOUSE - FROG - HAIR POPPER

No. 523EA6 EASTERN WET FLY ASSORTMENT. Contains a total of six dozen eyed Eastern Wet Flies. Packed three each of twenty-four popular and effective patterns, complete in a cellophane top multicolor counter display box. Each pattern clearly marked.
HOOKS: Sizes 10, 12, 14 or 16. Eyed only.
PATTERNS: Three each of the following:

Beaverkill	Cowdung
Black Gnat	Ginger Quill
Black Hkl Red	Gray Hkl Pink
Brown Hkl Pink	Grizzly King
Cahill	Ibis
Coachman	King of Waters

Montreal	Professor	Royal Coachman	White Miller
Pale Evg. Dunn	Queen of Waters	Seth Green	Wickhams Fancy
Parmachene Belle	Reuben Wood	Silver Doctor	Yellow Sally

PER ASSORTMENT (Retail 20c per fly).................**$14.40**
WEIGHT PACKED 8 ozs.

No. 523EAP6 EASTERN WET FLY ASSORTMENT. Here is an assortment for the fisherman who demands quick service. Twelve various patterns in a transparent top plastic box, each fly a distinct and different pattern.
HOOKS: 10, 12, 14 or 16. Eyed only.
PACKING: Six assortments in a two color counter display box. Six dozen flies in all.

PER ASSORTMENT
$2.40
PER SIX ASSORTMENT
DISPLAY BOX
$14.40

NEW!

WEIGHT PACKED: SIX DOZEN 8 ozs.

NO. 450 WORTH FLY ROD MOUSE

Skillfully tied and sculptured from all deer hair, this lifelike mouse lure is the perfect imitation of the real thing. Body and ears are all hair, tail is of chamois. Vivid eyes placed in front of the head adds to its appearance. Ringed eye hook neatly hidden in body pierces with quick certainty on the strike. A killer for large trout, bass and pike, in the smaller sizes for all pan fish.

HOOKS: Finest quality imported ringed eye, sizes 1/0, 2, 4 and 6.
PATTERNS: Natural Gray, Yellow, White and Black.
PACKING: One on a two color card, one dozen connected, in a counter display box. Larger sizes 1/0 and 2, each on two color card, in individual two color cellophane top display box.

No. 450 PRICE EACH. Sizes 4 and 6...**60c** PER DOZEN **$7.10**
PRICE EACH. Sizes 1/0 and 2 **70c** PER DOZEN **$8.30**
WEIGHT PACKED: 1 Dozen, 4 or 6, 4 ozs. 1/0 and 2, 5 ozs.

NO. 451 WORTH FROG LURE — A FLOATER

Enthusiastically recommended for luring all fresh water game fish, from bass and pike, to trout and pan fish. Body of all northern deer hair, with natural frog color and markings. Springy, weaving legs of untrimmed hair, make this lure realistic and tempting. Ringed eye hook hidden in the body, always ready for the strike. Truly a great lure.

HOOKS: Finest quality imported ringed eye, sizes 1/0, 2, 4 and 6.
PACKING: One on a two color card, each in a cellophane top two color display box.

No. 451 PRICE EACH. Sizes 4 and 6...**70c** PER DOZEN **$8.30**
PRICE EACH. Sizes 1/0 and 2 **80c** PER DOZEN **$9.50**
WEIGHT PACKED: 1 Dozen, 4 or 6, 4 ozs., 1/0 and 2, 5 ozs.

NO. 452 WORTH HAIR POPPER

A Worth creation that will be readily accepted by the angler who uses poppers. Tied very closely of finest northern deer hair, this popper will float for hours without dressing. Pops louder and sets up more commotion than most cork bodied types. Its unique design and shape, combined with springy weaving tail, makes it a sure fire attraction for bass, pike, trout and in the smaller sizes for pan fish. High quality imported ringed eye hook, fully hidden in the body, yields instantly on the strike.

HOOKS: Finest quality imported, sizes 1/0, 2, 4 and 6.
PATTERNS: Natural Gray, Yellow, White and Black, or any combination of these colors.
PACKING: One on a two color card, each in an individual cellophane top display box, or when specified, one in lusteroid tube.

No. 452 PRICE EACH. Sizes 4 and 6...**60c** PER DOZEN **$7.10**
PRICE EACH. Sizes 1/0 and 2 **70c** PER DOZEN **$8.30**
WEIGHT PACKED: 1 Dozen, 4 or 6, 4 ozs. 1/0 and 2, 5 ozs.

Worth catalog, page 12.

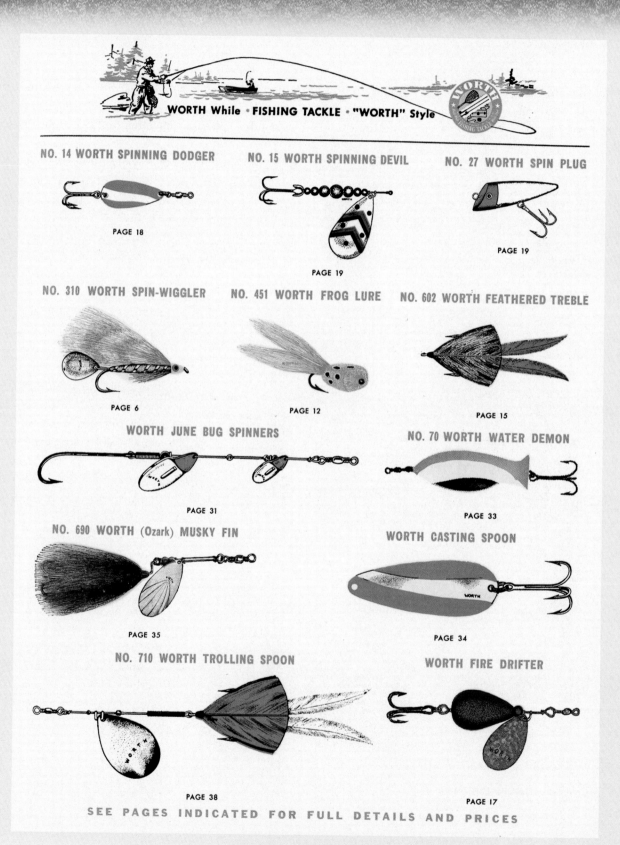

WORTH While · FISHING TACKLE · "WORTH" Style

NO. 14 WORTH SPINNING DODGER

PAGE 18

NO. 15 WORTH SPINNING DEVIL

PAGE 19

NO. 27 WORTH SPIN PLUG

PAGE 19

NO. 310 WORTH SPIN-WIGGLER

PAGE 6

NO. 451 WORTH FROG LURE

PAGE 12

NO. 602 WORTH FEATHERED TREBLE

PAGE 15

WORTH JUNE BUG SPINNERS

PAGE 31

NO. 70 WORTH WATER DEMON

PAGE 33

NO. 690 WORTH (Ozark) MUSKY FIN

PAGE 35

WORTH CASTING SPOON

PAGE 34

NO. 710 WORTH TROLLING SPOON

PAGE 38

WORTH FIRE DRIFTER

PAGE 17

SEE PAGES INDICATED FOR FULL DETAILS AND PRICES

Worth catalog, page 37.

Wright & McGill

Makers of modern Eagle Claw rods, reels, and hooks, of Denver, Colorado, also made many collectible plastic baits. Some of their baits, such as the Flapper Crab and the Bass-O-Gram, bring upwards of $100.00. However, most of their baits are worth $10.00 to $30.00 depending on model, box, etc. One unique item I found was a set of eight new-in-the-tube ¼ oz. spinning baits called the Dixie Dandy. These cute little baits are 1¾" long and look like a Bug-A-Boo with a tail spinner added. They have belly surface hardware and a screw tail hook hanger. The line tie has a little ringlet on it also. The colors shown are red/white, black, white shore minnow, yellow with black spots, perch scale, shad,

yellow scale with black back, and a sharp white with black head. These are the only lures like this I have seen in the thousands of plastics I have handled. They may not be rare, but they are a first for me. I purchased them by private treaty and got a deal, but I would think they should sell for at least $20.00 each in their mint condition new in the tube. Further, a set of lures such as this normally will command a premium, maybe $200.00 for the set. Tubes are only marked Wright & McGill Dixie-Dandy Trade Mark ¼ oz. Spinning Lure, no dates, no model numbers, no colors.

Wright & McGill also had a great two-piece cardboard box design. When one opened the box, the lure was displayed at about a 45 degree angle, great for collection display (see Volume 1's chapter on Doll Top Secrets). Some of the boxes are shown with new lures inside; these are worth $20.00 to $30.00 if the lure is mint in the box. The little red/white Miracle Minnow is Model 601-D, 1¹¹⁄₁₆" long, Miracle Minnow printed on diving lip. A Miracle Minnow without the box but in excellent shape sold for nearly $20.00 on eBay in May of 2001.

Wright & McGill lures out of the box are worth on the average $12.00 in excellent condition. There are some worth more, and the value of these lures is indeed on the increase as more people discover what they are as most were not marked. They have a nice appearance, and one can build a solid color collection of a number of the varieties. They also look great with Eagle Claw rods and reels or a Fre-Line spinning reel.

Dixie-Dandy Lures new in tubes. $20.00 – 30.00 each.

A second box type and its contents, surface hardware Bug-A-Boo. $20.00 – 30.00 boxed, $18.00 loose.

Miracle Minnows in their display type boxes. The Trout sold for nearly $50.00 on eBay in early 2002. The other lure should bring $30.00 – 50.00.

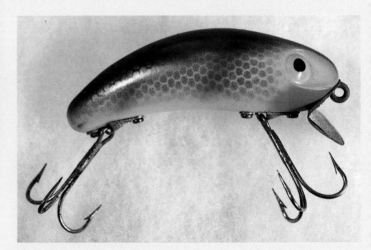

A nice color of W & M lure, 3" long, surface hardware, eyes are carved into molding process. $15.00 – 18.00 loose.

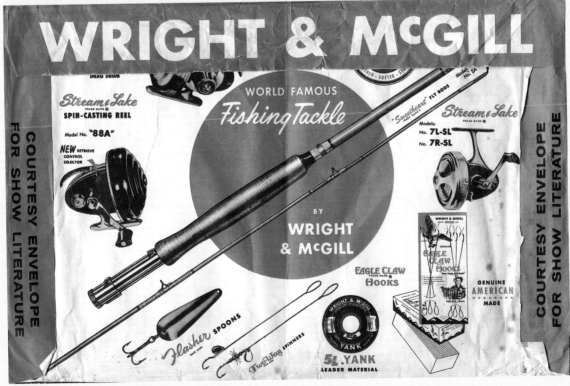

Front and back of dealer give-away packet from tackle shows. $25.00.

Zebco Fishing Lures

Zebco Division of Brunswick Corporation, P.O. Box 275, Knoxville, Tennessee 37901. These are covered earlier in Chapter 9 of Volume 1 but are mentioned again since Zebco also made Poe's and other lures. Shown is another shot of the Doll dealer dozen pack and close-ups of the box types. For as successful as Zebco (Zero Hour Bomb Company) has been in marketing reels and reel/rod combinations, an examination of their catalogs over the years informs one that they seldom produced and marketed lures. Thus, any of the older Zebco lures have potential for collectibility.

Dolls in a dealer carton and box shots. Dealer dozen, $600.00+.

Zimmy Plastic Plug

Manufactured by Tradewinds, Inc., P.O. Box 1191, Tacoma, Wash. Models S3-3 (3") and S4-3 (4") Zimmy Plugs shown new in their boxes were a recent discovery for me. I ran across about 40 of these in a trade from the Pacific Northwest, and they have turned out to be a very hot collectible, selling for $18.00 – 25.00 and up, new in the box, on eBay in 2001. This is a pre-zip code box, very colorful with a most stunning translucent reddish orange (color is called Red Glow) salmon plug inside. These were very well made baits and must date from the late 1950s, early 1960s. Again, this is one of the many smaller salmon plug companies we need to learn more about.

Zimmy Plugs new in boxes, $25.00+ in two-piece box.

Tiny But Growing In Value

This chapter concentrates on fly rod baits of the modern era in which collectors have some interest. This is one area that is often ignored in value guides, and it is hoped that some of the baits will be identified for the first time on their cards or in their packages. In Chapter 4 I refer to the use of sporting goods catalogs as a source of information about tackle. As it turns out, this is often our only source of information about the smaller, and sometimes even the large, fly rod bait companies. For instance, Robey Flies of Newaygo, Michigan, was located only a few miles from the lake that I grew up on located in north Kent County, Michigan. However, in all of my years hanging out in local tackle shops, I do not recall seeing one Robey catalog. These flies and fly rod baits are in wonderful packaging with fly graphics. I believe the history of the company dates post-war to about the mid-1960s. While scanning a jobber catalog from 1950 preparing to write this chapter, I recognized some of my "unknown" poppers as being made by Robey. Just imagine my delight!

Identification is the real challenge in fly rod bait collecting for sure. There are some books that are of great assistance, such as the brand new and most excellent guide by Mumas; however, we have so much to learn about this area of collecting that it will be years before many of these little critters are known with certainty.[12] I should say a word about fly rod baits versus flies. The flies tied by Carrie J. Frost and continued by Weber, Marathon, Worth and other major companies were initially intended for fly-fishing and were originally all aimed at trout species. Eventually, with the ideas of O. L. Weber and others, flies evolved in America to encompass flies for all species of fish, fresh and salt water alike. As the display cards by Weber demonstrated (Volume 1, Chapter 8), they were intended for use with spinners attached for baitcasting, well before spinning came to America as a fishing system.

However, there was another unique development going on in America regarding the fly rod, and later the spinning rod with a clear casting bubble, and that was the development of "miniature" versions of famous bass baits for fly and spinning rods. The classic fly rod baits were made primarily for use with fly rods and with spinners added for casting rods, as we did not have spinning rods and spinning available until the post-war era. There is some dispute in our collecting circles whether or not fly rod baits should include solely baits made as a model of the "big brothers and sisters" or if the category includes such items as the Callmac bug and other fly type lures made for species other than trout. In my opinion, I think we should include all fly rod type lures developed in America that deviate from the traditional salmon type flies of Scotland. In other words, we should include the larger bass bugs, tarpon flies, wooden fly rod baits, metal fly rod spoons, and all else made and developed for fly fishing in our native waters.

One can begin with the big names in lure production to examine this interesting area. South Bend catalogs of the 1930s had nice color displays of their bass fly rod baits, lures, and flies. The Callmac was a leader in the "bass bug" field and was often copied. South Bend also made fly rod size metal baits, the famous Trout-Oreno line, frogs, crabs, and many other items of interest. These were continued into the modern era. Heddon was also a leader in fly rod bait development, making miniature versions of River Runts, Punkinseeds, and a variety of poppers in their "spook material." These baits have gone through the roof in value because all collectors can spot the Heddon name, and they look so much like the bigger lures. Weber has already been discussed in detail; however, I need to remind the reader that a study of Weber catalogs from the early 1920s to the late 1930s is an excellent reminder of the evolution of fly rod baits. Weber's Dylite and cork fly rod baits are also very collectible. Pflueger made a wide array of fly rod baits in the early years of the modern era, Shakespeare also added a few, especially the Mack poppers, and Creek Chub Bait Company had one of the most complete lines of any of the big five companies in the arena of fly rod baits. Any of the above baits found on their cards or in a box will command a very high price.

Other companies of note include Burke for its addition of fly rod rubber baits in the 1950s, Glen L. Evans for its numerous contributions to fly rod poppers and other baits, Sam Peckinpaugh for his unique and famous Peck's lures (one of the hardest catalogs to find), and Wright & McGill. In addition to the baits themselves, a nice side collection is the addition of line dressing tins, solvent containers, and leaders on cards. There were also some nice fly tools made that would fit into this area of collecting, including knives, tying devices, creel baskets, staffs for wading rivers, stream guides — the list continues.

As to value, any bait not in the package or box if it cannot be identified is usually only traded for $5.00 at most shows. However, keep in mind that the seller may not know the bait but you might. Thus, I have purchased many big name baits by South Bend, Creek Chub, and Weber by recognition. When one finds a Creek Chub in its box, the value goes up 10 times. Of course, Heddon baits still bring even more money since we can all identify many of them. I would begin a collection of fly rod baits by collecting only items on cards, in boxes, or with identification of some sort. Once you get a feel for the differences, then expand your collection. I have been actively after fly rod baits for better than seven years and still cannot identify many in my permanent collection. Shown in this chapter are some baits new on cards, in boxes, and identified. Also shown are some nice displays of fly rod baits, some still unknown to me. One positive thing about collecting these diminutive baits is that they do not take up much room, and they display so very well. I am actually surprised that the values for fly rod baits have not become much higher, although, as I said earlier, they are on the way up as of this writing. One can indeed display a varied collection in two or three 9" x 12" glass covered cases.

In addition to this chapter, please see the Weber chapter in Volume 1 and this book's previous chapter for some fly rod examples. **Rather than assigning values for these baits, I have listed each item as common, scarce or rare.** The Pflueger Pippin is included in the following chapter on metals and quite a few Creek Chubs also appear earlier. Some of the Worth and Marathon items are common. Heddon fly rod plastics bring large dollars from some collectors while others have less interest. As we learn more about the rarity or commonality of all the baits, prices will reflect that status. Also, most of the following items were recently priced in the Mumas volume, sometimes low and sometimes high in my opinion. I think that we are just seeing the beginning of prices going up for excellent, in-the-box, and on-the-card fly rod items, and collectors should certainly try to find them in the field.

Weber's Lifelike Wigglakle Display Card, flies were sewn onto the card. Date unknown but probably an early piece.

Close-up of the beautiful flies at left.

THE JENNISON HARDWARE CO.

ARTIFICIAL BUGS
MARATHON POPPING MINNOW ASSORTMENT

Many prize bass have been taken with this new fly rod lure. It brings the bass from hidden depths with a rush.

Cork body, streamers and hackles are all securely tied and cemented to size No. 1 kinked shank turned down eye hollow point hooks.

Assortment consists of one dozen popping minnows in colors as follows: two each brown head, black hackle; brown streamers; pike head, black hackle, white streamers; pike head, black hackle, gray streamers; four each red-white head, white hackle and streamers, and one each pike head, black hackle, yellow streamers; black head, orange hackle, black streamers.

Per assortment
No. 527—One dozen popping minnows as enumerated above mounted on an 11x5½ in. easel back display card; wt. per assortment 6 oz. $5.40

One assortment in a box.

PAW PAW O-SO-LITE POPPING BUG ASSORTMENT

A bass bug style popper with feather wings and hackle tied on a floating cork body with cupped head.

Has a "stop and go" motion, giving that popping noise that will attract bass where nothing else will.

No. 1/0 Single Hook
Per assortment
No. 1/0—Consists of 6 popping bugs in assorted colors, mounted on a display card; wt. per assortment 5 oz. $2.40
One assortment in a box.

ARTIFICIAL BUGS
HEDDON POPPER-SPOOK

Bass and pan fish strike this little top-water fly rod lure.

Body with cupped front can be made to bubble or pop by a short twitch of rod tip. Has colored hackle at its rear. Hook molded into body and held fast. Indestructible transparent body.

1⅛ in. Body, No. 5 Single Hook
Per dozen
No. 940GR—Grey body and hackle.$7.20
No. 940WR—White body, red hackle 7.20
No. 940BW—Black body and hackle 7.20
No. 940BR—Brown body and hackle 7.20
No. 940Y—Yellow body and hackle. 7.20
No. 940DG—Green body and hackle. 7.20
Weight each 1/25 ounce.

One in a box, one dozen in a carton.

HEDDON POPPER-SPOOK ASSORTMENT

Assortment consists of twelve Popper-Spook minnows; two each of the following colors: gray body, gray hackle; white body, red hackle; black body, black hackle; brown body, brown hackle; yellow body, yellow hackle; green body, green hackle.

A new fly rod lure with transparent body and cupped front—can be made to bubble or pop by short twitch of rod tip. Hook molded into body and held fast. Cast easily and accurately.

Especially effective for bass and pan fish.

1⅛ in. Body, No. 5 Single Hook
Per assortment
No. 940CN—Wt. per assortment 4 oz. $7.20
One assortment in an attractive display carton.

ARTIFICIAL BUGS
HEDDON BASS-BUG-SPOOK

The last touch of lifelike appearance is given these bugs by the transparent body carefully decorated in natural designs. Very buoyant, and very serviceable as hook cannot pull out nor lure get water-logged.

2 in. Body, No. 1 Single Hook
Per dozen
No. 975BR—Brown body, wings and hackle $9.00
No. 975DG—Dark green body and wings and black hackle 9.00
No. 975GR—Grey body, wings and hackle 9.00
No. 975BW—Black body, black hackle 9.00
No. 975WR—White body and wings, red hackle 9.00
No. 975Y—All yellow 9.00
Weight each ⅛ ounce.
One in a box, one dozen in a carton.

HEDDON BASS-BUG-SPOOK ASSORTMENT

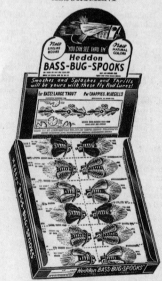

Assortment consists of twelve Bass-Bug-Spook lures; two each of the following colors: brown body, wings and hackle, dark green body and wings, black hackle; grey body, wings and hackle; black body, black hackle; white body and wings, red hackle; all yellow.

2 in. Body, No. 1 Single Hook
Per assortment
No. 975CN—Wt. per assortment 4 oz. $9.00
One assortment in an attractive display carton.

Catalog number 41, Jennison Hardware Company, 1941, page 45.

THE JENNISON HARDWARE CO.

ARTIFICIAL BUGS
ROBEY RED-HEAD POPPER ASSORTMENT

A popping bug that really pops with the minimum of rod movement. The broad head and deep-cupped front give the necessary water resistance, and the quick body taper assures hooking the fish. White cork body with red head.

No. 1 Humpshank Turned-Down Eye Hook

Per assortment

No. PRH—Consists of one dozen poppers, with assorted color feather tails; mounted on a scored card; wt. per assortment 4 oz. $3.60

One assortment in a box.

ROBEY KORK-O-BUG ASSORTMENT

A popular type bass bug, with durable cork head. It darts and swims with an erratic action very alluring to all game fish. Extremely light, weighing less than 1/20 oz. Picks up cleanly and cast with ease.

Each bug in a cellophane top box.

No. 1 Humpshank Turned-Down Eye Hook

Per assortment

No. J-1—Consists of one dozen bugs, two each of the colors enumerated below; mounted on a scored card; wt. per assortment 4 oz..$3.00

Colors

Head	Tail
White	White
Blue and gray	Gray
Black	Black
Green and yellow	Yellow
Brown and yellow	Brown
Red	Gray

One assortment in a box.

ROBEY MIDGET KORK-O-BUG ASSORTMENT

Same as above except smaller size for pan fish. A good floater and very durable.

No. 8 Humpshank Turned-Down Eye Hook

Per assortment

No. J-8—Consists of one dozen bugs, two each of the six finishes enumerated under No. J-1 above; mounted on a scored card; wt. per assortment 3 oz..........$2.40

One assortment in a box.

ARTIFICIAL BUGS
ROBEY HAIR WING MOTH ASSORTMENT

Sturdy moth shaped cork body, attractively finished in durable enamel. Both the wings and the tail are of hair securely imbedded in the body.

Each bug in an individual box.

No. 4 Humpshank Turned-Down Eye Hook

Per assortment

No. HL-4—Consists of one dozen bugs, two each of the six patterns enumerated below; wt. per assortment 9 oz. $6.00

Patterns

Body	Wing and tail
White and red	White
Black	Gray squirrel
Green and white	Yellow
Brown and yellow	Black and red
Tan and white	Black and yellow
Red	Brown squirrel

One assortment in a box.

ROBEY MIDGET FISH FIN ASSORTMENT

Wounded minnow type of cork bug in pan fish size. Glossy enameled cork head.

The live, crawly hair and feather tail imparts all the erratic action of a wounded minnow. A proven lure in both lake and stream.

No. 8 Humpshank Hollow Point Hook

Per assortment

No. K-8—Consists of one dozen bugs, two each of the six patterns enumerated below, mounted on a scored card; wt. per assortment 2 oz. $3.00

Patterns

Body	Tail
White	White and red
Blue and gray	Gray
Black	Black
Green and yellow	Yellow
Brown and yellow	Blue Dun
Tan and white	Gold

One assortment in a box.

ROBEY SPOTTY

Cork body, hair legs. Designed and finished for pan fish and trout.

No. 8 Humpshank Turned-Down Eye Hook

Per assortment

No. RS-8—Consists of one dozen bugs in assorted patterns; mounted on a scored card; wt. per assortment 3 oz. $1.80

One assortment in a box.

ARTIFICIAL BUGS
PAW PAW O-SO-LITE SURFACE BUG ASSORTMENT

A full floating cork body surface type bug with all the trimmings of feathers and hair to make it a real killer for all game fish. Has more erratic, lively action than the average.

No. 2 Single Hook

Per assortment

No. 2—Consists of 6 surface bugs in assorted patterns; mounted on a display card; wt. per assortment 5 oz. $2.40

One assortment in a box.

PAW PAW SILK WING HOPPER

The original silk feather fly rod lure. Its genuine oil-silk wing gives this bass bug a most natural action. Has a history of consistent success as a real killer.

No. 8 Turned Down Eye Hook

Per assortment

No. 550—Consists of one dozen lures in assorted colors; mounted on a display card; wt. per assortment 5 oz. $2.40

One assortment in a box.

Catalog number 41, Jennison Hardware Company, 1941, page 46.

THE JENNISON HARDWARE CO.

ARTIFICIAL BUGS
MARATHON CRAPPIE MINNOW ASSORTMENT

A snappy little fly rod feather minnow designed especially for taking crappies, but also very effective for trout, bass and other game fish. May be used just at it is or with a small spinner. This under surface lure has both fin and tail action, sinks readily, but casts easily with a trout weight fly rod.

Dressed on size 8 long shank Sproat hooks only with selected hackle streamer tail, tinsel ribbed wool body and enameled head. Fin or gill hackles are set at an angle to induce a pronounced lifelike action when the lure is retrieved with a "start-stop" motion of the rod tip.

Per assortment
No. 3577—Consists of one dozen crappie minnows, two each of the patterns enumerated below, mounted on a 11x5½ in. easel back display card; wt. per assortment 7 oz. $3.00

Patterns	Head	Hackle	Body	Tail
Silver Skipper	Red	White	White	White
Yellow Shiner	Red	Yellow	Yellow	Yellow
Blue Chub	Red	Gray	Gray	Gray
Red Skipper	White	White	Red	White
Yellow Tail	White	Yellow	Red	Yellow
Red Muddler	White	Gray	Red	Gray

One assortment in a box.

MARATHON MOSQUITO HOUN ASSORTMENT

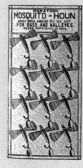

A deadly under surface fly rod lure that has every thing required to take bass and walleyes. A natural lake and river fly. Has both wing and tail action when retrieved or trolled with a jerky motion of the rod tip. Casts easily and accurately, hooks practically all strikes and is equally effective when used with or without the No. 0 nickel plated tail spinner with which it is equipped.

Well made, with genuine deer tail hair wings and a neat enameled composition body. Size 2 long shank Sproat hook.

Per assortment
No. 241—Consists of one dozen Mosquito Houn lures, three each of the patterns enumerated below mounted on a 11x5½ in. easel back display card; wt. per assortment 7 oz. $4.80

Patterns

Wing	Body	Back
Brown	Natural Green	Black
White	Natural Green	Black
Yellow	Natural Green	Black
Black	Natural Green	Black

One assortment in a box.

ARTIFICIAL BUGS
ED'S SURE HOOKER ASSORTMENT

Ed's Corker Minnow has a cork body enameled in colors, bucktail whiskers, feather tail and a double bend extra long No. 4 hook that prevents short strikes and fouling in weeds.

Ed's Sure Hooker Hopper is a popping bug with enameled cork body, heavily hackled, feather streamers and size No. 4 extra long shank inverted hook.

Ed's Corky Frog has a permanently floating cork body, heavily lacquered in green with black and brown spots. Legs are made of green and white feathers, imparting a lifelike action in the water. No. 4 double bend, extra long, inverted hook.

No. 4 Hook
Per assortment
Ed's Sure Hooker—Consists of six fly rod lures, two each of the three described above, assorted patterns, mounted on a display card; wt. per assortment 3 oz. $3.00

One assortment in a box.

ED'S IMPROVED GRASSHOPPER ASSORTMENT

Irresistible during grasshopper season. Its waterproof oiled silk wings form an airpocket which keeps it floating at all times. Unexcelled for trout and blue gills.

No. 10 Hook
Per assortment
Ed's Improved Grasshopper—Consists of one dozen lures mounted on a display card; wt. per assortment 3 oz. $3.00

ARTIFICIAL BUGS
ROBEY FUZZBUG ASSORTMENT

Tail of natural buck; body of closely tied hackle; wings of bucktail cocked upright to assure the lure lighting always in the right position.

No. 4 Hollow Point Turned Down Eye Hook
Per assortment
No. N-4—Consists of one dozen Fuzzbugs, two each of the patterns enumerated below; mounted on a scored card; wt. per assortment 4 oz. $3.00

Patterns

Wing	Body
White	Gray
Natural	Blue Dun
Natural	Badger
White	Claret
Yellow	Gray
Red	White

FLY ROD MOUSE
ROBEY ASSORTMENT

A perfect floating lure of buoyant hair. Casts and retrieves with ease and is a sure killer. Practically indestructible. Natural gray color.

Hollow Point Turned Down Eye Hook
Per assortment
No. G—Consists of one dozen lures, four each of No. 2, No. 6 and No. 10 hooks, mounted on a scored card; wt. per assortment 3 oz. ...$3.80

One assortment in a box.

ARTIFICIAL FLIES
ROBEY PARACHUTE DRY FLIES

Due to the unique method of construction, the Parachute fly alights on the water as softly as the natural insect. Only the hook point pierces the water; the body, hackle and wings remain on the surface. Dressed of the finest materials throughout.

Extra Fine Turned Down Eye Hook
Per dozen
No. 505—Size Nos. 10 and 12 hooks; wt. per dozen 1 oz. $2.40

Patterns

Adams	Lady Beaverkill
Black Ant	Professor
Cahill	Royal Coachman
Cowdung	Stone
Evening Dun	White Miller
Grizzly King	

One dozen in a box.

Note—In ordering flies, please specify size hook wanted.

Catalog number 41, Jennison Hardware Company, 1941, page 47.

THE JENNISON HARDWARE CO.

ARTIFICIAL FLIES
ROBEY GAUGED SPENTWING DRY FLY

Built with best quality stiff rooster neck hackle, gauged to size of hook. All other materials are equally high grade. Precision tied; properly balanced to float right.

Hollow Point Bronzed Hook

Per dozen
No. 100—Size, Nos. 16, 14, 10 and 8 hooks; wt. per dozen 1 oz......$2.00

Patterns

Adams	King of Waters
Female Adams	Lady Beaverkill
Beaverkill	McGinty
Black Ant	Montreal
Black Gnat	Mosquito
Black Prince	Parmachene Belle
Blue Bottle	Professor
Brown Mosquito	Queen of Waters
Cahill	Royal Coachman
Coachman	Seth Green
Cowdung	Silver Doctor
Dusty Miller	Max Sandy
Granger Quill	Whirling Dun
Gray Hackle	White Miller
Grizzly King	Wickhams Fowey
Hares Ear	Yellow Sally
Hopper Green	

One dozen in a box.

ROBEY LITTLE RIVER SPENTWING DRY FLY

Imitate drakes, duns, or other characteristic American trout stream insects which lie on the surface with gauze-like wings spread prone on the water.

Tied by experts, with good grade materials throughout. Unusually durable.

Turned-Down Eye Hook

Per dozen
No. 85—Size No. 10 hook; wt. per dozen 1 oz. $1.20

Patterns

Adams	Grizzly King
Adams Eggsack	Lady Beaverkill
Beaverkill	McGinty
Black Gnat	Mosquito
Brown Bivisible	Pale Evening Dun
Brown Hackle	Professor
Cahill	Queen of Waters
Coachman	Reuben Wood
Cowdung	Royal Coachman
Ginger Twill	Stone
Gray Bivisible	White Miller
Gray Hackle	Woodruff

One dozen in a box.

Note

In addition to the popular patterns listed on these pages, we can furnish all flies shown, in any standard pattern. Painstaking care is taken to tie all patterns accurately.

ARTIFICIAL FLIES
ROBEY LITTLE RIVER SPENTWING DRY FLY ASSORTMENT

Size No. 10 Turned-Down Eye Hook

Per assortment
No. 85-A—Consists of 12 dozen flies, ½ dozen each of the 24 patterns enumerated under No. 85; wt. per assortment 8 oz. $14.40

One assortment in a partitioned window top display box.

ROBEY DRY HAIR FLY

Natural untrimmed hair wings. For use either dry or wet and a good all season fly.

Extra Long, Hollow Point, Turned-Down Eye Hook

Per dozen
No. 215—Size Nos. 10, 6 and 8 hooks; wt. per dozen 1 oz............$2.00

Patterns

Adams	Gray Squirrel
Black Prince	King of Waters
Brown Squirrel	McGinty
Brown Squirrel Special	Professor
Coachman	Royal Coachman
Gray Drake	Silver Trude

One dozen in a box.

ROBEY DRY HAIR FLY ASSORTMENT

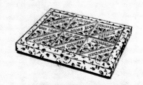

Size No. 10 Extra Long, Hollow Point, Turned-Down Eye Hook

Per assortment
No. 215-A—Consists of 6 dozen flies, ½ dozen each of the 12 patterns enumerated under No. 215; wt. per assortment 5 oz..$12.00

One assortment in a partitioned window top display box.

Note—In ordering flies, please specify size hook wanted.

ARTIFICIAL FLIES
ROBEY HACKLE DRY FLY ASSORTMENT

Wingless dry flies with soft chenille or worsted bodies. Ample hackle to float well. In twelve attractive patterns for trout or pan fish.

Size No. 10 Turned-Down Eye Hook

Per assortment
No. 50-A—Consists of 12 dozen flies, 1 dozen each of the 12 patterns enumerated below; wt. per assortment 8 oz.........$10.00

Patterns

Adams	McGinty
Black Gnat	Parmach. Belle
Brown Hackle	Professor
Cowdung	Royal Coachman
Gray Hackle, Yellow	White Miller
Grizzly King	Yellow Sally

One assortment in a partitioned window top display box.

ROBEY WET FLY ASSORTMENT

Closed matched wing wet flies with wool bodies. Dressed by the most skillful tiers with fine grade materials. In 12 attractive patterns.

Size No. 10 Turned-Down Eye Hook

Per assortment
No. 45-A—Consists of 12 dozen wet flies, 1 dozen each of the 12 patterns enumerated below; wt. per assortment 8 oz. $9.00

Patterns

Beaverkill	Grizzly King
Black Gnat	Partridge and Orange
Brown Hackle	Red Ibis
Cahill	Royal Coachman
Cowdung	White Miller
Gray Hackle, Yellow	Yellow Sally

One assortment in a partitioned window top display box.

Catalog number 41, Jennison Hardware Company, 1941, page 48.

THE JENNISON HARDWARE CO.

ARTIFICIAL FLIES

ROBEY AU SABLE STREAMER FLY ASSORTMENT

No. 240

Very long and slender wet flies. Extremely effective, imitating the action of a small minnow in the water. For lake or stream fishing.

Extra long hook prevents short strikes.

Feather Wing

Per assortment

No. 240—Consists of one dozen assorted patterns, all sizes No. 8 hollow joint turned down eye hook; mounted on an attractive display card; wt. per assortment 3 oz. $2.40

No. 245

Hair Wing

Per assortment

No. 245—Consists of one dozen assorted patterns, all sizes No. 8 hollow point turned down eye hook; mounted on an attractive display card; wt. per assortment 3 oz. $1.80

One assortment in a box.

PAW PAW O-SO-LITE STREAMER FLY ASSORTMENT

A popular assortment of long, slender wet streamer flies tied of best materials in a wide variety of color patterns. Highly recommended for any water where large trout are found.

Extra long hook prevents short strike.

Size No. 8 Turned Down Eye Hook

Per assortment

No. 451—Consists of one dozen flies, assorted patterns, mounted on an attractive display card; wt. per assortment 3 oz. $2.40

One assortment in a box.

ARTIFICIAL FLIES

ED'S MICKEY FINN STREAMER FLY

A very popular streamer consisting of a special combination of red and yellow hair with silver tinsel body.

Long Shank Turned Down Eye Hook

Per dozen

Mickey Finn—Size Nos. 8 and 6 hooks; wt. per dozen 6 oz.....$3.00

One-half dozen on a card.

ED'S BUCKHAIR STREAMER FLY ASSORTMENT

Made of good materials carefully dressed on long shank hooks. Can be used wet or dry and are very popular for trout or bass fishing.

Long Shank Turned Down Eye Hook

Per assortment

Ed's Buckhair Streamer—Consists of one dozen flies, Size Nos. 8 and 10 hooks, six assorted patterns; mounted on a display card; wt. per assortment 4 oz...$1.80

One assortment in a box.

ED'S BASS SPINNER FLY ASSORTMENT

Winged and hackle flies for use with spinners and trolling spoons.

Size No. 1/0 Ringed Eye Hook

Per assortment

Ed's Bass Spinner Fly—Consists of one-half dozen flies assorted patterns, mounted on a display card; wt. per assortment 3 oz...$0.90

One assortment in a box.

ARTIFICIAL FLIES

ROBEY WINNERS EYED HACKLE FLY ASSORTMENT

Plump bodies of genuine silk chenille; amply hackled. Fly can be used alone or in combination with a spinner.

Five assorted patterns put up in a transparent envelope.

Size No. 10 Ringed Eye Hook

Per assortment

No. 47—Consists of 5 dozen flies, one dozen envelopes of 5 assorted patterns each mounted on a display card; wt. per assortment 5 oz. $3.00

One assortment in a box.

ROBEY WINNERS SNELLED FLY ASSORTMENT

Wool body flies on 10 lb. test snells. Five assorted patterns put up in a cellophane envelope.

Size No. 10 Hook

Per assortment

No. A—Consists of 7½ dozen flies, 18 envelopes of 5 assorted patterns each; mounted on a display card; wt. per assortment 6 oz. $4.50

One assortment in a box.

Catalog number 41, Jennison Hardware Company, 1941, page 49.

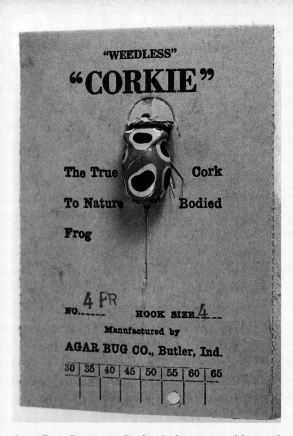

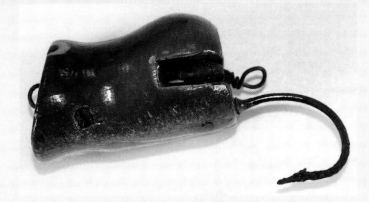

Frog Leg Kicker, **Halik,** rare.

Agar Bug Company, Butler, Indiana. An older card with an example of Corkie the Weedless frog, No FR, size 4. I do not know the significance of the 55 with a hole punched out, year or lot number, scarce.

Popping Bug, **Peckinpaugh,** scarce.

Trout-Oreno types, **A&I, H-I** or **Shur-Strike,** common.

Oreno Bass Bug, **South Bend,** scarce.

Another Trout-Oreno type, common.

Radiant Color Frog, maker unknown (found in U.P. Michigan), 2½" long, Dylite body, rubber legs, plastic glass type eyes, rare.

Paw Paw Floating Minnow, scarce.

Faulconer Co. Retriever?

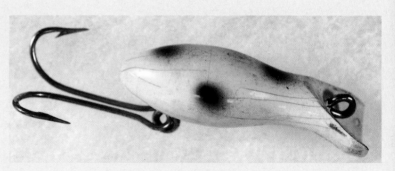

Unknown, same as Plate No. 1089 in Mumas' book, scarce or rare.

Amber plastic Devon type, unknown maker, common.

South Bend fly rod Flip-It, common lure, new in tube, scarce.

Falls Baits, Chippewa Falls, Wisconsin. These common fly rod baits, Rocky Sr. and Rocky Jr., above left and right, are gaining value as collectors discover their variety of size and color. Rocky Sr. is 1½" long. Also shown, below left, is a lure that could be considered fly rod or ultra light, but it is both my favorite lure and my favorite 135-pound white Labrador Retriever, Li'L Arty by Rockland Tackle Co., Inc., Color A, new in the box. I paid $45.00 for it on eBay three years ago. The other one shown, below right, may be an original or one made after Falls took it over. These are 1⅜" long wooden lures with a double spoon lip held on by two flat blade screws. the froglike legs are held on by one flat blade screw, the eyes are painted, and the line tie is a simple eye screw into the lip in front of the wobble plane. They are both scarce but actually Ultra Light lures, not fly rod lures.

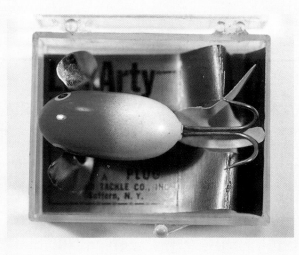

 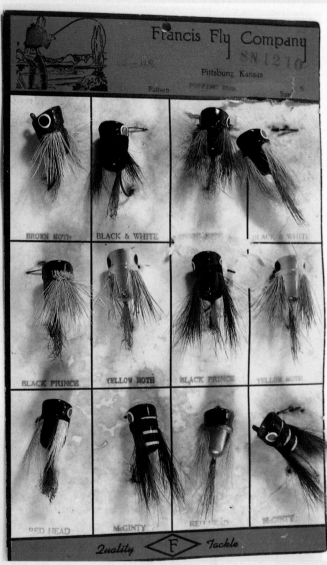

Francis Fly Company, Pittsburg, Kansas. Two new-on-card displays of some of their flies and poppers. The poppers shown at left are fairly common, they sold a lot of fly rod baits on the plains, especially. Display cards are rare. The poppers are SN 1210. The flies are shown at right and are SN 6010. The display cards with lures should be valued at $75.00 – 125.00 each.

A group shot showing clockwise from left: 1½" long Tin Liz by **Arbogast,** common; a very rare Colorado Moth, ¾" body size; a common **Marathon** Jack's Bass Houn, an unknown and common beetle (Millsite, Lur-All, Weber, etc.) and another one I am uncertain of (maybe a Cool Ripple), ¾" long.

Top row from left: **Weber** Pop-N-Wigl, semi-scarce; two **A&I, H-I** or **Shur-Strike** Trout-Oreno types, common; a rare **Halik** Frog Leg Kicker in fly rod size, legs worn off; another common Trout-Oreno type; very common Flatfish. Middle row from left: Unknown wobbler (**Shur-Luk** Shiner?); **Paul Bunyan** Fly Rod Transparent Dodger, semi-common; two **Paul Bunyan** Dinkies, semi-common (wood); two unknowns. The certain ones in the bottom row include the Jitterbug, semi-scarce, a semi-scarce small spinner, an **Eppinger** Trout-Eat-Us type lure, semi-rare. The poppers are likely common **Marathon** examples.

Three fly rod mouse baits, the middle one is a 1½" long Dylite type, but not a Weber known pattern. It has little tiny bead eyes and its ears are tufts of hair, tail is cloth. The one on the right could be a **Shoff's** or **Paw Paw.** It has leather ears, a leather tail, bead eyes, and is 1¾" long. The other one is not known to me but both Shoff's and Robey made striped ones. This one is 1¼" long, has hair ears and a thread tail. Scarcity unknown without a definite identification.

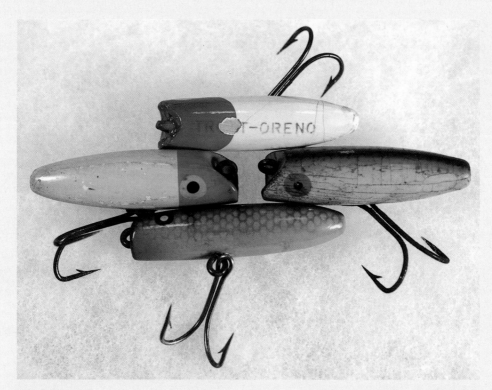

South Bend Trout-Oreno and some copies, rainbow is likely South Bend's own Best-O-Luck brand. Most colors are common.

Two unknown plastic fly rod baits and a Hula Popper, fairly common Hula, and others unknown.

A **Johnson** Sprite and a **South Bend** Trix-Oreno on cards, semi-common on cards, very common off cards.

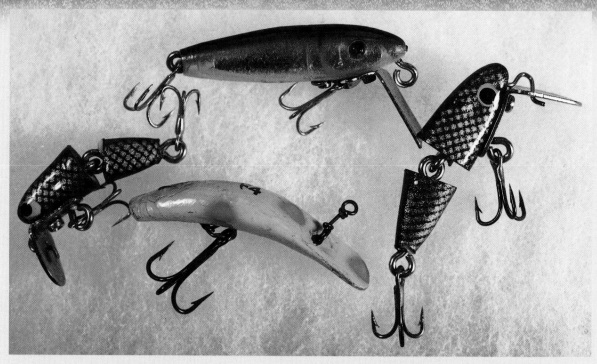

A very common fly rod Flatfish, a copy of a Mirrolure, and two copies of **Falls Minnows,** all common.

A small **Heddon** Wilderdilg, ½", in top left; a **Pflueger** Pilot Fly at top right; a **Pflueger** Pearl 1⅛" wobbler at bottom left; a **Pflueger** Fly Rod Wizard, 1½", in green crackleback at bottom right. All scarce, Wizard is scarce to rare.

Heddon, Widget from the early 1950s, semi-scarce.

Heddon, Wee Tads from 1982 – 1983. Very rare short production lure.

Heddon, Two Pop Eye Frogs and a Green Shore Wilderdilg Spook. All the Heddons are semi-scarce to rare with high demand.

Heddon, Wilderdilg, semi-scarce to rare with high demand.

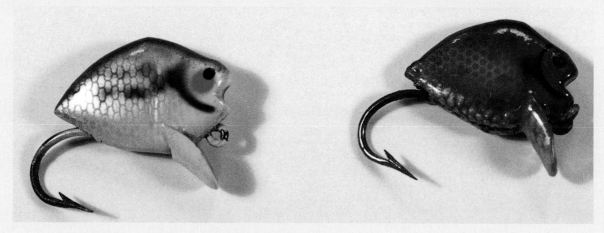

Heddon, two Punkie Spooks. A very high demand Heddon lure starting at $100.00.

Heddon, Bass Bug Spook, rare.

Heddon, River Runtie, marked Heddon. Very rare and in high demand.

Helin, F6 Wooden Fly Rod Flatfish, double hooks, common.

J&S Mfg. Co., Fresno, Calif. An example of a Jeff's Originals Cricket, new in very old box. The red in the box was a glue that held in the lure, very rare.

Loyd Peters' Fly Shop, 1738 West Sixth Street, Port Angeles, Washington, no zip code. The Macdonald's Secret Weapon giant fly for flasher or dodger new on the card, a great example of a localized lure from the 1960s or before. The package says, "tied to the specifications of Hector Macdonald of Macdonald's Boat House for use in the Famous salmon fishing grounds off Ediz Hook, Port Angeles, Washington by Loyd Peters' Fly Shop." Semi-scarce on card.

Marathon, another example of a Jack's Bass Houn, common.

Mermaid, made by **Stream-Eze, Inc.,** another example of a collectible Mermaid bait, with crown, very scarce, 1¾" long. Shown next to a 1¼" long (body size) **Peckinpaugh's** Parker's Feather Minnow for comparison of size, semi-scarce.

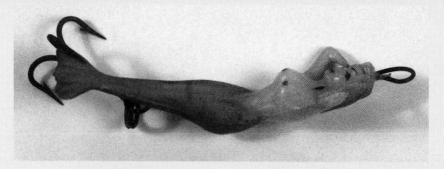

Mermaid, another very scarce fly rod **Mermaid** lure.

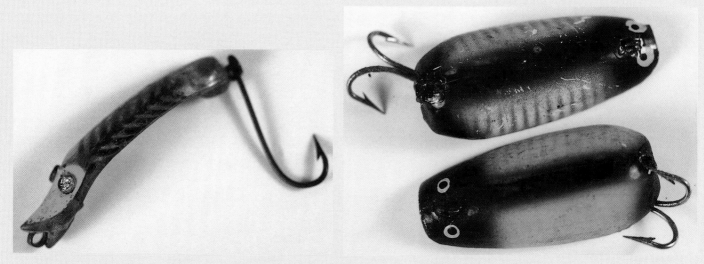

Paul Bunyan: Close-ups of a fly rod Dodger and two Dinkies, semi-common.

Phillips, a scarce Phillips & Phillips, Alexandria, Penna. two-piece cardboard box and its contents, new in box. The pattern is a Crippled Grey, Size SB, an Invincible Feather Minnow. A rare piece new in the box.

Schoenfeld-Gutter Co., also known as Silver Creek, a 1¾" Sea Gull in nice blue and white, rare and in high demand.

Shur-Luk Mfg. Corp., new on card Fly Rod Froggie, semi-common lure, scarce on card. Model 700, ¹/₂₃ oz., 1", painted eyes.

Shoff's Bass Flies, new in two-piece cardboard box with ripped insert, a Shoff's Wagtail Bass Fly in yellow, No. 298, rare in box, semi-scarce out of box.

Trylon, an example of the Japanese fly invasion from the 1960s. A nice wooden presentation box with the flies all nicely labeled. Very common flies, scarce presentation box in new condition.

Weezel Bait Co., three fly rod Weezels new in plastic box, common lures, less common in box.

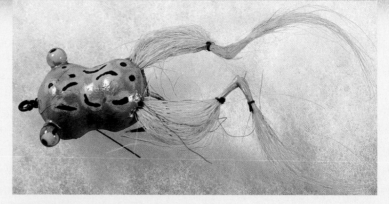

W. H. Brady Co., Eau Claire, Wisconsin. The Fish Dinner frog shown is a rare fly rod bait from the 1930s and early 1940s, a transitional bait for our book. But this exceptional bait is outstanding in its appearance. Very rare and in high demand.

Worth Tackle Co., some poppers in a box and fly rod baits on cards. Poppers and flies are common on cards, and in box semi-common.

Anything Special?

This chapter addresses the area of modern metal baits and seeks to identify anything of special collector interest in the field. Again, like fly rod baits, metal baits are usually relegated to the back seat or ignored altogether. It is hoped that this chapter can become a basis for more research into this field. Metal baits of the modern era have little value as a general rule; however, there is growing interest in the development of certain types of metal baits such as bass spinner baits[13] and some of the variations of spoons. Again, most of these baits have far more value if new in the package or new in the box. One thing to be aware of is that Heddon had some fairly short-run metal spoons, such as the Sculpin and Sounder, that should go up in value. Also, the Creek Chub Cohokie is worth finding. Pflueger continued to make metal baits into the modern era, and these make a nice display with new-on-the-card lures. Abu also made some really different metal baits, most of which did not show up in America. Some of the above baits might be worth keeping a few years.

Some of the more interesting metal baits are likely the ones shaped like fish, spoons with fins, etc. Many of these are of little cash value but still make nice display items and can even make an inter-esting collection by themselves. Atlantic Lures made a complete line of inexpensive metal baits, many of which looked like fish. New on the card or in a box, any of these baits would be of interest.

If you are going to build a collection of modern metal baits, including spinner baits, a good beginning source for research would be the BassPro catalogs beginning with the first one in 1970. Many of the spinner baits were short-lived productions, available in limited numbers and regions which makes for great collector interest. As Mayer points out in his article[14], attempting to find the first ones from the early 1950s is already a real challenge. Also, getting these items new on their cards is often as tough as finding a 1930 Heddon new in the box. Most fishing enthusiasts just threw away the cards of bubble-wrapped items, so these will ultimately become very collectible if still in the box or packaging.

I have already incorporated some metal baits into earlier chapters when appropriate so this chapter will be brief. I would like to expand it; however, it will be in future volumes as we learn more about dating metal baits since 1940. The main lesson is that anything new on the card or in the box will be of greater value than a loose metal item. Also, it is normal that the big-name companies' metal products will always hold greater value over small company productions. As a coincidence discussed earlier, a hardware store owner next to my office showed me a little container of 1960s baits he had kept, mostly metal, and I have capped this chapter off with a review of his modern metal baits.

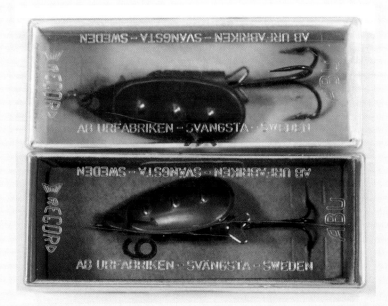

Abbey and Imbrie, New York, N.Y. A new-on-card Colorado Spinner, No. X2-0. I have sold similar A & I spinners on cards with trout graphics for $4.00 to $15.00 each, depending on crispness of card. This card will clean up some but is worth only about $5.00 as is.

Abu Spinners, two more Abu spinners as shown in Chapter 1. These are the ⅛ oz. and ¼" oz. sizes new in their boxes. Value is $5.00 – 10.00 each, new in a box.

Cop-E-Cat Spoons. These interesting Dardevle types were named Cop-E-Cat and made in Detroit. Shown is a Cop-E-Cat Model No. 7400, 2⅝" long, and a Cop-E-Cat, Jr., Model No. 7500, 3⅜" long, unknown value.

Heddon Spinner Baits. In addition to the Heddons shown in Volume 1, look for the Climax new on the diamond card as shown here, a Victor Comptometer/Recreation card containing a new ¼ oz. Model 471-WL Climax. These are already trading for $15.00 – 25.00 and are gaining interest with collectors of both Heddon and general bass spinners. Also shown here is the Heddon Buzz Bait. The card is merely marked James Heddon's Sons, likely 1983, Model 491-CHT, another short-lived late production Heddon metal bait that is becoming collectible. This one is marked that it was "Designed by Roy Marks, Owner Swamp Fox Lures."

A close-up of a **Pflueger** Pippin. This nice fly rod metal bait is gaining popularity and came in a variety of patterns, making it an ideal target for collecting. These trade for $10.00 – 20.00 loose.

Andy Reekers. This is a common example from a company that made many interesting metal baits, many shaped like fish. The older ones on cards are trading for $8.00 – 12.00 and the loose ones for about $3.00 – 6.00, depending on age and type. Some of the fish-shaped ones will likely become more collectible. The spoons usually have the name Andy Reekers and patent information of Pat'd U.S. Oct. 16-23, Can. Feb. 2-26.

C. Schilpp, Pat. Appld. For. This is my favorite modern metal bait, similar to an Al Foss, called a Crawler, body 1⅝" long. The Pat. Appld. For is on both the blade and the belly hook hanger device. Trade value $12.00 – 20.00.

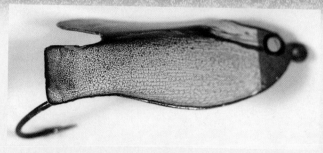

An interesting fish-shaped spoon/spinner bait, date and maker unknown.

Post-1988, but the type of short-lived bass spinner now attracting attention. This give-away bait dates from 1990.

Unknown, one of hundreds of little fish-shaped baits. This one has a scale pattern and what appears to be original coloration. The back is marked Japan in very small print.

Volcano Lure, an interesting example of a regional disaster leading to the creation of a fishing lure! This is The Mount St. Helens Volcano "Pennylure," A Hot New Item For Fish. It is merely a flattened one cent piece with a drilled hole and a treble hook. No trade data, likely scarce new in package, especially out of the Pacific Northwest region. Made by The Cimeter Group, 3447 Centennial Dr. NW, Salem, Oregon 97304. 1¼" long with impression of Mount St. Helens volcanic eruption on one side.

Hardware store goodies: Again, thanks to Larry Menard of L'Anse, Michigan, for allowing me to photograph his little container of lures he had kept in his local hardware store since the late 1960s. The contents are from top left, clockwise: Small Heddon Sonar, Model 431, 2", white eyes, price $1.15; Creek Chub Cohokie, yellow tail, 2¾", price $1.59; No. 2 Roy Self spoon, 2¾", silver back, orange/silver belly, no price; Garcia Lippy, rubber/plastic bait, 3¼", price $1.45; ½ oz. Roy Self "Long Wobbler" in yellow/silver, price 95¢; unknown metal wobble bait, 1¾" body, price 95¢; unmarked spinner with red bead, deteriorated rubber skirt, Marathon?, 1" body, price 95¢; balsa spinner with rubber skirt, made by Brevete SGDG, Pat. Pend., Made in France, all on spinner blade, 2¼" from spinner to hook, price 95¢; another unknown metal wobble bait, 1¾" body, price 95¢; Marathon Spoon Fly, 1", price 95¢. Most of these baits would trade for $3.00 – 5.00 with the Cohokie bringing $25.00+.

This chapter introduces the collector to such items as tackle boxes, fishing creels, bobbers and floats, worm boxes, minnow buckets, spears, fish decoys, fishing knives, and paper items related to fishing, especially catalogs. Again, the concentration is on items from the modern era that have already generated some interest due to either quality or rarity, and this gathering is far from exhaustive of the great possibilities in collecting.

Items made by the major lure manufacturing companies, such as Heddon, Pflueger, South Bend, Luhr Jensen, Creek Chub, Weber, Paw Paw, and Shakespeare, always have very high collector interest. Look for trade names and trademarks on the items. A nice little addition to any collection of lures or reels is a set of casting weights with the company names on them (see the Creek Chub and Shakespeare chapters in Volume 1 for examples). Sinker boxes also make a great addition, along with fly line dressing tins with company names.

As a general rule, most modern accessories are not worth as much as their antique counterparts, with a few exceptions. Modern UMCO tackle boxes are worth more than most "old" or antique tackle boxes. Many UMCO boxes sell for over one hundred dollars in excellent to mint condition, and for good reason. These boxes are sturdy, light, well designed and have a classic line to them. The Umcolite boxes are really amazingly light and store lures in a secure dust free environment. Beware in shipping these plastic boxes however; they will crack easily in the rough handling of our carriers. It is always advisable to double-box them for protection. An interesting collection would be as many UMCO boxes as possible with each one full of lures (my wife thinks this is already my goal)! This is a good storage system that also goes up in value.

Likely the most valuable of all items in the miscellaneous area are paper products and memorabilia. This includes advertising items such as store displays, counter displays, display cards, and catalogs. A catalog has great intrinsic and extrinsic value. A collection of catalogs from Heddon from 1940 to 1984 would cost one a king's ransom to purchase, however, one can certainly pick up one or two along the way without starving the children or the pets. A 1983 Heddon catalog recently sold on eBay for nearly $90.00, a sum unheard of a couple of years ago. The reason is that more and more collectors were seeking out references to plastic baits, even before the publication of this book.

Also, catalog reproductions are available through the NFLCC on CD-ROMs now and are a great way to learn. A goal for the collector could be to find the company catalog for the year that introduced his/her favorite lure and to add it to the collection. An often-overlooked area of catalogs is the "general distributorship" type catalog. These are normally more affordable than a single company catalog and often have vast amounts of information and sometimes the same exact color pages as appeared in the company catalog. A great example is the 1961 Supplement to the 1960 Sports catalog by Nu-Way Sporting Goods Co., Sioux City, Iowa.

This catalog supplement from 1961 shows the following: the Princess reel, discussed in Chapter 5, in full color; has a fold-out color page of Berkeley Tri-Lines; has a fold-out page in color of all Kautzky's Lazy Ike baits; has a color page of all Doll-Fly colors and lures from Thompson Fishing Tackle Company, Inc. (makers of the Doll Top Secret); has the full color chart reproduced from the actual Heddon Color Chart in the 1961 Heddon catalog; has a complete model and color listing, in color, of L&S Minnows; has one of the most complete Fred Arbogast listings in color I have ever seen that is dated October 1, 1960 and details all Arbogast lures in color; and, the list goes on to include Glen L. Evans lures in color, Mepps lures in color, jig flies from Mille Lacs in color, and a complete catalog of Burke's Flexo-Lures available in 1961, all shown in actual size and full color. I purchased this catalog on eBay for only a few dollars, and it is worth hundreds of dollars in terms of research and lure identification. In addition to all of the color photos, it has nearly all lures available in 1960 – 1961 shown in black and white with prices and model numbers.

The 1950 Nu-Way catalog is nearly as good and highlights another great year showing many new spinning size items and the introduction of many of the first plastic lures. Point Distributors from Stevens Point also put out a great jobber catalog that showed many new and interesting items each year and had catalog inserts as well. Gateway Distributors from Kansas also produced similar catalogs, as did Belmont Hardware. The list is really endless as to the additional sources of information about fishing lures and collectibles — simply enlarge your horizons and see what you can find.

A great reference for the 1970s is the American Wholesale Hardware Co., 1500 West Anaheim Street, Long Beach 1, California 1973 Fishing Tackle catalog, coming in at 228 pages chock full of information about fresh water and salt water lures, rods, reels, terminal tackle, accessories, and anything else to do with fishing. A great source to see which companies had merged, gone out of business, or introduced new products. It also has nearly complete model numbers and color charts for all major lures available in 1973, including Heddon, Arbogast, L&S, Speed Shads, Bombers, Water Dogs, Thin Fins, and the list goes on and on. This is the most complete source I have found on Plastic Research (Pradco) lures, makers of the famous Rebel line of plastic minnows. Last year I sold some of the small F25 series and P series plunkers for a pretty surprising price, bringing over $10.00 each without a package. The book also shows the Dura-Pak line for 1973 that included many "knock-off" baits that must have been made under license and marketed under the trade name "Golden Eagle" (see the Dura-Pak section in Chapter 1 for a list of these).

Additional sources of information include the pocket catalogs that came with many lures and reels, advertisements in trade journals and sporting magazines, and articles in magazines introducing new types of fishing and new innovations in lure and rod and reel design. Nearly every issue of sporting magazine from 1940 to date has a section of "new products" that is a wealth of information on "unknown lures." I have identified many lures by looking at advertisements that may have only appeared once or twice in a major publication. Remember, many of the plastic baits from the early 1950s were true "garage production" items and the maker could not afford to invest heavily in advertising. With this in mind, one may only see one or two advertisements for a new whiz-bang innovation in fishing lures. So, to find the names of some of the items, one must keep digging and look very carefully through publications in the 1950s and 1960s especially.

Once in a while a publisher made it easy for us, such as the great volume put out by *Popular Mechanics* magazine in May of 1953. The cover page says it all: "This great sport...SPIN FISHING, Page 81." This is an absolute treasure trove of information on the "new" type of fishing known as spin fishing and later known simply as spinning. The article entitled "They Call It Spin Fishing" written by the then-Secretary of the Sportsman's Club of America, outdoor writer Joe Godfrey, details rods, reels, and lures made specifically for this "new sport." It includes a color chart of most lures that were specifically designed for spinning and

most of the reels then on the market. The cost of this magazine purchased on eBay was less than $10.00, and its resource is worth thousands to compile all of the same data from catalogs from 1953!

In addition to the great article and accompanying photos in color and black and white, the makers of spinning equipment did not miss out on the opportunity to jam the May 1953 issue of *Popular Mechanics* with advertisements for their new and improved spinning reels, lures, and rods. This article, and others like it, also helps us document when spinning became "accepted" in our society as the "modern" fishing technique. By the mid-1950s spinning was here to stay, and large in-roads had been made into the classic bait casting markets that our lure collectors so dearly love. Fly fishing also went into its first major decline as the light tackle of spinning replaced the need of fly rods to get the same action in a trout stream or while fishing for panfish.

An excellent reference set for spin fishing from the 1950s is the three-volume set of articles on spinning reels found in the *Fisherman* magazine, March, April, and May volumes, 1954, Volume 5, Numbers 3, 4, and 5, published by the Fisherman Press, Inc., Oxford, Ohio. The back cover of the May volume shows the five Airex spinning reels then available. The issue is full of new spinning lures, reels, and rods. It also has an article evaluating spinning reels, the third in a series of three. But, the find of finds for spinning enthusiasts is the Trend Books, 5959 Hollywood Blvd., Los Angeles 28, Calif., edition titled: *Spin Fishing* written by Vlad Evanoff, Copyright 1957. It had the following articles: How to use spinning tackle; Improve your fishing; Take care of your equipment; How to catch more fish with light tackle; and, How to select and use the proper lures. The book details many rods, reels, and lures available to the public in the United States in late 1956 and early 1957. The cover most interestingly shows a Fin-Dingo, still with the Ropher markings, although the company had sold out to South Bend years earlier, and South Bend had quit offering the Fin-Dingo shortly before this time (see Volume 1). But, what a great little 125-page treatise on the art of spin fishing which was now well entrenched in the American fishing public's mind.

Maybe within the next generation of lure collectors we will see divisions among the modern collectors along the lines of 1940 – 1955; 1956 – 1965; 1966 – 1983; and post-1983. This is an even finer refinement than I suggest in the introduction. One could indeed argue that these time frames would make sense, given the historical developments of each era. So, let me be the first in print to suggest this idea as a way to further delineate modern fishing lure collectibles. The year 1940 for all the reasons already detailed in the introduction related to new materials coming onto the marketplace, the development of modern plastics, the impact of World War II on both materials and ideas, and is simply a good place to begin. The year 1955 is our first breaking period since spinning was well entrenched and most major companies had begun to make and/or distribute spinning tackle and baits by then. The next era of 1956 – 1965, the spinning era, is when most new tackle and lure developments were targeted for the new sport of spin fishing.

By 1966, some companies had started to re-introduce some of the classic tackle for baitcasting and fly-fishing. These were attempts by the major companies to expand the bait casting lure markets and met with only very limited success. Heddon reintroduced "vintage" wooden lures in the 1960s. Creek Chub did some final runs of wooden lures and brought back a number of classic lures in the late 1960s and early 1970s in hopes of revitalizing a dying market. Also, there was a national resurgence in the interest of fly-fishing that saw the birth of many new companies and products. However, these events did not succeed in turning the tide of the spin fishing fraternity. Maybe the era of 1966 – 1982 should be called the "vintage retro era."

By 1983, consolidation was well under way, and most of the big five were either being purchased or had already joined efforts to survive the onslaught. Companies that were once so strong and proud were now fighting for a share of the market due to new competition from abroad. The many changes in fishing techniques with the addition and expansion of the rubber worm, scented soft baits, the "jig 'n pig" craze of the bass fishing, and crankbaits of the walleye fishing tournaments only added fuel to the fires of destruction for classic tackle and lures. Add to this a total entrenchment of spinning and spincasting within the sport, especially for any of the newcomers to fishing, and there was little hope that the classic tackle would be able to survive. This era has given us some wonderful collecting possibilities again, especially in the area of color collecting with the new techniques of color and plastic blending and painting; however, it is too recent to identify collecting trends with any amount of accuracy. I am certain, however, that some of the smaller companies with limited productions during this period will again be of interest to future collectors. Storm Lures is an example of a very recent company with high collector interest. Also, the early Pradco lure varieties are already of fairly great value in some instances, especially the Heddon brand name.

What follows are just a few ideas and examples of ancillary items that a collector can find when looking for items related to fishing. As in previous sections, this is far from exhaustive of the possibilities but shows some rather nice additions to any collection.

Fish Decoys

The following are just a few of the many carvers that the world has yet to discover in great numbers yet who have been making great fish for years. I have included two fairly close-by Upper Peninsula carvers as examples, in addition to some well-known carvers.

Sherman Dewey, Manistique, Michigan. Dewey is in his early eighties and has been carving fish literally most of his life. He carves what are known as "functional fish" for use on some of the big ice spearing lakes in the Upper Peninsula. Most of his decoys have his initials stamped in the front fins. Dewey holds many personal spearing records and only makes a fish to swim, not to collect. However, over the past five years I have been selling his fish over eBay and at shows and have seen them continue to go up in popularity. Trading value is $15.00 – 25.00, unless very unusual in color or design. The one shown is a common pattern of his in the smaller 5" long size with painted eyes.

Walter Welch, Manistique, Michigan. Welch has been carving decoys for over 40 years and is currently in his mid-sixties. He is now retired, but when working at the Manistique paper company he carved fish for gifts for his friends and co-workers. Once he retired, just a few years ago, he started expanding his carving interests. He also made fish to use, and his early ones were all quite simple and effective in design. I have shown one of his in fire lacquer, a color he said is quite effective in drawing in large pike. It is 7¾" long, has carved gills, painted eyes, and is one of his earlier ones before he stamped his initials in the front fins. His current decoys are getting a little more advanced and some of his decoys have sold for $35.00 or more on eBay.

FJB, or **Floyd Joseph Bruce,** NW Lower Peninsula of Michigan. Bruce is a fairly well-known lure carver who also carved a few gorgeous duck decoys. Shown is a prototype of his "Pikie," 00 Proto of the ones he made, 25 production models only, this decoy is 6" long. Notice his use of "found objects" in his decoys. The value on this is negotiable due to rarity.

Randall Decoys, Minnesota, Mfd. By George L. Randall, Wilmar, Minn. An old factory decoy company that has very collectible fish. The two shown are both new from the two-piece cardboard boxes and loaned to me from a friend in L'Anse for this book. He purchased them in the Detroit area years ago on sale for 99¢ each and has never used them. Shown is a 7¾" sucker and a 6" perch, as marked on the box ends. The sucker has the original $1.75 price stamped in the weight bottom; the smaller $1.50 decoy does not have a price stamped on the weight. They should trade for $50.00 – 75.00 new in the box.

Bear Creek "Ice King" Spearing Decoy, a plastic decoy made in Kaleva, Michigan, and its cardboard box. These sell for $50.00 – 75.00 with regularity on eBay. Beware of the newer ones still being made and used. The only way to tell them for sure is in the box, but the newer ones are far lighter plastic and have "drain holes" in them. See the photo in Chapter 1 under Bear Creek for more examples.

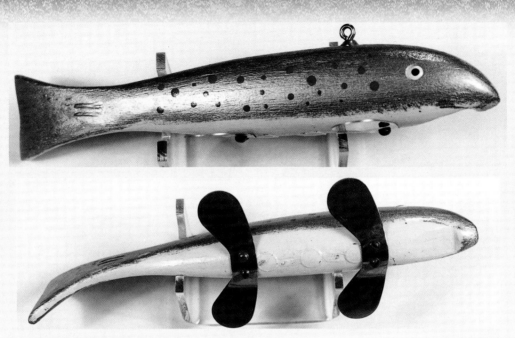

An older Bear Creek Ice King in wood, a sucker with gold paint and blue dots, valued at $75.00+.

Miscellaneous Items

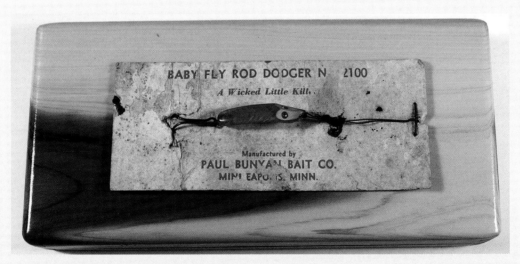

Fly rod box made in the late 1940s in Lapeer, Michigan, by Don Gapen. This was a beautiful cedar box with a magnetic clasp, and they also came with magnetic strips glued to the wood to hold the flies. The box is 7⅛" long by 3½" wide and was originally shipped in a cardboard sleeve wrapping. I have the remaining inventory of these and a number of different proto-types, some with fancy clasps. This was also distributed by Phillips Fly and Tackle Co. of Pennsylvania. They are valued at $15.00 – 30.00 each, depending on quality of wood and condition. The Artful Dodger is worth about $30.00 on its card. The Gapen family is still pro-ducing fishing items.

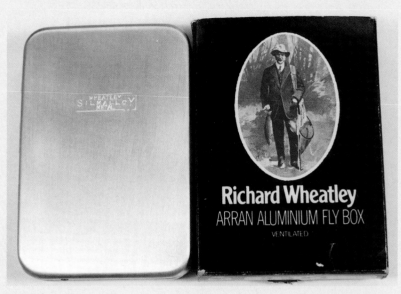

A nice Richard Wheatley Model 2303 fly, new in its box. Value: $20.00.

New-in-the-box Eagle Claw Hooks, Pattern 375, Size 1, ¼ gross. Value: $5.00.

Unique worm box, pull the plug and a worm comes out! Typical of our modern era. I paid $10.00 for it five years ago.

Barracuda Brand, by Florida Fishing Tackle Mfg. Co., Inc., St. Petersburg, Florida, U.S.A. Great graphics on this 108 lb. test stainless wire leader for deep sea fishing. No sales data.

Kalamazoo Tackle Company, Kalamazoo, Michigan. A very unusual find from a smaller tackle company that produced mainly reels. This is a stainless steel leader wire with a break strength of 140 – 146 lbs. Big enough for most of our Michigan bluegills! No sales data. This looks great displayed next to one of the Kalamazoo reels marketed in a black and silver tin can.

Ashaway line spools new in cardboard box. I sold over 20 of these on eBay in 2000 – 2001 for $15.00 – 22.00 each.

Gudebrod Bros. Silk Co., Inc. nice, wooden line spool, $10.00+.

Assortment of casting weights. Value: $5.00 – 10.00 each.

Examples of better old floats and bobbers. The value on these is one of the sleepers of modern collecting, many sell for upwards of $50.00, but many also sell for $5.00 at the most. It would take another chapter to do justice to just bobbers and floats. Look for the ones with brass end caps and rollers and also lure company bobbers. Also, there are some interesting electric bobbers made in the 1950s and 1960s that are great to find new in the package. The pencil type bobber is 8" long, and one end has a hole drilled for line; the tri-color model is 1¾" long; the green/white blended one with the pegs is 3" long and the other one with brass ends is 3¾"long.

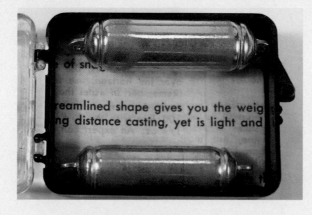

Keating's Floating Sinkers, one missing. This is a neat little set and sells for $10.00 – 20.00 complete. Made by Keating Manufacturing Corporation, 5060 Logan Street, Denver 16, Colorado. Circa March, 1957. The set included ⅛ oz., ⅙ oz., and ¼ oz. sizes.

An Abu-Garcia ⅜ oz., 2⅛" long casting weight ($5.00 – 15.00) and a unique find, the Pflueger grease tube still in the box ($10.00+).

A small assortment of sinker boxes, the key here is usually color. The blue Ideals are most common, red and yellow fairly rare, as are green and lavender. The little Best Ever is from H-I, and the Shurkatch is more unique than the Ideals. The Paul Bunyan was shown earlier. Shot boxes sell for $3.00 for common Ideals to over $100.00 for the rare round versions of early shot tins.

A Cortland 333 and an unusual Firestone square tin, Model No. 10-M-105. Both are examples of the variety to find in line dressing tins. These are colorful and fairly inexpensive additions to your lure collection, usually selling for $5.00 – 20.00, depending on rarity.

A common Orvis tin. $5.00 – 10.00.

A less common Fli-Line Dress tin. $10.00 – 20.00.

A nice J.C. Higgins leader holder, these also make a great addition to the collection. Colorful, never-ending variety, and usually $5.00 or less.

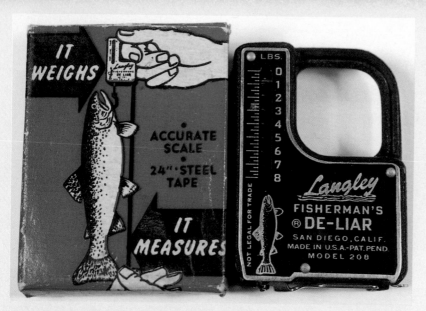

The common De-Liar in a less common small version in the introductory Pat. Pend. Box, Model 208. These sell for $5.00 up. This one should bring about $20.00 in its box, and if new, maybe more.

An Evinrude salesman's sample pin, 3" long, given upon entry to the convention, from a former Evinrude representative. Value: $85.00 – 125.00.

A reel oiler, likely an Orvis. Similar ones were sold by many companies, and some have the name stamped on the side, such as Shakespeare. Values: $10.00 – 30.00+.

Two examples of special "fish law" collectible rulers. They have the year and advertising for a bait shop on the other side. These sell for $5.00 – 25.00 depending on age and advertising on the back.

A gag fish call, a 4⅝" long plastic whistle. If the fish are not biting, just whistle. I have not tried it for fishing but it sounds like a regular whistle to me! Value: $5.00 – 10.00.

If your bait does not work, just coat it with this and it glows. A new in the 3¼" tube Lure-Glow, valued at $10.00 – 15.00. Made by Harrison Industries, Inc., Newark, N.J. A warning is on the tube that it is illegal in six states: Delaware, Idaho, Minnesota, Utah, Wyoming, and Iowa.

Depth-O-Plug in cellophane insert box, valued at $10.00 – 15.00, Mfg. by Bornemann Prod. Co., Aurora, Ill. Produced by Weber in the mid-1980s.

Depth-O-Plug in older cardboard box without cellophane. Value: $15.00 – 20.00.

A dealer display box carton for a most unusual fishing lure. The Fetch-It was a retriever lure used on a rod to retrieve your downed ducks or geese from a pond or lake when hunting without a dog. This new-in-the-box Fetch-It sold for $65.00 to $125.00 on eBay in 1999 when I broke up this carton. Dealer carton should bring $100.00+.

Magazines

In addition to the foregoing, make sure to keep an eye out for the useful magazines and catalogs available, in addition to the obvious company catalogs. I have not shown these publications since the descriptions speak for themselves.

Magazines are a great source of information, and as already outlined above related to spinning, magazines are a collectible in their own right. Age is the main factor coupled with condition. Figure if a magazine is 10 years old it is worth $5.00 in mint shape, add $5.00 more for every 10 year increment, double that once it is sixty or so years old.[15] Unique articles or artists will increase value. Musty smell, even on perfect issues, decreases value. Look for special issues on tackle, such as the *Field & Stream* January 1988 edition that has an article titled "New Tackle for '88." In this article, which is at the end of our collectible era for this book, we learn that Creek Chub/Dura Pak made one last attempt at marketing wooden pikies, darters, and injured minnows. These are the Sioux City, Iowa, plastic top boxes referred to in Volume 1. We also learn that 1988 saw the introduction of a baitcasting reel by Ryobi with a microprocessor computer chip to control the cast and an electronic hook sharpener called the Hook-Hone-R by Pointmatic Corp., a division of Burke Industries of Traverse City (see Flex Plugs on pages 39 – 48). Not many new lures and few companies are mentioned as most had gone by the wayside. I find it difficult to cozy up to the hook sharpener and computerized reel as fishing collectibles, but maybe a few generations from now these will be thought of as unusual items. The most amazing thing about this article is the demonstration of the lack of lure innovations and the concentration on electronic additions to fishing, such as sonar fish finders, reels, hook sharpeners and even seasickness preventers! Gone are the great new articles of hyperbole stating that a new lure design will catch every fish known to mankind, including perhaps Moby Dick. But this article is a great benchmark for ending our discussion of modern fishing collectibles.

Sports Liquidators

Sports Liquidators, P.O. Box 1338, Burbank, California 91505. This company produced a number of liquidation lure catalogs. I have shown the 10th Anniversary special volume as from 1970 which delineates for us the lures that were being liquidated that year. A close look at the cover shows dozens of spinning baits on their way out the door! Of course these were not all discontinued since the company purchased in volume for wholesale purchase through the mail. Many of the lures offered were actually knock-offs from Japan or copycat lures from Atlantic Lures and similar products. A source such as this is often the only place that one can ever document "off brand" names in rods, reels, and lures. It takes work to find things, but it is worth the search. A complete collection of these volumes from the companies beginning in 1960 would make a great addition to any research library. I have not seen these traded but would value it at $5.00 to $10.00 due to the recent publication date.

Front cover of Sports Liquidators 1970 close-out items.

SPORTSMEN-FISHERMEN

CLOSE-OUT
FAMOUS LURES

Again we acquired THOUSANDS of LURES!

The **VERY BEST!**...the **MOST POPULAR!**...the **FINEST QUALITY!**
All well known, Nationally advertised types.
...each Lure with a Good Reputation!

These Lures sell from **$1.25** to **$1.95** each.

Here's your chance to stock-up **NOW!**
...at our **BELOW** Wholesale Liquidator Prices.

SPECIAL ANY LURE ONLY .. 59¢ EACH.

#209 plus Letters.

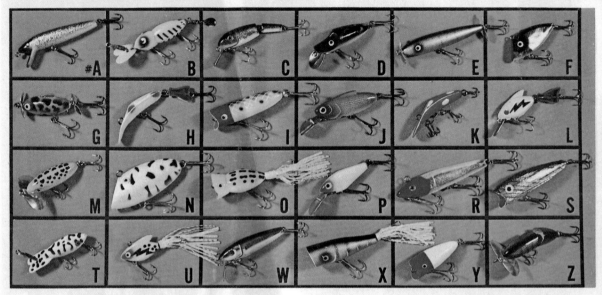

SOME MORE SPORTS LIQUIDATORS LURES ARRIVED!

THE MORE YOU BUY! ... the MORE YOU SAVE!

10TH ANNIVERSARY *Lure* SPECIAL

GET THAT ORDER IN NOW!

*Most orders shipped within 48 hours of receipt!

UNCONDITIONAL GUARANTEE!
We guarantee every item we sell!

Sports LIQUIDATORS
P.O. Box 1338, BURBANK, CALIFORNIA 91505

LOS ANGELES CALIF.

BULK RATE
U. S. POSTAGE
PAID
Permit No. 26851
Los Angeles, Calif.

Back cover of Sports Liquidators 1970 close-out items.

Universal Tackle & Sporting Goods Corporation

799 Broadway, New York 3, New York, wholesale distributors of fishing tackle catalog for Spring & Summer of 1950. It just doesn't get much better than this! This great volume of tackle listings shows numerous lures from 1950 in full color and has reproductions of catalog pages for many companies. Wood Manufacturing Co. of El Dorado, Arkansas, has its complete catalog of famous Wood's Lures reproduced here. This catalog also has the most complete listing of "new Paw Paw" plastic baits I have found to date. It shows all of the Paw Paw offerings for 1950 and has a complete color chart for their lures. The Francis Fly Company of Pittsburgh, Kansas, is also featured, and this is a rare reference to this company's baits, as shown under the fly rod section. Many of the smaller bait companies and two of the big five are well represented. I do note with interest, with no answer

as to why, Creek Chub, Heddon, and Pflueger were not represented at all. These companies are found in other references of the time period, but not here. It also shows many spinning items, rods, reels, and lures, all of which were new or very recent in the United States. It has a complete section on Action Glass Rods and details all the offerings. There is also a complete catalog page from the Langley Reel Company. This volume is worth hundreds of dollars of catalogs if purchased individually, and I found it in a deal of other items for virtually nothing. It just shows what those interested only in the very old items will sometimes give up for a good lure or a few dollars. I would value this as high as any company catalog from the 1940s, e.g., worth at least $100.00 if not much more.

Tackle Boxes

One example includes the Eagle Brand wooden tackle boxes shown on page 4248 of the American Wholesale Hardware Co. for 1973, a West Coast outfit. These tackle boxes were made in California primarily for salt-water fishing and are showing up on eBay with some regularity as antiques. They are not that old, but they are very nice and display well. They are easily recognized being made of plywood with a drop front. They came in Models 201, 301, and 601 in 1973, in a variety of sizes and configura-

tions. They usually sell for $75.00 to $125.00 each; new in 1973 they ranged from $18.25 to $26.20 at wholesale prices, so not a bad bargain in today's economy. In addition to this box, the collector should always be looking for tackle boxes by Kennedy, Heddon, Outing, Climax, early Old Pals, UMCO as already mentioned, some of the early BassPro Shop boxes, and anything else unusual.

Fishing Creels

Leather bound creels made in Hong Kong are quite popular with both the fishing collectible fraternity and home decorators, so the value is usually above $100.00 for a mint example. One can write forever on the subject of creels but be careful about

what you buy since many fakes are on the market, and too many unwary collectors have spent too much on a recently produced "antique creel."

Books

Again, an entire chapter wouldn't do a book survey justice, but be on the look-out for early books about fishing. These are collectible in and of themselves and can also assist one in learning about tackle types through history as in the Bates book mentioned earlier in this text. There are also early texts from the 1950s that discuss all of the tackle types and list many of the major and even the smaller companies' lures. Again, values vary from a few dollars to thousands of dollars for elusive first editions of rare works.

Pricing

The foregoing should give one an idea of the types of ancillary items available for the collector of fishing items. This is one area that is hard to determine values as people will often pay more than market value for something if it directly relates to their company of interest or specific collecting area. In other words, although a small Weber fly dressing tin may only be worth $5.00 – 10.00, a Weber collector will pay a little more to secure it for his or her collection. I believe the only test is to ask oneself if the price seems fair given the condition and rarity of any particular piece. The values I have assigned are suggestions based upon personal observations over the last few years and are certain to vary from region to region and as time passes. The best advice I can give is have fun looking for related areas and keep what you like.

Chapter 5: Modern Fishing Reels

This chapter highlights some of the more valuable reels of the modern era and discusses the evolution of spinning as an important addition to fishing. Collectors of reels have concentrated on the earlier models; however, there is growing interest and demand for high quality and/or rare models from the 1950s and 1960s. Especially of interest are reels made by Abu, Airex, Garcia, Heddon, Quick, and a few others. Also, early spinning reels are gaining popularity with collectors as we learn more about them. Spin fishing truly gained in popularity after World War II as veterans of the European theatre returned home with the equipment that was far more popular and readily available in England and Europe, spin fishing equipment. Early spinning reels had been around for decades and spinning, or spin fishing, had become popular in many European countries due to the modern spinning reels developed in England and France.[16]

The development and importation of spinning equipment led to new developments in manufacturing lures to meet the needs of the lighter tackle.[17] This development was also a "kiss of death" for much of the vintage tackle that collectors love. Baitcasting, with its ever-present threat of a "bird's nest backlash" on every cast, soon became part of American fishing history for many people as they picked up the simple to use spinning or spincasting gear being promoted by the manufacturers and the popular press. Of course, this also created collecting opportunities for the new tackle and the new smaller size lures that it spawned. Also, most of the newer lures were being created in plastic only as injection-molding techniques were well developed in the post-war economic boom in the United States. Baitcasting again made a come-back in the 1980s and 1990s as newer reels with sophisticated anti-backlash devices gained popularity. However, many of these newer baitcasting reels were now designed for lighter tackle as it too had gained in popularity.

The reels made by Abu have captured the hearts and pocketbooks of the collectors. This is not surprising as most of us in the Baby Boom generation spent hours staring at these reels in either catalogs or bait shops attempting to devise a plan to own one. They were out of the price range of most young American boys and girls. But now as collectors, we can purchase these items for admiration and use. Also, the Abu line of reels is being purchased for use and this keeps the prices up a bit higher than if only collectors were interested in the product. As others have discovered, I find it satisfying to go to my favorite large mouth lake and pick up a classic Heddon fiberglass Mark I rod in red color, matched to an Abu Ambassadeur 5000 in red color, and cast out a Zara spook in white with red head and wait for the action to begin. This is some of the fun of collecting, finding a use for the collectible tackle in addition to its display value.

Another area of interest in modern reels is to be on the look-out for reels with a special marketing angle such as the Pink "girls" reel made by Johnson in the early 1960s. I note that companies are again making color specific rod and reel sets for boys (blue) and for girls (pink) in the year 2001. Of course, the sexual revolution has broken down many barriers for females, and most now realize that it is their given right to participate in the sport of fishing and the hobby of collecting fishing items! I am surprised that companies still are making items with the stereotypical color schemes, but this may be a collecting "sleeper." At any rate, Johnson made the pink girls reel in Model 100AP in 1960, called the Johnson Princess, and even had a little heart with fleur de leis style engraving on it. This reel was obviously the ever-popular Criterion made by the thousands. However, another company was also marketing to girls through the use of color at the time (Lionel Trains, the famous "Girl's Train" in pink; engine/tender with pastel cars is a rare find.) and Johnson must have thought it a good idea. Few collectors even know the existence of the Johnson Princess, but if the Lionel Girl's Train is any indicator, and I think it is, this reel will truly go up in value over the years. One is shown below. Better yet, there is a matching "Princess Pink" tubular glass casting rod that for a time completed the set. I have never seen one, but they must be out there. Reels made specifically for kids would be a fun side collection, which could include reels, rods, and bobbers made with Disney characters, and tackle boxes made by Zebco.

A final area of interest in modern reels would be a reel associated with a personality or a specific event. Mitchell reels were leaders in the development of spinning tackle, and I am lucky enough to now

Pink Johnson's Reel. $25.00+ depending on condition.

own a like-new-in-the-box Mitchell 408 Ultra Light Spinning reel with an engraving of the name of the man to whom it was presented: Frank Borman, the astronaut who went to the moon! The story of the acquisition of the reel is as fascinating as the reel itself. Frank's son, Ed Borman, collects and restores duck decoys and had purchased a duck from me to be restored. In corresponding with him over the shipment of the duck, he asked me if I had any "better ducks" to trade, such as a Mason in need of some repairs. I said sure, what do you have to trade? He indicated he had a tackle box in the attic since the mid-1960s and that I could have it and all of its contents. So, sight unseen for both of us, we made a "handshake deal" over the Internet for an even trade.

Well, a day or two later Ed e-mailed me again and said there was a Mitchell reel in the box that he had forgotten about and that if I could figure it out, he would owe me a beer. I thought this was an odd e-mail, but then I started thinking about the name, Borman. Sure enough, the nice UMCO tackle box full of Creek Chub lures, Shakespeare Reels, and a presentation Mitchell with Frank Borman engraved on the reel arrived at my door a few days later. With excitement and interest I opened the box and immediately spotted the Mitchell reel. It looked absolutely common but when I removed the reel and looked at the side with the engraving, I thought, wow, Ed must be Frank Borman's son! I immediately e-mailed Ed and he confirmed his parentage and that the reel was one of many presentation items given to his father by famous companies after his missions for NASA. I offered him the reel back, but he insisted that a deal was a deal and that it was mine to keep. What a gentleman — we made a "blind trade," and he ended up parting with a very rare item that to me is priceless. Again, the power of the Internet is something else. One certainly never knows who is on the other end of an e-mail inquiry, so always expect the best and then be surprised when it is even better than the best!

A review of a Garcia Abu Ambassadeur 1962 Pocket Catalog shows the 5000 and 6000 and states that the reels are "Fit for a King." This 24-page pocket catalog has the address of 268 Fourth Avenue, New York 10, N.Y. for the Garcia Corporation and still refers to the fact that they carry rods, reels, lines, lures, kits, and accessories. Of course, the pocket catalog features the 5000 and 6000 Ambassadeur Baitcasting reels; the catalog in English was printed in Sweden. The value varies greatly depending on model variations, condition, rarity, boxed or not, etc., however, one can expect $50.00 to $150.00 for most of the better Abu Ambassadeur reels with the earlier Records fetching a premium price. I sold a 5500 Hi Speed in near mint condition to Japan for $495.00 in the summer of 2000. Not all Hi Speeds are rare, but some are, so beware

Presented to Frank Borman, serial number 771747. One of a kind item, price negotiable only.

of this small difference. Also, boxed reels, with tools and instructions, will bring more.

By 1968, Garcia had an address of 329 Alfred Avenue, Teaneck, N. J. 07666 as shown on the frontspiece of the little booklet called "How to Use Fresh Water Skills in Salt Water" by Mark Sosin and distributed in tackle stores where Garcia equipment was sold. This little booklet was one of 10 distributed by Garcia and would make a nice set to go with your Ambassadeur collection. Value is $5.00 to $10.00.

The other prime collectible in reels from this company is a Mitchell 300 reel, or any of its cousins. Again, values vary greatly but most of the new in box 300s will bring better than $50.00, likely closer to $75.00 if mint and complete. If you have never fished with either of these fine products, I encourage you to buy a good 5000 and a good 300 to use. They both work like a charm and are a joy to use day in and out. They were "top of the line" when made and still cannot be beat. Of course, the Frank Borman Mitchell will not be used and is priceless due to its unique character, but non-inscribed models make a great ultra-light reel.

When looking for fishing reel sources, do not overlook Lionel train catalogs! The 1958 Lionel train catalog not only shows the trains and accessories we Baby Boomer boys and girls drooled over, but look at the back of the catalog as shown on page 198 and see the nice selection of Airex reels made and marketed by Airex, A Division of the Lionel Corporation, Airex Corporation, 411 Fourth Avenue, New York 16, N.Y. It shows the Impala spin casting reel, three spinning reels, Spinster, Larchmont, and the salt water Mastereel. In addition, the Taurus and Ablette fly reels are shown. The

gold color Larchmont both looks and sounds expensive! Airex also distributed a few lures and also made nice glass rods. The prices of any Airex product usually brings more than its counterparts because there is competition for the item by both the Lionel collecting fraternity and the fishing collecting fraternity. One way to acquire good Airex items is through trading of Lionel items. I have acquired quite a few of their reels new in boxes by making train trades. The least that I have seen an Airex reel new in the box sell for is $50.00. The Airex Mastereel sold for $22.50 in 1953, $30.00 in a nice wooden presentation box kit. One should always consider the initial retail price of a reel or rod as it normally helps set collector prices; expensive reels sold less as a general rule and this results in fewer of them for us to find and fight over when we do find them. Reels that cost $30.00 in the 1950s should be worth at least twice that today given availability and demand. It is simple: finer items bring finer prices!

As a starting point in defining a direction for collecting modern fishing reels, note the following reel companies and types (see chart on page 198) featured in the 1950 Nu-Way Sports Catalog. A study of this list demonstrates that only small inroads had been made into the world of baitcasting by spinning reels. However, the tide had started to turn, and a review of the 1961 Supplement to the 1960 Nu-Way Sports Catalog (our same source 11 years earlier) shows many discontinued baitcasting reels, even some discontinued spinning reels, and many new additions in the new wave of spin-casting reels, or as some called them closed face baitcasting reels. As an example only, I have reprinted only a small part of the catalog changes (these appeared toward the bottom of many pages throughout the catalog supplement): 1960-61 Catalog Changes; Zebco 55 discontinued; Shakespeare Models 1920, 1964 (Marhoff), 1777 and 1798 discontinued; Pflueger Saturn discontinued; Bronson Green Hornet discontinued.

The same supplement introduced dozens of new reels and rods, mostly in the spinning or spin-cast categories. In addition the spin size baits were being introduced in the same proportions by the 1960s. The *Popular Mechanics* issue dealing with spinning referred to earlier is documentation of how fast the sport accepted spinning from 1950 to 1953. This issue detailed numerous new spinning reels available in the United States already by 1953.

As an example of what was on the market at the time in addition to all of the reels shown in the Nu-Way and Jennison Hardware catalog pages, I have included pages from Shakespeare and Pflueger catalogs, the two leaders in reel manufacturing during the modern era here in America. This should give the reader a good introduction to reels of the time period.

1950 Nu-Way Sports Catalog Reel Companies and Types

Baitcasting Reels

- Shakespeare: President, Marhoff, Wondereel Models 1920, 1921 and 1922, Tru-Axis, Criterion, Sportcast, Classic, Triumph, Tru Blue and Deuce.
- Langley: Lurecast, Streamlite, Deluxe Lakecast, Plugcast, Lakecast, Castrite, and Reelcast
- Bronson: Lashless, Mercury, Green Hornet, Fleetwing, Altoona and Aetna
- South Bend: all listed by numbers only, the most expensive to the least, 1250, 1000, 550, 450, 400, 300, 30 and 20
- J. A. Coxe: listed as South Bend by number, 25C, 25N, 10C, 30C, 60C and 95C
- Kalamazoo: Balchi No. 30, Balchi No. 20, Sportsman, Challenger, Atlas and the American Boy (this one was shipped in the tin can).
- Ocean City: listed by number, 2000, 1950, 1850, 1970, 1600, 1591, 1529, 11.

Trolling/Heavy Casting

- Bronson: Retriever
- J. A. Coxe: Do-All, No. 65-C and the model No. 1315L
- Shakespeare: Service Models 1944 and 1964
- Ocean City: Models No. 920, 910, 915 and 980
- Penn: Senator Models 113, 115 and 118, Peer Models 209 and 109, Bay Star Drag No. 180, Standard Penn 190 and the Bay Free Spool

Other

- Zebco: the introductory Zero Bomb Company "about to become famous" spincast reel with no model numbers, as it was the first and only in 1950
- Humphrey's: Model 3A Spinner (this was made in different sizes and was a spinning reel that looks like a fly reel, stainless steel)
- Bristol: Model 69 "light-lure Spinning Reel" (early open face)

Fly Reels

- South Bend: Models 1140 and 1130 Oren-O-Matic
- Perrine: Models 57, 50, 30 and 55 auto fly reels
- Kalamazoo: Models 1698, 1697 and 1695
- Shakespeare: Models 1837 and 1835 of the Tru-Art, Model 1821 O.K. auto
- Ocean City: Model 36 single action
- Ocean City: Model 90 auto-fly reel

Chart showing reel distribution by type available in 1950.

Back cover of Lionel catalog advertising Airex Reels.

Nu-Way Sporting Goods Company

New model, streamlined tear-drop design, handsome in appearance and quiet in operation. Frame of stainless steel; expertly hand-crafted. Capacity 100-yards.
SHAKESPEARE President
No. 1970____**$42.00**____$35.00 Ea.

A marvel of skilled workmanship and superior material. Green anodized aluminum head plate, nickel silver frame. Adjustable drag. Capacity 100 yards 15-℔ test line.
SHAKESPEARE Marhoff
No. 1964____**$18.00**____$15.00 Ea.

The reel that eliminates back-lashes. Spool spins fast at start of cast, loses momentum as line goes out. Capacity 100 yards 15-℔. test line.
SHAKESPEARE Wondereel
No. 1922____**$16.20**____$13.50 Ea.

Shakespeare reel built like a fine watch. Three-piece design frame of brass is chrome plated; adjustable casting drag; smooth running spiral gears.
SHAKESPEARE Tru-Axis
No. 1932____**$13.20**____$11.00 Ea.

Built like a fine watch. Brass frame, chrome plated; adjustable casting drag. Smooth running spiral gears. Capacity 100 yards 15-℔ test line.
SHAKESPEARE Criterion
No. 1960____**$13.20**____$11.00 Ea.

Aluminum end plates with plastic head ring. Attractive green anodized finish. No thumbing, long accurate casts without backlashes.
SHAKESPEARE Wondereel
No. 1921____**$13.20**____$11.00 Ea.

The standard model of that popular reel that eliminates back-lashes. Beginners learn to cast in 5 minutes. Experts enthuse over it too. Capacity 100 yards 15-℔. test line.
SHAKESPEARE Wondereel
No. 1920____**$12.00**____$10.00 Ea.

A featherweight member of the Shakespeare family. Experienced fishermen will enjoy the long effortless casts. Capacity 100 yards 15-℔. test line.
SHAKESPEARE Classic
No. 1972____**$12.00**____$10.00 Ea.

Fast, lightweight, narrow aluminum spool casting reels with level-wind feature. Popular with tournament casters and fishermen using light sporty rods.
SHAKESPEARE Sportcast
No. 1973____**$12.00**____$10.00 Ea.

This reel is truly a triumph of Shakespeare production engineering, for it contains many of the essentials of the higher grade reels, yet is offered at a very low price.
SHAKESPEARE Triumph
No. 1958_____**$9.00**_____$7.50 Ea.

Made of brass, chrome plated, circle finish and is an exceptional value at this low price. Has four gear train. Capacity 100 yards 15-℔. test line.
SHAKESPEARE True Blue
No. 1956_____**$6.60**_____$5.50 Ea.

All-metal, low-price level-winding reel. Heavily nickeled brass, circle finish. Capacity 100 yards 15-℔ test Wexford Wonder Line. Wt. 7.6 oz.
SHAKESPEARE Deuce
No. 1905_____**$5.40**_____$4.50 Ea.

''First in Sports''

Nu-Way Sporting Goods Company catalog, 1950, page 8.

Nu-Way Sporting Goods Company

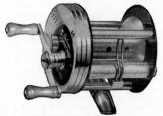

The narrow anti-inertia spool permits extreme casting accuracy and control. This reel is especially adapted for the new lighter lures.

LANGLEY Lurecast
No. 330_____**$18.00**_____$15.00 Ea.

Standard size bait casting reel gives outstanding performance to the expert and novice caster. Offering extreme accuracy.

LANGLEY Streamlite
No. 310_____**$15.00**_____$12.50 Ea.

Polished chrome trim with the new gear box control that allows easy accessibility to the gears without disassembling the entire reel.

LANGLEY Deluxe Lakecast
No. 370_____**$12.60**_____$10.50 Ea.

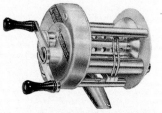

A narrow spool level wind reel in the medium price field. This narrow spool permits extreme accuracy and control.

LANGLEY Plugcast
No. 360_____**$12.60**_____$10.50 Ea.

Incorporating all of the outstanding features in Langley reels.

LANGLEY Lakecast
No. 351—150 Yd._**$10.50**_$8.75 Ea.
No. 350—100 Yd._**$10.50**_$8.75 Ea.

A new size standard level wind casting reel in the low price field. It incorporates all Langley features including box control.

LANGLEY Castrite
No. 380_____ **$8.10**_____$6.75 Ea.

The Reelcast is a level wind reel suitable for all types of fresh water fishing. Its light weight allows hours of back-lash-free casting without arm fatigue.

LANGLEY Reelcast
No. 500_____**$6.00**_____$5.00 Ea.

This reel is equipped with a newly devised spool bearing mechanism that permits highly sensitive anti-backlash adjustment to individual needs and casting techniques.

BRONSON Lashless
No. 1700_____**$9.00**_____$7.50 Ea.

High grade brass, chromium plated for long lasting durability and beauty. Jeweled adjustable spool caps are incorporated in this sturdy casting reel.

BRONSON Mercury
No. 2550_____**$6.60**_____$5.50 Ea.

An amazing new development to supply a growing demand for a lightweight reel at an extremely low price. New lightweight spool with snap-on plastic arbor.

BRONSON Green Hornet
No. 2200_____**$5.94**_____$4.95 Ea.

A full-size, 100-yard capacity, level-winding reel built in accordance with Bronson original three-piece construction. Chrome-plated brass throughout.

BRONSON Fleetwing
No. 2475____**$4.74**_____$3.95 Ea.

It is sturdily built, yet very low in price. It is full quadruple multiplying, level winding reel, constructed in three piece take down fashion.

BRONSON Altoona
No. 4250_____**$3.30**_____$2.75 Ea.

"First in Sports"

Nu-Way Sporting Goods Company catalog, 1950, page 9.

Nu-Way Sporting Goods Company

A new low price, sturdily constructed reel with bakelite end plates. Level winding and adjustable click. Full-100-yard capacity.
BRONSON Aetna
No. 2300____**$2.40**____$2.00 Ea.

Finest South Bend reel. End plates of stainless steel, maroon pearl plastic rings in head cap and tail plate.
SOUTH BEND
No. 1250____**$30.00**____$25.00 Ea.

One of the most famous South Bend Reels. Chrome plated frame with plastic head ring.
SOUTH BEND
No. 1000____**$18.00**____$15.00 Ea.

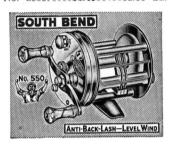

An all metal reel with chrome plated frame. Jeweled spool caps. Three-piece take-down construction, spiral gears. Capacity 100 yards 18-lb.
SOUTH BEND
No. 550____**$13.80**____$11.50 Ea.

A new improved model. Chrome plated plastic head ring. 3-piece take-down construction. Spiral gears, jeweled spool caps.
SOUTH BEND
No. 450____**$12.00**____$10.00 Ea.

A real value at a popular price. Chrome plated frame, jeweled spool caps. Spiral gears. Capacity 100 yards 18-lb. test line.
SOUTH BEND
No. 400____**$10.80**____$9.00 Ea.

Popular price, dependable South Bend reel with improved pawl retainer and thumb screw construction.
SOUTH BEND
No. 300____**$8.10**____$6.75 Ea.

Outstanding value, built throughout for hardest usage. Made of brass, take down construction.
SOUTH BEND
No. 30____**$6.60**____$5.50 Ea.

Outstanding value in a popular price reel of South Bend quality. Rugged and attractive in appearance.
SOUTH BEND
No. 20____**$5.40**____$4.50 Ea.

A custom built, level winding, free spool, bait casting reel designed for the discriminating fisherman.
J. A. COXE
No. 25C____**$44.00**____$33.00 Ea.

A narrow spool version of the 25-C, this model is especially designed for extremely light plugs.
J. A. COXE
No. 25N____**$44.00**____$33.00 Ea.

Custom built Coxe live axle reel. Exclusive take-apart cross bolt construction. Smooth effortless casts.
J. A. COXE
No. 10C____**$19.80**____$16.50 Ea.

''First in Sports''

Nu-Way Sporting Goods Company catalog, 1950, page 10.

Nu-Way Sporting Goods Company

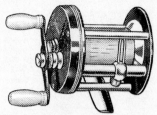

Lightweight, fast-running, 100-yard capacity. Coxe cross bolt construction provides effortless distance casting.

J. A. COXE
No. 30C_____**$15.00**_____$12.50 Ea.

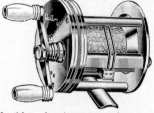

Macthless for its top performance, low cost, and smooth distant casting. Anti-backlash cross bolt construction used throughout.

J. A. COXE
No. 60C_____**$13.20**_____$11.00 Ea.

Model 95C

A new featherweight champion makes its bow. Noiseless operation and smoothness of performance make it an ideal casting reel.

J. A. COXE
No. 95C_____**$11.80**_____$9.75 Ea.

The matchless performance of this new BalCli DeLuxe drive level winding reel will convince any angler that here is a new and radically different reel that is tops at all times.

KALAMAZOO Balcli
No. 30_____**$24.00**_____$20.00 Ea.

This radically different reel has two gears instead of the usual four. It is engineered to stand the gaff of hard fishing. The kind that starts at sun-up and is still going at sun-down.

KALAMAZOO Balcli
No. 20_____**$11.64**_____$9.70 Ea.

One look at the new Sportsman level winding reel is enough to convince any angler that here is an unusual value in a high grade reel.

KALAMAZOO Sportsman
No. 1721_____**$11.52**_____$9.60 Ea.

The Neutral Quartz mottled plastic head ring with handles to match sets off the Challenger as an attractive reel which "challenges" comparison.

KALAMAZOO Challenger
No. 1718_____**$9.00**_____$7.50 Ea.

You will find exceptional value packed into this inexpensive level wind reel. Built of brass which is nickeled and then chrome plated.

KALAMAZOO Atlas
No. 1708_____**$7.20**_____$6.00 Ea.

Dealers everywhere have been waiting for a good, low priced reel. "American Boy" is it! Sturdily built of brass, heavily chromed over nickel.

KALAMAZOO American Boy
No. 1706_____**$5.76**_____$4.80 Ea.

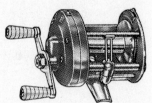

As precisely made as a fine watch. This superlative reel has proven itself to be both a tournament and a service reel.

OCEAN CITY
No. 2000_____**$24.00**_____$20.00 Ea.

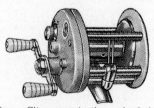

Ocean City presents the reel of the year! Streamlined and constructed entirely of Zephaloy, holding the weight to only six ounces.

OCEAN CITY
No. 1950_____**$12.00**_____$10.00 Ea.

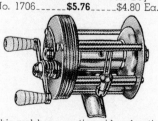

This reel has a casting aid and anti-backlash device to assure the fisherman longer, smoother casts without over-run.

OCEAN CITY
No. 1850_____**$10.20**_____$8.50 Ea.

''First in Sports''

Nu-Way Sporting Goods Company catalog, 1950, page 11.

Nu-Way Sporting Goods Company

A smart appearing, precision built level-wind reel. It has the Ocean City Smoothkaster control on left sideplate.

OCEAN CITY

No. 1970 _____ **$7.80** _____ $6.50 Ea.

New satin finish all metal reel with troubie free level-wind mechanism.

OCEAN CITY

No. 1600 _____ **$6.00** _____ $5.00 Ea.

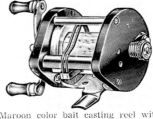

Maroon color bait casting reel with new Smoothkaster control, assures bachlash free casts. Aluminum spool with cork arbor.

OCEAN CITY

No. 1591 _____ **$4.80** _____ $4.00 Ea.

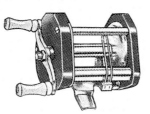

Streamline design, smooth running casting reel. Strong plastic frame, all metal parts plated. Dependable level-wind.

OCEAN CITY

No. 1529 _____ **$2.70** _____ $2.25 Ea.

A serviceable little reel for baitcasting or general use. Has been carefully machined and finished and is well worth its low price.

OCEAN CITY

No. 11 _____ **$6.48** _____ $5.40 Doz.

This new, level-winding, three-piece takedown reel is constructed to carry 150 yards of 18-lb. test line. Combination trolling and casting reel.

BRONSON Retriever

No. 2900 _____ **$8.34** _____ $6.95 Ea.

Beautiful new design. All purpose reel that can be used for salt water, river or lake trolling. Line capacity 150 yards 18-lb. test.

J. A. COXE Do-All

No. 65-C _____ **$15.00** _____ $12.50 Ea.

An excellent reel for heavy casting duties that will satisfy any fisherman under all circumstances.

COXE

No. 1315L _____ **$16.20** _____ $13.50 Ea.

Heavy duty fishing reel with star drag feature, operated by lever; non-reversing crank.

SHAKESPEARE Service

No. 1944-150 Yds. **$16.20** $13.50 Ea.
Nc. 1964-200 Yds. **$16.80** $14.00 Ea.

All purpose reel with level-wind; star drag and free spool features. Self-lubricating bearings for long life.

OCEAN CITY

No. 920 _____ **$15.00** _____ $12.50 Ea.

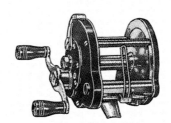

A level wind reel with new light weight spool. Rustproof pawl and worm. Free spool, 150 yard capacity.

OCEAN CITY

No. 910 _____ **$13.20** _____ $11.00 Ea.

The top lever on this model, when thrown, permits the handle to reverse —a feature favored by some fishermen over the conventional free spool.

OCEAN CITY

No. 915 _____ **$12.00** _____ $10.00 Ea.

"First in Sports"

Nu-Way Sporting Goods Company catalog, 1950, page 12.

Nu-Way Sporting Goods Company

150 yards Number 9 or 27-lb. test line. Has torpedo handle and heavily chrome plated spool. Gear ratio: 3 to 1.

OCEAN CITY

No. 980____**$4.80**____$4.00 Ea.

Equipped with a strong star drag, making it ideal for handling the heavier lake and river fish.

PENN-Bay Star Drag

No. 180____**$8.00**____$6.00 Ea.

Standard size trolling reel with light weight, easy casting spool. Bakelite end plates; all metal parts plated.

PENN

No. 190____**$4.66**____$3.50 Ea.

A trouble free, smooth casting, spinning reel with all the deluxe features fishermen insist on. Can't backlash no matter how hard the novice might try.

HUMPHREY'S Spinner

No. 3A-____**$27.00**____$22.50 Ea.

Big game fishing reels of distinction within the reach of all. Special order.

PENN Senator

No. 113—4/0____**$26.66**___$20.00 Ea.
No. 115—9/0____**$43.32**___$32.50 Ea.
No. 118—16/0__**$133.32**__$100.00 Ea.

ZEBCO: Will not backlash under any condition. Is fast, and affords the fisherman a long, effortless cast. Provides perfect casting control, it being possible to brake the cast by the slightest pressure of the thumb stop.

ZEBCO

No. 175_____**$21.00**_____$17.50 Ea.

A revolutionary new fly reel designed for the angler who appreciates the finest in automatic fly reels. Sturdy, one-piece die-cast aluminum frame. Offset reel stand. Smooth, highly polished and chrome-plated.

OCEAN CITY

No. 90_____**$12.00**_____$10.00 Ea.

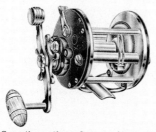

Smooth casting pleasure is yours with this high quality well constructed heavy duty reel. Capacity 200 yards 18-lb.

PENN-PEER

No. 209____**$20.00**____$15.00 Ea.

Especially designed for casting and bay fishing. Very fast gear action, and powerful star drag.

PENN-PEER

No. 109____**$13.32**____$10.00 Ea.

A small light weight, but sturdy reel that will add greatly to the pleasure of light tackle fishing.

PENN-Bay Free Spool

No. 185____**$6.66**____$5.00 Ea.

This new light-lure Spinning Reel gives accurate casting. Designed to operate simply and with as few adjusting parts as practicable.

BRISTOL

No. 69____**$18.00**____$15.00 Ea.

"First in Sports"

Nu-Way Sporting Goods Company catalog, 1950, page 13.

Nu-Way Sporting Goods Company

OREN-O-MATIC FLY ROD REELS

"THE BALANCED REEL"

Balanced, silent, free stripping reel; fits rod in natural balanced position. Anodized maroon finish; chrome plated steel line guide. Line is stripped without operating folding trigger lever; spring easily released when fully wound. Automatic line brake prevents broken leaders. Quickly, easily taken apart for cleaning.

SOUTH BEND
No. 1140—80 Yd. **$12.60** $10.50 Ea.
No. 1130—50 Yd. **$12.00** $10.00 Ea.

Shakespeare Tru-arT De Luxe Automatic Trout Reels make more fun out of fishing with a fly rod. Slack line, stripped off the reel by hand. can be quickly spooled back on the reel by pressing the lever with your little finger.

SHAKESPEARE
No. 1837—80 Yd. **$11.40** $9.50 Ea.
No. 1835—50 Yd. **$10.80** $9.00 Ea.

Fine construction and smooth action. Positive brake, friction clutch and hard chrome line guard. Silent winding device in the spring cap eliminates noises. A quality reel that will satisfy completely. Reasonably priced and truly an excellent value.

KALAMAZOO
No. 1695—50 Yd. **$6.96** $5.80 Ea.

Put on the market by popular demand for an upright model. Free stripping automatic, no brake manipulation needed to strip line. Finger tip line control.

PERRINE
No. 57—50 Yd. **$11.10** $9.25 Ea.

New rigid frame, lightweight single action reel. Metal alloy spool and frame, anodized finish; chrome steel line guide.

LANGLEY
No. 165_____**$4.50**_____$3.75 Ea.

Alloy metal reel, single action, light and strong. Black finish frame, chrome guide ring. Adjustable click and silent drag. Easily taken apart.

OCEAN CITY
No. 36_____**$3.60**_____$3.00 Ea.

Everything about the new Miracle reflects high quality. The fast, slide link release lever, the new safety lock—that's like a safety on a gun the way it prevents stripping a leader or breaking a rod tip. High quality silent wind, free stripping automatic reels. Chrome line guard and friction free clutch.

KALAMAZOO
No. 1698—80 Yd. **$9.24** $7.70 Ea.
No. 1697—50 Yd. **$8.40** $7.00 Ea.

Shakespeare's O. K. Automatic Reels offer exceptional features. They are free stripping, that is, you can strip line from the reel without depressing the lever. They are silent winding. When you need more spring tension to retrieve line simply wind the head cap of the reel—no noise—no fish scaring.

SHAKESPEARE
No. 1821—50 Yd. **$7.50** $6.25 Ea.

Low price, simple design automatic fly rod reel made by Perrine. Super strong dural-alloy, green alumilite finish. Stainless steel line guide. Features long spring, quick take-down and safety friction spool mounting.

PERRINE
No. 50—50 Yd.__**$11.10**__$9.25 Ea.
No. 30—30 Yd.__**$ 9.60**__$8.00 Ea.
No. 55—50 Yd.__**$ 6.60**__$5.50 Ea.

"First in Sports"

Nu-Way Sporting Goods Company catalog, 1950, page 14.

NEW...

Shakespeare DIRECT DRIVE Reels

with *Lighter Quieter Tougher*

NYLON GEARS

AMAZINGLY RUGGED
VELVETY SMOOTH
WHISPER QUIET

LOOK TO THE LEADER
FOR ALL THAT'S NEW!

Ben Hardesty, U. S. Professional all 'round bait and fly casting champion, has been field testing Shakespeare Direct Drive Reels with Nylon Gears for two years. He is shown above with a 55 pound Tarpon, one of several big ones—up to nearly 100 pounds—landed with these new reels.

TWO MODELS

SENSATIONAL LOW PRICES

No. 1924
HUSKY CHROME PLATED
BRASS MODEL $9.50

No. 1926
LIGHTWEIGHT ANODIZED
ALUMINUM MODEL $10.00

NEW PLASTIC PACKAGE

Shakespeare catalog, 1951, page 21.

Shakespeare catalog, 1951, page 22.

Shakespeare catalog, 1951, page 23.

Shakespeare catalog, 1951, page 24.

Four new pushbutton reels

Shakespeare

Special Values for our
75th Anniversary

New 7500
pushbutton reel

All-metal, American-made "7500"
will be specially promoted in 1972

No. 7500 ALL-METAL PUSHBUTTON REEL. Here's a headliner for our 75th year! Your Shakespeare dealer will be featuring this new reel at a special low promotional price. But you get a lot for your money: reel comes filled with 100 yards of 8-pound test premium 7000 mono and the removable spool can be easily, quickly filled with different weight line when desired. Attractively styled in Marina Green with fluorescent green stripe, the 7500 has an eight-point, foolproof pickup and star drag on handle that won't twist line when you're fighting a fish. Four-to-one retrieve ratio lets you bring in line fast. There's a stainless steel cone eyelet, too — to prevent wear at this critical spot, and to keep your line from fraying. Crank is permanently non-reversing so the drag is in operation even if you take your hand off the reel handle. (For extra reel spools, see page 55)

New 1700 II has rotating pickup pin (left) and new 7503 and 7504 reels have twin rotating pickup pins.

Shakespeare

7000

Now *all* Shakespeare reels displaying this label are supplied with our premium grade 7000 monofilament installed. It's the *best!*

Shakespeare catalog, 1972, page 10.

in Jubilee series

1700 II

Meet the new 1700II... with pin pickup

No. 1700 II PUSHBUTTON REEL. The "1700" was one of America's most popular reels — and now we've made it even better! The new, improved version has positive ceramic pin pickup that picks up line instantly and handles the toughest of monofilament without abrasion. There's a rubber line disc too. Other quality features include precision built, four unit construction of aluminum alloy; one-piece spool; permanent non-reverse; star drag that prevents line twist. The 1700 II comes filled with approximately 85 yards of 10-pound test premium quality Shakespeare 7000 monofilament. (For extra reel spools see page 55.)

7504

7503

These DeLuxe Models Have Twin Roller Pickup Pins

No. 7504 PUSHBUTTON REEL. Here's a star attraction among our new 75th Anniversary reels. The black and silver beauty has dual chrome pickup pins for less wear, quicker line pickup. Also a hard chrome plated pickup housing. The 7504 has level wind feature to wind line smoothly and evenly on the spool. Gear ratio is a hefty four-to-one. Foolproof star drag and permanent non-reverse are other features. Reel comes filled with 85 yards of 20-pound premium quality 7000 monofilament line.

No. 7503 PUSHBUTTON REEL. Smaller brother of the 7504, this model has all the features of the 7504 but is in a smaller, sportier size. Comes filled with about 90 yards of deluxe 8-pound 7000 monofilament. (For extra spools see page 55.)

Shakespeare catalog, 1972, page 11.

1767

Bill True, World Professional Casting champ, is a fisherman too. Bill used the S-177 outfit to set an all-time spincast accuracy record.

Champion Reel and Balanced Outfit

No. 1767

SHAKESPEARE TROPHY-WINNING PUSHBUTTON REEL.

This no-backlash spincasting reel is solidly built of aluminum alloy, has high strength drive gear and pinion (4 to 1 ratio). Eight-point pick-up is diamond hard chromed. Has epoxy finish, nickel-chromed crank and one piece die-cast spool. Equipped with lever type "on/off" non-reverse crank switch and adjusting star control. No line twist! Reel filled with 70 yds. 12 lb. line; extra spool filled with 100 yds. 8 lb. mono. Weight 10⅞ ounces. (For extra spools see page 55.)

No. S-177 The Bill True Champion balanced tackle outfit. Display-carded, contains No. 1767 push-button reel with 70 yards of 12-pound mono installed. Plus extra spool filled with 100 yards of 8-pound. Matched to the reel is a 6-foot, 2-piece pushbutton Wonderod. A free "How to Fish in Fresh Water" handbook is also included.

S177

1788

THE 1766 DELUXE WONDERFLYTE

No. 1766 PUSHBUTTON REEL

Four-unit, quick-take-apart design, with frame of die-cast aluminum alloy, epoxied in deluxe bronze. Off-set contoured thumb button for better control. Has 4 to 1 ratio, cut aluminum drive gear and metal pinion. Bayonet-locking outer cone for fast spool changes. Pickup head has large roller pin to prolong line life; rubber line guard disc. Star control drag adjustment. Lever control makes reel crank free or non-reversing with click. Wgt. 10⅝ ozs. Spool is filled with 100 yds. of 12-lb top quality monofilament line. (For extra spools see page 55.)

HEAVY DUTY DUAL DRAG WONDERCAST

No. 1788 PUSHBUTTON REEL

Comes with 20-pound test mono! Styled in silver, black and gray, the heavy duty 1788 has flare-shaped thumb button, bayonet-locking outer cone; 4 to 1 gear ratio with brass pinion and quality cut drive gear; oscillating level wind and chromed *roller pick-up pin*. Dual drag shifts from high to low pressure. Has permanent, silent, non-reverse crank. With two line-filled spools; 160 yards of 10-pound mono and 85 yards of 20-pound; weight is 13.7 ounces. (For extra spools see page 55.)

Shakespeare catalog, 1972, page 12.

Wondercast® Reels with Exclusive Micro-Drag

No. 1797 HEAVY-DUTY LEVEL-WIND has smooth Shakespeare level wind; beautiful Shakespeare black and gray Purist styling. Features: Four-unit construction, flare-shaped thumb button, brass pinion and high quality drive gear with 4 to 1 ratio; ceramic pick-up pin and diamond hard, chrome plated replaceable wear rings. Famous full circle micro-drag. Lever-type non-reverse is easy to reach. Wt. 10.2 ozs. Filled with approx. 100 yds. 12-lb. line. (For extra reel spools see page 55.)

No. 1777 Popular for heavy duty fresh water fishing. 4-unit, fixed spool construction with frame of aluminum alloy, bronze anodized aluminum side plates. Has aluminum alloy cut gear (4-to-1 ratio); diamond hard ceramic pick-up pin and replaceable, chromed wear rings; rubber bumper on pick-up head, machined spool, full circle micro-drag; lever-type non-reverse. Wt. 10.5 ozs. Filled with approximately 120 yds. 10-lb. mono.

No. 1778 Left hand crank model of **No. 1777**. Not illustrated. Filled with approximately 120 yds. 10-lb. mono.

Rugged reels with Cycolac* construction

No. 777 PUSHBUTTON REEL. Cycolac* molded reel with removable spool and capacity for 12 and 15-pound test mono. Ruggedly built, 4-unit (frame, spool, pick-up, cone); 4 to 1 retrieve ratio; metal pinion, aluminum alloy gear. 12-point, positive pick-up head. Designed with built-in automatic non-reversing crank. Star drag control prevents twisted lines when cranking against running fish. Filled with 12-lb. test mono.

No. 998 —Engineered with removable spool. Black molded Cycolac frame and cone with stainless steel guide ring; 12-point pick-up head. Has built-in non-reverse crank and adjusting star control to put drag pressure on a fish without fear of line twist. Filled with approximately 85-yds. 8-lb. mono. (For extra spools, see page 55.)

No. 999 FIREBIRD® — Constructed of Cycolac ABS material. Every part, every piece is made in America, and expertly constructed and assembled by Shakespeare's skilled craftsmen. Quality features: 1) High-impact Cycolac cone and frame; 2) stainless steel multi-point pick-up head for easy line retrieve; 3) star drag—no line twist; 4) four-to-one gear ratio—retrieves line fast; 5) filled with 10-pound quality monofilament.

*®Borg-Warner Corp.

Shakespeare catalog, 1972, page 13.

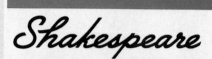

Famous Royal Maroon Spinning Reels

No. 2062 — FRESH WATER WEIGHT WITH SALT WATER POWER. Our incomparable 2062 is a spin reel powerhouse, with its 6-D drag (six metal and leather discs) for the steady pressure to lick any lunker. Ball bearing mounted gears give you brute retrieve power but with silky smoothness found in no other reel. The 3.7 to 1 gear ratio allows you to retrieve line fast with little effort. Other best-buy features include: baked epoxy finish over anodized dichromate sealed frame to deter corrosion; stainless steel line roller with Teflon bushing; stainless steel bail; nylon anti-freeze bushing on the on-off non-reverse lever. New one-piece crank is simple, fold-away type. Reel weighs approximately 10.7 ounces Three offerings are available:

No. 2062 with spool filled with 235 yards of 8-pound mono.

No. 2062NL with empty spool, no line.

No. 2062NL-2 with two empty spools, no line.

No. 2052 — LIGHT, COMPACT — FOR THE SPINNING SPORTSMAN. This little reel fits in the palm of your hand but it packs the power to handle any freshwater fish you're likely to tackle, and a lot of salt water fighters too. Weighing only nine ounces, the 2052 has ball bearing mounted gears, smooth, powerful 6-D drag, 4.7 to 1 gear ratio for fast line retrieve. Stainless steel bail and new handle folds for storage. Reel has lever for non-reverse control and molded Delrin line spool. Three offerings are available:

No. 2052 with 150 yards of 6-pound mono installed.

No. 2052NL with empty spool, no line.

No. 2052NL-2 with two empty spools, no line.

(For extra spools see page 55)

2062

2052

Shakespeare catalog, 1972, page 14.

Best spinning reels made, and they're 100% guaranteed!

Shakespeare Royal Maroon reels are backed by the strongest guarantee possible: buy a 2052, 2062, 2081 or 2091. If for any reason you are not satisfied, return the reel to us within 30 days with your dated sales receipt and get your money back. (Offer expires July 31, 1972)

Shakespeare Sea Wonders® For big, tough fish in salt water or fresh

When that really big trophy fish hits, be ready for him with a Shakespeare Sea Wonder spinning reel. The second he hits the smooth pressure of Shakespeare's exclusive 6-D drag starts to wear him down. Then, precision-running, ball-bearing-mounted gears give you all the brute retrieve power you need to land him. The stainless steel line roller has a Teflon sleeve to deliver line smoothly to the spool without abrasion.

No. 2081 SEA WONDER SPINNING REEL. This is the popular size for surf fishing, all-purpose salt water angling or fresh water fishing for salmon, muskies. steelhead, big lake trout, etc. Frame is anodized, dichromate sealed, epoxy enameled in Royal Maroon. Has all the Sea Wonder deluxe features mentioned above. Gear ratio is 3.2 to 1. Weight is 19.9 ounces. Capacity: 300 yards of 12-pound mono.

No. 2091 SEA WONDER SPINNING REEL. Our biggest spinning reel, this one fills the bill where the heavy spin fishing is...in the surf, from a boat, or off in the deep water. Has all Sea Wonder features plus big line capacity of 250 yards of 20-pound test mono. Reel weight is 20.9 ounces. (For extra spools see page 55)

2081   2091

Shakespeare catalog, 1972, page 15.

2200

2210

2230

2240

2250

Marina Green Ball Bearing Spinning Reels

Imported to save you money but made under Shakespeare auspices to assure top quality, the Marina Green series of spinning reels includes eight models from ultralight to heavy, including three models for left-hand use. All the Marina Green reels have ball bearing construction, are level winding, and have multi-disc drag systems. Each has two-piece crank for easy storage, on-off non-reverse lever, chrome plated bail with line roller. Finish of the lightweight aluminum alloy reels is in Marina Green enamel with chrome details. (For extra spools, see page 55.)

No. 2200 MARINA GREEN SPINNING REEL. Smallest in the series, this lightweight reel weighs only seven ounces. Its 5-to-1 gear ratio allows fast, effortless line retrieve. Spool capacity is 170 yards of six-pound monofilament.

No. 2200LH MARINA GREEN SPINNING REEL. Same as 2200 but with crank on right side for left-handed use. (Not illustrated)

No. 2210 MARINA GREEN SPINNING REEL. Medium size reel of three-unit design with ball bearing construction. Weighs 11 ounces and gear ratio is 3.75-to-1. Spool capacity is 180 yards of 8-pound mono, or 270 yards of 6-pound.

No. 2210LH MARINA GREEN SPINNING REEL. Same as 2210 but with crank on right side for left-handed use. (Not illustrated)

No. 2230 MARINA GREEN SPINNING REEL. For light salt water or tough fresh water use, this model weighs 15 ounces. Gear ratio is 4-to-1. Spool capacity is 240 yards of 10-pound test mono.

No. 2240 MARINA GREEN SPINNING REEL. For medium salt water use or for really big fresh water fish. Has 4-to-1 gear ratio, on-off non-reverse lever and all the other Marina Green features. Holds 260 yards of 12-pound test mono.

No. 2240LH MARINA GREEN SPINNING REEL. Same as 2240 but with crank on right side for left-handed use. (Not illustrated)

No. 2250 MARINA GREEN SPINNING REEL. For heavy spin fishing this is the reel. All Marina Green features including ball bearing construction. Weight is 17.5 ounces and gear ratio is 3.5-to-1. Holds 160 yards of 20-pound or 240 yards of 15-pound mono.

Shakespeare catalog, 1972, page 16.

2170

2171

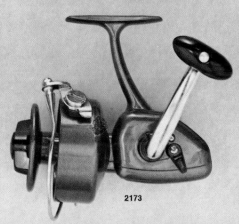

2173

Gold Medal Series

You get Shakespeare quality at a low, low price with these three spinning reels. All have multi-disc drag, on-off control lever. Finish is golden tan with bright chrome detail. Level-wind feature insures even winding of line on spool.

No. 2170 SPINNING REEL. Smallest in the Gold Medal series, this model has 4-to-1 gear ratio and weighs 8.5 ounces. Spool capacity is 185 yards of six-pound monofilament line.

No. 2171 SPINNING REEL. Standard size model weighs 10 ounces. Gear ratio is 3.5-to-1. Spool capacity is 280 yards of six-pound test monofilament.

No. 2173 SPINNING REEL. This dynamic reel is for rugged heavy duty fishing in fresh or salt water. Has a gear ratio of 3.8-to-1. The generous spool capacity is 215 yards of 15-pound test monofilament line. (For extra spools see page 55.)

Shakespeare Quality in Economy Spinning Reels

Closed-Face Spinning Reels

These Micro-Drag, under-the-rod, closed-face spinning reels are favorites of many fishermen. Two models are available:

1810

1756

No. 1810 DELUXE SPIN WONDEREEL®. This is a long-time favorite in a rugged under-the-rod, closed-face spinning reel. Purist gray styling with black detail. Four unit construction of anodized aluminum. Has smooth level-wind with easily adjustable full circle Micro-Drag. Other features: four-to-one gear ratio, chromed roller type pin pickup, chrome plated wear rings, lever-type non-reverse. Weight is 11.8 ounces and reel comes filled with approximately 190 yards of eight-pound premium quality 7000 monofilament.

No. 1756 SPIN WONDEREEL. Handsomely color styled in deluxe bronze, this smaller closed-face spin reel has four-unit construction, four-to-one gear ratio, Micro-Drag, lever-type non-reverse. Weight is 9 ounces and comes filled with approximately 145 yards of eight-pound test top grade 7000 mono. (For extra spools, see page 55.)

Shakespeare catalog, 1972, page 17.

SUPER SPORT NO. 1969 FREE-SPOOL REEL

The world's finest authentic free-spool reel for thumbs-off, no-backlash casting

No. 1969 SUPER SPORT BAIT CASTING REEL

Level-wind disengages when casting the 1969. Only the spool moves—not the gears, not the crank handle—just the spool. Another key feature is the adjustable Hydro-Film® spool-braking control. Here's how they work together: at the beginning of the cast, where half the backlashes occur, braking is greater to prevent the spool from overspeeding. At the middle of the cast the spool runs free—the lure flies farther. Then as the lure slows at the end of the cast (where the rest of the backlashes occur), braking takes over again to equalize the speed of the reel and the lure. Has 1-piece, solid spool for monofilament, adjustable star drag control; new design line carriage has Carboloy* ring. Capacity: 170 yds. 15-lb. mono. NOTE: *Counterbalanced, single-crank handle available from Service Dept., Fayetteville, Ark. See page 54 for address.*

*®General Electric Co.

THE 1969B —"ONE IN A THOUSAND"

This super deluxe version of the 1969 has smooth-running ball bearing bushings and is made in striking gold styling. Has all the other features of the 1969. The 1969B represents the finest example of the reelmaker's art. It's a reel for the master angler.

Shakespeare catalog, 1972, page 18.

Famous Shakespeare Level Wind Bait Casting Reels

No. 1924MS DIRECT DRIVE®. Designed and built to man-handle big fish. Three-unit construction, nylon gears; stainless steel bearings and phosphor bronze bushings. Dual plated nickel and chrome brass level wind and automatic thumb spool cap. Wt. 9 ozs. Capacity without arbor approx. 100 yds. 15-lb. braided line. Ty-bo crank drag.

No. 1973A DIRECT DRIVE SPORTCAST. No other reel quite like it for speed. Favorite of tournament casters around the world. Handsome gold and black styling. 3-unit, nylon gears and direct drive. Stainless steel bearings and bronze bushings. Level wind is dual plated nickel and chromed brass. Automatic thumb spool cap drag. Wt. 5.5 ozs. Capacity with arbor approx. 50 yds. 12½-lb.

No. 1950 DIRECT DRIVE. Three-unit construction, with steel pinion; machine aluminum alloy gear. Has stainless steel bearings, quality brass bushings and dual plated nickel and chromed level wind; "automatic thumb" – spool cap feature. Wt. 8.7 ozs. Capacity without

arbor approx. 100 yds. 15-lb. braided line.

No. 1950S TY-BO DIRECT DRIVE. Same as No. 1950 but with Ty-Bo Star Drag Crank. Wt. 9.4 ozs. Capacity without arbor approximately 100 yds. (50 yds. with arbor), 15-lb. braided line.

No. 1906 SUPERIOR. Built for rugged action and years of dependable fishing enjoyment. Has new beige vinyl covered head cap, aluminum frame. 3-unit construction with four gear train, stainless steel bearings and brass bushings. Wt. 5 ozs. Capacity without arbor 100 yds. 15-lb. braided line.

No. 599 NEW CASTING REEL. New, ultra light direct drive reel has frame of ABS material with precision molded glass-filled nylon gears. Also: adjustable spool cap for casting control, selective click, one-piece strong molded spool, level wind with plated mono pawl. Capacity is 125 yards of 12½-lb. test. Wt. 3.9 ozs.

Service Reels

No. 1944M SERVICE REEL – Rugged, dependable. Level wind. For fresh or salt water casting and trolling. Three-unit design with 4-gear train, adjustable star drag. Has brass level wind, nickel and chromed with stainless steel bearings and brass gears. Engineered with solid, 1-piece aluminum alloy spool, triple-coated for rust resistance. Spool diameter (1⅞"); pillar (1¾"); Wt. 13¼ ounces. Capacity: 200 yds. 18-lb. Squidding line or 200 yds. of 20-lb. mono.

No. 1946M SERVICE REEL – Plenty of line capacity and the guts to be used with monofilament in fresh or salt water. Three-unit, with 4-gear train, one-piece, solid aluminum spool. Has stainless steel bearings and phosphor bronze bushings. Comes with counterbalanced single grip handle installed (see page 25) plus extra double gripped crank. Reel has adjustable star drag. Spool diameter (1⅞"); pillar length (2¼"); Wt. 16.8 ounces. Capacity: approximately 310 yds. 20-lb. mono.

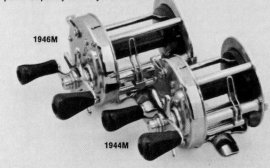

Shakespeare catalog, 1972, page 19.

Shakespeare

World's Finest Single Action Fly Reel for Salt Water, or Heavy Duty Angling

No. 1898 PURIST H.D. FLY REEL. This model has the same 6-D drag that makes Shakespeare spinning reels the envy of the world! With on-off non-reverse lever and built-in click on the drag (signals a running fish), this new Purist gray-and-black beauty is ready to tackle the toughest tarpon, coho salmon, chinook, or almost any other big gamester. Will hold any level or tapered fly line plus 200 yards of 20-pound braided line backing. This reel, matched to one of the FY940 Wonderods (page 30) is a favorite outfit of big game fly fishermen.

Extra spools and left-hand conversion kit are available from Fayetteville, Ark.; see page 54 for address.

Two Shakespeare single action fly reels of durable ABS material.

Mono-Blend®:

The Fly Line Made Like Monofilament

Shakespeare's long experience in manufacturing its own high quality fly lines was responsible for this latest development: Mono-Blend fly line. In the Intermediate class, Mono-Blend has the translucence of monofilament and the resulting invisibility to fish.

Available in both Floating and Intermediate types, Mono-Blend offers absolute line control because of the precise weight distribution of the coating over the uniform mono core. (See page 50 for more details on Mono-Blend.)

Economical

Single Action Fly Fishing Reels of Cycolac*

No. 1891 FLY FISHING REEL. Made of durable Cycolac ABS material, this model features a teakwood finish. Blends perfectly with new woodgrain fly rod series on page 30. Reel weighs only two ounces and has audible click which is easily converted to silent stripping. Felt friction pad prevents overrunning. Reel is 3⅝ inches in diameter and 1⅛ inches wide.

No. 1890 FLY FISHING REEL. Single action model is similar to No. 1891 but is molded of all black Cycolac. Strong and durable, it has audible click easily converted to silent stripping.

*© Borg-Warner Corp.

Shakespeare catalog, 1972, page 20.

Shakespeare Automatic Fly Fishing Reels

Choose from six models. All have dependable Shakespeare quality — and you retrieve line with the touch of a finger

VERTICAL MODELS

No. 1826 DELUXE VERTICAL TRU-ART® AUTOMATIC. Styled in Purist gray. Silent winding and free stripping with stainless steel line protector. Has fold-away retrieve lever, new longer wearing positive grip ratchet release coil and brake coil of square section spring wire. Safety button to prevent accidental line pick-up. Wt. 9.4 ozs. Will hold any level or tapered fly line.

No. 1827 VERTICAL TRU-ART AUTOMATIC. Beautifully finished in bronze and gold; silent winding and free stripping with handy fold-away retrieve lever. Has new longer-wearing positive grip ratchet release coil and brake coil of square section spring wire. Wt. 9.4 ozs. Will hold any level or tapered fly line.

No. 1824 OK AUTOMATIC. Attractively styled in light maple and dark brown and designed for either left or right hand use. It's free stripping and has a stainless steel line protector and new positive grip ratchet release coil with new brake coil of square section spring wire. Wt. 8.9 ozs. Will hold any level or tapered fly line. Has fold-away lever.

HORIZONTAL MODELS

No. 1836 HORIZONTAL DELUXE TRU-ART AUTOMATIC. The finest! Has stainless steel line protector; free stripping from either side and silent winding. Finished in Purist gray and black. Safety button lock to prevent accidental line pick-up. Wt. 9.3 ozs. Will hold any level or tapered fly line.

No. 1837 HORIZONTAL TRU-ART AUTOMATIC. Has deluxe bronze enameled aluminum frame; stainless steel line protector and longer wearing positive grip ratchet release coil and brake coil of square section spring wire. Free stripping from either side; silent winding. Wt. 9.3 ozs. Will hold any level or tapered fly line.

No. 1822 OK AUTOMATIC. Horizontal model has attractive gold metalescent baked enamel finished aluminum frame with dark olive enameled aluminum cap, stainless steel line protector, longer wearing, positive grip ratchet release coil of square section spring wire. Wt. 8.5 ozs. Will hold any level or tapered fly line.

Shakespeare catalog, 1972, page 21.

THE JENNISON HARDWARE CO.

FISHING REELS

PFLUEGER SUPREME

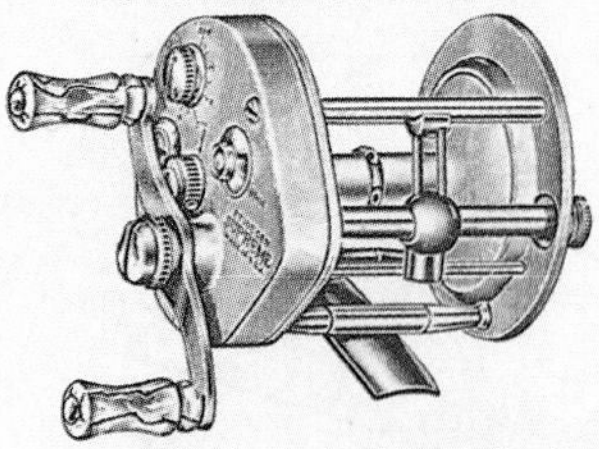

Level Winding, Anti-Back-Lash Quadruple Multiplying

Satin finish nickalum and polished diamolite; phosphor bronze bearings; phosphor bronze generated spiral tooth gear; tool steel generated spiral tooth pinion; adjustable back sliding click; balanced crank; pyralin handles, mottled black and pearl.

Complete with cork arbor spool filler. Speede reel oil, Runfree gear grease, Little Giant screw driver wrench, soft rubber back plate ring, one pair soft rubber handle grips and fine leather bag.

Each

No. 1573—Cap. 130 yds. 18 lb. test silk line, diam. of plates 2¼ in., length of pillars 1⅞ in.; wt. each 7½ oz..............**$25.00**

No. 1573-A—Left hand model..... **32.00**

PFLUEGER SUMMIT

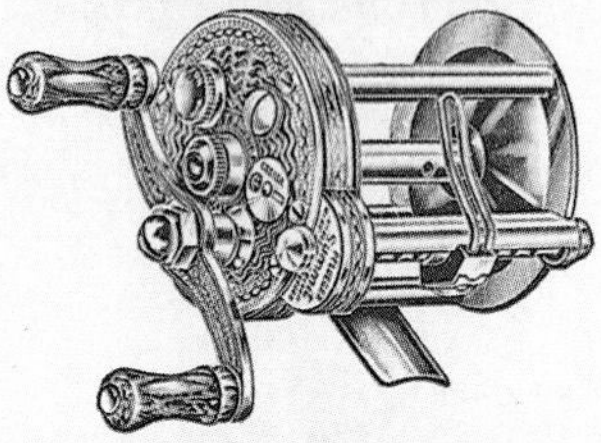

Level Winding, Anti-Back-Lash Quadruple Multiplying

Polished diamolite finish on fancy nickel silver; phosphor bronze bearings; diamalloy pivots; bronze gear; tool steel pinion; adjustable back sliding click; genuine scarlet agate jewels; fancy balanced crank with two pyralin mottled grips.

Cap. 110 yds. 18 lb. test silk line, diam. of plates 2 in., length of pillars 1⅞ in.

Each

No. 1993—Standard spool; wt. each 8 oz. **$10.00**

No. 1993L—Lightweight aluminum alloy spool; wt. each 7½ oz. .. **10.00**

FISHING REELS

PFLUEGER NOBBY

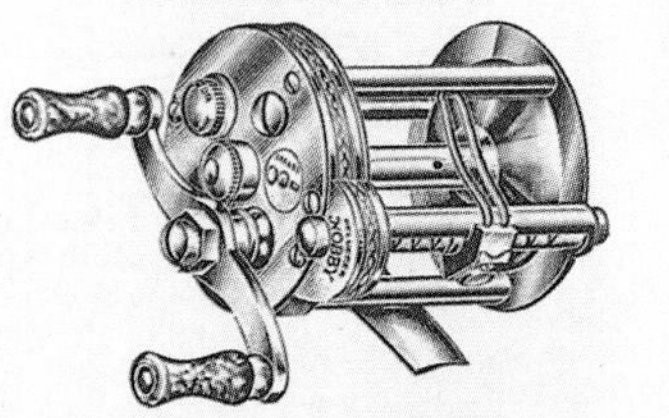

Level Winding, Anti-Back-Lash Quadruple Multiplying

Satin finish nickalum trimmed in polished diamolite; phosphor bronze bearings; rustproof diamalloy spool pivots and gear post; spiral cut bronze gear and tool steel pinion; adjustable back sliding click; genuine scarlet agate jewelled oil cups; fancy balanced crank.

Each

No. 1963—Cap. 100 yds. 18 lb. test silk line, diam. of plates 2 in., length of pillars 1⅞ in.; wt. each 5¾ oz...................**$7.20**

PFLUEGER SKILKAST

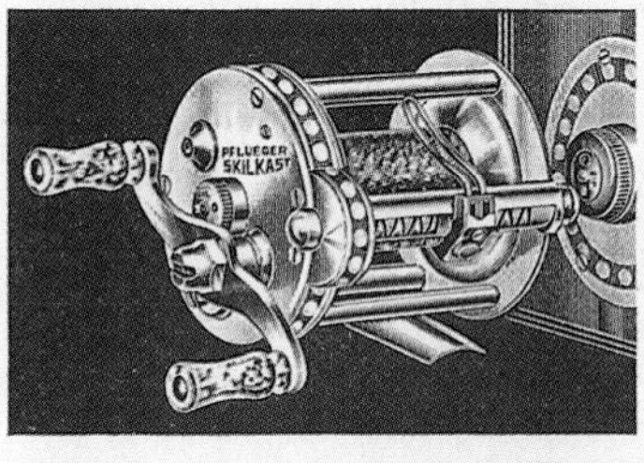

Level Winding, Anti-Back-Lash Quadruple Multiplying, with Mechanical Thumber

Polished diamolite finish; light weight aluminum spool with cork arbor cemented in perfect balance; spiral cut gears; replaceable bearings for double thread shaft; precision built extra wide phosphor bronze line guide.

Mechanical thumber does away with all need for thumbing the reel after cast is started. Adjustable with micro-precision to suit line and lure used, it affords distance casts without any tendency to overrun or back lash. Thumber operates only when line is running out.

Each

No. 1953—Cap. 75 yds. 18 lb. test silk line, diam. of plates 2 in., length of pillars 1⅞ in.; wt. each 11 oz...................**$7.00**

FISHING REELS

PFLUEGER AKRON

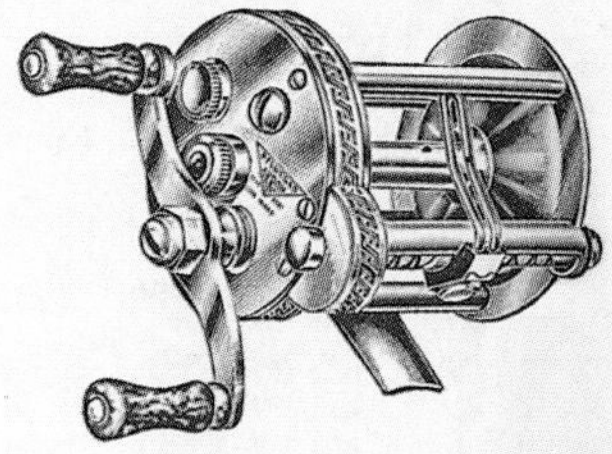

Level Winding, Anti-Back-Lash Quadruple Multiplying

Polished diamolite finish; phosphor bronze bearings; spiral cut bronze gear and tool steel pinion, diamalloy spool pivots and gear post; adjustable back sliding click; tension oil cups, each with bearing oil feeder, inset with large scarlet red jewels; fancy balanced crank.

Cap. 110 yds. 18 lb. test silk line, diam. of plates 2 in., length of pillars 1⅞ in.

Each

No. 1893—Standard spool; wt. each 10 oz. **$6.00**

No. 1893L—Lightweight aluminum alloy spool; wt. each 9½ oz..... **6.00**

PFLUEGER TRUMP

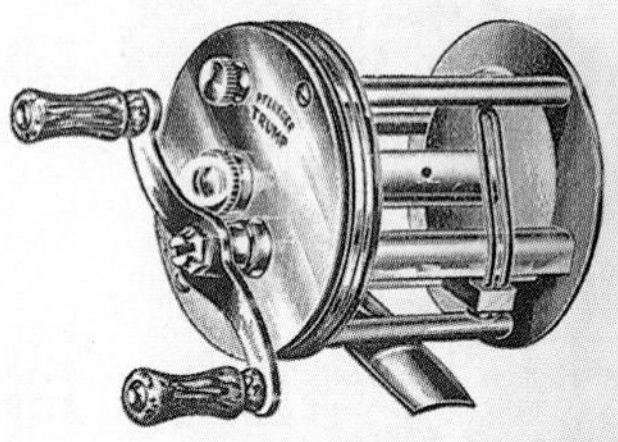

Level Winding, Anti-Back-Lash Quadruple Multiplying

Polished diamolite finish; tension oil cups inset with scarlet jewels; hardened steel pivots; adjustable back sliding click; steel pinion; fancy balanced crank; mottled brown pyralin grips.

Light in weight, distinctive in design, built for long wear and satisfactory service.

Each

No. 1943—Cap. 90 yds. 18 lb. test silk line, diam. of plates 2¼ in., length of pillars 1⅞ in.; wt. each 7⅞ oz...................**$3.25**

FOUR BROS. PARD

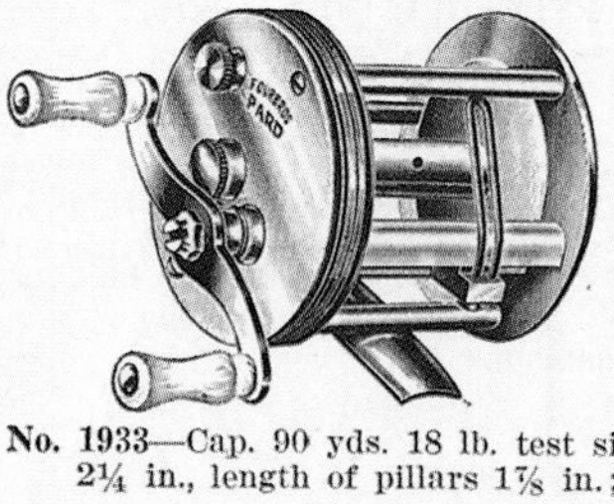

Level Winding, Anti-Back-Lash, Quadruple Multiplying

Finished in combination of highly polished and satin nickel; tension oil cups; hardened steel pivots; adjustable back sliding click; pyralin ivory handles.

Each

No. 1933—Cap. 90 yds. 18 lb. test silk line, diam. of plates 2¼ in., length of pillars 1⅞ in.; wt. each 7½ oz.......**$2.50**

PORTAGE PASTIME

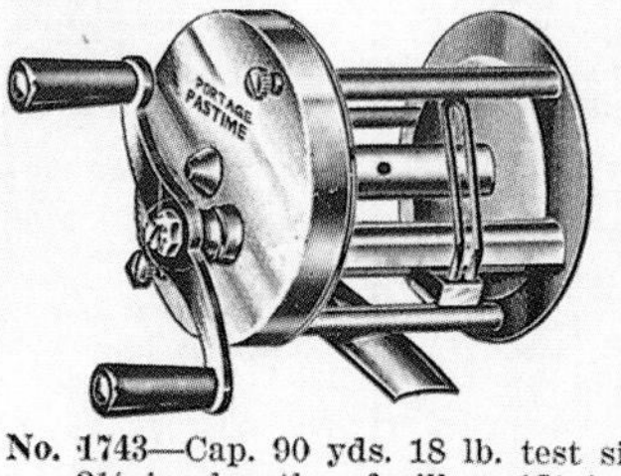

Level Winding, Quadruple Multiplying

Polished nickel finish; hardened steel pivots; bushed for bearings, with oil holes; adjustable back sliding click; take apart feature provides for easy cleaning; substantial level winding mechanism; fancy crank with double handles.

Each

No. 1743—Cap. 90 yds. 18 lb. test silk line, diam. of plates 2¼ in., lengths of pillars 1⅞ in.; wt. each 7⅝ oz......**$1.80**

All above, one in a box.

Jennison Hardware Company, Catalog Number 41, 1941, page 8.

THE JENNISON HARDWARE CO.

FISHING REELS
BRONSON LASHLESS

Level Winding, Anti-Back-Lash, Quadruple Multiplying

Heavily chromium plated brass; new aluminum spool, 28% lighter, fitted with cork arbor; adjustable click on tail plate; four gear train, two spur and two spiral; duo-pawl; "S" crank with comfortable shaped colored handles.

A newly devised spool bearing mechanism provides a highly sensitive anti-back-lash feature. Accurately adjusted to all variations in lure weight, style of anglers cast, by turning tail plate spool bearing on left end of reel.

Each

No. 1700—Cap. 100 yds., diam. of spool 1½ in., length of pillars 1¾ in.; net wt. each 9 oz......$6.00

BRONSON SILVER PRINCESS

Level Winding, Quardruple Multiplying

Silver-like chromium plated brass; decorative design on head, tail and crank plates; ebony bakelite head ring. Three-piece take-down; adjustable jeweled spool caps; duo-pawl; duo-click; spiral gears; adjustable drag. New locking device for crank handles. Mottled black and white ivorine handle grips; tension spring beneath grips to eliminate vibration; extended line carriage.

Each

No. 3720—Cap. 100 yds., diam. of spool 1½ in., length of pillars 1¾ in.; net wt. each 9 oz. $6.00

BRONSON SPARTON

Level Winding, Non-Back-Lash, Quadruple Multiplying

Heavily chromium plated brass; attractively knurled head cap; three-piece take-down. Knurled, adjustable spool caps; four gear train, two spirals and two spur gears; adjustable click on tail plate; phosphor bronze click spring with hardened steel ratchet and pawl; chromium plated phosphor bronze level winding screw; black and white shaped grips. Equipped with new improved non-back-lash device.

Each

No. 3500—Cap. 100 yds., diam. of spool 1½ in., length of pillars 1¾ in.; net wt. each 8½ oz. $3.50

FISHING REELS
BRONSON VETERAN DELUXE

Level Winding, Quadruple Multiplying

Heavily chromium plated brass; new light weight aluminum spool fitted with cork arbor. Two spiral and two spur gears; improved design for smoother, quieter operation and longer life. Jeweled adjustable spool caps; adjustable drag; adjustable click; accurately balanced crank with comfortable handle grips.

The newly designed light weight spool allows more accurate, easier and longer casts and also tends to reduce backlashes.

Each

No. 1400—Cap. 100 yds., diam. of spool 1½ in., length of pillars 1¹³⁄₁₆ in.; net wt. each 9 oz.....$5.50

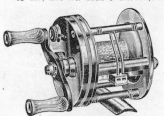

Narrow Frame, Level Winding, Quadruple Multiplying

Identical to No. 1400 above except that it has a narrow frame. It is an ideal reel for "Skish" casting and tournament casting or it will serve very nicely as a standard casting reel.

Heavily chromium plated brass; aluminum spool fitted with cork arbor; pillared rod clip.

Each

No. 1401—Cap. 50 yds., diam. of spool 1½ in., length of pillars 1⅜ in.; net wt. each 8 oz. $6.00

BRONSON MERCURY
Level Winding, Quadruple Multiplying

Chromium plated brass frame; head cap and tail plate decorated. Aluminum spool fitted with cork arbor. Jeweled, adjustable spool caps; duo-pawl; adjustable click with hardened steel ratchet and pawl; chromium plated level winding screw; pillared rod clip; balanced crank with black and white grips.

Each

No. 2550—Cap. 100 yds., diam. of spool 1½ in., length of pillars 1¾ in.; net wt. each 8¾ oz. $3.00

No. 2551—Narrow frame; otherwise same as No. 2550; cap. 50 yds.; diam. of spool 1½ in., length of pillars 1⅜ in.; net wt. each 8 oz. 3.25

FISHING REELS
BRONSON VETERAN

Level Winding, Quardruple Multiplying

Heavily chromium plated brass; decorative knurl on outside of head cap; three-piece take-down. Knurled, jeweled, adjustable spool caps; improved click, new duo-pawl; adjustable thumb drag; locking device for crank handle; black and white handle grips.

Each

No. 1010—Cap. 100 yds., diam. of spool 1½ in., length of pillars 1¾ in.; net wt. each 9 oz. $4.50

BRONSON RETRIEVER

Level Winding, Quadruple Multiplying

Heavily chromium plated brass; three-piece take-down construction. Adjustable spool caps; four gear train with bridge construction; two spiral and two spur gears; duo-pawl; adjustable click with hardened steel ratchet and pawl and phosphor bronze click spring; large full shaped green handle grips.

Each

No. 2900—Cap. 150 yds. 16 lb. test silk line, diam. of spool 1⅞ in., length of pillars 1¹¹⁄₁₆ in.; net wt. each 10 oz. $3.50

All above, one in a box.

Jennison Hardware Company, Catalog Number 41, 1941, page 9.

THE JENNISON HARDWARE CO.

FISHING REELS
BRONSON GLADIATOR

Level Winding, Non-Back-Lash, Quadruple Multiplying

Chromium plated throughout. Adjustable click on tail plate; hardened steel ratchet and pawl; chromium plated level winding screw; new crank nut assembly; nicely shaped green and white handle grips on perfectly balanced S shaped crank.

Each

No. 3400—Cap. 100 yds., diam. of spool 1½ in., length of pillars 1¾ in.; net wt. each 9 oz..........$2.45

One in a box.

BRONSON METEOR

Level Winding, Quadruple Multiplying

Circle chromium plated brass; three-piece take-down construction. Knurled adjustable spool caps; duo-pawl; adjustable click; balanced "S" crank with black and white shaped grips.

Each

No. 2500—Cap. 100 yds., diam. of spool 1½ in., length of pillars 1¾ in.; net wt. each 8¼ oz....$2.45

One in a box.

FISHING REELS
BRONSON FLEETWING

Level Winding, Quadruple Multiplying

All metal, chromium plated; three-piece, take-down construction. Two spur and two spiral gears; duo-pawl; adjustable click; hardened steel level winding and click pawl; phosphor bronze click spring; screw-off, non-adjustable jeweled spool caps; S shaped balanced crank with white shaped handle grips.

Each

No. 2475—Cap. 100 yds., diam. of spool 1½ in., length of pillars 1¾ in.; net wt. each 7 oz......$1.75

One in a box.

BRONSON COMET

Level Winding, Quadruple Multiplying

All metal, chromium plated; three-piece take-down. Duo-pawl; adjustable click; hardened steel ratchet and pawl; new crank nut assembly; "S" crank with green and white shaped grips.

Each

No. 2400—Cap. 100 yds.; diam. of spool 1½ in., length of pillars 1¾ in.; net wt. each 9 oz..........$1.45

No. 2433—Same as No. 2400 except nickel plated and without duo-pawl 1.20

One in a box.

FISHING REELS
BRONSON ALTOONA

Level Winding, Quadruple Multiplying

Bright nickel plated finish; walnut bakelite head and tail plates, with tapered crank handle grips to match; three-piece take-down construction. Improved click; metal bridge molded into bakelite head cap serves as bearing surface for points of wear and affords perfect alignment of reel.

Each

No. 4200—Cap. 100 yds., diam. of spool 1½ in., length of pillars 1¾ in.; net wt. each 7 oz.....$1.15

One in a box

BRONSON ARROW JR.

Single Action

An all metal reel of light yet sturdy construction; nickel plated finish. Adjustable click; double handles with green grips.

Each

No. 4400—Cap. 80 yds., diameter of spool 1½ in., length of pillars 1⅝ in.; wt. per box 3 lbs......$0.25

Twelve in a box.

HEDDON LONE EAGLE

Level Winding, Quadruple Multiplying

Chromium plated throughout; three-piece take-down construction. Silent, smooth running spiral gears of hardened brass and steel; click button on bottom plate; crystal-agate jewel spool caps; chromium plated level-winding screw and carriage; double crank with mottled ivoroid grip.

Each

No. 206—Cap. 100 yds. 15 lb. test silk line; diam. of spool 1½ in., length of pillars 1¹¹⁄₁₆ in.; wt. each 8½ oz..........$4.00

One in a box

UNION

Level Winding, Quadruple Multiplying

Nickel plated, satin finish. Free running and durable; with click; well balanced double grip handle with white grips.

Each

No. 7225S—Cap. 60 to 80 yds., diam. of plates 2 in., length of pillars 1⅞ in.; wt. each 7 oz......................$1.00

THE JENNISON HARDWARE CO.

FISHING REELS
UNION

Double Multiplying

Nickel plated; with click and balanced handle. A large size reel at a popular price.

Each
No. 7076—Cap. 40 to 60 yds. diam. of plates 2 in., length of pillars 1⅝ in.; wt. each 3½ oz........$0.60
One in a box.

Nickel Plated

Nickel plated finish, good grade steel; permanent click; raised pillars; wood handle.

A pattern familiar with all fishermen.

Each
No. 35—Cap. 40 yds. 18 lb. test silk line; diam. of plates 1⅝ in.; length of pillars 1 in.; wt. each 5 oz. $0.25
Six in a box.

PFLUEGER PAKRON, TROLLING

Extra Large, Single Action

Satin diamolite finish. Powerful adjustable drag and adjustable click, both operated from back plate. Drag adjustable while fish is being played—operates only while line is going out, no tension or drag while reeling in. Spool has bearings both front and back; balanced crank with large grips.

Designed especially for lake trout fishing with wire line but a splendid trolling reel for many purposes.

Each
No. 3180—Cap. 1200 ft. No. 20 B.&S. gauge copper wire or 600 yds. 12 thread linen line; diam. of plate 6⅛ in., length of pillars 1¼ in.; wt. each 38 oz. $6.00
One in a box.

FISHING REELS
PFLUEGER MEDALIST

Single Action; with Right Hand Polished Diamalloy Line Guard

Satin nickalum, gunmetal finish; light weight perforated spool flanges. Spool can be instantly detached from frame without pinching line. Adjustable weight feature permits increasing weight up to about 50 per cent.

With Adjustable Drag and Click

Adjustable while fish is being played; operates only while line is going out; very light click when winding in.

Each
No. 1494—Cap. 90 yds. "G" line; diam. of plates 3¼ in., length of pillars 1⅜ in.; wt. each 5¼ oz..$5.75

With Dual Click Mechanism; No Drag

Either or both clicks may be engaged, providing light or heavy click action.

Each
No. 1492—Cap. 60 yds. "G" line; diam. of plates 2⅞ in., length of pillars 1⅜ in.; wt. each 4 oz.....$5.25
One in a box.

PFLUEGER GEM

Single Action; with Right Hand Line Guard

Nickalum, gunmetal finish; very light weight yet strong. Click mechanism of latest improved design; hardened steel click tongue, smooth in action and built for long wear. Spool quickly and easily removed by a simple but positive latch mechanism operated with one finger—no screws to twist off or become lost. Cross plate of neat and substantial construction will fit all standard rods.

Each
No. 2094—Cap. 90 yds. "G" line; diam. of plates 3¼ in.; length of pillars 1⅜ in.; wt. each 4 oz..$3.50
One in a box.

FISHING REELS
PFLUEGER SAL-TROUT

Single Action

For fly casting and trolling. A large capacity reel—distinctively light in weight.

Satin gunmetal; one-piece perforated back plate; perforated removable spool; non-corrosive diamalloy axle; adjustable back sliding tempered steel click; black rubber handle.

Oiling system is provided whereby the reel can be oiled at every frictional point without taking it apart.

Each
No. 1554—Cap. 100 yds. "G" line; diam. of plates 3¼ in., length of pillars 1⅜ in.; wt. each 4¼ oz...$1.80
One in a box.

PFLUEGER SAL-TROUT, TROLLING
Single Action

Outstanding in line capacity this model was especially designed for steelhead deep lake fishing and general trolling purposes. It is particularly adapted for wire line fishing.

Adjustable drag—a very simple but positive mechanism permits adjusting drag tension on spool to serve any requirement.

Mat nickel finish; diamalloy non-corrosive axle; adjustable back sliding click; black rubberoid double handles.

Each
No. 1558—Cap. 210 yds. No. 20 B.&S. gauge copper wire; diam. of plates 5½ in., length of pillars 1 in.; wt. each 18 oz. $3.50
One in a box.

PFLUEGER CAPTAIN
Single Action

Mat nickel finish; non-corrosive diamalloy axle; adjustable axle drag.

Upright cross plate and line guard are screwed together whereby the reel easily can be made either right or left hand wind. Readily oiled without taking reel apart.

Each
No. 4128—Cap. 365 yds. No. 12 cuttyhunk line, diam. of spool 4¾ in., length of pillars 1 in.; wt. each 10 oz. $2.50
One in a box.

THE JENNISON HARDWARE CO.

FISHING REELS
PFLUEGER TAXIE

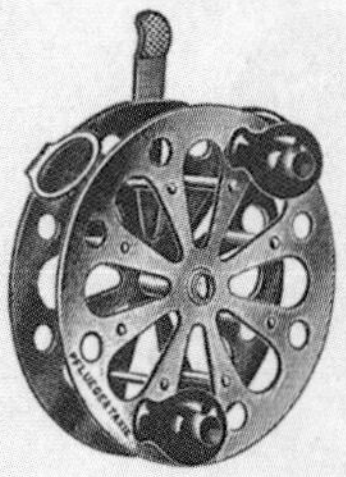

Single Action

Mat nickel finish; front and back plates are of one piece construction and firmly riveted together; perforated side plates. Has double line guard for either right or left hand use; diamalloy non-corrosive axle. For mounting flat on rod, suitable for all standard fresh water rods.

With Spring Lever Drag

Each

No. 3128—Cap. 365 yds. size 12 cuttyhunk line; diam. of spool 4¾ in., width of spool 1 in.; wt. each 9 oz. **$1.65**

One in a box.

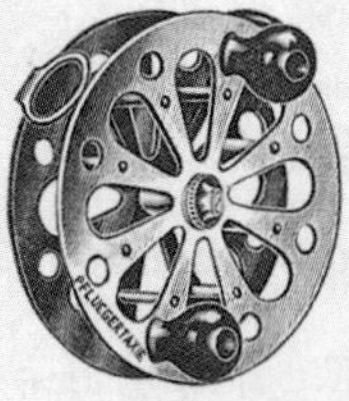

With Adjustable Axle Drag

Otherwise identical with No. 3128 above.

Each

No. 3138 .....**$2.00**

One in a box.

PFLUEGER PROGRESS

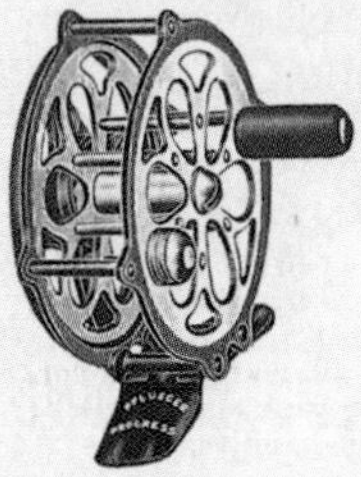

Single Action

Satin gunmetal finish; one - piece perforated back plate; perforated removable spool; steel axle; adjustable back sliding tempered click; rubberoid handle.

Each

No. 1184—Cap. 80 yds., diam. of plates 2¾ in.; length of pillars 1 in.; wt. each 3¾ oz.....**$1.10**

One in a box.

UNION, FLY

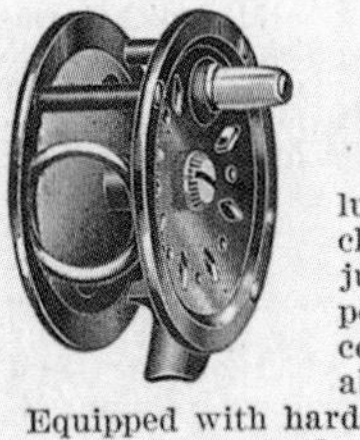

Single Action Lightweight

Black finish duralumin; permanent click with three adjustable wearing points; open plate construction; removable spool.

Equipped with hardened chrome plated steel ring line guard.

Each

No. 7169—Cap. 50 yds., diam. of plates 3 in., length of pillars 1 in.; wt. each 4¾ oz.........**$1.50**

One in a box.

FISHING REELS
UNION, FLY

Single Action Lightweight

Black nickel finish, light weight steel frame with click.

A good grade single action trout reel.

Each

No. 7115-S—Cap. 90 yds. 18 lb. test silk line; diam. of plates 2⅞ in., length of pillars 1 in.; wt. each 4¾ oz. **$0.75**

One in a box.

MARTIN AUTOMATIC

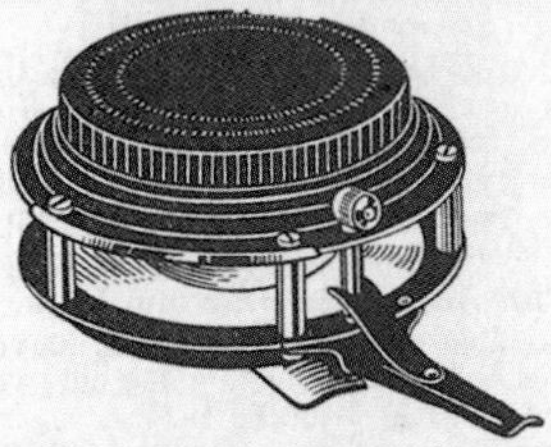

Black Finish; Free Stripping

Sturdily made of aluminum throughout; complete with line protector.

A slight touch on the brake lever and all slack line is reeled in as fast as it is retrieved. No slack line, snarls or knots. A throw-off releases spring tension on the spool, permitting a free-running spool, allowing line to be removed without causing spring tension.

Equipped with a new "reel click."

Nos.	2	3	4
Cap. "G" line, yds.	90	150	225
Diam. spool, in.	2 11/16	2 11/16	2 11/16
Width spool, in.	7/16	11/16	13/16
Wt. each, oz.	6¾	7	7¼
Each	$5.00	5.50	6.00

One in a box.

MARTIN FLY-WATE AUTOMATIC

Black Finish; Free-Stripping

Developed especially for the fly caster, light in weight and gives a perfect balance to any light fly rod; by a slight touch on the brake lever the Fly-Wate automatically reels in line as rapidly as it is retrieved. No slack line, knots or snarls.

Equipped with a proven, practical, free-stripping feature that permits stripping line from spool without winding spring, and a new "reel click."

Nos.	27	28
Cap. "G" line, yds.	90	150
Diam. spool, in.	2 11/16	2¾
Width spool, in.	7/16	⅝
Wt. each, oz.	6¼	6½
Each	$7.00	8.00

One in a box.

FISHING REELS
PERRINE AUTOMATIC

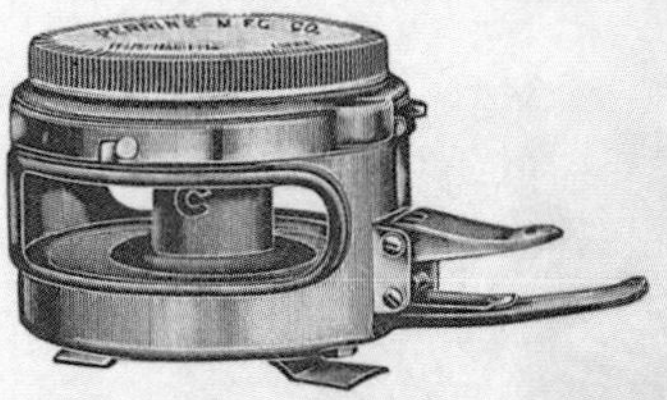

Black Alumilite Finish, Free Stripping

Light weight. Strong construction of tempered Dural aluminum alloy; stainless steel line guides; smooth and flush on inside of shell; right or left hand use. Quick takedown without tools for cleaning.

No brake manipulation necessary to strip line; entirely free of brake resistance. All the freedom of a single action reel in fly casting and the advantage of the automatic for retrieving the line by a touch of the finger.

Exceptionally long spring, retrieves 70 to 90 feet of line.

Nos.	30	50	80
Cap. "G" line, yds.	35	50	80
Diam. spool, in.	2¾	2¾	2¾
Width spool, in.	⅜	½	¾
Wt. each, oz.	7¾	8¼	8¾
Each	$6.30	7.40	7.90

One in a box.

HEDDON AUTOMATIC

Heddon
AUTOMATIC FLY-REEL
Free-Stripping

Rich Mahogany Alumilite Finish, Free Stripping

Strongly constructed of Dural aluminum alloy; the finish is very durable and nonlight-reflecting. Stainless steel line guides; smooth and flush on inside of shell; for right or left hand use; quick take-down without tools.

Has all the freedom of a single action reel in casting, plus the advantages of an automatic, as stripping is done without manipulating the brake, entirely free of brake resistance. No necessity to lock-off the brake.

Spool is mounted on the pinion with frictional contact, adjustable by nut on upper end, to permit line to be stripped after spring is fully wound without damage to the gears or spring.

Takes almost any line generally used for trout, small mouth bass, crappies, etc.

Each

No. 57—Cap. 50 yds. "G" line; diam. of spool 2¾ in., width of spool ⅝ in.; wt. each 8¼ oz. **$7.50**

One in a box.

Jennison Hardware Company, Catalog Number 41, 1941, page 12.

THE JENNISON HARDWARE CO.

FISHING REELS
PFLUEGER OHIO, SALT WATER

Double Multiplying

Metal bound plates, polished diamolite trim; satin chrome finish spool. Internal drag, operated by star wheel permits adjusting tension as desired, while fish is being played. Free spool controlled by shifting lever conveniently located on upper edge of front plate. Perma-mesh gears; always in mesh. Hardened end bearing steel pivots; generated spiral tooth gear and pinion; adjustable back sliding click; fancy balanced crank with mottled black and white torpedo handle. All working parts can be oiled without taking reel apart.

Each

No. 1978—Cap. 275 yds. No. 12 cuttyhunk line; diam. of plates 3¼ in., length of pillars 2⅛ in., gear ratio 2¼ to 1; wt. each 2⅜ oz.................................$6.50

One in a box.

PFLUEGER INTER-OCEAN, SALT WATER

Double Multiplying

Black bakelite and polished chromium plates; reverse metal bound; satin chromium finished spool. Free spool controlled by shifting lever conveniently located on upper edge of front plate. Perma-mesh gears; gear and pinion always in mesh. Generated spiral tooth gears; and bearing steel pivots; adjustable back sliding click; patented adjustable tension oil cups; leather thumb drag; balanced crank with torpedo style handle. Extra strong cross plate will fit any rod.

Each

No. 1888—Cap. 275 yds. No. 12 cuttyhunk lines; diam. of plates 3¼ in., lengths of pillars 2⅛ in., gear ratio 2 to 1; wt. each 24 oz.................................$4.50

One in a box.

PFLUEGER GOLDEN WEST, SALT WATER

Double Multiplying

Black bakelite and satin nickel. Free spool controlled by shifting lever conveniently located on upper edge of front plate. Perma-mesh gears; gears always in mesh. Generated spiral tooth gears; end bearing steel pivots; removable bronze spool pivot bearings; adjustable back sliding click; patented adjustable tension oil cups; leather thumb drag; balanced crank with hard rubber handle. Extra strong crossplate will fit any standard rod.

Each

No. 1878-F—Cap. 275 yds. No. 12 cuttyhunk line; diam. of plates 3¼ in., length of pillars 2⅛ in., gear ratio 2 to 1; wt. each 21 oz. $2.70

One in a box.

REEL LUBRICANT
REELSLICK

In Collapsible Metal Tubes

The ideal lubricant for reels and all fishing equipment. Saves rods—positively eliminates frozen joints. Absolute protection against rust, moisture and salt water damage.

Per dozen

No. 500—Wt. per dozen tubes ½ lb........................$1.20

One dozen tubes in a display carton.

REEL GEAR GREASE
PFLUEGER RUNFREE

In Collapsible Tubes

A combination of the best known, proven lubricants that clings to the teeth of the gear and does not gum or retard the speed of the drive.

Gears frequently and properly greased with "Runfree" will run smoothly almost indefinitely.

Per dozen

No. 2120—Wt. per dozen tubes 7⅘ oz.........$1.20

One tube in a box, one dozen boxes in a carton.

REEL OIL
PFLUEGER SPEEDE

In Glass Bottles

Free from all perfumes, acids and other corrosive elements. A smooth, lasting lubricant, prevents a sticky and jerky action, will not gum or thicken. A wire oil dropper is part of the bottle cap; oil will flow out of any form of oil can. Screw cap will hold bottle oil tight.

Per dozen

No. 379—About ⅔ ounce; wt. per dozen bottles 3½ lbs.....$2.40

One-half dozen bottles in a display carton.

POCKET OILERS
PFLUEGER "MARVEL"

Nickel Plated Brass

A convenient size and shape for the angler. Feeds oil promptly in hot or cold weather by compressing the sides of the oiler with the fingers. Each compression delivers a drop of oil.

To seal the oiler, put tapered needle in center of cap into opening in spout, then screw cap down.

Per dozen

No. 2103—Wt. per dozen ½ lb.......$3.00

One dozen in a box.

Jennison Hardware Company, Catalog Number 41, 1941, page 13.

Pflueger catalog, 1966, front cover.

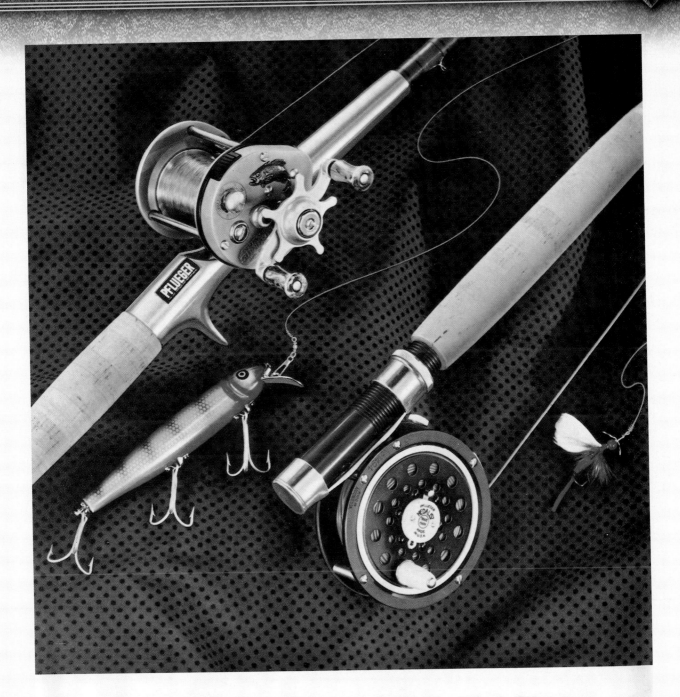

For Those Who Appreciate The Finest

Bait Casting

No where in the world will you find a bait casting combination to compare with the Supreme and this new, exclusive, balanced-action rod. For over a century the "most copied" yet, never matched for performance.

Fly Casting

Let the flies be wet or dry. Let the fish be trout or tarpon and you will find the experts using the Pflueger Medalist . . . they know there is no reel that can compare. Beginner or old hand . . . invest in the best.

Pflueger catalog, 1966, inside front cover.

"Watchlike" Precision that makes Pflueger "The Tackle of Champions"

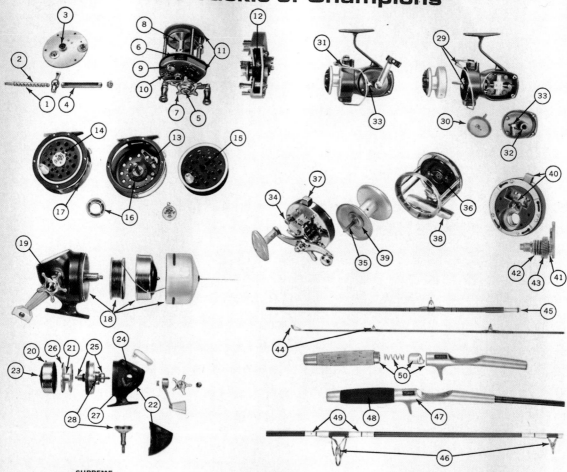

SUPREME

1. Finest quality line guide mechanism.
2. Stainless steel double thread shaft.
3. Phosphor bronze bearings for long life.
4. Double thread shaft removable without taking entire reel apart.
5. Free spool.
6. Optional anti-reverse.
7. Star drag.
8. One-piece precision cut spool made of solid aluminum bar stock.
9. Adjustable anti-backlash.
10. Storage of extra half-nut in front cap.
11. Die cast aluminum front and back caps.
12. Watch-like gearing mechanism.

MEDALIST

13. One-way actuating brake.
14. Quick take-apart push button.
15. If weights are desired for better balance, split shot can be inserted into the drum of the spool.
16. Reversible right or left handed ratchet.
17. Stainless steel chrome plated line guard.

99 JUPITER

18. Quick take-apart.
19. Star drag.
20. Carboloy pin pick-up.
21. One-piece anodized machine-cut spool.
22. Die cast aluminum frame.
23. Neoprene line snubber.
24. Oilite bearing.
25. Reciprocating spool mechanism.
26. Brushes on spool to prevent line fouling.
27. Built-in anti-reverse.
28. Stainless steel pinion—precision machine cut, heavy duty brass gear.

1200 FREEFLITE

29. Stainless steel bail and line roller.
30. Micro-precision cut gears.
31. Fold-away bail for easy storage.
32. Oilite bearings.
33. Optional, silent, anti-reverse mechanism.

CAPITOL

34. Quick take-apart button.
35. Stainless steel spool axle.
36. Phosphor bronze, non-corrosive bearings.

37. Push button free spool—automatic re-engagement when crank is turned.
38. One-piece crossplate.
39. Reinforced spool flanges.
40. Push button free spool mechanism.
41. Built-in anti-reverse.
42. Nine disk drag for maximum braking power.
43. Heavy duty, precision, machine-cut gears.

RODS

44. Carboloy guides and tip top.
45. O-ring ferrules.
46. Chrome plated stainless steel braced guides for salt water rods.
47. Silverflite handle—simplicity of design.
48. Finest quality molded composition grip for casting ease and durability.
49. Windings—high quality threads attractively wrapped on guides and ferrules to match colors of rod shafts.
50. Reel locking assembly—minimum working parts.

HIGHLIGHT QUALITY PFLUEGER FEATURES
(Additional features shown on following pages)

Pflueger catalog, 1966, page 1.

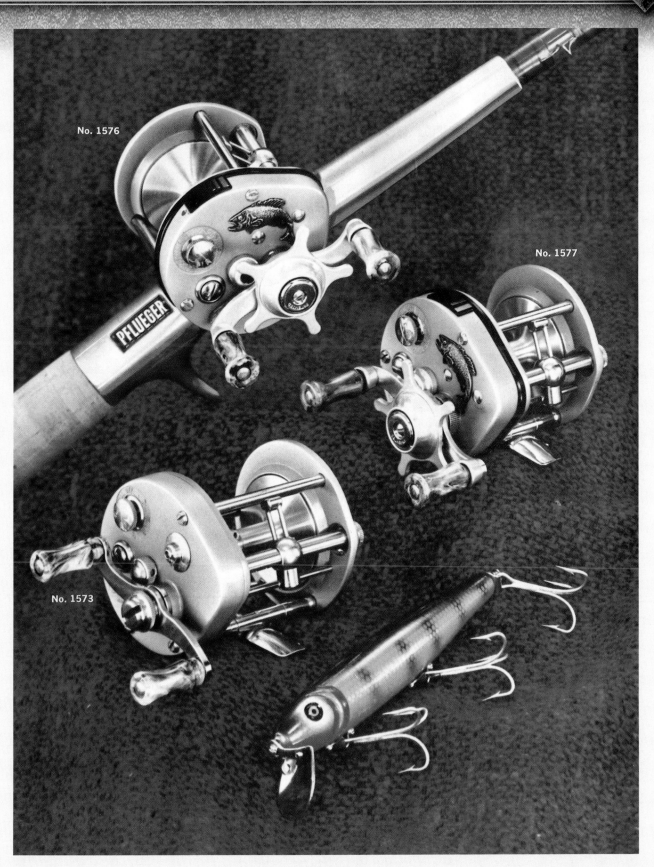

Pflueger catalog, 1966, page 2.

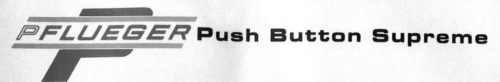

PFLUEGER Push Button Supreme

Nos. 1576-1577 PFLUEGER SUPREME WITH FREE SPOOL & STAR DRAG

Best of all bait casting reels. Provides everything the most demanding fisherman can want. Extremely light yet strong with tough aluminum alloy. Precision built with exacting tolerances that assure smooth as silk performance. Automatic push-button Free Spool gives extra-long casts even with light lures. Handle stands still while spool spins. Handle engages automatically at retrieve. Star Drag gives fingertip control even while playing fish.

Has infinite selection of anti-backlash settings. Optional Anti-Reverse on top of cap for instant use. Phosphor bronze gears are spiral-cut and hand-lapped with watch-like precision for longest wear and dependability. The double thread shaft is chrome plated stainless steel. Satin finished by patented process for greatest corrosion resistance. Handles monofilament or braided line. Fast retrieve with 4 to 1 gear ratio.

NARROW SPOOL SUPREME
No. 1577
Spool width 1¼". Weight 7¼ oz.
Capacity 15# mono, 135 yards.
$57.50

STANDARD SPOOL SUPREME
No. 1576
Spool width 1¾". Weight 8 oz.
Capacity 15# mono, 200 yards.
$57.50

GIFT BOXED
Black molded plastic case, white stain top and red velvet base.

FREE ACCESSORIES
Both the Supreme Reels 1576 and 1577 plus the Classic Supreme 1573 are equipped with soft rubber Comfo ring plus the popular E-Z Grips for handles and combination wrench-screwdriver.

PFLUEGER Classic Supreme

No. 1573 PFLUEGER CLASSIC SUPREME

An aristocrat among even the finest reels, this model appeals to the experienced bait caster because of its smoothness and life-long dependability. Both its satin-finished frame and its micro-machined aluminum spool are extremely corrosion resistant and will withstand the rigors of salt water tarpon fishing as well as the challenge of fresh water bass, walleye, or northern pike. All gears are spiral cut and hand-lapped with meticulous care to assure a smooth, effortless action with every cast. Its

level wind mechanism can be removed for cleaning without taking the reel down. Has jeweled oil cups, stainless steel chrome plated double threaded shaft, sliding click, and is equipped with a special compartment in the reel cap for a spare pawl (which guides the line back and forth across the reel). This reel handles either monofilament or braided line easily. Gear ratio is 4 to 1, with line capacity of 200 yards 15 lb. test nylon line. Weight of 7½ ounces.
$44.50

When ordering please specify our stock numbers and sizes.

Pflueger catalog, 1966, page 3.

Pflueger catalog, 1966, page 4.

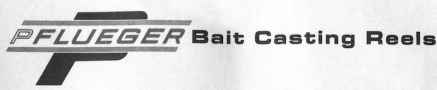

PFLUEGER Bait Casting Reels

* No. 1995 SUMMIT

A handsome reel of tough nickel alloy with brightly polished chromium plate that defies wear or rough action. Triple-unit construction with stainless steel shaft. Its patented push button Free Spool can be disengaged when casting heavier lures. Sturdy Star Drag. Handsome engraved design on cap and back plate, jeweled oil cups, adjustable anti-backlash and sliding click. Brass gears, bronze bearings. Gear ration 4 to 1, 175 yd. capacity of 15 lb. test nylon. Wt. 7-5/6 oz. **$24.95**

No. 1993L SUMMIT

A medium priced reel well known for its always-smooth action and good looks. Precision built for all-around fishing, it's dressed up with engraved cap and crank, and has the big extras: jeweled oil cups, chromed parts, brass gears, long-life bronze bearings, and stainless steel double thread shaft. Has spare pawl, removable level wind mechanism. All moving parts can be oiled without take-down. 4 to 1 gear ratio, with line capacity of 175 yds. 15 lb. test line. 7¾ oz. **$18.95**

* No. 1895 AKRON

For fishermen who want a luxury reel minus the big price tag. An action reel that speeds out line smoothly with either light or heavy lures. Has patented Free Spool feature. Star-type drag gives fingertip control of line at all times. Level wind mechanism is removable, and all moving parts easily lubricated. Spare pawl included. Jeweled oil cups, adjustable anti-backlash, and sliding click, brass gears, bronze bearings, stainless steel shaft. 4 to 1 gear ratio, reel takes 175 yds. 15 lb. nylon line. Weight 7¾ oz. **$19.95**

Nos. 1893 and 1893L AKRON

For the caster who wants a highly serviceable reel that can take plenty of action. Ruggedly built with solid brass, has handsomely plated chrome finish and bronze bearings. Its easy-moving level wind mechanism is removable. Stainless steel double thread shaft, jeweled oil cups, adjustable anti-backlash, and sliding click. Spare pawl, line capacity of 175 yds. of 15 lb. test nylon. Gear ratio is 4 to 1. No. 1893 with standard chrome spools (8⅓ oz.). No. 1893L with lightweight aluminum spool (7⅔ oz.).
.... **$14.95 ea.**

No. 1960 DELUXE NOBBY

Here's the reel for precision casting—one of the fastest, smoothest, lightest reels made. Moving parts develop 20% less inertia, resulting in a faster spool, greater ability to cast lighter lures. Has polished pivots, gears, and pinions, and hollowed gears that are stronger, lighter. Nylon thrust bearing on each side of gear for less friction. Anodized aluminum frame. Entire reel weighs only 5 oz. 4 to 1 gear ratio, 175 yd. line capacity of 15 lb. line. **$16.95**

* No. 1965 FREE SPOOL NOBBY

The reel itself is light—only weighs 6 oz. because it's aluminum. Strong enough to handle big game fish—and light enough for tournament casting. Free Spool operation is optional at the discretion of the angler. Star Drag helps land larger fish with lighter line. Materials and Construction: Attractive red anodized aluminum construction. Light weight spool, strong machined skeleton gears, extra pawl in compartment. Data: Gear ratio 4 to 1. Line capacity—175 yds of 15 lb. test nylon line. 1⅞" pillars, 2" plates. Wt. 6 oz. **$22.95**

No. 1963C NOBBY

A rugged, lightweight reel for longer, lighter-action rods and ⅜ to ½ oz. lures. Has jeweled oil cups, adjustable anti-backlash, sliding click, and special compartment in cap for spare pawl. Level wind mechanism can be removed, moving parts lubricated without take-down. Satin-finished with chrome for long wear. Has stainless steel shaft, brass gears and bronze bearings for quiet operation, long life. Aluminum spool. 4 to 1 gear ratio. 175 yds. 15 lb. nylon test. Weight 5½ oz. **$15.95**

No. 1953 SKILKAST

Makes any caster an expert. Mechanical thumber prevents spool from overrunning. No backlash since the spool is thumbed automatically at the end of lure flight. Removable level wind mechanism. Ruggedly built of brass, plated with brightly finished chrome. Precision-machined brass gears, bronze bearings for long, trouble-free life. Gear ratio 4 to 1. Takes 175 yds. of 15 lb. test nylon line. Weight 8 oz. **$16.95**

No. 1510 FAS-KAST

A direct-drive type reel with extra fast rate of retrieve and rugged enough for any fresh water fish. Converts easily to left hand retrieve and handles either monofilament or braided line. Smooth, adjustable anti-backlash and strong gears give long effortless casts without backlash. Has stainless steel shaft, satin silver finish with black Tenite trim, aluminum spool and Delrin gears. 4⅛ to 1 retrieve rate, 200 yd. 12 lb. mono test or 175 yd. 12 lb. braided line. Weighs 6 oz. **$16.95**

* FREE SPOOL! A BIG EXTRA!

With Free Spool construction, the reel's spool rotates freely, but the handle does not turn. This results in less inertia, faster starts, and the ability to cast lighter lures farther. Simply press button to activate—handle re-engages automatically as reeling starts.

When ordering please specify our stock numbers and sizes.

Pflueger catalog, 1966, page 5.

PFLUEGER Bait Casting Reels

No. 1943 TRUMP

A smart looking economical bait casting reel with extra features the experienced fisherman wants and expects to pay big money for; both a jeweled oil cup and a patented anti-backlash on rear oil cup. Moving parts easily oiled. Soundly constructed of soild brass plated with polished chrome, brass and nylon gears and brass bearings. Stainless steel double thread shaft. Gear ratio 4 to 1, line capacity of 175 yds. 15 lb. test nylon, Weight 7⅞ oz.....**$7.95**

No. 1944 PFLUEGER

The unique "Gold Rush" model with brightly polished brass finish that gleams like gold, including the spool. A solid gold performer, too, that whips out the line as smoothly as a premium model. Both frame and spool are of solid turned brass, while gears are nylon and brass. Comes equipped with Pflueger's patented anti-backlash on rear oil cup. Double thread shaft is made of stainless steel. 4 to 1 gear ratio, line capacity is 175 yds. of 15 lb. test nylon. Weight 7⅞ oz............................**$9.95**

No. 1923 TRUSTY

Here's the reel that's great for the beginner or a spare for the experienced angler. An improved lightweight model, it has smooth patented anti-backlash and sliding click. All moving parts are easily lubricated. Built of machine-tooled aluminum, with dark green anodized cap, front plate and back plate. Aluminum spool and crank are satin-finished to resist corrosion. Gear ratio 4 to 1. 175 yds. 15 lb. nylon test. Stainless steel shaft. Weight 5¼ oz. **$6.95**

No. 1933 TRUSTY

Because this amazingly strong reel is Pflueger built, it gets the approval of everyone who buys it. The same reel as the No. 1923 Trusty but with satin aluminum finish. Cross plate is of stamped construction, shaft of stainless steel. Despite its low price, it still has Pflueger's patented anti-backlash. Gear ratio is 4 to 1, with full 175 yd. line capacity of 15 lb. test nylon. Weighs 5¼ oz.................**$5.95**

Pflueger catalog, 1966, page 6.

𝙿𝙵𝙻𝚄𝙴𝙶𝙴𝚁 Service Reels

No 1355 ROCKET

No other reel can surpass this Rocket for speed, zest, and excitement. Anglers whose sporting blood runs heavy use this reel for salmon, steelhead, and muskies with solid confidence. Has instantaneous anti-reverse by moving shift lever. Equipped with Star Wheel Drag. Wind mechanism can be removed without take-down. Anti-backlash and click, spare pawl in cap. Brass finished with extra heavy chrome, stainless steel shaft, brass gears and bronze bearings. Smooth working handle crank. 3⅜ to 1 gear ratio, line capacity of 190 yds. 27 lb. braided. Weight 14½ oz. **$18.95**

No. 1365 ROCKET

Identical in features to Model No. 1355 above, except it has balanced torpedo crank and salt water cross plate. Brass spool is chrome plated. Weighs 14½ oz. **$18.95**

No. 1375 ROCKET

Solid Pflueger construction is quite evident in this premium-built reel that will manhandle the big fish with ease. Designed for monofilament line, its special spool is finished in chrome and reinforced to withstand the pressures of monofilament. Equipped with torpedo crank. Will take 300 yds. of 12 lb. test monofilament line. All other features same as No. 1355. Weight 14⅞ oz. **$19.95**

No. 2000 BOND

For fresh or salt water trolling, heavy casting, or pier fishing, this reel's in a class by itself. A fast retrieve performer, it handles either monofilament or braided line, and will run when the main gear is in Free Spool. New Patented Anti-backlash, extra pawl in cap. Has balanced torpedo handle crank, chrome plated brass gears, red bakelite plates and chrome binding rings. Gear ratio is 3.77 to 1. Line capacity is 200 yds. of 27 lb. braided nylon test or 300 yds. 15 lb. monofilament. Weight is a sturdy 15½ oz.

No. 2000 with casting rod cross plate **$15.95**
No. 2002 with salt water cross plate 15.95
No. 506 Bond rod clamps 75

No. 2004 NEW BOND

A heavy duty performer for fresh water trolling, the New Bond has fast retrieve, New Patented Anti-backlash, extra pawl in cap, Star Drag, and extra-wide Free Spool, and up to 475 yard level wind capacity with 12 lb. test line. Adaptable for light and medium salt water fishing, it takes lead core trolling line, braided, or monofilament nylon. Level wind runs with main gear in Free Spool. Has balanced torpedo handle, chromed parts, bakelite plates with chrome binding rings. Gear ratio is 3.77 to 1, weighs 16 oz.

No. 2004 . . . . **$17.95**
No. 506 Bond Rod Clamps 75

When ordering please specify our stock numbers and sizes.

Pflueger catalog, 1966, page 7.

No. 1050

No. 1200

No. 1000

PFLUEGER Spinning Reels

No. 1050 SEA STAR
Though it weighs in at only 16 oz., this versatile heavy duty spinning reel takes on salt water and fresh water both. Beefed up with an exceptionally strong aluminum spool and a frame with a baked-on epoxy finish, the Sea Star can take the big ones even under the crushing pressure of monofilament line. Bail, line roller, bail holder, axle, and trip lever are of weather-defying stainless steel. Non-locking drag with slow take-up and adjustment, silent anti-reverse on spool for smooth, level winding. Gear ratio is 3¼ to 1, retrieve rate 20 inches per revolution. 200 yd. 20 lb. monofilament line capacity.................$36.95
No. 520 Extra Spool.............................. 4.00

No. 1200 FREEFLITE
Lightning fast retrieve is the reputation of this medium sized reel. Built with large line capacity spool, it holds 200 yds. of 8 lb. test monofilament. Roller on bail prevents line damage. Bail folds for easy storage. Finished in rich epoxy grey with satin silver spool. Ultra-smooth machined gears and pinion of aluminum alloy and stainless steel. Smooth-flowing drag with slow take-up and fingertip adjustment. Gear ratio 3⅛ to 1. Wt. 8 oz.................$24.95
No. 536 Extra Spool.............................. 2.50

No. 1000 FREESPEED
An All-American performer that outwears and outvalues all other under-$20 reels on the market. Like all Pflueger reels, its component parts are of the finest materials available; a rugged spool, frame, and bail carrier of tough die-cast aluminum, all-metal gears, and oilite bearings. All exposed parts are protected by a chip-resistant baked-on finish that defies corrosion and gives the reel a handsome look. The stainless steel bail folds for storage, has hardened line roller. Gear ratio 3⅛ to 1, with 175 yd. line capacity of 6 lb. test mono. Wt. 11 oz.........................$16.95
No. 513 Extra Spool.............................. 2.00

Pflueger catalog, 1966, page 8.

PFLUEGER Spin Casting Reels

No. 86 POLARIS
A push button spin casting reel with "the sensitized touch." You can feel your casts right down to your fingertip with this reel. Drag is extremely smooth and can be adjusted while playing a fish. Has long wearing epoxy housing, blue handle, chrome finished cone and side plates. Carboloy pick-up pin. Filled with 80 yds. of 8 lb. test, super soft-monofilament. Weight 7½ oz. Free ⅜ oz. No-bounce practice casting weight included......**$17.95**
No. 538 Extra Spool (no line)........................ **1.25**

No. 99 JUPITER
A heavy duty spin-casting reel tough enough to tackle anything that swims in fresh or salt water. Filled with 150 yds. of 12 lb. test line, it features an efficient Star Drag that smooths the take-up and is easily adjusted while playing the fish. Comes with a ⅝-oz. Pflueger No-Bounce practice plug. Long-wearing Carboloy pick-up pin, precision

machined gears, tough epoxy finish. Reel weight with line is 12 oz...**$34.95**
No. 534 Extra Spool (no line)..................... **3.00**

No. 84 SATURN
No better spin-casting reel in its price range than this snazzy Saturn. Its adjustable drag with nylon brake shoe has one of the smoothest take-ups of any enclosed reel. Three-to-one ratio metal gears retrieve 17 inches of line per revolution. Equipped with ⅜-oz. No-Bounce practice casting weight. Cone and side plates are anodized in maroon, housing is an aluminum casting with lacquered satin finish. Brass carrier, hard chromed for long wear. Extremely durable stainless steel pick-up pin. 80 yards of 8 lb. test monofilament on spool. Total weight with line is 8 oz...**$14.95**
No. 524 Extra Spool (no line)..................... **1.25**

Adjustable drag has smooth take-up nylon brake shoe. Drag is adjusted while playing the fish.

New long-wearing stainless steel line pick-up pin firmly fastened into Zytel pin holder.

Tooled metal gears that run smoothly—no bind or grind. Highest quality.

When ordering please specify our stock numbers and sizes.

Pflueger catalog, 1966, page 9.

PFLUEGER New Salt Water Sport Reels

No. 1777-2777 SEA KAST

Two brand new reels designed especially to meet the needs of fishermen who want finest quality, rugged construction and light weight. They are ideal for bay fishing, surf casting and for trolling. While they are built to withstand salt water fishing, they will be popular for use in fresh water where big, hard hitting fish can be expected. The brightly polished spools are made of aluminum and the flanges have been reinforced. In addition they have been covered with the new Leonite 201. This clear Silicone-Epoxy Acrylic coating is extremely hard and tough. It is completely resistant to salt, acid, alkali, oil and will keep spools bright and shiny after years of hard fishing. The axle bearing pivot points have been polished to a mirror-like finish to provide smooth, easy performance. The new free-spool clutch mechanism prevents gear jamming and will allow the fisherman to put these reels into free-spool at any time he chooses. For those who want to use lighter line with the minimum danger of breaking, a new strong,

smooth-stripping Star Wheel Drag has been installed. All moving parts can be thoroughly oiled without the inconvenience of taking the reel apart. A high speed gear train provides very fast retrieves and helps the fisherman maintain a constant pressure on the hooked fish. Gear ratio 3.58-1.

No. 2777 SEA KAST (Extra wide spool)
Capacity 750 yds. of 15 lb. test monofilament; 550 yds. of 20 lb. test monofilament; 300 yds. of 27 lb. test Tarpsail Nylon Squidding line. Wt. 15 oz...**$22.95**

No. 777 Extra bakelite spool (not recommended for monofilament line)..........................**$2.75**

No. 1777 SEA KAST (Regular spool)
Capacity 550 yds. of 15 lb. test monofilament; 370 yds. of 20 lb. test monofilament; 200 yds. of 27 lb. test Tarpsail Nylon Squidding line. Wt. 13.8 oz............**$19.95**

No. 177 Extra bakelite spool (not recommended for monofilament line)... ....**$2.50**

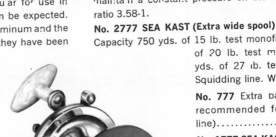

No. 1777

Pflueger catalog, 1966, page 10.

No. 1778

No. 2275

No. 1785

No. 2288

No. 1775

No. 1788

PFLUEGER Salt Water Reels

No. 2288 SEA KING

The outstanding performer that takes the roughness of surf casting in stride. A hefty 18½ oz. reel, it features a unique mechanical thumber which operates only when line is running out and slows the spool automatically. Other extras are quick take-apart, effortless Star Wheel Drag with easy take-up, push button Free Spool that engages at start of retrieve, extra wide spool with nylon bearings, balanced torpedo crank handle. Free rod clamps included. 3-1/13 to 1 gear ratio. Wt. 18½ oz. Takes 320 yds. 27 lb. test nylon line.

No. 2288 with bakelite spool....................$19.95
No. 2288M with aluminum spool.................. 21.95
No. 485 Extra bakelite spool 2.80
No. 486 Extra aluminum spool.................... 3.90

No. 2275 SEA QUEEN

Smoothness and distance are the buy-words of this light-weight surfing reel. Its extra-wide spool and 320 yard line capacity are usually found only in higher priced reels. It's loaded with extras, including a free spool with shift lever located on the front plate, a Star Wheel Drag that smooths the take-up. Spool is red bakelite with close-fitting spool flanges and adjustable nylon bearings. The flashy red caps are finished in polished chrome to give the reel a jaunty look. Balanced torpedo crank handle, free rod clamps. Wt. 14½ oz. Gear ratio 2½ to 1.....................$15.95

Nos. 1788-1785 CAPITOL

Strike a sail, tuna, or a marlin with this deep-sea trolling reel and it will dish out the speed stamina needed when

they hit. Has an extra strong aluminum spool adaptable to monofilament or braided line. The entire reel is finished to fight salt water corrosion, and its unique take-apart feature allows a spool switch in less than 20 sceonds. The push button free spool automatically engages at the start of retrieve while the Star Drag allows a slow, even take-up, Torpedo crank handle is balanced. Gear ratio is 3-1/13 to 1. Screwdriver wrench included. Two models are available.

No. 1788 Capacity 350 yds. of 27 lb. test nylon.
Wt. 21¾ oz.......................................$22.95
No. 1785 Capacity 270 yds. of 27 lb. test nylon.
Wt. 17½ oz.......................................$19.95

No. 1778 SEA LION

Salt water fishing or fresh water trolling meets its match in this tough-as-a-nut lightweight reel. Its sturdy, deep spool has 350 yd. line capacity. Free spool with throw-off lever, Star Wheel Drag for smooth take-up. Balanced torpedo crank handle eases the pull. No take apart necessary to lubricate, and screwdriver-wrench is furnished for emergencies. Chrome-bound red bakelite cap and backplate, tooled brass spool, and nylon front bearing to adjust spool end play. Has 2½ to 1 gear ratio. 350 yds. of 27 lb. braided nylon line capacity. Wt. 18¼ oz....................$15.95
No. 506 Rod Clamps............................. .75

No. 1775 SEA LION

Smaller version of the 1778, with line capacity of 220 yds. of 27 lb. braided nylon line. Weighs 14 oz........$14.95
No. 506 Rod Clamps For Sea Lion and Capitol Reels...75

When ordering please specify our stock numbers and sizes.

Pflueger catalog, 1966, page 11.

No. 1498
No. 1494
No. 1492
No. 755
No. 1558
No. 3178
No. 1554
No. 1774

Pflueger catalog, 1966, page 12.

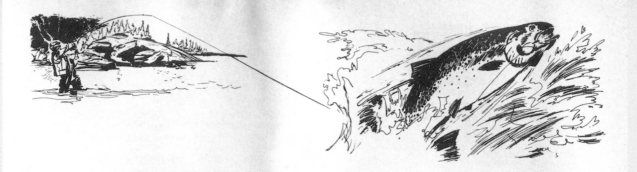

PFLUEGER Fly Casting Reels

MEDALIST REELS

Here are six single-action fly reels that have won the hearts of both the experts and the amateurs. In each model, the fly enthusiast will find a smooth-acting drag that operates only when the line is flowing out. There's no pressure to fight while retrieving. Each model features quick take-apart for easy cleaning or line changing; just press the button and the spool pops out. Quiet, two-way click, husky reinforced aluminum frame and reverse ratchet, and stainless steel guide that won't fray or scour line. Pillars and cross plate are chrome plated while the finish is in satin black. All but Model No. 1492 are easily convertible to left or right hand retrieve.

No. 1492 $^{13}/_{16}$" pillars, 2⅞" plate, 4 oz...........$12.95
No. 1494 $^{13}/_{16}$" pillars, 3¼" plate, 5¼ oz......... 14.95
No. 1494½ 1"   pillars, 3¼" plate, 6 oz......... 15.95
No. 1495 $^{13}/_{16}$" pillars, 3⅝" plate, 6 oz......... 15.95
No. 1495½ 1"   pillars, 3⅝" plate, 6¾ oz......... 16.95

Heavy duty model for tarpon, salmon, bonefish, with large line capacity. Reinforced spool and back plate, larger drag for extra braking power.

No. 1498 1" pillars, 4" plate, 6¾ oz................$19.95

EXTRA SPOOLS

	Suggested Retail Price
No. 496 Spool for 1492 Medalist.........	$4.35 Each
No. 497 Spool for 1494 Medalist.........	4.55 Each
No. 494 Spool for 1494½ Medalist.......	4.80 Each
No. 498 Spool for 1495 Medalist.........	4.80 Each
No. 495 Spool for 1495½ Medalist.......	5.05 Each
No. 499 Spool for 1498 Medalist.........	5.25 Each

"QUICK TAKE APART" FEATURES

When ordering please specify our stock numbers and sizes.

No. 755 SUPEREX

Fills the bill all the way with quality and style. The Superex is an automatic, with Pflueger's quick take-apart that allows almost instantaneous spool change with the push of a button. A tough, lightweight reel, it weighs only 9 oz., yet holds 32 yds. of C line and retrieves 24 yards on one spring winding. Free-stripping clutch lets more line go out after spring is wound to capacity. Nylon release lever folds against reel for easy storage. Aluminum housing is finished in rich grey epoxy, cross-plate is stainless steel. Brass machined gears with stainless steel pinion. **$15.95**
No. 490 Extra Spool............................... 2.15

No. 3178 PAKRON

An ace in the hole among single-action reels designed for wire-line trolling. Takes on lake trout and rainbows with power to spare. Adjustable drag operates only when line is rolling out, and there's no drag on the retrieve. Spool slips out easily. Adjustable click, single balanced torpedo handle. Conversion to left-hand model is simple. Brass construction with satin chrome finish. Line capacity 400 yds. of 45 lb. test monel wire.....................**$29.95**

No. 1558 SAL-TROUT

Built for steelhead fishing or for deep lake-trout trolling. A Pflueger quality single-action reel for wire line. Easily removed spool, adjustable drag and sliding click, single torpedo handle. Brass construction with satin nickel finish, it weighs 20¼ oz. Line capacity is 400 yds. of 45 lb. test solid monel wire or 210 yds. of 15 lb. test nylon...**$14.95**

No. 1554 SAL-TROUT

A dependable single-action fly reel that doubles in brass for trolling. Light but sturdy, it has extra line capacity for such a moderate price. Removable spool, adjustable click. Built with aluminum frame, gun-metal finish, aluminum spool that's satin-finished. Takes C level line plus 75 yds. of 15 lb. backing. Weight 5 oz......................**$4.95**

No. 1774 PROGRESS

An inexpensive single-action fly reel that gives reliable service every time. Weighs only 4½ oz., but is unusually strong and sturdy. Spool removes by loosening one screw. Has light click, brass frame with a gun-metal finish, aluminum spool. Takes C level line plus 50 yds. of 15 lb. backing...**$3.50**

Pflueger catalog, 1966, page 13.

Heddon Imperial Fly Reel, Model No. 125, $125.00 – 150.00.

Two Winchesters, a nice fly reel in box, Model 1600S, the label says "One Single Action Fishing Reel, Steel, Gun Metal Finish, 60 yds.," it sold new for $1.29 and would bring $125.00 – 200.00 today new in the box. The other reel is an Arrow Jr. Fishing Reel, single action, nickel plated, wooden handles, 80 yd. It is Model 4400, also in a Winchester box, with an identical label design, but the boxes are not marked Winchester, nor is this reel. This inexpensive bait caster should bring at least $50.00 today in the box. Remember they took over Hendryx so this is likely an earlier Hendryx model.

Abu Ambassadeur 5000, $50.00 – 75.00 for common models.

A Cardinal spinning reel, $75.00+.

Pflueger Pelican Spinning reel extra spool box, Model 518, $20.00.

Pelican extra reel and box, same as above.

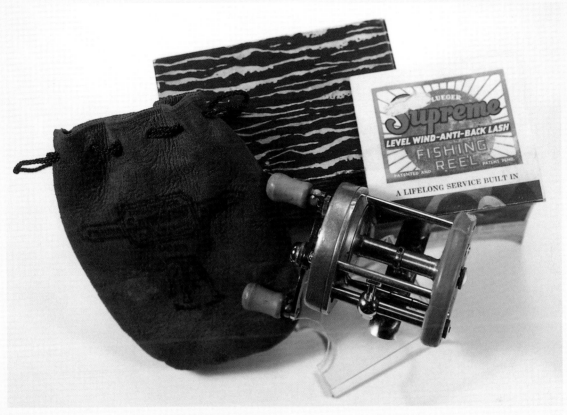

Classic Pflueger Supreme with leather bag, inserts, palm guard, rubber knob covers, patent pending model, $100.00+.

A modern South Bend Bait Casting reel, Model Cast-Oreno Model 16, $30.00+.

A hard to find early Jamison Model No. 11 spinning reel, patent pending model, an early American model, $20.00 – 40.00.

An early Record spinning reel, handle removed, with paper insert, $75.00+.

The classic Shakespeare, a President Model 1978 in the box with all accessories, $65.00 – 90.00, sold new for $32.50.

New in the box Model 2065 Spin Wonder, spinning reel by Shakespeare, $50.00+ for new in the box version.

Box end for the Model 2065.

Model 1765 Shakespeare Wonder-Flyte from the Borman tackle box.

Box end for the Wonder-Flyte, no trade data, unique history.

Shakespeare Model No. 17 Wonder-Cast from the Borman tackle box.

H-I "The Utica Reel", early auto fly reel, values vary by models. $20.00 – 60.00.

Johnson Reels patch, $5.00 – 10.00.

J. C. Higgins Model 312.31130 fly reel, shown also on back cover of book, $30.00 – 40.00.

Unusual Johnson Model 80, demonstrator in bag, no trade data but should bring $40.00+ as it is unusual.

A two-piece cardboard box for a post-war baitcasting reel from my old neighborhood, Rockford, Michigan. This was a unique development inasmuch as the company used early marketing surveys to determine what the fishing public wanted in a bait casting reel and then made it. Thus, the slogan, "The reels the Fishermen asked for" on the box. I interviewed a close relative of the founder of Ranger Reels and was informed that they also developed the Model 80 shown in bottom photo on page 249 but decided to license it/sell the development rights to Johnson Reels as the owners of Ranger thought the future remained in bait casting reels. But, in fairness to Ranger, keep in mind that this was right after the war, and spinning was still not fully established. Later Ranger developed a prototype spinning reel, but it never went into full production, according to my source. The photos at top right and left center show the end view of a Ranger and a front view of the same reel, new from the box shown.

The Ranger Prototype spinning reel that was not produced. The cut-out shown is only for explanation, and the model was to have the line come out of the little hole in the top with a half-bale releasing it. Also, not the thumb release trigger on the rear of the reel. No trade data on this item. Ranger bait casting reels sell for $20.00 – 50.00 depending on the quality, condition, and presence or absence of box.

The concentration in this chapter is on fishing rods related to the new field of spinning and spin casting. Also covered is the development of the fiberglass rod in the 1940s and beyond and what the collector should be looking for when in the field searching for items.

Rods are often an overlooked item by the beginning collector. For one thing, they seem rather common and very similar. However, as with lures, there are very rare items even from the 1960s and 1970s that have either held their value or gone up greatly. As with most collectibles in the field of fishing, any Heddon product seems to grow in value. However, there are some other fine fiberglass rods of great collector interest including Phillipson, St. Croix, Garcia, Eagle Claw, Wonderods by Shakespeare, Fenwick, even Fenwick blanks, some of the Pflueger and South Bend rods, certain Tru-Temper rods, Airex rods, Action rods, some handle designs, most of the pack rods made in the 1960s and 1970s, and more. Values vary from a few dollars to a few hundred dollars, so it pays to have at least some familiarity with this interesting category of fishing collectible. Like lures, the more fishing rods one actually examines in detail, the more one learns. The next time you are at a garage sale and the person says all they have are some old rods, do not fail to look! Also, as a bonus, you may find an Abu Ambassadeur 5500 Hi Speed on an old Garcia rod. One day while visiting an antique store, I found a Phillipson glass rod mint in a case purchased for $45.00 and later sold to a Japanese dealer for $400.00 who in turn sold it for $700.00. So, when you find that "old rod," look twice before deciding not to buy it.

Also, think twice before you sell one. I have one regret in rod sales to date: I once owned a presentation rod given to Joseph D. Bates, Jr. by Phillipson Rods. I traded this for some Julias Vom Hoffe and Orvis reels in a good trade. However, I wish I still had this rod in my collection as I have learned that a little history added to an item makes it far more interesting in the long run. That is why the Frank Borman reel is so important to me now. South Bend offered a series of rods named after Mr. Bates as well, but the Phillipson was a rod made for him personally, and one simply does not find such items very often. So restrict your urge to make a quick buck and hang on to those one-of-a-kind items,

because they cannot be replaced at any cost.

One can also display rods by hanging them or designing a nice rack for that purpose. Of course, some of them are great fishing rods, such as the Phillipson. But, regardless of the ultimate use for the rods, they are an important part of our sport and hobby, and the collector should take the time to learn more about them.

I would begin by collecting the classic Shakespeare Wonderods as they epitomize our cultural fascination with the "new and improved" version of products. Plastics and modern nylon were direct outcomes of product developments during the war years, and Shakespeare was prompt in taking advantage of these new and improved materials for rods, reel components (nylon gears), and lures (the Glo line). The classic Shakespeare products to me would have to include a Wondereel lined with Wexford Wonder line with a Shakespeare Mouse tied on the end, all mounted on a Wonderod. This "is" Shakespeare of the 1950s! Begin with a 1951 Shakespeare catalog for reference and the cover shows the premium Fly Wonderod (Model No. 1290) in full flex, reeling in a trout. Open the catalog, and the frontispiece has the four colors then available for the Wonderods. Pages 2 through 7 then detail all of the various Wonderods available in baitcasting, surf, spinning, fly, trolling, and other models. The catalog also explains how to identify a Wonderod from its copies. This is an excellent source of information, and anyone interested in this classic rod should begin by finding this catalog, or another of the late 1940s or early 1950s catalogs by Shakespeare as a resource. When I started seriously expanding my collection a few years ago, my wife brought home a premium Shakespeare baitcasting Wonderod mounted with the new in 1951 Shakespeare President baitcasting reel and a box of assorted Shakespeare tackle that included a Mouse and a line spool box for Wexford lines from at a local garage sale. As I said, such a combination epitomized a company for better than a decade.

Rather than take a lot of photos of rods, I thought catalogs would best show the important rods of the Modern Era. I again wish to thank Shakespeare for permission to use Shakespeare and Pflueger materials in Chapters 5 and 6 and in Volume 1.

Shakespeare catalog, 1964, front cover.

Shakespeare BALANCED TACKLE GUIDE

These charts will make it easier to assemble balanced outfits of Shakespeare reels, Wonderods and lines for a particular kind of fishing.

"PUSH-BUTTON" TACKLE ASSEMBLY GUIDE

Class and Reels	Rod Action and Length	Lb. Test Lines	Weight of Live Bait or Plugs
LIGHT 1773-1774-1775-1776- 1792-1794-1799	EXTRA LIGHT 6'0", 6'6" or 7'0"	4 to 8	Best, ¼—Good, ⅛ to ½
MEDIUM-1765 (8 lb.) 1777-1778-1779- 1799-1794-1792	LIGHT or Kwik-Taper 6'0", 6'6" or 7'0"	8 to 10	Best—⅜—Good, ¼ to ⅝
MEDIUM HEAVY 1765 (12 lb.) 1772-1793-1795-1797	Omni-Action or Kwik-Taper 6'0" or 6'6"	12-15-20	Best, ⅝—Good, ⅜ to 1

BAIT CASTING TACKLE ASSEMBLY GUIDE

Type of Fishing	Suggested Reels	Action and Length	Lb. Lines	Lures (oz.)
LIGHT . . . Bass, panfish, sporty casting	1973A, 1928, 1929, 1970A	XL—5'2" or 5'8" XL—6'0"	6-10	¼ Best ⅛ to ½ Good
MEDIUM LIGHT . . . Bass, pickerel, fresh water or salt water casting	Reels above; also 1982, 1924-1950-1964-1958 1956-1937	XL—5'8" L—5'8" or 6'0" Kwik-Taper 5'8" & 6'0"	10-12½	⅜ Best ¼ & ⅝ Good
MEDIUM— . . . All purpose casting & trolling. Big bass, walleye, northern, fresh water trolling or S.W. casting	Reels immediately above, also 1924S, 1950S, 1933, 1935, 1937, 1992	L—5'2" or 5'8" M—5'2" or 5'8" Kwik-Taper 5'8" & 6'0" Omni-Action 5'8" & 6'0"	15-20	⅝ Best ⅜ & ½ Good
MEDIUM HEAVY . . . Heavy duty fresh water trolling, s.w. casting	1944M-1944-1946-1946M- 1949	H-action, Omni or Special Models	20-30	¼ to 1

FLY FISHING TACKLE ASSEMBLY GUIDE

Type of Fishing	Reels	Wonderods Suggested	Line		
1. LIGHT Bluegills, sunfish, crappie, perch, rock bass, brook trout, etc.	Tru-ArT or OK	Light Sporty Specialized— A848, A922, 929, A829 838, A816, A814, A812, 809	Select from Rod-to-Line Chart Level	Double Taper	Weight Forward
2. MEDIUM-LIGHT Spotted, white, small-mouth, largemouth bass; brown and rainbow trout; grayling, etc.	Tru-ArT or OK	Versatile all-Around—Most Wonderods will be fine. Use: A855, 844, 949, A822-8' A818-7'9" & 8' & 8'6", A816, A814, B812	Select from Rod-to-Line Chart Level	Double Taper	Weight Forward
3. MEDIUM Large bass, snook, steel-head or cutthroat tr., jack salmon, etc.	Tru-arT or OK	Rods in Omni-Action or 9'0" models, A818, A855, A924, 819, 824, 832, A849 A928, A824-9', 832-8'6" for sporty fishing try 818-9'0"	Select from Rod-to-Line Chart Level	Double Taper	Weight Forward
4. MEDIUM HEAVY Atlantic salmon, bonefish, tarpon, etc.	Single action type	No. A928 recommended for Omni Action models in 8'6" length: A819, A824, A832	Select from Rod-to-Line Chart Level	Double Taper	Weight Forward

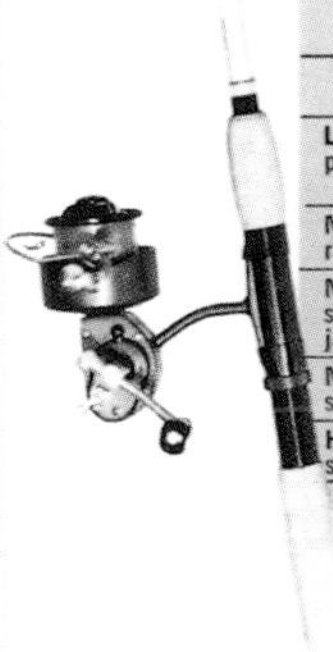

SPINNING TACKLE ASSEMBLY GUIDE

Type of Fishing	Suggested Reels	Action & Length Rods	Lb. Lines	Lures
LIGHT . . . Crappie, bluegill, perch, sunfish, trout, bass, etc.	1725-1732-1735 1756-1870-1875 2064-65-62-68	Comb. 620 or 621 Ex. Light 5'-6'-6'6"	2-4-6	Live bait or lures ⅛ to ⅜ oz.
MEDIUM LIGHT . . . Brown, rainbow, bass, grayling, etc.	1810-1870-1875 2064, 2065-62-68	Light 6'6" or 7'0" also Kwik-Taper	4-6-8	¼-½ oz. of pop. live bait hookups
MEDIUM . . . Large bass, snook, steelhead, cutthroat, Dolly Varden, jack salmon, etc.	1810-2062 2064-65, 2068 2070	Med. 7'0" or 6'6" Kwik-Taper and Omni-Action	6-8-10	⅜ to ¾ oz. lures; live bait in this wt. range
MEDIUM HEAVY . . . Atlantic salmon, bonefish, etc.	2062-2064-2065 2068-2070-2080	Salt water class. 7'0" to 8'6"; Omni.	10-12-15	½ to 1 oz. lures, or live bait
HEAVY . . . Salt water surf and boat	2080, 2080RH, 2082, 2090, 2090RH, 2092	Salt water, surf 9'0" spinning rods	12-15-20	1 to 4 oz. lures or live bait

"Secrets of Successful Fishing"
by Henry Shakespeare

200 Page Fishing Book for only 50c

Written by one of America's great sportsmen who makes the sport of fishing easier and more fun. Filled with illustrations, charts, instruction, and How to do it information.

- Locating Hot Spots
- Getting the Big Ones
- Choosing the Best Lures
- Tips on Knots and Lines
- How To Play a Big Fish
- Cast Like a Pro
- Importance of Balanced Tackle
- Types of Fish and Feeding Habits
- Equipment Care

Send 50 cents in check, coin or stamps to: Shakespeare Co. Dept. 4A Kalamazoo, Michigan

ABOUT MATERIALS and PRICES

Shakespeare tackle is manufactured of the best obtainable materials commensurate with product price. Federal excise tax is included where applicable. Specifications and prices as given here were in effect at the time of printing. But if costs are increased by material and/or manufacturing costs and/or Federal wage regulations, the Shakespeare Company reserves the right to change prices, specifications, design or discontinue models without incurring obligation. All prices shown are base prices from which trade discounts are computed. They are not represented to be retail list prices, or usual or customary retail prices. All prices are effective August 1, 1963. Prices are F.O.B. Kalamazoo, Mich.

INDEX TO 1964 CATALOG

		PAGE
TACKLE OUTFITS	R-7304, R-7309, R-6512, R-9718, R-9922 S-183, S-184, S-186, S-191, S-192, S-193, S-194 164, 165, 166, 167, 168, 169, 171, 172 B-147, 1302 set	4 4 4 4
PUSH BUTTON REELS	1765 1772, 1773 1774, 1775, 1776, 1777, 1778, 1779 1792, 1793, 1795 1794-1797 1799	9 8 11 6 11
CASTING AND TROLLING REELS	1901, 1905, 1909 1924, 1924S, 1928 1933, 1935, 1937 1941, 1944, 44M, -46-46M-49 1929, 1970A 1950, A950S 1956, 1964 1973A 1982, 1992 20 & 30	14 16 13 15 12 16 14 16 13 5
FLY REELS	1821, 1822, 1824, 1825, 1926, 1826L, 1827 1835, 1836, 1836L, 1837, 1895	17 17
SPINNING REELS	1725 1732, 1735, 1756 1782 1810, 1870 1875 2062, 2064, 2065, 2068, 2070, 2080, 2090	18 19 20 19 18 21
PUSH BUTTON RODS	A204, A205, A207, A209, B212, B214, A216, A304, 307, A404 A218, A219, 319 B222, A224, A227, A229, A239	24 25 22
CASTING RODS	A404S, B406, B408, A409, B410, B412, B414, A416 A417, B419, A422, A424, A427, A436	27 26
FLY RODS	809, B812, B814, A816, A818, A819 B822, A824, A829 A922, A924, A928, 929, 949 A832, 838, 844, A848, B849, B855	30 29 28 28
SPINNING RODS	607 & 707, A609 & A709, 710, B612 & B712 B614 & B714, A616 & A716, A618 & 718 A717, A619 & A719, A620, A621, B622 & B722 A723, A624 & A724, A628 & A728, A629 & A729 A639 & A739, A649 & A749	31 32 33 34 35
SALT WATER RODS	1169, 1181, 1187, 1189 1223, 1229, 1235, 1237, 1239, 1276 1062, 1064, 1067, 1068, 1069, 1071 1031, 1032, 1038, 1051, 1055 1306-09, 1311-25, 1329-31 1072, 1085-90, 1095, 3012-20, 3030-50, 3130-80 1014, 1015-16, 1017, 1028, 1047-48-49-50 1057-58-59-60 2900 & 2905, 2910 & 2915, 2920-25-30 2935-40, 2945-50, 2955-2960	36 36 40 38 38 39 37 37 41 41
WONDER POLES	1312, 1314, 1316	41
FLY LINE	4300, 4330, 4315-20-20T Mill Ends 4333, 4335, 4337, 4339	42 43
CASTING LINE AND SPINNING LINE	4400, 4485, 4487, 4489, 4500, 4500X, 4550 4444 4490C-B-I, 4491 & 4492 Mill Ends 6100, 6300, 6800 4495 5500, 6200, 6500, 6900 5040, 5046 bulk mono 5042, 5045, 5047, 6950, bulk mono. 5048, 5049, 5050, 5300, 5303-04 5900-G-D-S, 5900XG	44 45 44 46 46 47 47 46 47 47
MISC. SUPPLIES	Misc. Parts & Accessories Handles, Grips, Parts Rod Carrying Cases	42 42 42
SPARE SPOOLS	Push Button Spools . . . 8-9-10-11 Push Button Spools . . . 8-9-10-11 Closed Face Spinning Spools Spin Wonder Spinning Spools Sea Wonder Spinning Spools	19 20 21

Printed in U.S.A.—SAFRAN—64A

Shakespeare catalog, 1964, page 2.

NEW...

for that WONDERFUL YEAR - 1964

ALL FASHIONED BY *Shakespeare*

FOR THOSE WHO TAKE PLEASURE IN FINE FISHING TACKLE

Here's some of the important *brand, spankin' new* Shakespeare tackle taking its place on the American fishing scene for 1964. Reels, Wonderods and lines all made to delight the hearts of America's sport fishermen.

NEW —**No. 1826L** reel (Omni size fly line installed) with matched No. A832 Presidential Wonderod.

NEW —**No. 1765 Wonderflyte** (with 8 and 12 lb. line-filled spools) and new styled No. B212 Wonderod.

NEW —**No. 1929** Direct Drive Mono-Cast reel with No. B414 Wonderod, styled in rich brown.

NEW —**No. 2068** Spinning reel with deluxe No. A749 Executive Wonderod.

SHAKESPEARE WARRANTY POLICY

Shakespeare reels are guaranteed against defective workmanship and material. Adjustment or replacement is subject to delivery and inspection at the factory or at a Shakespeare Authorized Reel Service Center. Any defective condition will be taken care of by repair or replacement without charge. Shakespeare dealers are NOT authorized to make replacements.

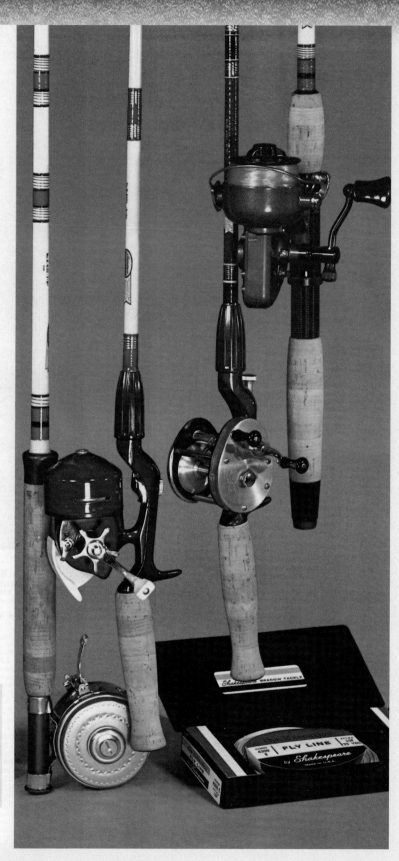

Shakespeare catalog, 1964, page 3.

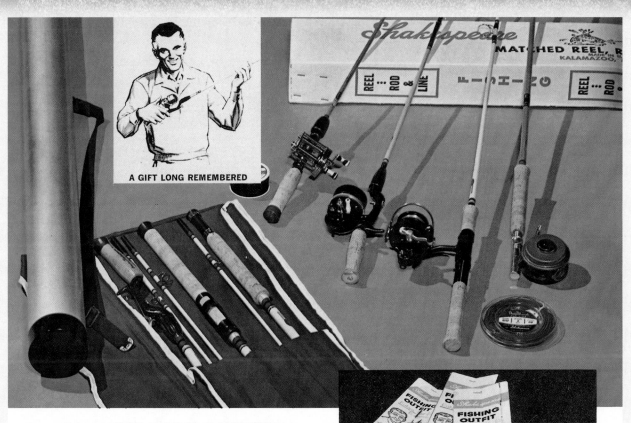

SHAKESPEARE OUTFITS
DISPLAY-BOXED FOR GIFT OR PRESENTATION

No. 1302 MATCHED WONDEROD PRESENTATION SET

Here's a *matched* set of Presidential Wonderods that starts a sport fisherman's heart doing flip-flops on sight.

Consists of: No. A832—8'6" fly Wonderod; No. A639—7" spin Wonderod; and No. A229—6'—2 pc. Wonderod for casting or push-button fishing. Rods come in brown canvas roll (white trimmed) and aluminum carry-case. In reshippable parcel post carton. **No. 1302,** Each...**$100.00**

GIFT-PACKAGED SETS

Attractively assembled in 2-color cardboard carton; reel and rod display-mounted for presentation.

No. 174 Push button combo, budget-priced. Packaged: No. 1773 (8-lb. line on reel.) No. A209 Wonderod, 2-pc. Ea..........**$21.50**

No. 165 Braggin' Tackle, Push button type, Packaged: No. 1765 reel with two spools (12-lb. and 8-lb. mono-filled); No. B212L-6' Wonderod, 2-pc. Set.................................**$29.50**

No. 166 The Push button fisherman's favorite. Packaged: No. 1777 reel (10-lb. mono on reel). No. A209—6' Wonderod, 2 pc. Each..**$31.50**

No. B147 "Top drawer" Push button tackle, built for all-around fishing. Packaged: No. 1797 reel (12-lb. mono installed.) No. A218L—6' Wonderod, 2-pc., Each..........................**$45.50**

No. A145 Push button set containing No. 1774 WonderCast reel and No. A209—6' Wonderod, 2-pc. Each...........**$26.50**

No. 167 BAIT CASTING fishing set, perfect for the occasional angler contains: No. 1901 level wind reel, No. A404—5' Wonderod, 50 yds. No. 4444—15-lb. casting line. Set, Each..........**$12.95**

No. 168 Close-faced spinning set, expertly matched. Contains: No. 1725 under-the-rod spin reel with punch button (8-lb. mono on reel) with No. 710—7' rod. Set......................**$22.50**

No. 169 Open face spinning outfit, for fresh or salt water. Contains: No. 2062 reel (8-lb. mono installed) with No. B712—7' Wonderod. Set...**$44.50**

No. 171 FLY FISHING SET "Reel go-togethers" for all round fly fishing. Contains: No. 1824 reel, No. 809—8' Wonderod, No. 4337-D Level line. Set................................**$26.25**

No. 172 SALT WATER SET for light trolling, pier, jetty or dock. Contains: No. 1944 service reel, No. 2920—5'6", No. 4485T (tan) 24-lb. Squidding Line. Set.........................**$31.50**

DISPLAY CARDED KITS
Reel—Rod—Line All Set for Fishing Fun

No. S-183 PUSH BUTTON KIT. For general purpose fishing. Contains No. 1773 maple tone push-button reel with star drag. Color matched No. A204—6' rod. 8-lb. line installed on reel. Complete..**$14.90**

No. S-186 PUSH BUTTON KIT. Excellent for heavier lake or river fishing. Features the No. 1772 WonderCast reel with star drag, 12-lb. line installed; No. A204—6' glass rod is color styled to reel. Complete set...**$17.90**

No. S-184 PUSH BUTTON KIT. Good for bass, pickerel and pan fishing. No. 1773. WonderCast reel has line installed and matches with 2-pc. glass rod, No. A204—5'. Mounted on short 30" display card. Complete.......................................**$14.90**

No. S-191 PUSH BUTTON KIT. Contains No. 1773 WonderCast Reel (8-lb. line installed) and No. A209—6' Wonderod, 2-pc. Set...**$19.90**

No. S-192 PUSH BUTTON KIT. Contains No. 1772 WonderCast reel (filled to capacity with 12-lb. mono) and matching No. A209—6' Wonderod, 2-piece. Complete set.................**$22.90**

No. S-193 PUSH BUTTON KIT. The beautiful tackle combination featured on front cover. Contains No. 1765 reel (two spools, filled with 8 & 12-lb. mono.) No. B212L—6' Wonderod. Complete **$27.90**

No. S-194 BAIT CASTING KIT. Perfect for the vacation-type fisherman. Contains: No. 1901 level wind casting reel and 2-piece No. A204—5' glass rod. Complete................**$10.90**

No. S-195 PUSH BUTTON KIT. The popular set for 1964, with No. 1765 WonderFlyte reel (two spools, filled with 8 & 12-lb. mono) combined with No. 307—6' Wonderod. Complete.....**$22.90**

Shakespeare catalog, 1964, page 4.

Shakespeare BRAGGING TACKLE

USE THE SHAKESPEARE "WONDER BEND" TEST
Shows how a glass fishing rod should be built for best performance

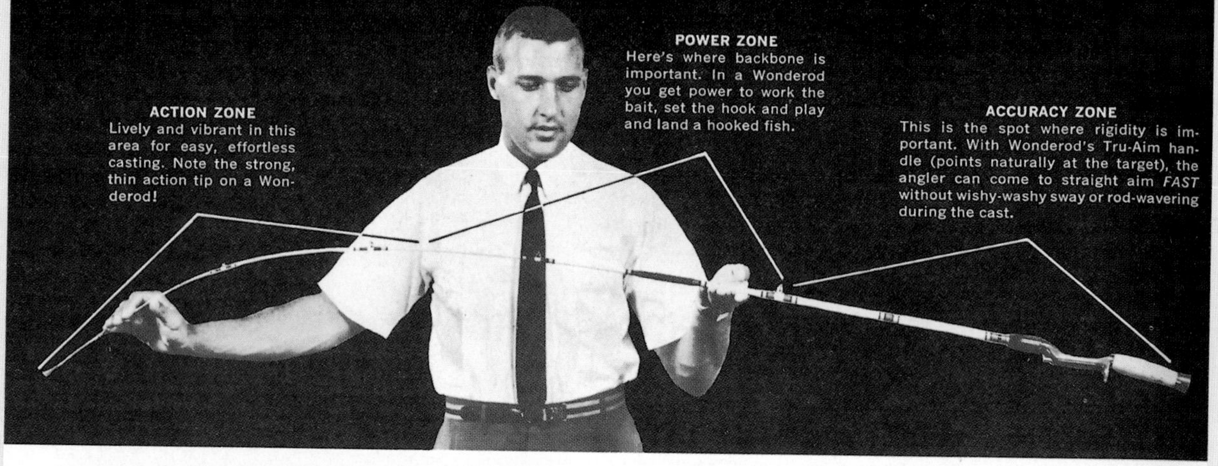
POWER ZONE
Here's where backbone is important. In a Wonderod you get power to work the bait, set the hook and play and land a hooked fish.
ACTION ZONE
Lively and vibrant in this area for easy, effortless casting. Note the strong, thin action tip on a Wonderod!
ACCURACY ZONE
This is the spot where rigidity is important. With Wonderod's Tru-Aim handle (points naturally at the target), the angler can come to straight aim *FAST* without wishy-washy sway or rod-wavering during the cast.

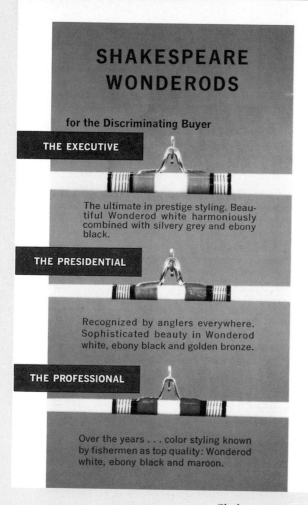

SHAKESPEARE WONDERODS

for the Discriminating Buyer

THE EXECUTIVE

The ultimate in prestige styling. Beautiful Wonderod white harmoniously combined with silvery grey and ebony black.

THE PRESIDENTIAL

Recognized by anglers everywhere. Sophisticated beauty in Wonderod white, ebony black and golden bronze.

THE PROFESSIONAL

Over the years . . . color styling known by fishermen as top quality: Wonderod white, ebony black and maroon.

No. A329 PRESIDENTAL THREE-PIECE PUSH-BUTTON WONDEROD. Popular suitcase model for anglers who like to travel . . . "always prepared." Three-piece, tubular glass, swelled butt construction, for casting live bait and spin lures from ¼ to ½ ounce or bait casting lures from ⅜ to ⅝ ounce. Wonderod white with light bronze winds, black extended trim and two decorative bands. Carboloy® spin-type guides and tip-top. In deluxe cloth bag and new plastic case.

No.	Length	Action	Guides	Price
A329	6'0"	Light	4	$29.95

No. A239 EXECUTIVE WONDEROD. The ultimate in rod construction, craftsmanship and quality. Kwik-Taper construction casts live bait or spinning lures from ¼ to ½ ounce. Prestige Wonderod white with silver grey winds, black extended trim and two decorative bands. New rubber bumper on the black anodized aluminum butt cap gives added protection as well as styling coordination. Tru-Aim double offset aluminum handle has Shark Fin Grey color and extra long, extra select specie cork grip. Carboloy® spin-type guides and tip-top, of course! In super de luxe padded leatherette carrying case.

No.	Length	Action	Guides	Price
A239	6'0"	Light	7	$39.95

No. A229 PRESIDENTIAL WONDEROD. THE PRESTIGE BUY. Spectacular Omni-Action plus Presidential styling. Casts spinning lures from ¼ to ½ ounce and bait casting lures from ⅜ to ⅝ ounce. Wonderod white blade, light bronze winds, black extended trim and two decorative bands. Omni design Tru-Aim double offset aluminum handle—styled in dark metallic brown finish plus complimentary brown anodized aluminum butt cap with rubber bumper. Carboloy® spin-type guides and tip-top. Has a deluxe cloth bag and plastic tube tip protector.

No.	Length	Action	Guides	Price
A229	6'0"	Omni	4	$29.95
A229	6'6"	Omni	5	$29.95

No. A227 PRESIDENTIAL WONDEROD. Extremely fine rod craftsmanship plus versatile Kwik-Taper action put this Presidential rod high on the WANTED List. Casts live bait or spinning lures from ¼ to ½ ounce or bait casting lures from ⅜ to ⅝ ounce. White blade with bronze tone winds, black extended trim and two decorative bands. The dark metallic brown finish on the Tru-Aim double offset handle is complimented by a brown anodized aluminum butt cap with a rubber bumper. Carboloy® spin-type guides and tip-top. Comes in deluxe cloth bag with plastic tube tip protector.

No.	Length	Action	Guides	Price
A227L	6'0"	Light	4	$27.95
A227L	6'6"	Light	5	$27.95
A227XL	6'6"	Extra Light	5	$27.95
A227M	6'0"	Medium	4	$27.95

No. A224 PROFESSIONAL WONDEROD. Here's luxury, quality and professional performance. Exciting Omni-Action for live bait, spin lures or casting plugs from ⅛ to one ounce. Prestige Wonderod white with contrasting black winds and red nylon extended trim, two decorative bands. Strong, Tru-Aim double offset aluminum handle has beautiful Shark Fin Grey finish. Rear grip is extra select specie cork with a protective black anodized aluminum butt cap. Stainless steel wire frame spin-type guides and Carboloy® tip-top. Comes in cloth bag with fiber tube tip protector.

No.	Length	Action	Guides	Price
A224	6'0"	Omni	4	$24.95
A224	6'6"	Omni	5	$24.95

No. B222 PROFESSIONAL WONDEROD. Fine craftsmanship is very evident in this Professional model, Kwik-Taper Wonderod. Used for live bait, spin and bait casting lures from ⅛ to ⅝ ounce. Wonderod white blade, with maroon nylon winds and black extended trim, plus two decorative bands. Stainless steel wire frame spin-type guides and Carboloy® tip-top. Maroon Tru-Aim double offset aluminum handle with color matched anodized aluminum butt cap and extra select specie cork grip. Reel-Tyte-Lock. Cloth bag with a fiber tube tip protector.

No.	Length	Action	Guides	Price
B222L	6'0" and 6'6"	Light	4	$22.95
B222XL	6'6"	Extra Light	4	$22.95
B222M	6'0"	Medium	4	$22.95

(See Center Spread (Pages 24 & 25) for illustration.)

Shakespeare catalog, 1964, page 22.

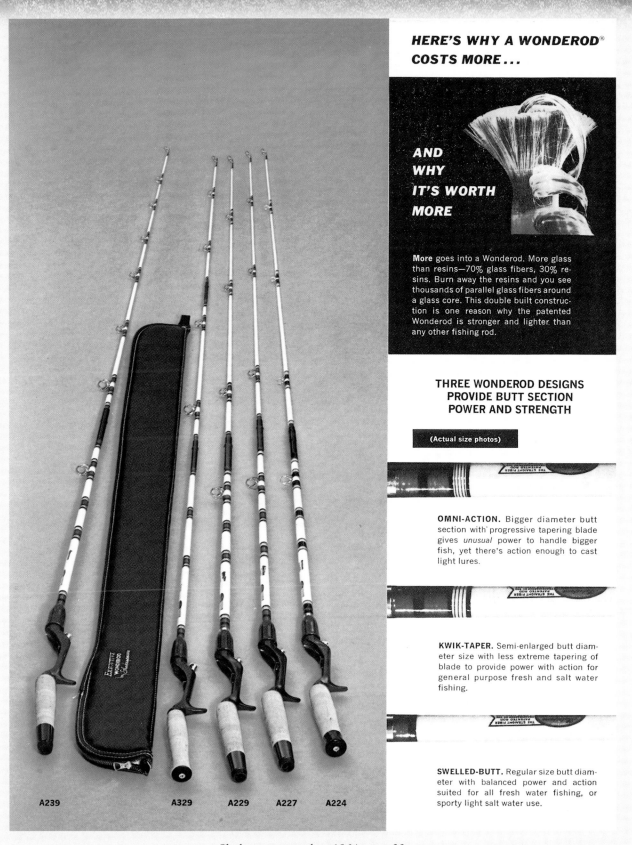

HERE'S WHY A WONDEROD® COSTS MORE...

AND WHY IT'S WORTH MORE

More goes into a Wonderod. More glass than resins—70% glass fibers, 30% resins. Burn away the resins and you see thousands of parallel glass fibers around a glass core. This double built construction is one reason why the patented Wonderod is stronger and lighter than any other fishing rod.

THREE WONDEROD DESIGNS PROVIDE BUTT SECTION POWER AND STRENGTH

(Actual size photos)

OMNI-ACTION. Bigger diameter butt section with progressive tapering blade gives *unusual* power to handle bigger fish, yet there's action enough to cast light lures.

KWIK-TAPER. Semi-enlarged butt diameter size with less extreme tapering of blade to provide power with action for general purpose fresh and salt water fishing.

SWELLED-BUTT. Regular size butt diameter with balanced power and action suited for all fresh water fishing, or sporty light salt water use.

A239   A329   A229   A227   A224

Shakespeare catalog, 1964, page 23.

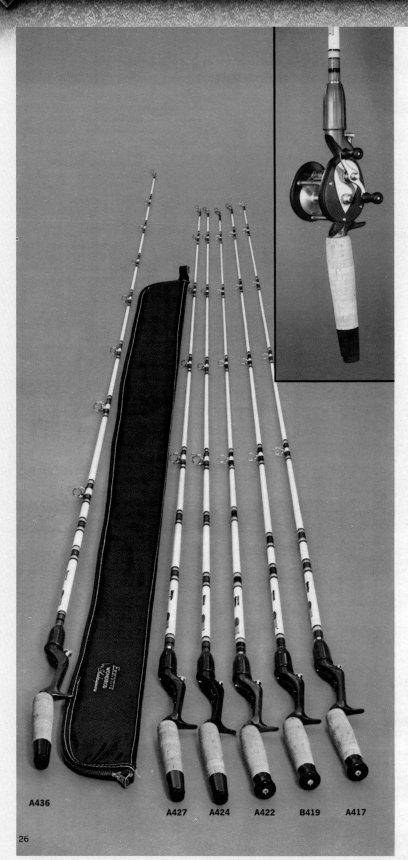

BAIT CASTING
BY SHAKESPEARE

ACTION · POWER · ACCURACY

No. A436 EXECUTIVE. The ultimate in casting rods. Kwik-Taper design casts live bait and spin or bait casting lures from ¼ to ⅝ ounce. Prestige Wonderod white with silver grey winds, black extended trim and two decorative bands. A new rubber bumper on the black anodized aluminum butt cap gives protection as well as styling coordination. Tru-Aim double offset aluminum handle has Shark Fin Grey color and extra long, extra select specie cork grip. Carboloy® spin-type guides and tip-top. Rod comes in super deluxe padded leatherette carrying case.

No.	Length	Action	Guides	Price
A436	6'0"	Light	7	$36.95

No. A427 PRESIDENTIAL WONDEROD. Omni-Action and Presidential styling make this rod tops on the "Braggin' Tackle" list. Casts spin and casting lures from ⅛ to one ounce. White blade; light brown winds, black extended trim and two decorative bands. Tru-Aim double offset aluminum handle has extra long specie cork rear grip and Reel-Tyte-Lock seat, plus a new brown anodized aluminum butt cap and rubber bumper. Carboloy® spin-type guides and tip-top. Packed in deluxe cloth case and plastic tube and tip protector.

No.	Length	Action	Guides	Price
A427	5'8" and 6'0"	Omni	4	$27.95

No. A424 PRESIDENTIAL WONDEROD. Popular Kwik-Taper construction for casting live bait, spin or bait casting lures from ¼ to ⅝ ounce. Wonderod white blade, light brown winds and black extended trim with two decorative bands. Tru-Aim double offset aluminum handle has select, extra long specie cork grip with Reel-Tyte-Lock seat, plus a new brown anodized aluminum butt cap and rubber bumper. Carboloy® spin-type guides and tip-top. Packed in deluxe cloth case with plastic tube tip protector.

No.	Length	Action	Guides	Price
A424L	5'8" and 6'0"	Light	4	$24.95

No. A422 PROFESSIONAL WONDEROD. Here's an extremely versatile rod. Omni-Action casts lures from ⅛ to one ounce. Prestige Wonderod white blade, with black and red nylon extended winds with two decorative bands. Tru-Aim double offset aluminum handle has shark fin grey finish; extra select, extra long specie cork rear grip with Reel-Tyte-Lock seat and a black anodized aluminum butt cap. Stainless steel wire frame spin-type guides and Carboloy® top. Packed in cloth bag with fiber tube tip protector.

No.	Length	Action	Guides	Price
A422	5'8" and 6'0"	Omni	4	$22.95

No. B419 PROFESSIONAL WONDEROD. It's "happy fishing" with this popular Kwik-Taper Wonderod. Casts live bait and spin or bait casting lures from ¼ to ⅝ ounce. Famous Wonderod white blade, with maroon and black nylon extended winds, plus two decorative bands. Handle is Tru-Aim double offset aluminum, maroon finish. Has extra select specie cork, extra long, rear grip with Reel-Tyte-Lock reel seat, and maroon anodized aluminum butt cap. Stainless steel wire frame and spin-type guides and Carboloy® top. Comes in cloth bag with fiber tube tip protector.

No.	Length	Action	Guides	Price
B419L	5'8" and 6'0"	Light	4	$19.95

No. A417 WONDEROD. An Omni-Action model for those who take their fishing seriously. Casts all the popular lures from ⅛ to one ounce. Famous Wonderod white blade has maroon nylon extended winds. Handle is maroon Tru-Aim double offset aluminum with matching anodized aluminum butt cap. Extra select specie cork (extra long) rear grip with Reel-Tyte-Lock. Stainless steel wire frame guides and tip-top. Comes in plastic bag with fiber tube case.

No.	Length	Action	Guides	Price
A417	5'8" and 6'0"	Omni	4	$17.95

A436 A427 A424 A422 B419 A417

26

Shakespeare catalog, 1964, page 26.

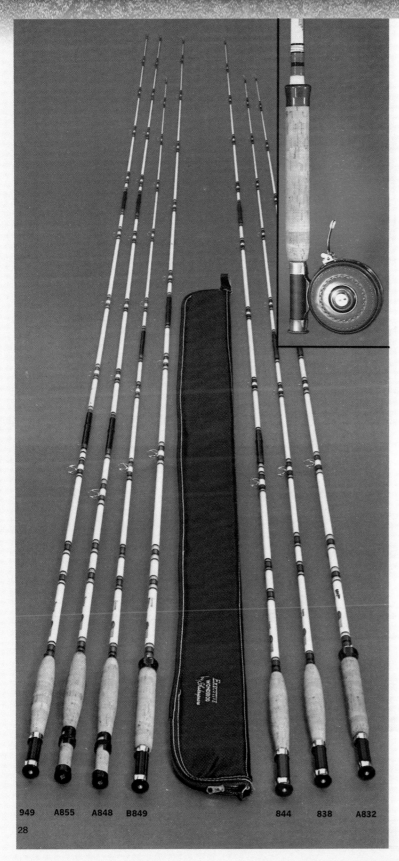

SHAKESPEARE FLY WONDERODS

No. 949 EXECUTIVE FLY WONDEROD. The ultimate in styling for an all-around three-piece fly rod. Handles bugs, bait, spinners, streamers and dry flies for all types of fishing. Wonderod white with grey nylon winds, black extended and two decorative bands. Has 6¾-inch extra select specie cork cigar-shaped grip with black anodized aluminum snap lock reel seat. Stainless steel guides with rustproof tip-top. Comes in super deluxe padded black leatherette carrying case. Weighs 4.9 ounces.

No.	Length	Guides	Lines	Price
949	8'6"	7	C, HCH & 6MH	$49.95

No. A855 EXECUTIVE FLY WONDEROD. The finest fly rod ever built. For all 'round use with bugs, spinners, streamers and dry flies. Three-piece, tubular construction. Prestige Wonderod white blade with grey nylon winds, black extended trim and two decorative bands. Has 6¾-inch extra select specie cork cigar-shaped grip with black skeleton-style screw locking reel seat; stainless steel stripping guide and snake guides, with rustproof tip-top. Packed in super deluxe padded black leatherette carrying case. Weighs 4.9 ounces.

No.	Length	Guides	Lines	Price
A855	8'6"	7	C, HCH & 6MH	$55.95

No. B849 SHAKESPEARE EXECUTIVE FLY WONDEROD. All-purpose for flies, bugs, spinners; trout, bass and panfish. Kwik-Taper action design. Blade is Wonderod white, silver grey winds, black nylon extended trim, and two decorative bands. The 7½-inch extra select specie cork grip has black anodized aluminum snap lock reel seat with matching fore cap. Stainless steel guides with rustproof tip top; deluxe padded black leatherette carrying case. Weighs 4.9 ounces.

No.	Length	Guides	Lines	Price
B849	8'6"	6	C, HCH & 4M	$49.95

No. A848 EXECUTIVE FLY WONDEROD. Feather light for sporty use on small trout streams and pan fishing. White blade with grey nylon winds and black extended trim, plus two decorative bands. Has 6¾-inch extra select specie cork cigar-shaped grip with black skeleton style screw locking reel seat. Stainless steel stripping guide and snake guides with rust-proof tip-top. In super deluxe padded black leatherette carrying case.

No.	Length	Guides	Lines	Price
A848	7'9"	6	D, HDH & 4M	$48.95

No. 844 PRESIDENTIAL FLY WONDEROD. All 'round three-piece deluxe fly rod. Handles bugs, bait, spinners and dry flies—for all types of fishing. Wonderod white with light brown winds, black extended trim and two decorative bands. Has 6¾-inch extra select, specie cork cigar-shaped grip. Has brown anodized aluminum snap lock reel seat. Stainless steel guides with rustproof tip-top. Comes in cloth bag and deluxe aluminum screw top case. Weighs 4.9 ounces.

No.	Length	Guides	Lines	Price
844	8'6"	7	C, HCH & 6MH	$44.95

No. 838 PRESIDENTIAL FLY WONDEROD. Two-piece, tubular glass construction, extra light action for flies and small streamers, White blade, light brown and black extended winds, with two decorative bands. The 6¾-inch extra select specie cork cigar-shaped grip has snap lock reel seat. Stainless steel guides and rustproof top. Weight: 7'9"—4.5 ounces.

No.	Length	Guides	Lines	Price
838	7'9"	6	C, HCH and 4M	$38.95

No. A832 PRESIDENTIAL FLY WONDEROD. Omni-Action, fly Wonderod with fast taper for dry or wet flies, streamers and small bass bugs. Wonderod white with light brown and black trim winds with two decorative bands. The 7½-inch specie cork grip has brown anodized aluminum snap lock reel seat and matching brown anodized aluminum fore cap. Stainless steel guides with rustproof tip-top. Comes in cloth bag and aluminum case. Weights: 7'9"—4.7 oz. 8'6"—4.9 oz.

No.	Length	Guides	Lines	Price
A832	7'9"	5	C, D, HCH, HDH, Omni and 8H	$32.95
A832	8'6"	6	Same	$32.95

949 A855 A848 B849 844 838 A832

28

Shakespeare catalog, 1964, page 28.

SPIN WONDERODS

No. 607 SPINNING ROD. Solid glass, quality at a low price. Casts live bait and lures from ⅛ to ½ oz. Two-piece in a rich green color with dark green extended winds, silver foil underwrap, white trim and decorative band. Grip is 12-inch specie cork with sliding ring lock reel seat; stamped frame guides and top. Comes in a plastic bag.

No.	Length	Action	Guides	Price
607	6'6"	Light	4	$7.95

No. 707 SPINNING ROD. Similar to above but with fixed seat. Specie cork, 2½-inch foregrip and 4-inch rear grip with fixed screw lock, sliding hood reel seat; stamped frame guides and top. Comes in a plastic bag.

No.	Length	Action	Guides	Price
707	6'6"	Light	4	$7.95

No. A609 SPIN WONDEROD. Top value. Tubular glass model casts live bait and lures from ⅛ to ½ ounce. Two-piece blade is maple color with dark brown extended winds, decorative band with gold foil underwrap. Has 12-inch specie cork grip with sliding ring lock reel seat; stamped frame guides and top. Comes in a plastic bag.

No.	Length	Action	Guides	Price
A609	6'6" & 7'0"	Light	4	$9.95

No. A709 SPIN WONDEROD. Fixed seat model of No. A609 above. Has specie cork 2½-inch foregrip and 4-inch rear grip with fixed screw lock, sliding hood reel seat; stamped frame guides and top. Comes in a plastic bag.

No.	Length	Action	Guides	Price
A709	6'6" & 7'0"	Light	4	$9.95

No. 710 SPIN WONDEROD. Companion rod to closed-face under the rod reels. Has cork 6½-inch foregrip and 3½-inch rear grip. Fixed aluminum screw lock, sliding hood reel seat. Tubular glass swelled butt model casts live bait and lures from ⅛ to ½ ounce. Blade is maple color with dark brown extended winds, decorative band with gold foil underwrap. Stamped frame guides and top. Comes in plastic bag.

No.	Length	Action	Guides	Price
710	6'6" & 7'0"	Light	4	$10.95

No. B612 SPIN WONDEROD. A real Shakespeare value at this low price. Ideal for live bait and lures from ¼ to ⅝ ounce. Two-piece. Blade is sparkling ivory with maroon extended winds, decorative band with silver foil underwrap. Has 12-inch specie cork grip with sliding ring lock reel seat. Stamped frame guides and tip-top. Comes in plastic bag.

No.	Length	Action	Guides	Price
B612	6'6"	Med. Light	4	$12.95
B612	7'0"	Med. Light	4	$12.95

No. B712 SPIN WONDEROD. Fixed seat model of No. B612. Has cork 2-inch foregrip and 5½-inch rear grip. Natural anodized aluminum fixed screw lock, sliding hood reel seat. Stamped frame guides and top. Comes in plastic bag.

No.	Length	Action	Guides	Price
B712	6'6"	Med. Light	4	$12.95
B712	7'0"	Med. Light	4	$12.95

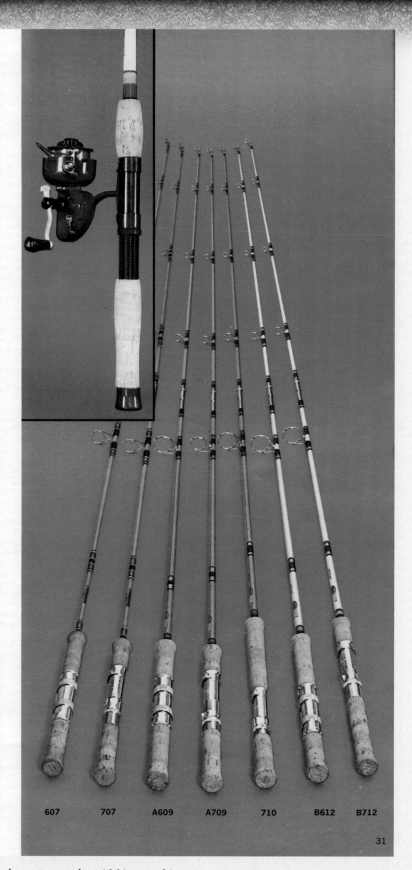

607 707 A609 A709 710 B612 B712

31

Shakespeare catalog, 1964, page 31.

Heddon®

GOLDEN MARK®

The first to use Heddon's exclusive all-glass ferrules for positive fit and smooth, superior actions. Tubular fiberglass rods in translucent amber. Gold-plated stainless guides. Carbide tip tops. Nylon locking reel seats on spinning and fly rods.

Casting Rods 1 piece
6442 5'6" Controlled Flex™ Action

Spin-Casting 2 piece
*6444 6' Vari-Power™ Action
6446 6'6" Controlled Flex Action
6448 6'6" Controlled Flex Action, 4 piece

Spinning Rods 2 piece
*7640 5' Ultralight™ Action
7642 6'6" Controlled Flex Action
7643 6' Lightweight Action
7644 7' Controlled Flex Action
*7646 6'9" Vari-Power Action
7648 7' Controlled Flex Action, 4 piece

Fly Rods 2 piece
8540 6'6" Ultralight Action
8542 7' Controlled Flex Action
8545 8' Controlled Flex Action
*8546 7'6" Controlled Flex Action
8547 8'6" Controlled Flex Action
8548 8' Controlled Flex Action, 4 piece
*SHOWN

Heddon catalog, 1974, page 21.

Heddon is by far the most recognizable name in fishing lure collectibles. Anyone on eBay seems to think that it is made of gold if made by Heddon, even if really a Pradco 1997 Heddon release! But, Heddon did indeed make some classic rods in metal, bamboo, and glass. This book is not meant to reexamine all the other great works on Heddon, and one can simply buy the book *Heddon Rods: The Rod with the Fighting Heart* for a complete discussion of Heddon bamboo rods and a history of Heddon rods. However, any treatise on modern fishing collectibles would be grossly incomplete without a discussion of some of the more popular recent Heddon rods for collecting. In the 1960s Heddon introduced a beautiful amber glass rod that is superb in construction, appearance, and function. I purchased an 8' Trail Fly Rod (four sections) in this model new in 1968, coupled it with a Pflueger Medalist 1496 Fly Reel and Scientific Anglers Dry Cell fly line, and went "Brookie hunting." This fly rod outfit has held up beautifully through the years and for the last 10 years has not missed an "opening day" (the last Saturday in April here in Michigan) looking for trout action. I now wish that I had purchased a complete line of these rods in 1968!

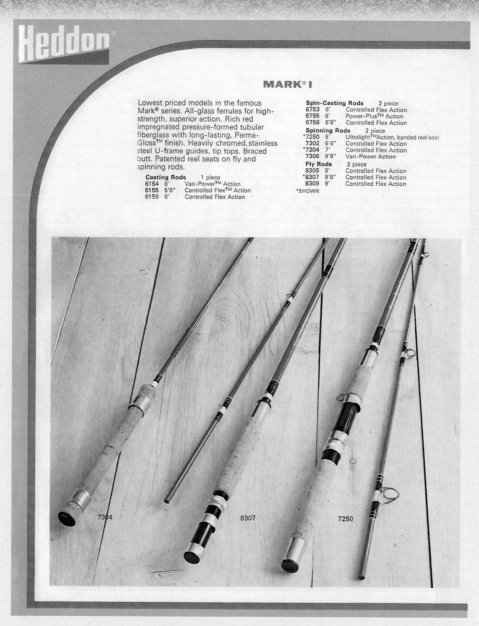

Heddon catalog, 1974, page 23.

Heddon also introduced the Mark series of rods in the early 1970s, and these red glass rods are also excellent for both fishing and collecting. Again, I have used a Mark I baitcaster for years and still do. These are starting to bring a good dollar amount for collecting, but one can still fish them too.

Miscellaneous rod companies could fill another book; however, some are highlighted here. Tru-Temper is a classic rod company and also an early maker of fine glass rods. Jobbers, through wholesale houses, hardware stores, and Western Auto outlets, often sold these rods. I believe the early Sears and

Wards glass rods were likely made by Tru-Temper also. Look for some of the following names: Abercrombie & Fitch, Actionglas and Actionrod*, Bristol*, Ezee-Cast*, Gep Metal*, Gephart Glass*, Glasscaster*, J.C. Higgins (Sears), Heddon, Horrocks-Ibbotson, Longcaster*, Michigan Rods, Montague*, Pflueger, Phantom Glass Casting Rod*, Shakespeare*, South Bend* (same quality as Heddon), Stubcaster* (unique rod for "casting where… brush in the way"), Tru-Temper, Western Auto, and Wright & McGill*.

*Indicates the rod was featured in the 1950 Nu-Way Sporting Goods Catalog shown on the following seven pages.

Nu-Way Sporting Goods Company

The finest solid glass rods money can buy. Round tapered blade with live action.

ACTIONGLAS AG 4'7", 5'1", 5'7" __**$28.20** $23.50 Ea.

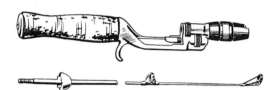

Triangular for lighter weight. TRIANGULAR for faster action, triangular for perfect balance.

ACTIONROD AT 4'7", 5'1" _____**$28.20** 23.50 Ea.

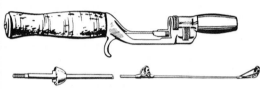

The perfect rod for fishermen who want ACTIONGLAS quality at a moderate price.

ACTIONGLAS AGB 4'7", 5'1", 5'7" __**$21.00** $17.50 Ea.

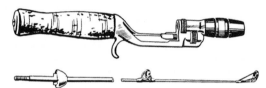

The rod with SQUARE grain structure, uniform hardness and de-luxe tip-action.

ACTIONROD AS 4'7", 5'1" _____**$25.20** $21.00 Ea.

New Actionglas rods at popular prices.

ACTIONGLAS AGC 4'7", 5'1", 5'7" __**$16.20** $13.50 Ea.
ACTIONGLAS AGD 4'7", 5'1", 5'7" **$11.94**   9.95 Ea.

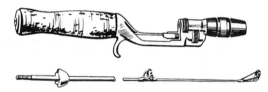

Perfectly balanced ROUND tapered steel blade with a bamboo-like feel.

ACTIONROD AR 4'7", 5'1" _____**$21.60** $18.00 Ea.

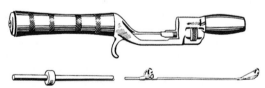

This rod offers the holiday sportsman a good rod at an exceptional price.

ACTIONROD ARC 3'7", 4'7", 5'1" ___**$11.94** $9.95 Ea.

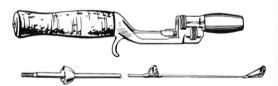

For sportsmen who want quality at a price.

ACTIONROD ASB (Square) 4'7",5'1"**$19.30** $16.00 Ea.
ACTIONROD ARB (Round) 4'7",5'1" **$16.74** $13.95 Ea.

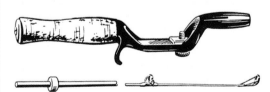

NOW—New rods, at popular prices with good action.

ACTIONROD ARD 3'7", 4'7", 5'1" ___**$8.34** $6.95 Ea.
ACTIONROD ARL 4', 4'7", 5'1" _____**$6.00** $5.00 Ea.

A fast-selling rod with slip-fit blade lock at an exceptionally low price.

ACTIONROD ARE 3'6", 4'6" _____**$4.20** $3.50 Ea.

''First in Sports''

Nu-Way Sporting Goods Company catalog, 1950, page 1.

Nu-Way Sporting Goods Company

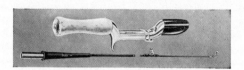

A rod made of durable weight blade stock, and designed for the fisherman who desires good tip-action.

BRISTOL No. 36-Hex—4½' and 5' **$8.40**___$7.00 Ea.

A Hex telescope bait casting rod with detachable handle. Four joints telescoped to 18 inches.

BRISTOL No. 7-Hex-5'2"_____**$ 7.20**_____$ 6.00 Ea.

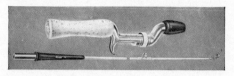

A fine quality rod in the middle price range constructed to meet the severest test.

BRISTOL No. 38-Hex—4½' and 5' **$6.00**___$5.00 Ea.

A good quality rod in the low price field yet with tapered and heat-treated round steel blade—nickel plated finish.

BRISTOL No. 39-RD-4½'_____**$ 3.60**_____$ 3.00 Ea.

The finest quality tubular steel rod made. A special process gives the rod "life" in the right place, improves casting action and enables you to real fishing pleasure.

GEP No.HF-Tubular-5½' & 6'___**$21.60**___$18.00 Ea.

A solid, triangular shaped steel rod. Chrome finished for beauty and added strength. This is an exceptional value with many deluxe extras on the blade surface.

GEP No. 198-Solid Hex-4½' & 5'__**$14.40**__$12.00 Ea.

With the adjustable Nu-Grip and cork handle. Special analysis alloy steel hexagonal shaped. Balanced for light flexible action. Grained backed brown enamel finish with walnut colored celluloid hosel at butt of rod. Offset handle with cloth carrying case.

GEP No. 88-Hex-4½' & 5'_____**$12.00**_____$10.00 Ea.

The finish and streamlining of these rods make them outstanding in both appearance and performance. Evenly balanced solid square steel forged to meet the stiffest tests any fisherman can put them through.

GEP No. 550-Hex-4½' & 5'____**$10.80**____$ 9.00 Ea.

An outstanding value in chrome finished square blade rods. The evenly balanced action is tops. Has three quality chrome guides and tip.

GEP No. 250-Sq—4½' and 5'____**$8.40**____$7.00 Ea.

Solid square steel blade. Special alloy, conventional handle, light flexible action. A quality usually found in much higher rods. Blade an attractive cream color.

GEP No. 300-Sq.-4½' & 5' _____**$7.20**_____$ 6.00 Ea.

Special analysis solid steel at a price that can't be beat. No. 195 is available in the Hexagonal steel with the famous Gep actionized feel and tip-action.

GEP No. 195-Hex-4½' & 5'_____**$ 6.00**_____$5.00 Ea.

An exceptional value that is hard to beat. In the low priced field No. 210 is available in the solid steel round blade with screw lock reel seat.

GEP No. 210-Round-4½'_____**$ 4.20**_____$ 3.50 Ea.

''First in Sports''

Nu-Way Sporting Goods Company catalog, 1950, page 2.

Nu-Way Sporting Goods Company

'Glasscaster'

**Solid Fiber Glass
Bait Casting Rod**

Here at last a perfected fibreglass rod at a price any of your customers can afford. A new technical process makes it possible to fuse thousands of glass fibres into one flexible, translucent, solid shaft to form one of the toughest substances known.

Glasscaster Rod 4½'__**$14.34**__$11.95 Ea.
Glasscaster Rod 5'____**$15.54**__$12.95 Ea.
Glasscaster Rod 5½'__**$16.74**__$13.95 Ea.
Glasscaster Blade 4½'**$11.94**__$ 9.95 Ea.
Glasscaster Blade 5'__**$13.14**__$10.95 Ea.
Glasscaster Blade 5½'**$14.34**__$11.95 Ea.

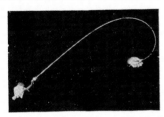

Here's the casting rod you've been looking for. Action in the tip where you need it for long effortless perfect spot casting. Power to handle the big ones under any condition. Will not rust, rot or set.
PHANTOM GLASS CASTING ROD
No. 55—5' and 5½'__**$28.20**__$23.50 Ea.
Southwester—4½' & 5'_**$9.54**__$7.95 Ea.

Truly a deluxe combination! The new all-chromium plated steel tip . . . 3 sturdy chromium plated stainless steel bridge type guides and tip top . . . plus the offset polished chromium plated handle with positive reel locking ring.

EZEE-CAST No. 40—4½' and 5'_**$6.00**_$5.00 Ea.

Now you can have a standard casting rod of fine quality which will also interchange with that very popular stub-caster.
Longcaster No. 20—Rod_____**$9.54**_____$7.95 Ea.
Longcaster No. 19—Shaft_____**$5.94**_____$4.95 Ea.

Nothing else like it. Ideal for trolling or casting where overhanging brush is in the way. Handy and compact.
Stubcaster No. 21_____**$7.14**_____$5.95 Ea.

Action! Strength! Ability to stay straight after long use. These are the qualities you'll find in the new Wonderod by Shakespeare. An attractive 1950 model in translucent amber.
Shakespeare No. A1180L—5' 2"_____**$21.00**_____$17.50 Ea.
Shakespeare No. 1175L—5'2"_____**$18.00**_____$15.00_Ea.
Shapespeare No. 1177—3'6"_____**$13.50**_____$11.25 Ea.

Deluxe quality criterion split bamboo casting rod designed for light to medium weight lures.
Shapespeare No. A1114L—5½'_____**$18.00**_____$15.00 Ea.

Eye catching with the appearance of a much higher priced rod. Off-set die cast aluminum handle with positive action ring type reel lock—has bright aluminum finish, natural cork grip and plastic forward grip. The taper ground oil tempered steel tip has attractive green baked enamel finish.
EZEE-CAST No. 20—3½' and 4½'_____**$3.90**_____$3.25 Ea.

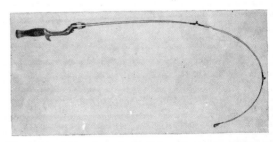

The outstanding value of all steel casting rods. Made of specially treated high grade silicon chrome vanadium steel, with positive reel locking device and natural cork grip handle.
EZEE-CAST No. 30—3½' & 4½'____**$4.00**____$3.30 Ea.

"First in Sports"

Nu-Way Sporting Goods Company catalog, 1950, page 3.

Nu-Way Sporting Goods Company

WRIGHT & McGILL GRANGER FLY RODS

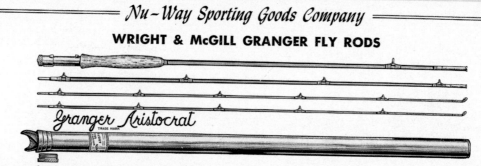

Granger Aristocrat TRADE MARK

These are the finest split bamboo rods possible to make. Built to exacting standards by skillful workmanship, they have perfect taper, accurate dimensions, effective action, power and balance. Every user of these rods is well pleased with the great amount of joy and satisfaction they have given. Especially designed for both wet and dry fly fishing.

GRANGER No. GA—8½'—4½ Oz., 9'—5 Oz._____**$48.00**_____$40.00 Ea.

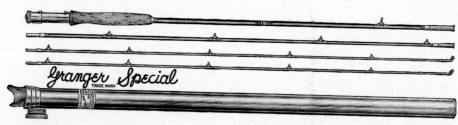

Granger Special TRADE MARK

Only the most exacting standards are used in making these handsome rods. They have perfect taper, accurate dimensions and effective action, balance and power. Especially designed for wet or dry fly fishing. They are highly praised by the thousands of fishermen who have used these rods during the past 30 years.

GRANGER No. GS—8½'—4½ Oz., 9'—5 Oz._____**$36.00**_____$30.00 Ea.

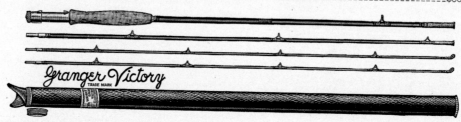

Granger Victory TRADE MARK

These rods are made to exacting standards. They have perfect taper, accurate dimensions and effective action, balance and power. Especially designed for wet or dry fly fishing and a thrill to the proud possessor of this truly fine rod.

GRANGER No. GV—8½'—4½ Oz., 9'—5 Oz._____**$30.00**_____$25.00 Ea.

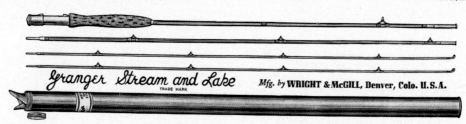

Granger Stream and Lake TRADE MARK   Mfg. by WRIGHT & McGILL, Denver, Colo. U.S.A.

These rods are special favorites of skilled fishermen. Their perfect taper and accurate dimensions give them power, balance and action especially suited for both wet and dry fly fishing.

GRANGER No. SL—8½'—4½ Oz., 9'—5 Oz._____**$24.00**_____$20.00 Ea.

"First in Sports"

Nu-Way Sporting Goods Company catalog, 1950, page 4.

Nu-Way Sporting Goods Company

"COMFICIENT" GRIP

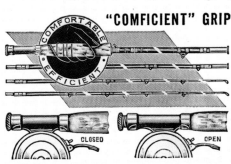

"LITE-LOCK" END-LOCKING REEL SEAT

For many years the choice of many anglers. Carefully built three-piece (with extra tip) singlebuilt split bamboo fly rods. Newly designed Lite-lock reel seat, South Bend "Comficient" cork grip.

South Bend No. 47—8½' & 9' **$24.00**__$20.00 Ea.

The famous South Bend Singlebuilt rod construction principle is shown above. It consists of six strips of carefully matched triangular sections of cane milled from the dense, outer section of the bamboo stem. Only the finest Tonkin cane is used.

A series of extremely attractive three-piece (with extra tip) single-built split bamboo fly rods. Newly designed light weight thread lock maroon and chrome reel seat.

South Bend No. 57—8½' and 9'_____**$12.00**____$10.00 Ea.

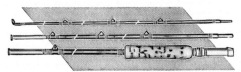

Wonderfully attractive rods. Three-piece singlebuilt split bamboo. Screw-locking reel seat of mottled yellow Tenite and chrome plated brass. Truly a great value.

South Bend No. 55—8½' and 9'___**$9.00**___$7.50 Ea.

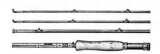

An excellent all-around rod with sporty action—plenty of backbone. Three-piece selected flame finish split bamboo, with extra tip.

Shakespeare No. 1305—8½' & 9'__**$24.00**__$20.00 Ea.

BEAUTIFUL ACTION, light weight and great strength are combined in the new Shakespeare Glass Fibre Wonderod. Rod does not take a "set".

SHAKESPEARE

No. 1280—7'9"—3.9 Oz._____**$42.00**_____$35.00 Ea.
No. 1280—7'9"—5.02 Oz._____**$42.00**_____$35.00 Ea.

A rod with perfect balance, powerful action, long life and moderate price. Reel seat Tenite, screw type locking band. Three piece natural finish split bamboo. Extra tip. Dry fly action.

Shakespeare No. 1362—8½' & 9'__**$18.00**__$15.00 Ea.

New DeLuxe Glass Rods. Combines lightness, strength, and action to give angler complete control of his fly and get new thrills from the battling action of fish.

Shakespeare No. 1390—8½'—5-Oz. **$60.00** $50.00 Ea.
Shakespeare No. 1380—8½'—5 Oz. **$48.00** $40.00 Ea.

This fly rod is guaranteed for 3 years and includes yearly factory inspection, varnishing and normal repairs. The fine balanced action gives the registered Gep a "feel" all its own.

GEPHART Registered 8½' & 9'____**$30.00**__$25.00 Ea.

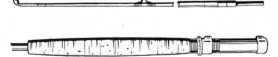

A durable all-purpose glass fly rod for wet or dry fly fishing and sturdy enough for trolling or still fishing.

ACTIONGLAS No. AG8—7½' **$33.00**____$27.50 Ea.
PHANTOM No. BG—7½'_____**$42.00**____$35.00 Ea.
PHANTOM No. BG—8½'_____**$42.00**____$35.00 Ea.

The Gep tubular spinning rod is an item of genuine beauty. The sturdy action and willing response to assist in backward and forward casts endears it to the fisherman. Perfectly balanced.

GEPHART No. 196—7'_____**$30.00**__$25.00 Ea.

"First in Sports"

Nu-Way Sporting Goods Company catalog, 1950, page 5.

Nu-Way Sporting Goods Company

Tops in the low-priced field. Three joints and extra tip. Selected flame finish split bamboo. Ferrules: Straight rolled welt, bronze finish wound over. Reel Seat: Black plastic Scrulock. Bronze fittings.

Montague No. 1RF--8', 8½', 9'____**$21.00**__$17.50 Ea.

Three joints and extra tip. Stock: Brown tone split bamboo. Ferrules: Improved, rolled welt, nickel plated. Reel Seat: Titelock, nickel plated and blue plastic.

Montague No. 1SUF—8½' and 9'__**$14.40**__$12.00 Ea.

The best fly rod value on the 1950 market. Three joints. Stock: Dark colored split bamboo. Ferrules: Nickel-plated rolled welt. Reel seat: Nickel-plated plain band.

Montague No. 1CF—8½' and 9'____**$8.40**___$7.00 Ea.

A DeLuxe quality bait rod. Light weight, sporty action hard to beat for cat-fishing. Handle has positive thread locking reel seat.

South Bend No. 480—10'_____**$12.00**__$10.00 Ea.

Bristol Hexagonal Telescopic Fly Rod made especially for the fly fisherman who always wants a fly rod conveniently stowed in his car—4 joints, 7⅓ feet in length.

Bristol No. 4—7⅓'_____**$8.40**___$7.00 Ea.

A round telescopic rod 4 joints, 7¾ feet long. Its reduced length allows for ease in fly casting. Aluminum die cast handle gray-tone finish with reversible feature and good grade cork grip.

Bristol No. 12—7¾'_____**$6.00**___$5.00 Ea.

Here is a rod that offers real versatility. With the various combinations of tips and reversible butt it gives you . . . (1) a 9 ft. Fly Rod with reel below hand . . . (2) a 6½ ft. light Fly Rod . . .(3) by reversing grip, either rod may be used for still fishing . . . (4) a 6 ft. Baitcasting or No. 1 or No. 2 Light Trolling Rod . . . (5) a 3½ ft. Baitcasting or Light Trolling Rod . . . (6) grip may be reversed on No. 4 and No. 5 if desired. Four joints and grip. Stock: Browntone split bamboo.

Montague No. 4ERC_____**$16.20**__$13.50 Ea.

Three joints. Stock : Browntone split bamboo. Ferrules: improved nickel-plated, rolled welt. Reel Seat: Nickel-plated Titelock.

Montague No. 1HF—8½' and 9'____**$9.00**___$7.50 Ea.

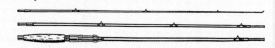

This rod is particularly suited for cat-fishing, for perch and other pan fish and also for bass. This is a particularly good seller. Stock: Natural color split bamboo neatly finished.

Montague No. 1CLB—9'_____**$12.00**__$10.00 Ea.

Natural Split Bamboo. Grips: Double natural knurled. Rubber button. Reel seat: Nickel-plated, Titelock. An ideal rod for river fishing.

Montague No. 12 MOB—7½'_____**$9.00**___$7.50 Ea.

Hexagonal telescopic rod 4 joints 9 feet long. Another fine rod for all fishermen ,equipped with snake guides mounted on brass sleeves, chrome plated. Aluminum die cast handle with reversible feature and good quality natural cork handle. Spring steel joints. Cloth case.

Bristol No. 9—9'_____**$6.60**___$5.50 Ea.

Round telescopic rod 3 joints 8½ feet long which is most satisfactory for all types of still fishing. Aluminum die cast handle brightly finished with reversible feature and cork grip handle. Finished in brown baked enamel. Stainless steel guides.

Bristol No. 15—8½'_____**$4.80**___$4.00 Ea.

''First in Sports''

Nu-Way Sporting Goods Company catalog, 1950, page 6.

Nu-Way Sporting Goods Company

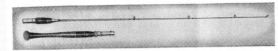

Recommended for salmon, lake trout, and fish of similar size. One piece special analysis solid steel actionized. Corrosion proof Gep-armor-oid finish. Positive reel locking device. Hardened steel guides chrome plated. Solid birch butt with rubber butt cap. Cloth case.

GEPHART No. 500-5½'_____**$19.20**_____$16.00 Ea.

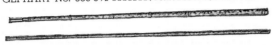

High quality materials and expert workmanship make these fish poles a real value, priced to sell in volume.

L3M—3 Piece, 12'_____**$20.00**_____$16.68 Doz.

An outstanding value for weekend fishing and beginners. Equipped with brass reel seat, tip, guide and non-level winding reel. Every pole an outfit.

MONTAGUE No. JOR_____**$20.16**_____$16.80 Doz.

Extra strong for bluefish, lake trout, bonefish, muskelunge and other large fish. Also used to satisfaction as boat rods on bays and salt water. Made of the same special alloy steel used in Gep casting rods but of heavier stock which gives greater stiffness and strength.

GEPHART No. 505-5½'_____**$14.40**_____$12.00 Ea.

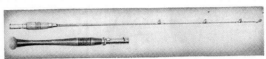

Machine made rolled edge ferrules riveted to the bamboo. Ends are plugged with doweling to increase strength. All metal nickel plated "band eye" tip top. Mottled finish.

L4M—3 Piece, 14'_____**$22.90**_____$19.08 Doz.

Made of the finest imported bamboo. Restraightened and tempered. Only available in the natural clear finish. It has no competition at this price.

No. 10—2 Piece, 8-10'_____**$6.48**_____$5.40 Doz.

Made of selected imported Bamboo. Solid brass Ferrules with rolled edges to give maximum strength. Each ferrule is fitted and fastened to insure a lasting tight fit.

No. 112—3 Piece, 12'_____**$17.14**_____$14.28 Doz.
No. 114—3 Piece, 14'_____**$20.00**_____$16.68 Doz.

Processed Oriental First Quality Straightened Bamboo Fishing Poles To Insure Uniform Top Quality.

BAMBOO FISHING POLES

Length	Approx. Weight Per 100	List Price Each	Packed in Bundles of		
12'	50 Lbs.	17c	100	**$20.30**	$16.92 Per Bdl.
14'	65 Lbs.	22c	100	**$26.00**	$21.70 Per Bdl.
16'	80 Lbs.	27c	50	**$16.00**	$13.34 Per Bdl.
18'	100 Lbs.	34c	50	**$20.54**	$17.12 Per Bdl.

CALCUTTA SMOKED BAMBOO POLES

Genuine short jointed finest quality Calcutta poles. Pre-smoked, semi-solid ranging from 14' to 16'. Assorted 50 poles per standard bundle.

Length	Approx. Weight Per 50	List Price Each		
14'—16'	60	$1.88	**$112.80**	$94.00 Per 50

NOTICE: Prices on Oriental Bamboo and Calcutta Poles are Subject to Change Based on Ocean and Rail Freight Rates

"First in Sports"

Nu-Way Sporting Goods Company catalog, 1950, page 7.

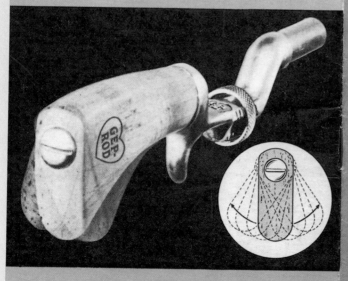

Gep-Rods catalog, 1940, front and back cover.

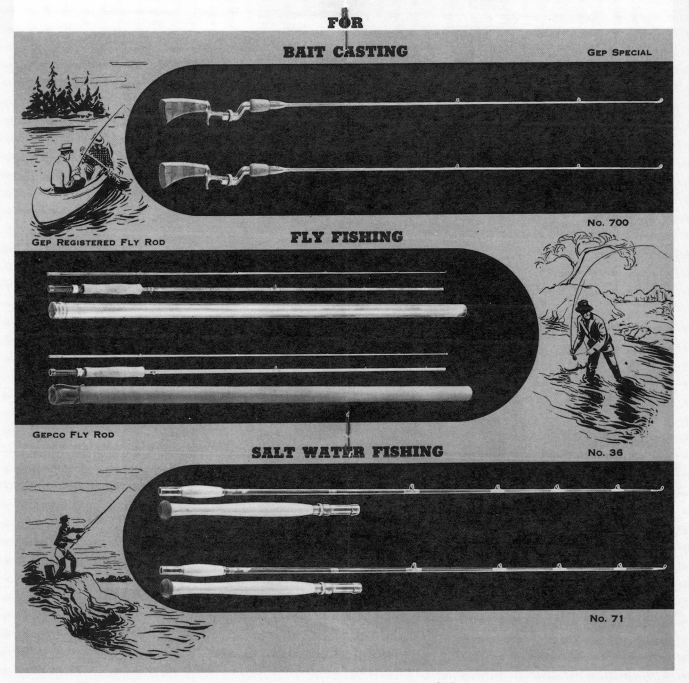

Specialists in Steel Fishing Rods

FOR

BAIT CASTING — GEP SPECIAL

No. 700

GEP REGISTERED FLY ROD

FLY FISHING

GEPCO FLY ROD

SALT WATER FISHING — No. 36

No. 71

Gep-Rods catalog, 1940, pages 16 and 17.

Top of Abercrombie and Fitch carrying case in leatherette. The multi-section glass pack rod like new in the case known as the Passport Rod. Each section is approximately 6" long, cork handle is exactly 6" long. Total of nine sections and handle. Glass is solid fiberglass with glass ferrules. The rod is marked Abercrombie & Fitch, New York-Short Hills-Chicago-San Francisco on first section and Passport on second section. Leatherette box is hinged with a snap hinge and trimmed in gold foil. The glass ferrules are 1½" long on eight sections, the first section fits into the handle. Assembled, it would make a nice snappy Brookie rod. $500.00+.

One interesting side collection would be pack rods and travel rods. In 1973 Berkley introduced a "complete travel kit" with multi-section fiberglass rod, two reels, a tackle box, lines, and extra line spools. I purchased one new for a trip to the Yellowstone River and have used it ever since. Eagle Claw also produced a beautiful four-piece travel rod in a tube in the 1970s worth noting. Of course, one can go back in time and collect "gentleman's rods" made of tubular steel. These were made for the inside vest pocket of a trench coat so the fisherman could stop off on the way home from work or take the rod with him on his business trips. These actually date back to the 1800s and were made throughout fishing history until replaced by fiberglass. One of my favorites is a rod I have seen only once, the Abercrombie and Fitch multi-section glass rod in a small vest pocket box. This must date from the 1960s or earlier and is an exceptional addition to any collection of modern fishing items. I have turned down offers of $500.00 for this rod. Again, it may not be all that scarce, but I have run across only one of them in the last few years (shown above).

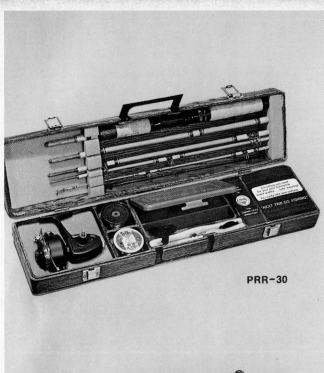

PRR-30

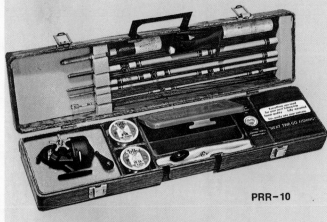

PRR-10

BERKLEY'S DELUXE ROD AND REEL TRAVEL PACKS

Complete outfits, including the finest quality Berkley reels, Trilene monofilament line, para/metric rods, and pocket-size tackle/bait boxes.

All items are neatly packed in a custom-made, handsome and extremely durable "simulated wood" presentation case. The case has two key-lock latches and a flush folding handle. Truly a compact innovation for the traveling angler. Eliminates scattered tackle and reduces the risk of rod breakage.

PRR-30 SPINNING OUTFIT

Para/metric Custom 5 pc. 7' Spinning Rod with tubular glass ferrules and the famous curved taper design.

4201A Adapter Spinning Reel — for fresh or salt water fishing. Fitted with the Berkley adapter for "instant line change."

Berkley Trilene monofilament line on instant-change spools. One 100-yd. spool of 6 lb. test on reel, plus an extra 100-yd. spool of 10 lb. test. Also 125-yds. 17 lb. on reel's regular spool, packed as a spare.

Pocket-size Tackle Box. Handy for baits, hooks, etc. Tough polypropylene, molded in one piece.

PRR-10 SPINCASTING OUTFIT

Para/metric Custom 5-pc. 6½' Spincasting Rod. Tubular glass ferrules and curved taper design provide a unique casting sensation, you'll cast farther and more accurately with less effort.

310 Spinning Reel. Berkley's best closed face reel. Star drag, positive pickup, 3 to 1 retrieve, all-metal construction.

Berkley Trilene monofilament line. 100 yds. of 10 lb. test pre-wound on reel. Two extra 100-yd. spools in case — one of 6 lb. and one of 10 lb.

Pocket-size Tackle Box. Tough polypropylene, molded in one piece. Compartments for sinkers, hooks, baits, etc.

A "ONE-PIECE FEEL"

Berkley's exclusive patented Double-flex "hidden" ferrules make these many-sectioned travel rods practical — for easy carrying and fine fishing action. Made of the same material as the rod, these hollow-glass ferrules flex with the rod. Gone are the days of dead-weight, "dead" spots and dull, heavy action. This ferrule gives a one-piece feel and one-piece action — and light weight. It looks like fine trim on a one-piece rod, too.

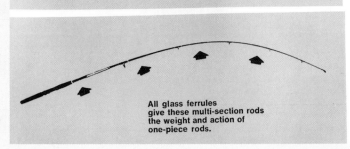

All glass ferrules give these multi-section rods the weight and action of one-piece rods.

Berkley catalog, 1972, page 16.

BERKLEY'S DELUXE ROD AND REEL TRAVEL PACKS

PRR-5C Combination *FLY FISHING AND SPINNING OUTFIT*

Para/metric Custom — 5 pc. 7' combination Spinning Rod/Fly Rod with convertible handle.

4201A Adapter Spinning Reel — for fresh or salt water fishing. Fitted with the Berkley adapter for "instant line change".

540 Fly Reel — New single action adjustable drag. Light weight, fully aerated. Removable spool. 1 to 1 retrieve.

Berkley Trilene — line on instant-change 100-yd. spools. One spool 6 lb. test on spinning reel, plus an extra spool of 10 lb. test. Also 125 yds. 17 lb. test on reel's regular spool, packed as a spare.

Fly Line — 30 yds. Berkley double taper with Trilene backing wound on fly reel.

Pocket-size Tackle Box — 3TB. Tough polypropylene with compartments for various terminal tackle items and flies. Tapered Leader and Fly included.

PS8C - 8 RODS-IN-ONE *TRAVEL PACK*
The most versatile fishing outfit ever made!

A. Multi-piece Berkley para/metric Custom rod with tubular glass ferrules for one-piece feel. Handles for spinning/fly and bait/spincasting rod assembly.

B. 4201A Adapter spinning reel with "instant change" 100-yd. spool of 6 lb. test Berkley Trilene monofilament line.

C. Berkley's best spincasting reel, 310, star drag, spooled with 100 yds. 10 lb. test Trilene.

D. Single action 540 Berkley fly reel, spooled with 25 yds. Berkley floating fly line.

E. Extra "instant line change" spool of 100 yds. Trilene. Also 125 yds. 17 lb. test on spinning reel's regular spool, packed as a spare.

HERE ARE THE 8 DIFFERENT OUTFITS
you can assemble by varying your selections or rod sections and handles:

4 SPINNING OUTFITS
1. 6'8" medium-light action spinning rod.
2. 7'2" medium action spinning rod.
3. 5'10" spinning/trolling rod.
4. 8' steelhead/salmon spinning rod.
Each with matching 4201A reel and line.

2 FLY FISHING OUTFITS
1. 6½' light (trout) action fly rod.
2. 7'9" fly rod for bass/pan fish.
Each with matching 540 reel and line.

2 SPIN/BAIT OUTFITS
1. 5'10" medium action baitcast/spincast rod.
2. 6'8" light action baitcast/spincast rod.
Each with matching 310 reel and line.

Easy assembly instructions and pictures included with each pack.

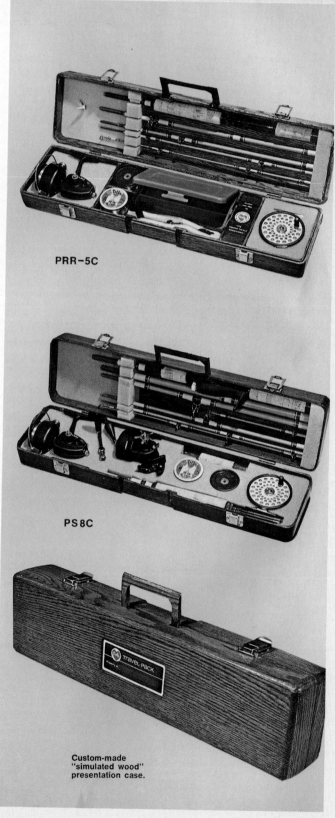

PRR-5C

PS8C

Custom-made "simulated wood" presentation case.

Berkley catalog, 1972, page 17.

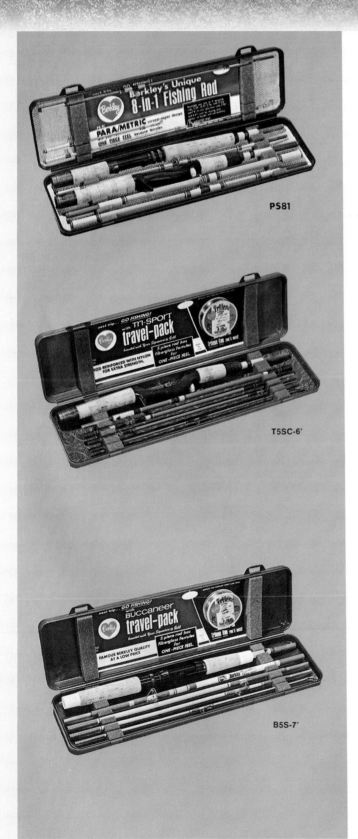

PS81

T5SC-6'

B5S-7'

BERKLEY
MULTI-PIECE RODS
IN TRAVEL PACK

"next trip, go fishin'"

This attractive, compact case fits into small luggage. Measures 18¾" x 5¼" x 1¾".

Para/metric Rod

PS81 new 8-rods-in-1, rod only.

Multi-piece Berkley para/metric custom rod with tubular glass ferrules for one-piece feel. Handles for spinning/fly and bait/spincasting rod assembly.

1. 6'8" medium-light action spinning rod.
2. 7'2" medium action spinning rod.
3. 5'10" spinning/trolling rod.
4. 8' steelhead/salmon spinning rod.

5. 6½' light (trout) action fly rod.
6. 7'9" fly rod for bass/pan fish.

7. 5'10" medium action baitcast/spincast rod.
8. 6'8" light action baitcast/spincast rod.

Tri-Sport Rods . . . with line.

Berkley's popular Tri-Sport rod is now offered in these 5 versions — without sacrificing the excellent fishing qualities. The Berkley glass ferrules preserve the Tri-Sport's distinctive fast tip action. Each pack includes appropriate Berkley fishing line. Removable point-of-sale card included.

T5SC-6' includes 5-piece 6' Spincasting Rod and 200 yds. of 8 lb. test Berkley Trilene monofilament line.

T5S-7' includes 5-piece 7' Spinning Rod and 200 yards of 8 lb. test Berkley Trilene.

T6F-8' includes 6-piece 8' Fly Rod and 30 yards No. 6 double taper fly line.

T5C-7' includes 5-piece 7' Combination Spinning-or-Fly Rod with 100 yards of 8 lb. test Berkley Trilene line and 30 yards of Berkley No. 6 double taper floating fly line.

Buccaneer Rods . . . with line.

Berkley's high quality — low priced Buccaneer series moves up in class to become a great series of Travel Pack rods. The addition of Berkley's all glass ferrules makes the big difference. Each pack includes a multi-piece rod (with a one-piece feel) and appropriate Berkley line. Removable point-of-sale card.

B5SC-6' includes 5-piece 6' Spincasting Rod and 200 yards of 8 lb. test Berkley Trilene monofilament line.

B5S-7' includes 5-piece 7' Spinning Rod and 200 yards of 8 lb. test Berkley Trilene.

B5F-7' includes 5-piece 7' Fly Rod and 25 yards of Berkley floating level fly line.

B6F-8' includes 6-piece 8' Fly Rod and 25 yds. of Berkley floating level fly line.

B5C-7' includes 5-piece 7' Combination Spinning-or-Fly Rod with 100 yards of 8 lb. test Berkley Trilene line and 25 yards of Berkley floating level fly line.

Berkley catalog, 1972, page 18.

BERKLEY FLY FISHING OUTFITS IN TRAVEL PACK

"Next trip, go fly-fishin'"

Extra value! These travel-fly fishing outfits come in the attractive, durable case.

(For easy shelf identification, the case is packed in the wood-grain box with end label shown above).

Extra value features include rods with all glass ferrules and specie cork grips, Berkley fly line, a Berkley knotless tapered leader, and a popular dry fly. Perfect for personal use, ideal for **gift-giving!**

Tri-Sport Fly Outfit TPK

. . . includes 6-piece rod, reel, line, leader and fly. This outfit features a sensitive 6-piece rod that fishes, feels and reacts like a one-piece rod. Lots of backbone, but light in weight. Everything needed for fly fishing is included in the compact carrying case.

TPK includes 6' 6" fly rod, Berkley's 510 single action fly reel with 30 yards of Berkley No. 6 double taper floating fly line on the reel, Berkley's knotless tapered leader and a popular dry fly.

Buccaneer Fly Outfit BPK

. . . includes 6-piece rod, reel, line, leader and fly. This outfit features a 6-piece Buccaneer fly rod that feels like a one-piece rod: sensitive — full of action — light weight. Everything you need to enjoy the fun of fly fishing is included in compact carrying case.

BPK includes 6' 6" fly rod, Berkley's 510 single action fly reel with 25 yards of Berkley's C level fly line on the reel, Berkley's knotless tapered leader, and a popular dry fly.

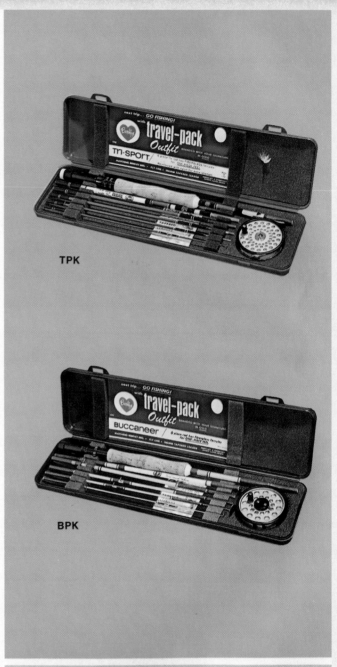

TPK

BPK

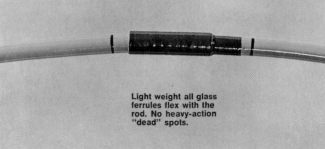

Light weight all glass ferrules flex with the rod. No heavy-action "dead" spots.

Berkley catalog, 1972, page 19.

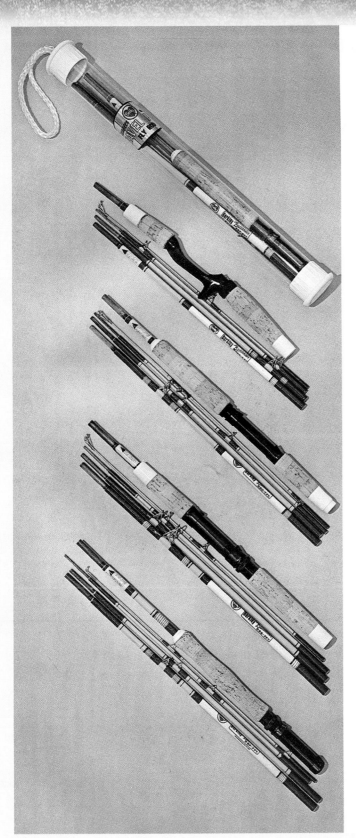

NEW BERKLEY BUCCANEER PACK RODS

in compact carrying tubes

Berkley Buccaneer multi-piece rods offer compact convenience for packing, with the live action, light weight and feel of a one piece rod, thanks to all-glass ferrules. Choose from spincasting, spinning, spinning/fly combination, or fly rods. Each is packed in an extremely durable, heavy gauge, clear Tenite* tube, 18" long. Each end of the tube has a soft foam cushioned poly cap, and each tube has a lariat-braided carrying handle.

BT6F-8' . . . A six-piece 8' fly rod with anodized aluminum reel seat and specie cork grips.

BT5SC-6' . . . A five-piece 6' spincasting rod with live-action nylon/glass handle and specie cork grips.

BT5C-7' . . . A five-piece 7' rod for spinning or fly fishing. Convertible handle has removable specie cork butt grip.

BT5S-7' . . . A five-piece 7' spinning rod with anodized aluminum fixed reel seat and specie cork grips.

BT5F-7' . . . A five-piece 7' light weight fly rod, with anodized aluminum reel seat and specie cork grip.

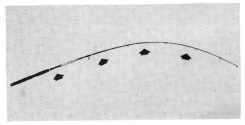

All glass ferrules

Berkley Buccaneer pack rods transmit live-action into the user's hand because weak and heavy "dead" spots created by ordinary metal ferrules are completely eliminated. Illustration above shows the uninterrupted curve, under load, provided by Berkley's all-glass ferrules.

Berkley catalog, 1972, page 20.

Heddon®

TRAIL BLAZER™

Made for the sportsman on the go. Rod packed in cloth case inside of back pack aluminum tube. Amber translucent fiberglass blank. Gold guides and top. Braced butt guides. Spinning rod has Heddon's patented nylon locking ring on reel seat.

Spin-Casting Rod   4 piece
*6450 6'   Medium-light Action

Spinning Rod   4 piece
*7650 6'   Medium-light Action

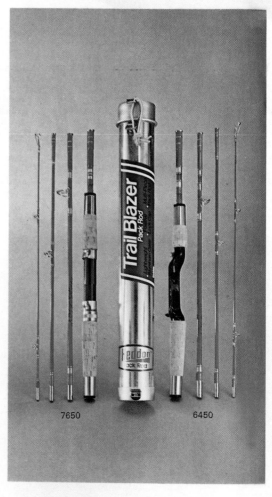

7650   6450

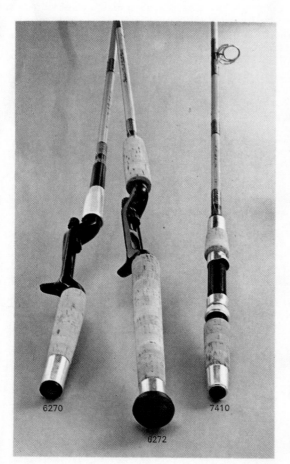

6270   7410

6272

MARK® BRUTE™

Heddon's newest series, designed for the specialty fisherman who needs something extra. Quartz-cured, tubular glass rod blank for extra strength. Exclusive Heddon® stainless Wire/Wrap™ cannot stretch, rot, fray, slip or corrode. Carbide guides on casting rods. Carbide tip tops and chromed steel guides on spinning rods.

Casting Rods   1 piece
*6270 5'6"   Medium Heavy Action, detachable handle
6271 6'   Medium Heavy Action, detachable handle
*6272 5'10"   Heavy Action

Spinning Rods   1 piece
7408 5'3"   Medium Heavy Ultralight
*7410 5'7"   Medium Heavy Ultralight
*SHOWN

Heddon catalog, 1974, page 24.

Wonderpoles and Ice Rods

ICE RODS BY SHAKESPEARE

Designed to give the nation's millions of ice fishermen Shakespeare quality in ice fishing rods.

No. IR300 BEST QUALITY. Here's the deluxe version for the serious ice fisherman. Rod is 4½-feet long with 9¼-inch hardwood handle with nickel end cap fitted to solid white fiberglass blade. Rear grip section of handle is specie cork with sliding rings for seating reel. There are three stainless steel guides and a stainless steel tip-top. Rod is trimmed with maroon and black extended winds. Overall weight is 3⅝ ounces.

No. IR200 BETTER QUALITY. A 3½-foot model with solid white glass blade mounted on 16⅜-inch hardwood handle with nickel end cap. There's a chrome-plated nickel line winder. Rod has two wire formed snake guides. Rod trim is maroon and black. Weight: 5 oz.

No. IR100 GOOD QUALITY. One-piece solid glass blade with 9-inch hardwood handle makes a dandy two-foot ice rod. There's a steel wire, zinc plated line guide and tip-top. Nickel-chrome plated line winder on handle. Weight: 2 oz.

No. IR101 READY TO FISH. This rigged ice fishing outfit includes IR100 rod but comes completely assembled with line, styrofoam bobber and ice fishing jig.

Glass Telescoping Wonderpoles

Brings "class" to still fishing. Maple color, with sensitive fast-action tip. With rubber caps, it forms its own case! Three convenient lengths.

Number	Length Extended	Length Closed	Number of Sections
TP-12	12 feet	55 inches	3
TP-16	16 feet	55 inches	4
TP-20	20 feet	55 inches	5

Jacket Patch

Join the "Shakespeare Fishing Club." Jacket patch 5" by 4", is gold, black, blue, green and white. If your dealer cannot supply, write direct to Advertising Department, Shakespeare Company, Kalamazoo, Mich. 49001 and enclose $1.00 for each patch, postpaid. Order **No. JP-1.**

No. 3848 FERRULE CEMENT. Handy for minor rod repairs, fixing loose tips, etc. Just heat and apply.

TP-20   TP-16   TP-12

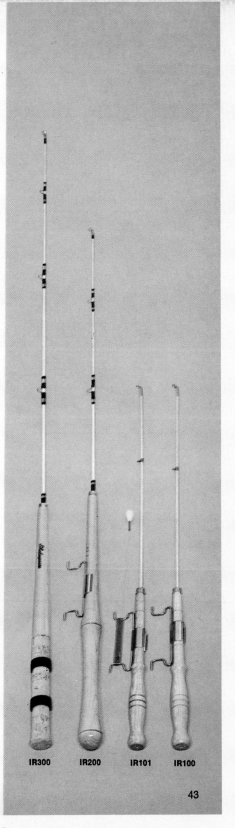

IR300   IR200   IR101   IR100

43

Shakespeare catalog, 1972, page 43.

Novelty rods would be another interesting sideline or centerpiece of a rod collection. The odd-looking Michigan rods are quite hot as a collectible, commanding well over $50.00 each; Hurdcasters will bring up to $200.00 in mint condition; the Popiel Pocket Fisherman (of television fame), and any other unusual rod will be sought after in the future. Also be on the look-out for unusual grips.

This is not a book about bamboo rods, however, I have bought and sold over 200 high quality bamboo rods and must add a word or two here. First of all, condition is extremely important, and poor rods bring poor prices. Secondly, this is the one exception to the rule that individually made items normally sell for far less than company items. Well, a classic rod made by a well-known individual rod maker will command premium prices, sometimes in four or five figures. Not one Heddon or South Bend bamboo rod will ever compete with a Payne or a Young for example. Finally, this is one area that I would rely upon only a noted expert or qualified dealer in bamboo rods for advice on purchases. Sure, if you are at a garage sale and you find a four-piece rod with both tips mint in its bag for $25.00, buy it. But, if you are spending hundreds of dollars for a unique piece, you better know that it is authentic, that it has not been rebuilt, that the varnish and wrappings are correct, that the tip has not been replaced, etc. Bamboo collectors are very particular about their rods, and the phrase "caveat emptor" has no better place in this book than in reference to purchasing fly rods made of bamboo.

I would start with known rods by Heddon, South Bend, Montague, H-I, Weber, and Shakespeare. Add to that collection some quality rods from current or recent diviners of this art with great care and expense. Round off the collection with some show-and-tell goodies like a handcrafted wooden net from Ed Cummings in Flint, Michigan, and some display cards from Weber of Stevens Point, Wisconsin. As a general rule, rods with any flaws are worth only a small portion of their book value. A missing tip on a two-tip rod hurts its value greatly but not as much as a rod having both tips but missing line guides, ferrules, etc. Also, as a general rule, shorter rods (7½' or less) are worth more than longer rods. One obvious reason is that with most of our modern homes having eight-foot ceilings, it is tough to display an 8' rod. Rods, especially bamboo rods, should never be kept in any position but upright, whether in their tubes or put together! Another reason short rods command a premium price is that those of us in the trout territories of the upper Midwest and the East fish with our collectibles.

Finally, do not overlook bamboo casting rods, especially if made by a major company such as Heddon.

What Now?

In this chapter I attempt to predict some hot areas for future fishing collectibles and give the beginning collector some organizational tips on how to help the collection grow with a plan. This plan is one area that many early collectors face with uncertainty and often have a giant accumulation of items with no sense of purpose. Some tips from one who has been down that road may assist future collectors in avoiding some costly mistakes.

When my wife first read the above paragraph, she laughed out loud, and rightly so. My collecting life has been one of total chaos at times with the main goal of accumulating "more toys" than anyone else; however, in all fairness to myself, I believe that period is now over and I have reached a more mature level of collecting. What is meant by the phrase "more mature level of collecting" is that there is some direction to attaining specific goals regarding specific items. In other words, now I want the "most toys" related to certain fishing collectibles. For instance, one can simply not own enough Fin-Dingos! But, seriously, one needs to have some guidance and some idea of a goal or the collection is merely an accumulation of items.

The best lesson can be learned from my former academic life as an archaeologist: catalog all items! If I had it to do over again, I would have written down every lure, rod, reel, and accessory ever purchased, the source, the cost, the condition, and whether it was for trade, sale or my permanent collection. With this master list data, all else becomes easy. However, most of us get caught up in the moment and always think we can record that information later. Well, you cannot. You forget, you get busy, you get lazy, you get tired, and something interferes. So, do yourself a favor and record everything as you find it, not later. This also helps you document scarce colors, scarce baits, lures with an unusual history or ones owned by someone special, etc., and becomes an invaluable tool for insurance purposes as well.

The following is a suggested means of recording data related to your collection. Make a 5" x 7" card (a little more room to write on than a 3x5 card) and record the following information as you acquire items. Record the item purchased, the purchase price, a description of the item, from whom purchased, whether it was acquired for trade, sale or the permanent collection, any special comments about the item, its history, or its value. Then, if you are comfortable with a computer, when you return home immediately put this information into a spreadsheet format for ease of record keeping. I have all four hundred plus of my Sonics on a spreadsheet,[18] and it is the only way I can keep track of the colors, eye variations, printed name color variations, and the myriad of other minor differences in a Heddon Sonic.

I do the same for my Jitterbugs, Tadpollys, Punkinseeds, and Fin-Dingos. Eventually, I hope to add all of my permanent collection to a spreadsheet format for record keeping purposes and filling in the gaps in my own collection.

Your interests will likely change, evolve, grow, widen, narrow, and in general be refined over the years. However, with a solid record of your items you can better decide what is of value to you and your collection.

The main thing in collecting is to attempt to find a focus and zero in on that focus. Only the collector can make that determination. For me, I have a very broad interest and want to expand to all areas that my budget and space allow. However, I know I like rainbow-colored lures more than most, Fin-Dingos, and Dolls are very special, that I find it easier to sell doubles than singles, and I still do not own every color Heddon ever made. Is this a focus? Well, it is for me, but it may not work for you. If you like fish-shaped lures such as Punkinseeds, Fin-Dingos, and Dolls, then do not buy the others, concentrate on one area until you are happy with the state of your collection and then expand. Expand only when you are happy with the state of your initial collection.[19]

The foregoing is easy advice but hard to follow for we all seem to get "bitten by the bug" and go a little nuts. After all, fishing lures are "little pieces of art" as my wife always says, and who does not like to be surrounded by art? But try to stay organized, within your budget and space limits, focused on what you really enjoy, and all will be smooth.

Regarding forecasting the future, I hold myself and my publisher harmless for any of the following comments; they simply seem possible given the history of lures, fishing collectibles, and collectibles in general:

- lures that look like fish seem to hold their value or go up;
- lures in limited production are usually a better investment;
- colorful lures, such as Rainbows, have held their values;
- novelty lures and advertising lures have great potential;
- lures in boxes or on cards are always a better investment;
- display cards and unique advertising items increase in value;
- prototypes of anything have great intrinsic and extrinsic value;
- paper products usually increase due to rarity and natural deterioration of paper;
- find an area no one else wants to collect, start buying everything in sight at great prices, and you are soon joined by a few hundred others; and,

Ignore everything above, and buy only what you like!

A 1970s BassPro
Tackle Box and Contents

A recent purchase on eBay seems to typify the lures one would find in a typical tackle box from the 1970s. The ever-present Jitterbugs and Hula Poppers, a wide selection of Bomber Baits, an offering from Eddie Pope, some nice bass spinners still on their cards, and all kinds of other goodies just waiting to be discovered. This box was from a retirement community in the Phoenix, Arizona region and found its way back to the Midwest via eBay. I am not showing this box as statistical proof in an empirical or scientific sense as I do not have the chain of evidence for the box. However, the provenance seemed to be legitimate and it appears rather untouched for most of the last decades, with the possible exception of the addition of some newer South Bend terminal tackle, snaps, leaders, and a box of sinkers. But the box had a new Heddon Prowler, typical Bombers of the era, Bayou Boogies in post-box packaging, and a Glen L. Evans Co. buzz bait from when they were still owned by Gladding, pre-1982. It also contained the Frog Pikie by Shakespeare/Paw Paw made in Hong Kong shown in the Shakespeare chapter (Volume 1) that dates from the early to mid-1970s. At any rate, the box is shown as an example of two things: (1) a field find of modern collectibles with most items from the 1970s; and (2) what one could find on eBay for about $160.00 in the spring of 2001.[20]

Spinning size Jitterbug in frog, catalog is from 1971, the year Tru-Shad was introduced by Arbogast. $12.00+.

Large size, 3⅜" as measured on the curve, Eddie Pope Fishback, Sinker Model, in silver scale. $8.00 – 12.00.

A casting size, spinning size, and two fly rod Hula Poppers. $8.00 each, more boxed.

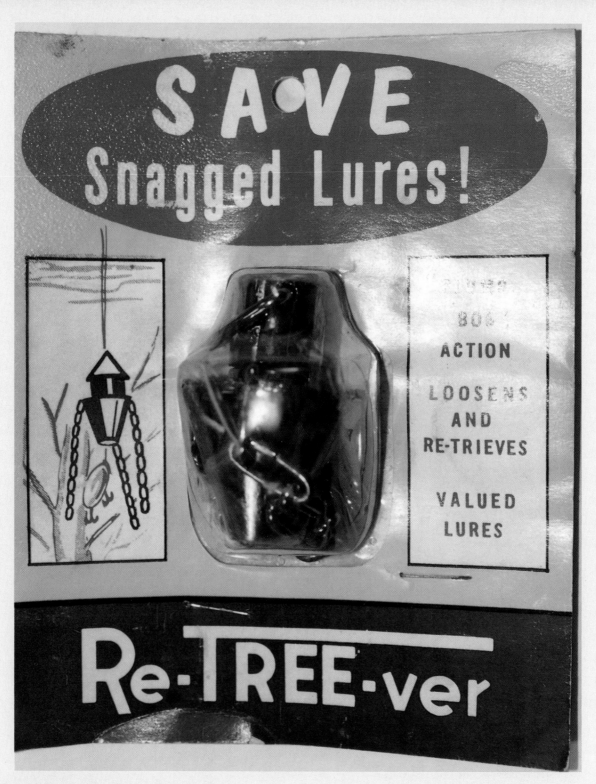

One of the many lure retrievers invented for bass plugs, this one new in its package called the Re-Tree-ver, made by Kar-Gard Company, Kansas City, Missouri, pre-zip code card. In addition to the plug knocker, it also made fish stringers. $30.00+ new on card.

Glen L. Evans Booby Trap Model 3254, ¼ oz. bass spinner new on card. This pre-dates 1982 for certain. $15.00+ new on card.

Two Cordell Topo Spoons new on cards, no model numbers, address on cards is Post Office Box 2020, Hot Springs, Arkansas 71901. $5.00 each.

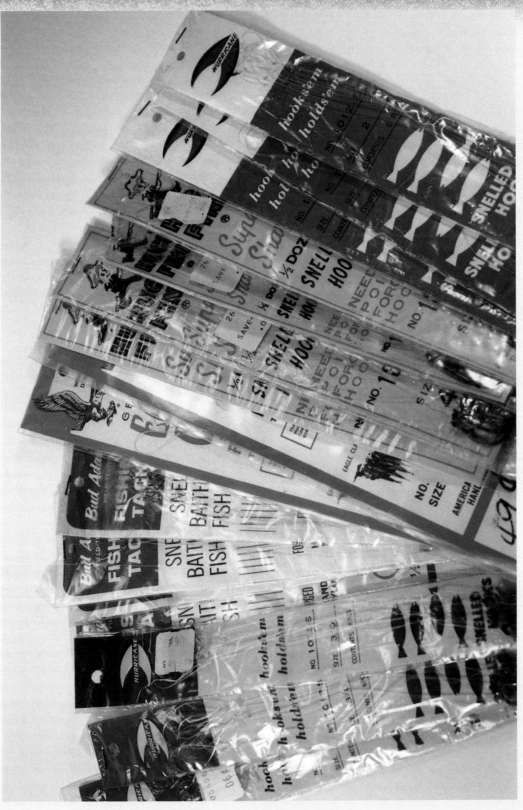

A wide variety of snelled hook packets, from left to right, Hurricane (Korean made), Bud Adams (Japanese made), Eagle Claw (Mexican and U.S.A. made), Huck Finn (Korean made), and more Hurricanes. $1.00 – 3.00 each.

Mann's Baits on blister packs, three Wooly Bullys, and a Jelly Worm. Evidence of the jig 'n pig phase being upon us. Wooly Bullys have a box number of P.O. Box 607 in Eufaula, Ala. 36027 and the Jelly Worm is at P.O. Box 604. The three-pack is Model 315-P and weighs in at ⅜ oz. $3.00 – 8.00 each on cards.

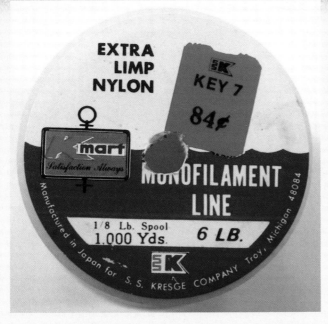

"Blue Light Special" line from K-Mart, still old enough to have the SSK trademark of Kresge Company but post-zip code. Made in Japan, 1,000 yards, cost 84¢. $2.00 – 5.00.

South Bend terminal tackle and some Mustad snelled hooks. The South Bend tackle all has the older address at 1950 Stanley Street, Northbrook, IL 60062, and prices ranged from 57¢ to $1.47. It was made in both Korea and Japan. $2.00 – 5.00 each.

A "Roo-Tur" Model RO-14 by Rabble Rouser, new in the box; a Bomber Water Dog Model 1514, wooden, new in Gainesville, Texas slide-top box; and a Rebel "MiniR Noisemaker," Model F-94R-03, new in the plastic slide-top box. $12.00 – 25.00 each new in the box, Rabble Rouser being the most desired followed by the Bomber then the Rebel. Colors, of course, could create a higher price if rare.

bayou boogie *The original swimming, vibrating lure deadly to all game fish.*

7000 Series
Wt. 1/4 oz.   Length 1-1/2"
For spinning and slow trolling

6500 Series
Wt. 1/3 oz.   Length 2"
For spinning, casting and trolling

6000 Series
Wt. 1/2 oz.   Length 2-1/2"
For casting and trolling

5000 Series
Wt. 3/4 oz.   Length 3"
For deep casting and fast trolling

Bayou Boogie is a sinking type lure with a fast vibrating action designed to quiver, shimmy, and swim just like real fish. It will run only as deep as allowed to sink creating a very versatile lure for most water depths. Functions ex... ...g and casting. In both trolling and ...t the mood of the fish. In casting, ...es deadly. For bottom bumping, ...n slack and sharply raise rod tip. ...d with a distinct vibration that can be felt in ... the lure a certain amount of fre... fall to impart a... action. Be alert at all ti... for the strike!

COLOR NUMBER **6501**

Whopper Sto...r, Inc. P.O. BOX 1111 SHERMAN, TEXAS 75090

MADE IN U.S.A.   LITHO IN U.S.A.

Bayou Boogie, cost $1.19 new, in seal top plastic bag on a cardboard background, 6500 Series, Model and Color 6501 (it casts a blue tone on top due to reflective color of paper; the lure is actually a gray shad color), 1/3 oz., 2", new in package but removed to photograph. An unusual find new in the package. I would rate this card more difficult to find than the boxed lures shown in Volume 1 and value it at $25.00+ in this condition.

A 1½" ¼ oz. screw hardware model and the previous lure. There was also a 2" screw hardware model in black/yellow scale. $25.00+ with card, $8.00 – 12.00 loose.

The Finnish invasion: two Rapalas. Early boxes with advertising still in both Finnish and English. Model 9S, 3½" floating and Model 5G, 2" floating. Both new in boxes with papers. It would take a powerful computer to calculate the fish caught on just these two lure styles! $5.00 – 8.00 for early ones shown here.

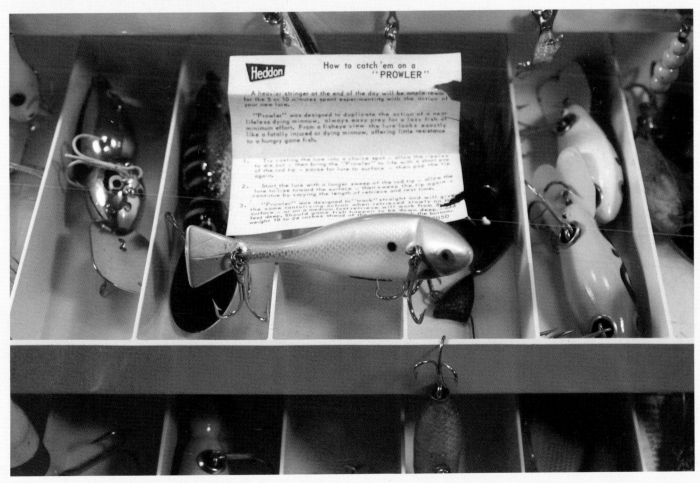

Heddon Prowler, Model 7025, in Shad. New with instructions but no box. This is an early 1970s lure. $25.00+.

Top of box from left to right: Top row: Weller's "Shimmy Tails" from Erwin Weller Co.; a tray of jig heads; a Rapala is behind in far tray; Doll (same company as Chapter 9, Volume 1) worm or fly heads (jig 'n pig again); hanging down is a small 1½" Big O from Cordell in flesh color, orange belly, yellow eyes, and red gills, pupils protrude, simple screw hardware with hooks on split rings; a Mepps #2 and a Rooster Tail; far tray has another Rapala; middle tray has the Heddon Prowler in "O" above; little tray has some Nature Faker Inc. of Windsor, MO eyelets for E F & G lines; far corner tray has a #1 Aggravator Bass Spinner in yellow body, red eyes, and a black/yellow tail; the front corner tray has a wooden Bomber, 2⅜" body, in yellow coach dog, orange eyes with black pupils, appears never fished; and hanging in front of the Bomber is a fish-shaped Phoebe lure in gold scale, 1½" long and a Mepps #5 Aglia with the British/French Pat. Bottom row: A purple headed Lazy Ike diving plastic worm rig (see the four-pack under Kautzky), a small yellow jig head, a large rounded jig head with worm, and a small lizard tail jig rig; the second tray has a 3¾" skirted Rebel Top Water plug, protruding yellow eyes with black pupils, silver sides, black back, molded in hook hangers with swivels connecting hooks, appears unused; a wooden 2⅜" body length, using my calipers, Bomber in a neat silver speckled sides with white stripes on a black back, slight age lines only; unmarked plastic silver/chrome green back, Water Dog type lure with square lip, tail spinner, surface hardware with two flat blade screws on each hanger, "Carrot Top" type eyes, new; Bomber Water Dog, 3" long in same color pattern as the Bomber two trays to the left and also in perfect unused condition; hanging above the empty tray is a Cordell Spot, 3" long, silver with red mouth and spot and a Bomber Slab Spoon in white; next tray has a "Little George" in green back, red eyes, marked tail spinner, and two unmarked lures with the plastic lure molded around the combination hook hanger/line tie, each with a spinner blade and a feather duster type tail, the body is ¾" long and one is dark gray scale and the other is light gray scale; the next tray has two Bombers 2⅜" body length, both wooden, some age lines but little damage, the white with black dots may have been fished and the Shadow-Wave pattern appears unused; and the end tray has a Black Fury #3 by Mepps and a Kastmaster by Acme Tackle Co., 3⅝" length, this was a competitor of Weber's Mr. Champ. Most of these lures were not collectible until the past couple of years but now most lures would bring $5.00 – 12.00 if in decent shape as shown here.

The top row was covered above as the bottom row on page 294; starting on the left of the bottom row is a lizard type jig 'n pig set new in its package and two small Doll type jigs; next over is a Cordell Big-O in gold chrome with black back, 3" long, fished; hanging is the small Bayou Boogie type described above and a Japanese plastic plunker type, 1½" long with plastic protrusion where screw hardware is mounted into the tail; next is another Cordell Big-O, 3" in Silver Chrome with black back, also used but in good shape; next is a larger Water Dog, wooden, 3¼" long, frog back, yellow belly, appears unused; next is another Big-O type lure but unmarked, protruding orange plastic eyes, plastic dive lip, molded in very small hook hangers with hooks on split rings, body is 2¹⁵⁄₁₆" long, like new; next is another Bomber, same size but plastic and rattler, Shad pattern, used, above the Bomber hanging is a Lucky 13 copy from Japan, 1⅞", white eyes, perch color, Japan in small letters on bottom of mouth (Herter's?); next is a smaller, 2⅜" long lure made exactly as the one two trays to the left, but not marked; a 2⅜" long plastic Bomber in black with silver specks, like new, and papers for Bomber Baits and two Rapala inserts. Again, most of these lures are now worth $5.00 – 12.00 loose, more if new in box. Cordell Big-Os and Bombers could be worth much more for rare colors.

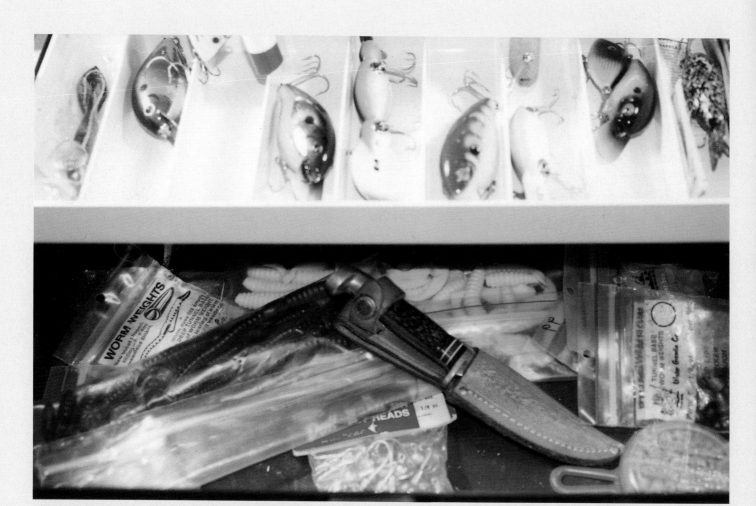

The bottom was full of some of the items already shown, more Doll jig heads in the smaller ¼ oz. size, the Water Gremlin sinker box, Water Gremlin worm weights, swivels, etc., two assortments of plastic worms new in bags from the Northwoods, Tackle Sales Division, PO Box 4169, Milwaukee, Wis. 53210, and best of all, a very nice Western knife with a 2¹⁵⁄₁₆" blade, like new in leather sheath. One thing that adds credence to the possibility that this box was in storage for years is the fact that the knife and sheath snap have the green corrosion found only after a prolonged storage period. Most of these items are of little value with the exception of the knife, $20.00+.

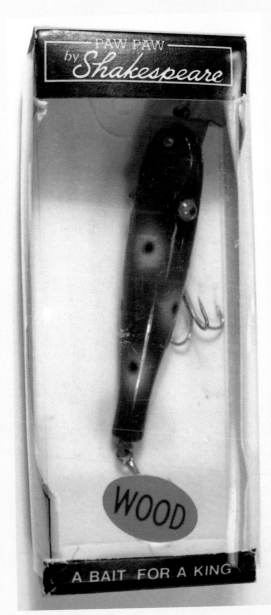

And, do not forget the Shakespeare/Paw Paw Frog colored Piky Getum lure new in the box with pocket catalog. This rare set from the mid-1970s would bring $50.00+ if only for its difficult to find pocket catalog.

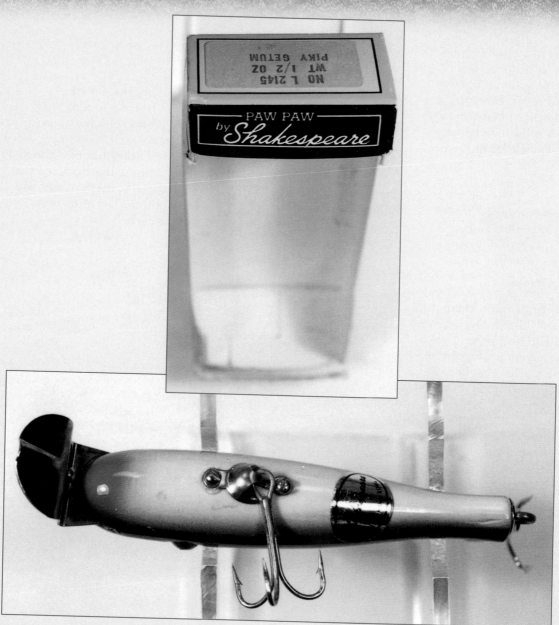

Bottom view of the Shakespeare/Paw Paw Frog colored Piky Getum lure and end view of the box. $50.00+.

Well, there we have it, one last look at modern fishing lure collectibles through the experience of one tackle box. Not bad, 48 lures not counting any accessories or jigs. A nice Western knife. Ten lures new in packaging. An unusual "Plug Knocker" new in its package. Assorted goodies new in their packages, the ever dangerous plastic/rubber worms, one Lazy Ike worm not counted in the total of 48, all in a dandy three-tray BassPro box. Not bad for $160.00, $3.33 per lure, and most in great shape or new.

But, not all eBay buys are as fortunate. Some buys net[21] beat-up old junk that is worth little to anyone. But with time and experience, you will be able to add to your collection of modern items by also making some decent buys at shows and on the Internet. Whatever your source, attempt to buy from someone with experience and a strong positive reputation for knowledge and honesty. And, most importantly, arm yourself with as much knowledge as you are able.

Good luck, and enjoy!

The following book list is not necessarily exhaustive but is presented in the order of what this author thinks is of most importance in learning about modern fishing lure collectibles and their history. None of the books will replace the experience of actually viewing and handling fishing lures and related items; however, with the following books in your basic reference library, you will be ahead of the game in seeking out a solid foundation on which to build your own specialized knowledge of the field of fishing tackle collectibles.

Slade, Robert A. *The History & Collectible Fishing Tackle of Wisconsin*, 1999, Bob & Tess Slade. Published by and available from the author, Robert A. Slade, S. 75 W. 18983 Circle Drive, Muskego, Wisconsin 53150.

This book is one of the first a beginner should acquire because it really does justice to both history and collecting. Unlike so many lure picture books, this book goes to great lengths to detail numerous small and large companies in Wisconsin, or ones that took over Wisconsin companies. A new collector could find at least two to three years of "head start" collecting experience by reading this volume and paying attention along the way. Bob does a great job covering all types of collectible fishing items and does not have a bias toward only the "very old" or the "very valuable." One final reason to read it is that Wisconsin was really only second to Michigan in terms of sheer numbers of lure companies, although only home to one of the real big names: Weber. But, Heddon had a research center in Chetek, and many great lures still show up in that northwestern region of Wisconsin.

Richey, George. *Made in Michigan Fishing Lures II*, 2000. Published by and available from the author at Honor, MI 49640 and some other tackle book retailers.

This is the book I would have written if Mr. Richey had not already beat me to it! The first edition (1995) of this wonderful book was one of the first I purchased because it covered small companies, metal baits, and plastic baits in addition to the vintage bass and pike plugs. The book details numerous companies from my native state of Michigan that produced fishing lures and related tackle from the beginning to the zip code introduction in 1963. Also, like Bob Slade's treatise on Wisconsin, Richey does not show any bias toward only the rare and valuable but does justice to the most common of Michigan baits. He also has detailed historical data on each company and helps the beginner and advanced collector alike trace the development of lure making in the great lure making state of Michigan. Mr. Richey is the editor of the *NFLCC Gazette*, and his knowledge of Michigan companies is truly not surpassed by anyone. My only regret with the book is that the illustrations are in black and white but that has allowed the publisher to keep the price of the book affordable.

Luckey, Carl F. *Old Fishing Lures and Tackle*, 5th Edition, 1999, Krause Publications, 700 E. State Street, Iola, WI 54990-0001.

This is undoubtedly my favorite of the general lure guides currently available as it details the very old to the fairly new. The 5th Edition also has an expanded section on plastics and some great resources for the "modern" collector. It is our loss that Mr. Luckey has now passed away and will not be able to keep revising this tried and true book now in its fifth printing. Hopefully, the publisher will continue this work using another author. The other reason I like this book so much is that it also gives some detailed history of companies and lure developments not found in most other books.

Murphy, Dudley and Rick Edmisten. *Fishing Lure Collectibles*, 2nd Edition, 2002, Collector Books, P.O. Box 3009, Paducah, KY 42002-3009.

This is the best reference book for photo quality, layout, and presentation of the big companies and miscellaneous lures prior to 1940. The photos are large enough to see detail which really helps in identifying subtle differences on lures. This is one of the must-have reference books.

Streater, R.L. with Rick Edmisten and Dudley Murphy. *The Fishing Lure Collector's Bible*, 1999, Collector Books, P.O. Box 3009, Paducah, KY 42002-3009.

This great classic has recently been edited and updated by Murphy and Edmisten. This book has many little notes, leads, and details not available elsewhere. The graphics at times are not the best, but it is a big help in identifying small companies, old and new alike. This great reference was for years available only directly from the author, R.L. Streater, and was often used by collectors in the NFLCC. Thanks to the efforts of Murphy and Edmisten and Collector Books, this wonderful volume is now available to the general collecting public.

White, Karl T. *Fishing Tackle Antiques*, Revised Edition, 1985, P.O. Box 169, Arcadia, OK 73007.

This is the classic "picture book" of fishing lures, reels, rods and other fishing collectibles. My wife can attest that this book was on my lap nearly every night for the first few months I owned it, with me poring through memorizing lures, old and new, and company data. My only complaint with White's book is that the photos are too small and the detail is at times hard to see. But, it is a great source of photographic information. Also, some of the limited data is wrong, the data is too limited, and the prices were originally far too high. Now, the hobby has actually grown into his prices, and many times they are too low for the more difficult to find items. With this said, I still would not recommend building a general collection without this volume on your shelf, or better yet, in your lap!

Smith, Harold. *Collector's Guide to Creek Chub Lures and Collectibles, Second Edition*, 2002, Collector Books, P.O. Box 3009, Paducah, KY 42002-3009.

A must-have for any Creek Chub collector. This wonderful history has superb graphics and is very complete. Dr. Smith does a great job even of covering the modern era up to the closing of the main operation in Indiana. His book gives a good overview of one company's history from the beginning to the end of its existence as an independent company. This would be a good reference for any collector to help understand the type of historical developments that all companies were experiencing. It is especially helpful to the collector of modern Creek Chub lures in its coverage of rare colors and models.

Wong, Terry. *Identification and Value Guide To South Bend Fishing Lures*, 2000, Terry Wong. Published and available from the author at 1657 Acoma Dr., Phoenix, AZ 85023 for $33.00, shipping included.

This is a superb introduction to South Bend lures prior to their sale to Gladding in 1964. The photography and color charts are of the highest quality, and the layout is to be commended. It is a very easy to use and highly researched volume on one major company which contributed so much to both vintage and modern lure collecting. Actually, Terry stole a little of my thunder by having some nice photos of Fin-Dingos, Fish-Obite, and other plastics available from the South Bend stable out in print prior to this volume! But, this gives me the great advantage of now referring to his work for more details! I would not imagine collecting South Bend without first buying this book, but it is far more useful than that, it is a necessary reference to show many changes from vintage to modern and does an excellent job of covering South Bend up to 1964.

Wong, Terry. *Collector's Guide to Antique Fishing Lure Colors*, 1997, author published and available from him at address above.

This book has 13 pages in full color, showing over 200 lure colors for the "big five" lure companies. This is an excellent working reference that helps identify items found new-in-the-box according to the color codes. The only source book showing such detailed color layouts with the accompanying code numbers on the market.

Takeyama, Masami and Tetsuya Kumada. *Heddon Plastics Collectibles*, 1st Edition, 1999, printed in Japan.

This book is published in Japan and available at this time only in Japanese; however, it is an excellent and complete photographic reference for modern Heddon plastics. It will

be published in English at some date, according to the authors. Regardless, with this book in hand, one can discern the small differences in Heddon plastics that developed over the last 50 years of the company and become very well informed indeed. Again, this book stole a little of my thunder as I had anticipated being first to demonstrate many of the same differences and must now say, see this reference for more details. However, as much as I love this book, there are some omissions on modern box types and lures that my book covers, so it is hoped that the reader will be able to use my book as the history of Heddon plastic developments and this book as an accompanying photo journal, as it is most complete and beautiful in that regard.

Harbin, A. Clyde, Sr. *James Heddon's Sons Catalogs* (from 1903 to 1953), 1977 by the author. Originally published by CAH Enterprises, 1005 Marlin Road, Memphis, TN 38116 with the current Second Printing available from Highwood Bookshop, P.O. Box 1246, Traverse City, MI 49685.

This wonderful source of early Heddon catalogs is the best way to acquire early Heddon catalogs at a reasonable price, although only 12 pages are in color. It certainly assists the "modern" collector in two ways: it builds a strong foundation of knowledge of Heddon and shows the changes in detail from 1940 until 1953. I recommend it highly.

Sinclair, Michael. *Heddon: The Rod With The Fighting Heart*, copyright by Michael Sinclair and available from Highwood Bookshop at the above address.

This work is the only one in the bibliography that I have not read, but I have a friend who recommends it highly. As it deals primarily with the bamboo rod line, it is a little off this book's central interest, but I would recommend it for any person specializing in Heddon items.

Kimball, Art and Scott. *Early Fishing Plugs of the U.S.A.*, 1989, P. O. Box 252, Boulder Junction, WI 54512.

Although this book is technically out of our historical era, it is a great early work on lure collecting and identification and is itself now a collectible volume. A recent reprint was made available which is good news for those of us that did not own one of the first volumes. There are a few "plugs" referred to from the post-war era, but most are prior to 1940. But, the history alone is worth reading.

Muma, John R., et al. *Old Flyrod Lures*. 1991, Natural Child Publisher, 3811 62nd Drive, Lubbock, TX 79413.

John Muma is the main author in collaboration with nine others on the very tricky area of fly rod baits. If you are interested in fly rod baits but not flies, you must own and study this book. Without it the collector is wandering in a maze with very few exits! With this book, at least you have a beginning point to attempt to identify these most illusive little lures. The book covers most large producers of fly rod baits and many smaller ones. It also has a section of yet to be identified baits.

Muma, John R. and Jim Muma. *Old Flyrod Lures*, 2nd Edition, 2001, published by the authors (Great Lakes Initiatives) and available for $64.00, shipping included, from either John R. Muma, Box 5092, USM, Hattiesburg, MS 39406 or Jim Muma, 1706 Pine, Belleville, IL 62226-4256.

This book is a much expanded version of the first edition and has contributions from more than 50 NFLCC members and far greater attention paid to smaller companies. It has nearly 1,200 color photos of over 3,000 fly rod lures and is a great buy given its extensive color treatment of fly rod baits. Many of the previously unidentified baits are identified and corrections to the first edition are included. Of course, the pricing is far more accurate as it is updated given recent trends. A collector of fly rod baits simply cannot afford not to own this volume.

Lawson, George S., Jr., *Lawson's Price Guide to Old Fishing Lures*, 1996 edition.
Lawson, George S., Jr., *Lawson's Price Guide to Old Fishing Rods & Misc. Tackle*, 1997 edition.
Lawson, George S., Jr., *Lawson's Price Guide to Old Fishing Reels*, 1997 edition. All of these volumes or the updated versions are available from the publisher at Monterey Bay Publishing, P.O. Box 796 (97-2), Capitola, CA 95010.

These price guides are very useful for those already "in the know" but of less use to the rank beginner as some knowledge is already assumed on the part of the user. If the item can be identified, it can be valued by using the guide(s). These volumes are excellent in determining values on special colors and rare pieces as the prices given are from actual trade data that has been compiled by Mr. Lawson during the past few years. These were the first volumes to identify color variation of lures as an important factor in determining valuation.

Homel, Dan. *Collector's Guide to Old Fishing Reels*, 1995 edition, Second Printing. Forrest-Park Publishers, P.O. Box 29775, Bellingham, WA 98228-1775.

This volume is a good basic introduction to the different types of fishing reels available and is one of the first to address the collectible nature of some of the "modern" reels, including spinning reels. The book still is biased toward more antique reels but does give an excellent introduction to the general field. The illustrations are in black and white

but are crisp and clear and will really assist the beginning collector in identifying the large variety of reels available.

Homel, D. B. *Classic Fishing Lures & Angling Collectibles*, 1998. Forrest-Park Publishers, P.O. Box 29775, Bellingham, WA 98228-1775.

By the same author as above, this is a very nice introduction to all the variety of fishing collectibles available, including fly fishing items. The illustrations are in black and white, but the history of different items is excellent and gives a good general introduction for the beginner. Also, the book is oriented primarily to the time period that I refer to as vintage, meaning the pre-1940 era.

Apfelbaum, Ben, Eli Gottlieb, and Steven J. Michaan. *The Art of the Spearfishing Decoy*, 1990, Museum of American Folk Art, published by E. P. Dutton, 2 Park Avenue, New York, NY 10016.

This is one of my favorite fish decoy volumes as it shows a wide variety of decoys from all regions in America and gives one an instant idea of the differences seen from region to region. It also has an excellent introduction on how the decoys were used in spearing fish and an interview with a great carver, Ben Chosa, about fish spearing, spears, and decoys. The photography is superb.

Kimball, Art, Brad and Scott. *The Fish Decoy Volumes 1-3*. Available from the authors at Aardvark Publications, Inc., P.O. Box 252, Boulder Junction, Wisconsin 54512.

Organized by states and carvers, these books are an expensive resource to acquire, but the serious decoy collector should not be without all of the volumes. The Kimballs have an extensive collection of decoys and have been privy to knowing many of the great carvers. The personal historical information is excellent. The photography and details on the carvers are most helpful in identifying that "unknown" decoy.

Peterson, Donald J. *Folk Art Fish Decoys*, 1996, Schiffer Publishing, Ltd., 77 Lower Valley Road, Atglen, PA 19310.

This would likely be the first book for a new collector of fish decoys to buy. Professor Peterson has done a wonderful job introducing the novice and more advanced collector alike to a fine array of fish decoys and their carvers. I like the book as it has a good sense of the history of spear fishing, a nice variety of spears and other items, and a coverage of "company" decoys. The book is heavy on Minnesota fish and carvers. The photography is superb.

Endnotes

[1] This sale may not necessarily be typical of the true value of this lure, and it is likely more of these lures will now "show up" as people search for them due to the high sale price. This lure was in a green diamond Heddon box.

[2] A perfect example of this is demonstrated by the two summer 2001 offerings from the NFLCC, both the *Gazette* and the *Magazine* feature articles on modern collectibles, something unheard of just a couple of years ago. Also, the December 2001 *NFLCC Magazine* has an article on Heddon from 1939 – 2000.

[3] Zippy was the cartoon character developed by the postal service to convince consumers to use the new, improved, addressing system of the addition of Zip Codes. The character appeared in advertisements, on posters, on the corners of plate blocks, etc., until we all learned enough to use the proper zip code in our destination address.

[4] Fortunately, Shakespeare has a nearly complete run of catalogs, and Luhr Jensen has maintained a solid archival record of its many purchases. Hopefully, forthcoming volumes by this author will detail this information for the collecting world to share.

[5] See the chapter on Luhr Jensen in Volume 1 for a specific example of why that company was one of the first to recognize the ultimate importance of spin fishing.

[6] Again, I remind the reader that this treatise is meant to be illustrative of "modern" fishing lures and collectibles and is by no means exhaustive. I have a lifetime of work ahead of me to research and document additional companies and lures that will be added to future volumes. Major companies were covered in Volume 1.

[7] The mystery was solved by Phil Jensen, president and owner of Luhr Jensen, the current owner of Accetta brands. He informed me that indeed Accetta simply produced the Champ since Weber was in receivership at the time and had ceased production of the Champ and all other items. So Accetta simply started producing the lure, knowing there would likely be no ramifications from Weber Tackle Company due to its financial position. Weber closed its doors one year later, in 1988.

[8] Again, my thanks to Phil Jensen for informing me that indeed Atlantic Lures produced its items without any permission or licensing agreements, to the best of his knowledge. Much like Herter's, a simple name change and a slight design change would be made, and the knock-off lures were simply marketed in the hopes of no legal ramifications forthcoming. Atlantic was able to do this partly because of the large amount of imported knock-offs that were already eroding the markets of the major manufacturers, and it was simply not cost effective to be suing every maker of a copycat lure.

[9] As I said earlier speaking of Sonics, these were really made for the Ultra Light Spinning market.

[10] *Bud Stewart: Michigan's Legendary Lure Maker*, by Frank R. Baron and Raymond L. Carver. Copyright 1990 by the authors. Published by Ferguson Communications, Hillsdale, MI 49242.

[11] This reminds me of Nick and myself out fishing. He always called me his "guide" and "let me" row the boat for him while he cast for bass under the overhanging logs and next to the lily pads and docks. Actually, this service as his guide taught me a lot about fishing, patience, and the peace of being on the water, even when not reeling in a "big one." I seriously wonder if this lesson is now lost on the high speed tournament fishing crowd?

[12] This chapter is not intended to compete with the wonderful work done by the Mumas and all the contributors to their recent work on fly rod baits, and any serious collector of fly rod baits should rush out and buy their volume. Rather, I wanted to include this chapter simply to alert the collector to an important and growing area of interest within the hobby.

[13] See "Spinner Baits As Collectibles" by Larry Mayer in Volume 26, No. 89, June 2001, Summer Issue of the *NFLCC Gazette*, copyright 2001.

[14] Ibid.

[15] In other words, value as follows: 1990-1999: $5.00; 1980-1989: $10.00; 1970-79: $15.00; 1960-69, $20.00; 1950-59: $25.00; 1940-49: $30.00 and now add about $10.00 a year again back to 1920. Earlier than 1920 they can bring $50.00-100.00 each if mint, non-musty, and have graphics by known artists or important introductory advertising or articles of historical merit.

[16] According to a veteran fishing tackle salesman, the best spinning reels are still made off-shore.

[17] See the specific example given in the chapter on Luhr Jensen in Volume 1.

[18] See the example earlier in Chapter 1, Volume 1, in the section on Sonics.

[19] A comment is in order about accumulating versus collecting. Most of us accumulate in the beginning, and I see nothing wrong with it as a final goal either. However, you will likely enjoy your items a little more once you have some plan in mind for organizing them, displaying them, and keeping track of them. The main point is that only you can decide how to go about collecting, and you should only collect "for you" and not because someone else tells you that a particular item is worth collecting.

[20] I had also planned to show an entire chapter of the lures of Charles (Bud) Hartman, which I purchased earlier this year (2001), due to its wide coverage and Mr. Hartman's 28-year history in tackle company representation. However, space limits prevented the inclusion of the photos as planned. But, as credited earlier, many of the photos in this book are of lures recently received from Mr. Hartman through the generous brokering of my friend Tony Zazweta. Without Mr. Hartman we would be missing Wee Tads, Burke Flex Lures, many, many of the miscellaneous companies, the mint Jitterbugs with red plastic lips, etc. So, what I have done is integrate his lures, but I still think a great presentation would be all 600 or so of his accumulation of nearly 50 years (1951 – 1999) in the lure industry. I am just so glad that he kept every color of Widgets, all those hard to find plastics, each of the Original Wood Bassers, and so many other nice lures to pass on to me. Thanks, Bud (and Tony too)!

[21] I couldn't resist one parting pun.

Index

Page numbers in bold indicate Volume 1 location.

303

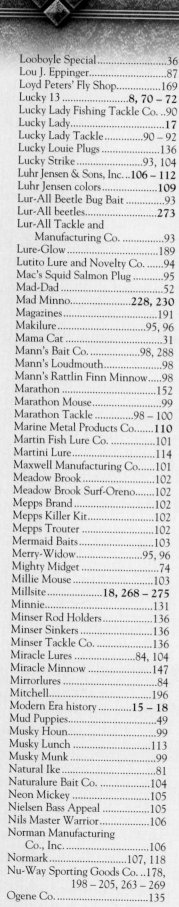